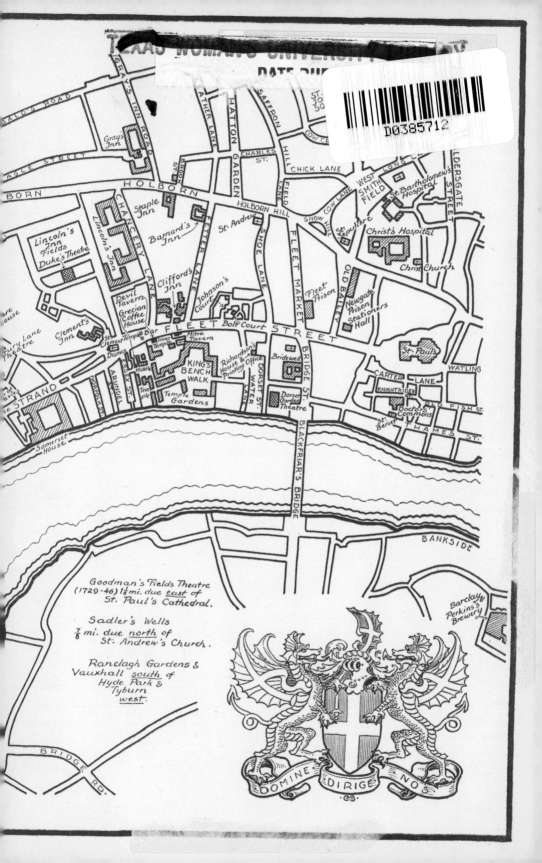

Goodman's Fields Theatre
(1729-46) 1½ mi. due *east* of
St. Paul's Cathedral.

Sadler's Wells
⅞ mi. due *north* of
St. Andrew's Church.

Ranelagh Gardens &
Vauxhall *south* of
Hyde Park &
Tyburn
west.

DOMINE DIRIGE NOS

BOX, PIT, AND GALLERY

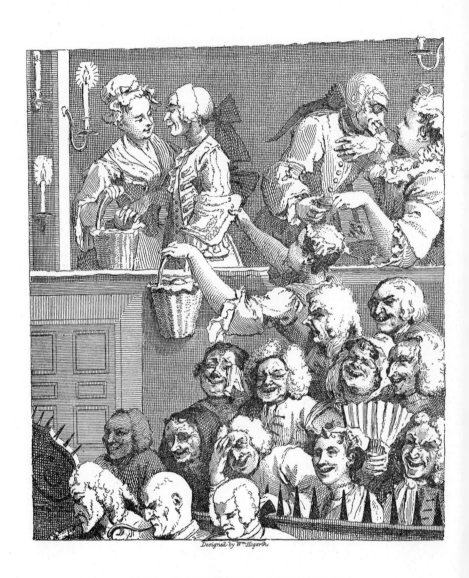

Designed by Wm Hogarth

THE LAUGHING AUDIENCE.

Box
Pit and Gallery

STAGE AND SOCIETY
IN JOHNSON'S LONDON

BY JAMES J. LYNCH

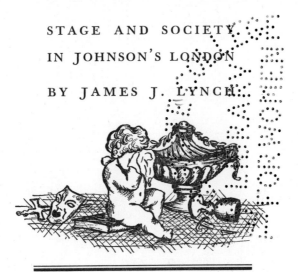

UNIVERSITY OF CALIFORNIA PRESS
Berkeley and Los Angeles
1953

UNIVERSITY OF CALIFORNIA PRESS
BERKELEY AND LOS ANGELES
CAMBRIDGE UNIVERSITY PRESS
LONDON, ENGLAND
COPYRIGHT, 1953, BY
THE REGENTS OF THE UNIVERSITY OF CALIFORNIA
PRINTED IN THE UNITED STATES OF AMERICA
DESIGNED BY WARD RITCHIE

TO

Jean Lupton Lynch

Preface

EIGHTEENTH-CENTURY *England is full of paradoxes, not the least important of which is to be found in the theater. Circumstances were right to encourage the resurgence of drama—a drama that was fresh, timely, and vital; moreover, activity in dramatic composition was abundant. Yet, anyone who has read many of the plays written in the eighteenth century must have been struck by the result of that activity—a drama that, almost without exception, is no more than mediocre. Although occasionally moving by its rhetoric or entertaining by its manipulation of plot, it succeeds neither in fully capturing the spirit of its time nor in generating the power that would make it timeless. The tragedies are either frigid or feeble; the comedies, sugary or solemn. We should not, therefore, expect to find much that can be called literature among the plays written for the theater of Dr. Johnson's London. But a history of dramatic performance may serve ends other than those which are purely literary. As long as it finds expression on the stage, drama is in a real sense a communal activity. It reflects the profound and abiding as well as the trivial and transient interests of its audience. The drama may serve, then, as a kind of social yardstick by which many of the characteristics of the age can be measured. To the extent that it was represented by contemporary audiences, society itself therefore may be a principal object of study even in a book on theatrical history. One important qualification must, of course, be added: only as those professionally concerned with the stage were able and willing to provide the kind of dramatic performance that audiences wished to see can the repertory serve to mirror social history.*

In the following chapters I have attempted to unravel the various threads of influence on the mid-eighteenth-century London theater and, by beginning with the known facts—the identity of the plays that were actually presented on the stage, the propensities of the dominant theater managers, the abilities of the leading actors, and the slender gifts of the playwrights—to discover what the repertory reveals about contemporary society.

vii

Preface

To trace these threads it has been necessary to compile a considerable amount of detailed information, and much of this has been included in the text. But I have assumed throughout that the reader may find at least as much of value and interest in the details as in the generalizations. Numerous and widely scattered contemporary sources have been drawn upon for this essential information—letters, diaries, newspapers, magazines, theater annals, and the like; but two more recent works I wish particularly to mention as convenient compilations of stage performances and, while doing so, to acknowledge my indebtedness to them: John Genest's Some Account of the English Stage, from the Restoration in 1660 to 1830 *(Bath, 1832), and* Dougald MacMillan's Drury Lane Calendar, 1747-1776 *(Oxford, 1938). A third work of this kind, exhaustive in its field and eminently usable, appeared after this book had gone to press:* Charles Beecher Hogan's Shakespeare in the Theatre, 1701-1800 *(Oxford, 1952).*

A word should be said about the chronological boundaries of this investigation. There have been, of course, numerous treatments of the drama both by types—for example, pastoral drama, sentimental comedy, domestic tragedy, and by periods—particularly, for the eighteenth century, Allardyce Nicoll's invaluable handbooks. Most studies of the drama, whether by type or by period, are concerned more or less exclusively with the plays written during the time under consideration, with what I have called throughout this book "new drama." Drama as literature is perhaps necessarily so treated. But in a stage history of drama, plays written earlier that continue to show signs of theatrical vitality must also be taken into account. And for eighteenth-century England the inclusion of such works is especially important because stock pieces and "revived drama" constitute a large element in the repertory. Without them an adequate picture of the time could not emerge. As I read further into the dramatic literature and the theater history of the century, the value of bringing together within the bounds of a single study the total repertory and all the important circumstances determining its composition became increasingly evident. It also became clear that, rather than an arbitrary division like the last half of the century, a stretch of forty years from 1737 to 1777 had sufficient unity to justify designating it as a "period"—if not in literary history, at least in the history of drama. In addi-

Preface

tion to a rather surprising degree of homogeneity in theatrical affairs, the period had considerable sociological importance. As the theatrical period coincided with that which saw a significant change in the make-up of society, I was led to accept those years as my terminal dates. It was a happy accident that the period also coincided with that called the "Age of Johnson."

It is a pleasure to make acknowledgment for assistance and helpful counsel: to Dr. William Van Lennep of Harvard College Library and Mr. Tyrus G. Harmsen of the Huntington Library for aid in finding the illustrations; to Miss Catharina Maria Barnas for drawing the map that appears on the end papers; to Mrs. Carma Fackrell for assistance with the typing of the manuscript; to the Committee on Research of the University of California for grants in aid; to Professor Josephine Miles for advice that pointed the way out of a difficulty; to the editorial staff of the University Press, especially Miss Lucie E. N. Dobbie and Mr. John H. Jennings, for their friendly coöperation and many helpful suggestions; to Professor Brewster Rogerson for reading the manuscript at one of its early stages. Particularly I must thank Professors B. H. Bronson and Willard H. Durham, who not only encouraged and guided my investigation but also read the manuscript with patience and perception; it would be impossible to exaggerate my indebtedness to them. Finally, there is a debt difficult to put into words, which I have acknowledged in the dedication.

J.J.L.

Berkeley, California

ix

Contents

Illustrations

CHAPTER ONE

The Mid-Eighteenth Century

The mid-eighteenth century was an important formative period in English history. It came between two events of far-reaching influence: the Revolution of 1688, which made real the dream of parliamentary government; and the First Reform Bill of 1832, which not only served to establish a "bill of rights" for the English people but also made the humanitarianism advocated by poets from the time of Thomson the official law of the land. In 1688 the centuries-old doctrine of the divine right of kings was at last given its death blow, and the government, although still far from democratic, was placed in the hands of a much broader segment of the population than formerly. By 1832 the classes in the social hierarchy whose voices were once unheard or disregarded had succeeded in making their influence felt to such an extent that the government found it expedient to recognize them by parliamentary action.

The years 1737 to 1777, coming halfway between these two events, saw many important developments in the making. The Industrial Revolution was gaining momentum, and with it came about the impoverishment of the small farmer, the destruction of much of village life and tradition, the rapid growth of the cities, and the gradual urbanization of a large part of the population. The very framework that had made the older social structure possible was crumbling. At the same time, methods of agriculture were being improved, a movement that was later to be led by no less a person than George III, the "farmer king." The small holdings of the villagers were consolidated, the commons were broken up, and the produce went to the new factories in the cities.

While these changes were taking place at home, Englishmen abroad were expanding their colonial holdings and establishing world-circling trade routes. Products of remote countries were making their way back to England, where they not only lent variety to English fare but also helped to broaden the intellectual horizon of those who remained at home. Ever increasing travel to foreign ports brought more and more Englishmen into contact with the native populations of other lands and made the nabobs almost a new social class.

The influence exerted upon drama and the theater by these developments was twofold: the playwrights were supplied with new material, new backgrounds, and new attitudes; and the audience itself reflected the changing nature of the social structure. The new material included characters drawn from natives of other lands and from English nabobs and merchants, plots in which situations were based upon the possession of wealth, and such distant settings as the Americas or the East. New attitudes were to be seen particularly in the exploitation of English history. As industrialization and colonial expansion increased, the sense of England's national greatness became more pervasive and a quickened awareness of her imperial destiny arose. This broadened outlook actuated a curiosity about the springs of national entity—the men and events of her historical and legendary past. Like the philosophers and historians, the playwrights turned to those past times, with the result that more plays using themes and characters drawn from English history reached the stage during the eighteenth century than ever before or since.

The mid-century audience also mirrored the changing conditions. Because of the developments in industry and commerce, a new class of society was coming into existence, one whose position and influence were based upon the merchandise in its ships and warehouses rather than upon the blood in its veins. The aristocracy was still respected for its taste and noblesse, but the middle class was gathering into its own hands the power formerly vested in the aristocracy. Among this new class were merchants and misers, puritans and parvenus, the conscientious and the hypocritical—men of all kinds. And among this new class were also many theatergoers—some only casual spectators, but many habitués and connoisseurs also—who made up an increasingly important part of the audience.

The socio-political scene and the world of the theater were strikingly different. Whereas the social order was changing and the empire was expanding, the theater remained remarkably homogeneous for the entire forty-year period. The Licensing Act, which was passed in 1737, not only was in a real sense the formal and parliamentary recognition of the theater as a powerful social instrument, but it also, by limiting the number of theaters, made the history of the stage the history of the two patent houses, Drury Lane and Covent Garden. Although legitimate drama was sometimes produced elsewhere, notably at the theater in Goodman's Fields and at the Little Theatre in the Haymarket, most of the important events in mid-century drama took place at the two theaters-royal.

The personnel of the acting companies at the two playhouses showed almost the same degree of constancy as the number of theaters. The late 1730's were a relatively barren period between the days of the famous triumvirate—Booth, Wilks, and Cibber—and the generation of actors that was soon to follow. Booth and Wilks were dead, and Cibber, who had retired from the stage, returned to act only infrequently. Except for Cibber, James Quin, who first appeared on the stage in 1714, was the only important member of the older generation still active in 1737. Charles Macklin had already begun his long stage career before 1737, but he could hardly be regarded as an important actor before his appearance as Shylock in 1741. He continued on the stage throughout most of the century, and at the age of ninety created the arduous role of Sir Pertinax Macsycophant in his own play *The Man of the World* (1781).

Quin and Macklin met a powerful rival in 1741 when David Garrick made his first appearance on the London stage, and until his retirement Garrick dominated the theater. Spranger Barry, who first acted in Dublin in 1744, soon came to London and was Garrick's only serious competitor for acting honors after Quin's retirement. During the following three decades a generation of extraordinarily able actors and actresses arose: Henry Mossop, William Powell, Henry Woodward, Ned Shuter, "Gentleman" Smith, Thomas King, John Henderson, Thomas Sheridan, John Moody, Richard Yates, and Samuel Foote; Susannah Cibber, Hannah Pritchard, Kitty Clive, Peg Woffington, George Anne Bellamy, Miss Macklin, Mrs. Spranger Barry, Frances Abington, Jane Pope, Mary Ann Yates, and Miss Nossiter. These players entertained audiences season after season throughout the period, with surprisingly little change in the personnel of the acting companies. But only a few of them were still on the stage when Garrick retired in 1776; and by 1777, the year of Barry's death and of the retirement of Woodward and Miss

Macklin, almost everyone who had shared the greenroom during the mid-century was gone from the stage, and a new generation —that of Mrs. Siddons and the Kembles—was about to establish itself.

An almost equal degree of homogeneity is to be seen in the repertory between 1737 and 1777. During the first third of the century Shakespearean drama had made up only a small part of theatrical offerings whereas Restoration drama bulked relatively large. The situation was reversed shortly thereafter. Restoration plays, except for a few favorites that remained as stock pieces, became less and less important. At the same time the amount of attention given to Shakespeare showed a remarkable increase, and Shakespearean drama retained an important position in the repertory throughout the rest of the century. Other older drama showed a noteworthy degree of persistence, such pieces as *The Beggar's Opera, The Conscious Lovers,* and *The Provok'd Husband* having been acted twenty-five or more of the forty seasons at each theater. New drama, on the whole, followed certain familiar patterns: tragedy in the styles popularized earlier by Addison's *Cato* and Rowe's *Jane Shore,* and comedy after the fashion of Steele and Cibber.

The repertory remained, therefore, pretty much the same throughout the period. But there is a noticeable change during the last quarter of the century. New types, such as Gothic tragedy and comic opera, came to compete on almost equal terms with the drama that had previously dominated in the theater. Closely related to this development is the growing divergence between literary drama and the theater; 1777 is the date of Sheridan's *The School for Scandal,* one of the last important dramas to combine suitability for the stage with literary quality. Thereafter, with few exceptions of consequence, original plays given stage performance consisted of popular farces and melodramas that were often hardly more than outlines for the actors. The literary tradition gradually deserted the theater, ultimately to result in such closet drama as the plays of Scott, Shelley, Byron, and Browning in the next century. An era in the history of drama as well as in the history of the theater had indeed come to an end by 1777.

From the standpoint of the critic, there is also some justification for regarding these years as a well-defined period in dramatic history. Mid-century critics had never lost sight of the

theater in their discussion of dramatic pieces; indeed their remarks found their inspiration in theatrical performance. Likewise editors of older dramatic works, in spite of their concern
with matters of text and allusion, showed by their comments that
stage presentation had not been forgotten. But with few exceptions later critics looked at the drama almost as if it had been
written exclusively for the closet instead of the stage. Shakespeare's characters, for example, were no longer merely poetic
vestures to be donned by the actor while he "strutted his brief
hour"; they had become flesh-and-blood figures to be dissected
in public lecture and periodical essay. How nearly this changed
attitude accords in time with the end of the period is suggested
by an announcement in *The Public Advertiser* for 1774 of what
is perhaps the earliest lecture on Shakespeare's characters.[1]

There are other traits also that may be regarded as characteristic of the time. When Garrick came to the stage in 1741, he
brought with him a new style of acting, somewhat incorrectly
called "naturalistic" but certainly more realistic than the studied
declamatory periods of Quin. Quin himself recognized that a
new age of acting had arrived. After seeing Garrick perform,
he remarked, ". . . if the young fellow was right, he, and the
rest of the players, had been all wrong." [2] Macklin had also
been moving in the direction of greater realism, and he and
Garrick were followed by many of the younger performers. Although the older style of acting continued to be cherished by
some of the actors, and probably by many older members of the
audience, it was soon apparent that the newer style had won
out. When finally Garrick and Quin appeared together in roles
of equal importance, as Horatio and Lothario in *The Fair
Penitent* in 1746, Garrick received the greater applause. Richard
Cumberland, reminiscing long after, recalled that when Garrick
made his first entrance ". . . it seemed as if a whole century
had been stept over in the transition of a single scene." [3]

Along with this innovation was a growing tendency to regard
a dramatic piece as a vehicle for a principal or "star" actor. The
tendency ultimately became so strong that it resulted in the
practice popularly called the "possession of parts." This practice remained in vogue and had a considerable influence in
determining the repertory. It contrasts sharply with the situation at the beginning of the century, when parts had been

[1] For notes to chap. 1, see p. 311.

shared with much greater freedom; it was a point of pride to the triumvirate at Drury Lane that a play be mounted strongly cast "all around." But with the advent of the star actor, mid-century audiences often filled the theater to see the actor in a favorite role rather than the play itself as a total production.

Finally, there are matters pertaining to stage spectacle that help to characterize the period. Realistic settings were rarely used, and it was not an uncommon practice to press into service the "flats" that had been designed for an earlier play. Neither verisimilitude nor novelty in the use of backgrounds had been sufficiently regarded to warrant large expenditures for new sets. There were some exceptions, notably for *The Chinese Festival* in 1755 and *Antony and Cleopatra* four years later; but the exceptions are few. It is noteworthy that the gorgeous scenery and spectacular stage effects in these two productions were not sufficient to make the plays succeed. But when Garrick brought De Loutherbourg to Drury Lane in 1771 to serve as stage architect, his employment heralded the end of an age, an age in which the stage carpenter and the scene painter had been of much less importance than they were to be in the later eighteenth and early nineteenth centuries. Thereafter spectacle was given increasing attention until, toward the end of the century, while the theaters were vying with each other for precedence in "sound and shew," there was what would have seemed to the preceding generation a brazen indifference to the play itself. Similarly, accuracy in costuming had been little regarded. The actors wore contemporary clothing with no concern for the historical period represented, and the actresses often dressed in cast-off gowns given to them by fashionable ladies of the court, although new dresses brought over from Paris were employed on occasion. Theatrical tradition made demands, and innovation in costuming was not encouraged. It was not until late in the century that realistic costuming became prevalent.

These two developments are of more than incidental importance. For two centuries English drama had depended almost entirely for its effectiveness upon the poetic beauty of its language and the viability of the dramatist's cosmos. But all that was changing. Dialogue was supplanted by scenario, and the conceptual realism of the poet's characters and situations made way for the scenic realism of the producer's settings and costumes. Such changes were responsible for a revolution of far-reaching consequence in the history of English drama. Not only were the theatrical superficies of drama altered, but interposed between spectator and actor, and especially between spectator and playwright, was a realistic hindrance to that very illusory power upon which drama had so long depended.

A homogeneous theatrical society with firmly established traditions, a more than adequate acting company, governmental patronage and protection, and actable dramas both new and old numbering in the hundreds—such was the state of affairs in the mid-century. And this was to be found at the palpitating heart of a vigorous, proud, and self-conscious nation just then struggling into the oversized and unaccustomed garments of empire. Why a great national drama did not develop must remain an unanswered question in literary history, for the conditions of drama were present par excellence. Instead there was a great national theater in which a study of the circumstances of dramatic performance is at least as rewarding as that of the largely mediocre drama that those circumstances helped to produce.

PART I: THE REPERTORY

CHAPTER TWO

The Theatrical Season

A current play at a Broadway or London theater may run for one, two, or even three years, during which time it is acted every night and on frequent matinees. The population of a large metropolitan area—and especially as it is frequently augmented by visitors from other parts of the country—can support a long run, for the number of both habitués and casual theatergoers is large. As a result, changes of program are infrequent. Unless there are several theaters, each offering different entertainment, the opportunity for the theatergoing public to find variety on the stage is small.

Different indeed was the situation in the eighteenth century. A run of nine or ten nights was considered good; fifteen, unusual. Moreover, a play—even a popular new piece—did not always hold the stage for all the nights of its run consecutively, but was interchanged with stock plays and revivals of various kinds. Within a comparatively short period—even in a week's time—it was therefore possible for a spectator to see several complete changes of program at a single theater. Consequently standards different from those of the present must be used to measure the success of theatrical performances in the eighteenth century. The success of a new piece must be judged, not by the length of its initial run, but by the number of performances it had throughout the entire season and by the number of seasons in which it was later revived.

Two important differences between the eighteenth-century theatrical season and that of today are at once suggested. First, there is likely to be at least as much significance in the fact that a new tragedy ran, for example, six instead of nine nights as there is in the fact that a contemporary play runs for six rather than nine months. Even though the performance of a new play then was no less a significant event for a theater-minded public than it is today, the eighteenth century was a time of greater prodigality in drama—new plays then were more expendable.

Second, there was, paradoxically, an obvious unwillingness to let a play that survived its first season disappear completely from the boards. Thus arises a situation that to us may seem inexplicable: a new play, which had perhaps no more than a dozen performances in its first season, was revived for a half dozen more the next year and two or three in each of the following several seasons. Many of the new dramatic compositions had such pertinacity and at the same time such a tenuous and sporadic stage life that the complexion of the typical season during the mid-eighteenth century is characterized chiefly by its variety, its alternations of offerings, and its frequent changes of program.

The two patent houses, Drury Lane and Covent Garden, often called the "winter theaters," ordinarily opened for the season about the middle of September and remained open until late May or early June. During the first few weeks of the season it was customary for each theater to schedule performances on only three nights in the week and to alternate with the rival house, which offered plays on the other three week nights.[1] But after the season was well under way, each theater advertised six performances a week. Thus, if both houses were open for about eight and a half months, a total of four hundred performances would be possible during the season. There was seldom, however, such a large number. No plays were performed on Christmas Eve or Christmas Day, on the fast days of Lent, or during Holy Week. Moreover, the theaters were closed because of special circumstances, such as during the mourning period following the death of a member of the royal family.[2]

Misfortunes of a purely theatrical nature might also cause one or both of the playhouses to close down for a time. Covent Garden, for example, opened much later than usual in 1747—the year Garrick assumed the management of Drury Lane—owing to the impoverished state of the acting company at Covent Garden, from which Garrick had lured several of the important actors. And that theater closed again for a time in the following January and February, ordinarily the height of the season, when Rich's inferior company found that it could not compete on anything like equal terms with the strong troupe at Garrick's theater.[3]

There were on the average about 180 nights each season on which both patent houses offered the playgoing public some

[1] For notes to chap. 2, see p. 311.

kind of dramatic entertainment. In terms of the whole forty-year period, there were approximately 14,000 performances in London between 1737 and 1777, exclusive of those at the summer theaters and the "minors." The records of these performances have not all been preserved, and those extant are scattered widely and unsystematically.[4] But by collating titles of plays, names of characters, appearances of actors, and dates of performances as they appear in a large number of contemporary documents,[5] it has been possible to compile for the period a record accounting for three-fourths of the total number of performances that would have been possible. Since it is quite unlikely that any event of importance to the theater would have been entirely overlooked by the authors of the diaries, journals, memoirs, biographies of actors and playwrights, histories and annals of the theaters, or in the contemporary newspapers and magazines, the general picture of each theatrical season can be delineated with a considerable degree of accuracy.

The opening date of each season seldom varied more than a week from September 15, and the closing date came near the end of May. The benefit performances commenced in the middle of March and were a large part of the repertory during the following two months. Relatively few new plays were produced, and there were even fewer revivals of plays that were no longer regarded as stock pieces. The new plays were ordinarily brought forward during December, January, and February, the last month being the most popular for first performances. New afterpieces appeared with less regularity, although the greatest number were produced for the first time during the months of March and April. Revivals followed the same pattern as new plays, the largest number being mounted in the middle of the season.

The plays chosen to open the season were for the most part stock pieces, selected from Elizabethan, Restoration, and early eighteenth-century drama, although a few relatively new plays were occasionally used. The plays performed during the closing nights of the season show the same variety except that new plays bulk larger in the total. Although the choice of play for the opening night of a season may not always have been of special significance, the selection of plays for that purpose accords largely with those most often performed during the forty-year period.

13

From every point of view, the season seems to have been planned with an eye to the maintenance of a large number of stock pieces. These stock plays were ordinarily the ones used by both regular and new members of the company for their first appearances in the early part of the season; they alternated with new plays or were joined with new afterpieces during the height of the season, from Christmas through March; and they were selected more frequently than newer plays for the actors' final appearances in the late spring. Consequently, throughout the season the stock piece was the principal ingredient in the theatrical diet.

So infrequently was there any significant change in the repertory from season to season, at least until about 1760, that each season seems to have been planned on the example of the preceding. In the repertory there were a few invariables that the mid-century had inherited from an earlier day. Thus Rowe's *Tamerlane* was performed at both theaters on or about each November 5 to commemorate the landing of William III in England. A practice less frequently followed was the performance of Ravenscroft's *The London Cuckolds* each year on October 29, Lord Mayor's Day. The play was, however, objectionable to a moral age and was finally abolished in 1751 at Drury Lane, whereupon Rich quickly followed Garrick's example.[6] But aside from these arbitrarily established performances, there was often a strikingly similar arrangement of plays from season to season, a circumstance that seems to indicate that the managers believed they had found a suitable and profitable order for the staging of their plays.

During the first few weeks there was a representative sampling of the older pieces in the entire repertory. During this time at least two or three of Shakespeare's plays were performed, most frequently *Richard III, Hamlet, Macbeth,* or *Romeo and Juliet* of the tragedies and *The Merchant of Venice* or *As You Like It* of the comedies. Restoration comedy was represented by such plays as *The Way of the World, The Provok'd Wife,* and *The Recruiting Officer;* late seventeenth-century tragedy, by *Venice Preserved* and *The Mourning Bride.* Early eighteenth-century drama presented early in the season commonly included *The Beggar's Opera, The Conscious Lovers,* and *The Provok'd Husband.* Once the season was under way, other plays of each category were added and arranged to provide alternation between tragedy and comedy, between Shakespearean and Restoration or early eighteenth-century drama, the arrangement interrupted only occasionally by the insertion of a more recent play, usually a comedy such as *The Suspicious Husband* or *The Jealous Wife.*

In mid-season much the same situation prevailed; if new plays or revivals of long-unacted plays were added, they merely replaced some of the stock pieces of lesser popularity. While the benefits were in progress no special arrangement seems to have been enforced, since the beneficiaries had the right to select any plays they wished; but during the closing weeks of the season some of the most popular stock plays were again performed— for example, *The Beggar's Opera, The Fair Penitent, King Lear,* and *Henry IV, Part I*—except on those rare occasions when a new play had become so popular that it dominated the latter part of the season, as *The School for Scandal* did in 1777.

These various plays were ordinarily accompanied by shorter plays that served as afterpieces. The latter might be of several varieties—farces of two or three acts, pantomimes, comic operas, or even regular dramas abridged to provide shorter pieces. In addition, there was often an "entertainment" between the full-length drama and the afterpiece. Moreover, an occasional prologue, a prelude, or a special epilogue, sometimes regarded as sufficiently important to be announced in the playbill, helped to fill out the evening's program. The playgoer therefore did not suffer from lack of variety during the course of the evening.

Of these various lesser offerings, the afterpiece was the most important. It was most commonly a farce or pantomime that had already proved successful. It could be added to almost any five-act drama, apparently with little thought as to its appropriateness; if it struck the public fancy at the moment, it might be performed as many as fifty times in a season. Obviously such pieces soon lost their novelty and rarely survived the season, although there were several notable exceptions, such as *Lethe, High Life below Stairs, Harlequin Sorcerer,* and *Miss in Her Teens.* At Drury Lane it was a common practice to introduce two such pieces in a season and, by alternating the farces or by combining them with different pieces, to provide the audience with a greater variety of fare. At the same time the life of the afterpiece was thereby prolonged. The frequency with which a single farce or pantomime might be performed resulted naturally in the limitation of the number that could be acted during a season. As a result there were fewer new afterpieces staged than new full-length plays, in spite of the greater difficulty involved in the composition and performance of the latter.

Consequently the repertory of the patent theaters between 1737 and 1777 was remarkably uniform in several different ways from one season to the next. There are, however, some indications of change in the nature of the season, particularly after about 1760. For one thing, the practice of adding the new plays to the repertory earlier in the season than formerly was becoming more common, so that during the last third of the period the performance of new plays, including afterpieces, was quite frequent in November and early December. The inclusion of revivals of long-unacted plays followed the same pattern. Second, the theatrical season was gradually undergoing change in the selection of plays for early autumn. Whereas earlier the first weeks were devoted almost exclusively to Shakespearean and Restoration plays and to such early eighteenth-century favorites as *The Beggar's Opera* and the sentimental comedies of Steele and Cibber, during the later years the plays of contemporary playwrights—for example, Colman, Cumberland, Garrick, Goldsmith, Hoadly, and Sheridan—were deemed suitable as vehicles for the actors' early appearances. Third, a slow but steady increase in the number of new dramas brought to the stage is apparent during the last fifteen years of the period. Finally, the growing interest in musical pieces is reflected in the constitution of the seasons during the later years. Although never so popular as *The Beggar's Opera*, musical comedies such as those of Bickerstaffe came to be used during the early part of the season and to be alternated with the more conventional dramatic types. Thus, in spite of the uniformity of seasons in several important aspects, there was also a gradual change, indicating an awareness that greater variety was needed in the repertory than had been demanded by the mid-century audience.

Perhaps the season can be understood best, however, by examining in greater detail two fairly typical seasons, one early and the other late in the period. Although no season can be regarded as entirely representative, as the personnel of the company, the political situation, current interests and fashions, and other factors were constantly making themselves felt in the theater, the seasons of 1751-1752 and 1774-1775 correspond generally with those before and after and at the same time have no unusual characteristics that are reflected in the repertory.

In the 1751-1752 season seventy different full-length plays were performed at the two patent houses, sixteen of which were given performance at both Covent Garden and Drury Lane. Shakespearean drama was represented by four comedies (*The Merchant of Venice,* * Much Ado About Nothing, Twelfth Night,* and *As You Like It*), five tragedies (*Romeo and Juliet,* * Hamlet,* * Othello,* * King Lear,* and *Macbeth* *), and four histories (*Richard III,* * Henry IV, Part I, Henry V,* and *Henry VIII*). Other early drama was represented only by comedy (*Eastward Hoe, Every Man in his Humour, Rule a Wife and Have a Wife,* and *The Pilgrim*). Twenty-seven comedies written in the half century after the Restoration were acted, including five by Farquhar, five by Vanbrugh, three by Congreve, and two by Mrs. Centlivre. Of these the most frequently acted were *The Recruiting Officer,* * The Provok'd Wife,* * and *The Way of the World.* * Late seventeenth-century tragedy was represented by *Venice Preserved, The Orphan,* * Oroonoko,* * The Mourning Bride, The Earl of Essex,* and *Theodosius.* Later comedies in the repertory included *The Miser, The Conscious Lovers,* * The Provok'd Husband,* * The Refusal,* and *The Drummer.* Eighteenth-century tragedy was represented by four plays of Rowe (*Tamerlane,* * The Fair Penitent,* * Lady Jane Grey,* and *Jane Shore* *), Young's *The Revenge,* Smith's *Phaedra and Hippolytus,* Lillo's *The London Merchant,* Philips' *The Distrest Mother,* Hughes' *The Siege of Damascus,* and Hill's *Zara.* No new comedies were acted at either theater, the most recent being Hoadly's *The Suspicious Husband* * (1747). Thomson's fairly new tragedy *Tancred and Sigismunda* (1745) was revived, and Francis' new *Eugenia* was given its first performance. The latter tragedy was the only new first piece of any kind acted at either theater during this year, and it survived for only six instead of the usual nine nights.

The selection of plays for this season is significant. For example, it is noteworthy that several of Shakespeare's romantic comedies were performed at the very time when the romantic temperament was making itself felt in other ways and in other

---

* Performed at both theaters in the season.

literary forms. The influence of the acting company is also suggested by the repertory. Shakespeare's tragedies, for example, provided powerful roles for Garrick at Drury Lane and Barry at Covent Garden, who were then at the height of their rivalry. The popularity of *Romeo and Juliet,* the play most frequently acted during the season—twenty-one nights at the two houses— is the result of both kinds of influence. The part of Romeo was ideally suited for Barry, who excelled in portraying the stage lover. At the same time the frequency with which this tragedy was acted was also the result of the spirit that gave favorable reception to the romantic comedies. That many Restoration pieces were revived indicates that comedies of manners and wit had not yet lost their popularity, but the survival of the pathetic tragedies of Rowe, Otway, and Southerne is less surprising in view of the appeal that such fare had to the sensibilities of the mid-eighteenth-century public—a public that had already idolized Richardson.

During this season the nights devoted to Shakespearean drama constituted one-fourth of the total—striking testimony of the continuing popularity of Shakespeare on the stage. A greater number of performances was given to early eighteenth-century tragedy, however, than to Shakespearean tragedy, and Shakespearean comedy was outranked in frequency of performance by both Restoration and eighteenth-century comedy. Although a greater number of comedies of manners was revived, sentimental comedy had as many performances in the repertory. Although the comedies of all types brought to the stage outnumbered the tragedies by three to two, the tragedies had a slightly larger number of performances than the comedies. It is perhaps not surprising that such should be true in an age that took itself as seriously as did the eighteenth century.

Two notable revivals occurred during this season, those of the long-unacted *Eastward Hoe* and *Every Man in his Humour,* both performed at Drury Lane. But the two plays had sharply contrasting fates. The Jonsonian play met with immediate success and was long retained on the acting list. That it was acted sixteen times during the 1751-1752 season is no doubt owing in part to the strong cast, which included Garrick, Woodward, Yates, and Shuter. But it may also be that the spectators were ready to enjoy the eccentricities of characters whom they would not readily identify with themselves; in the mid-century it was this disinterested kind of satirical comedy that could compete with the sentimental genre. On the other hand, Chapman's play was performed only once and then was "driven from the stage." [7] It also had a strong cast, but that did not prevent the audience from rejecting it. The occasion was Lord Mayor's Day, when the licentious *The London Cuckolds* was traditionally staged; but during this season Garrick substituted the older play in keeping with his policy of improving the morals of the stage. Perhaps the audience objected to the change; but it is also likely that the Elizabethan's satirical treatment of social climbers and carpet knights proved too strong fare for an audience that included many of the *nouveau riche* and self-conscious "connoisseurs."

During the 1774-1775 season a greater number of different first pieces was performed—ninety-eight full-length plays at the two patent houses, and again sixteen were acted at both Covent Garden and Drury Lane. Seventeen plays by Shakespeare were acted, an increase of four over the 1751-1752 season. These included eight comedies (*As You Like It,** Much Ado About Nothing,** The Tempest, Twelfth Night, Measure for Measure, All's Well That Ends Well, The Winter's Tale,* and *The Merchant of Venice*), six tragedies (*Hamlet,** Cymbeline,** Macbeth, Romeo and Juliet, King Lear,* and *Othello*), and three histories (*Richard III,** Henry VIII,* and *Henry IV, Part I*). Other early English drama was represented by one tragicomedy (*Philaster,* in Colman's 1763 alteration) and six comedies (Jonson's *Every Man in his Humour* and *The Alchemist,* Shirley's *The Gamester,* Brome's *The Jovial Crew,* Fletcher's *Rule a Wife and Have a Wife,* and a version of *The Chances* that contained the alterations of both Villiers and Garrick).

Only thirteen Restoration comedies, or less than half the number acted in 1751-1752, reached the stage during this season, of which only one—the perennially popular *The Beaux' Stratagem* —was performed at both theaters. None of Vanbrugh's plays was performed, and of Congreve's only *Love for Love.* However, Mrs. Centlivre and Farquhar continued as popular authors, and one play by Wycherley, its licentiousness expunged by Garrick in 1766, was given performance. Late seventeenth-

* Performed at both theaters.

century tragedy was represented by several old favorites—
*Oroonoko, The Mourning Bride, Venice Preserved, All for
Love, The Rival Queens,* * *Theodosius,* and *The Fatal Marriage*
(in Garrick's alteration titled *Isabella*).

Although fourteen eighteenth-century comedies were presented, these included only four written early in the century
(*The Drummer, The Provok'd Husband,* * *The Conscious
Lovers,* * and *The Miser*). One mid-century comedy, *The
Suspicious Husband* (1747), held its place in the repertory, but
most of the comedies were quite new—*The Jealous Wife*
(1761), *The Clandestine Marriage* (1765), *The Hypocrite*
(1768), *The West Indian* (1771), *The Fashionable Lover*
(1771), *The School for Wives* (1773), *A Christmas Tale* (1773),
She Stoops to Conquer (1773). The situation was similar for
eighteenth-century tragedy. The plays of Rowe (*Jane Shore,* *
Tamerlane, The Fair Penitent, and *Lady Jane Grey*) continued
to be acted, as did Hill's *Zara,* Philips' *The Distrest Mother,* *
Lillo's *The London Merchant,* Young's *Revenge,* and Smith's
Phaedra and Hippolytus, all of which were written early in the
century. But most of the tragedies were of more recent composi-
tion—*Elfrida* (1752), *The Gamester* (1752), *The Brothers*
(1753), *The Earl of Essex* (1753), *Douglas* (1756), *The Earl of
Warwick* (1766), *Medea* (1767), *Timanthes* (1770), *The
Grecian Daughter* * (1772), *Henry II* (1773), and *The Heroine
of the Cave* (1774). Musical pieces included *The Beggar's
Opera,* two of Bickerstaffe's comic operas (*The Maid of the
Mill* * and *Love in a Village**), and Arne's serious opera, *Artaxerxes.* Of these, all but the first were also of recent composition.

The most noteworthy difference between this season and the
earlier one is to be seen in the number of new plays. In all, eight
plays were introduced during the 1774-1775 season. Two of
these were comedies—Cumberland's *The Choleric Man* and
Sheridan's *The Rivals;* one—Burgoyne's *The Maid of the Oaks*
—was a comic opera. But more than half were tragedies—
Francklin's *Matilda,* Jephson's *Braganza,* Hoole's *Cleonice,*
Hull's alteration of Thomson's never-acted *Edward and Eleanora,* and Francklin's translation of Voltaire's *Orestes,* which
appeared as *Electra.* Several of these were among the most frequently performed plays during this season. *The Maid of the*

* Performed at both theaters.

Oaks led all plays, both new and revived, with twenty-five performances, followed by *The Rivals* and *Braganza* each with fifteen, *The Choleric Man* with thirteen, *Matilda* with eleven, and *Cleonice* with nine.

These plays succeeded for a variety of reasons. Burgoyne's comic opera was a success, not only because of its novelty and the current fashion of musical pieces, but also because of its connection with the famous *fête champêtre* at Banstead Downs earlier that year. Sheridan's comedy owed its success to its eminently stageable nature, a quality that helped it to survive the century whereas the other new plays of this season soon disappeared from the acting list. The temporary success of the comedy of Cumberland and of the tragedies of Francklin, Hoole, and Jephson can be attributed to novelty as well as to the custom of encouraging new pieces for the benefit of the author.

Only one older play—*The Distrest Mother,* which was performed on fifteen nights—approaches the frequency with which most of these new plays were acted, and its sudden popularity resulted from the spirit of rivalry between the two theaters. Both theaters revived the play early in January, and Barry and his wife at Covent Garden successfully outrivaled Smith and Miss Younge at Drury Lane for the public's favor. But the rest of the older plays fall far short of the number of performances accorded the new pieces. Of them, the most frequently revived were *As You Like It* and *Richard III* (seven nights each), *The West Indian* (six performances), and *Twelfth Night, Hamlet, The Rival Queens, School for Wives,* and *Love in a Village* (five times each). This small group of stock plays may suggest the kinds of dramatic fare that still appealed to audiences in 1774-1775: Shakespearean comedy and tragedy, high-sounding but highly actable poetic tragedy that exploited the emotions, sentimental comedy, and comic opera.

Relatively little change between 1751-1752 and 1774-1775 is noticeable in the ratio of performances of tragedy and comedy, and the only significant change in the complexion of the season is the inclusion of a larger element of musical pieces. More important, however, is the considerable shift from earlier to more recent drama. Whereas in 1751-1752 one-fourth of the nights during the season were devoted to Shakespeare, the proportion had declined to one-sixth in 1774-1775. Similarly the number of performances of other Elizabethan and Jacobean drama decreased from 7 to 5 per cent of the total for the season, and Restoration drama dropped from 31 to 15 per cent. On the other hand, only 36 per cent of the season had been given over to the performance of later plays in 1751-1752; but in 1774-1775 eighteenth-century plays were acted on 65 per cent of the nights during the season, half of which were devoted to plays never acted previously. Thus in the theater's own version of the "battle of the books," the victory was inclining toward the contemporary.

CHAPTER THREE

New Drama on the Stage

Full-length plays by contemporary dramatists formed a large part of the theatrical repertory, constituting more than one-third of the total number of plays of all types brought to the stage between 1737 and 1777; they account, however, for less than one-fifth of the total number of performances. This fact is itself significant in assessing the theatrical history of the mid-eighteenth century: there was much dramatic activity, but the resultant plays lacked the vitality necessary to keep them on the stage. Of the sixty-four tragedies and fifty-two comedies that had their first performances in the period, thirty-four and twenty-seven respectively—that is, more than half—did not survive their first season. Thus, much of the new drama had no more than a momentary influence on the repertory. And of the ones that had a better reception, only five tragedies and seven comedies were performed in as many as ten seasons.

That the new drama lacked the ability to compete successfully with stock plays for a place in the repertory is particularly apparent to the modern student of the period. But contemporaries were often aware of the unhappy situation also. In 1739, for example, the Countess of Pomfret wrote that nothing was quite "so rare a thing as a good play in these days." [1] Seventeen years later, Dr. Grainger remarked, "If my intelligence is true, the town will be fed no better fare this winter than it was last." [2] In 1769 Walpole said that the theater "swarms with wretched translations, and ballad operas, and we have nothing new but improving abuse." [3] And at the end of the period, young Johnson of Torrington wrote of Francklin's *Matilda*, ". . . they say this is the Queen, what must the rest be?" [4] Eighteenth-century drama is best known, perhaps, for its general level of mediocrity.

It must be constantly borne in mind that the ratio between old and new drama in the repertory was determined largely by

[1] For notes to chap. 3, see p. 312.

the inability of mid-century dramatists to provide the stage with plays that had the histrionic effectiveness of older drama. Consequently, it is not surprising to discover that the new plays, although amounting to one-third of the comedies and more than half the tragedies that reached the stage, furnished only one-fifth of the performances. In other words, rarely more than one night a week on the average was given over to plays written during the period.

It is illuminating to compare the stage history of these plays with that of other groups of dramatic compositions. Produced between 1737 and 1777 were 116 comedies and tragedies that can be called new—more than were revived from any earlier time. Yet this large body of drama was outranked in number of performances by Restoration drama, although only fifty-four plays in the latter group were revived; and the sixty-five plays written between 1700 and 1737 were given 400 more performances during the period than were new plays. The contrast with Shakespearean plays is even more striking, for these, although only one-fourth as numerous as new comedy and tragedy, were performed with such frequency as to outrank all contemporary drama in the repertory by a ratio of six to five.

Thus, the new drama consisted of a large body of plays, most of which had short runs, infrequent revivals, and early deaths. In order to deal adequately with such a numerous group, it is necessary to find a suitable method of classifying them. The most obvious classification is, of course, into comedy, tragedy, and musical pieces (serious opera, ballad opera, comic opera, and masque), for these three categories include all new plays that were brought to the stage as first pieces. After such a classification has been made, it is apparent that there were more new tragedies than new comedies given their first performances in the period. Moreover, new tragedies were more numerous in the repertory than all the revived tragedies combined, regardless of the time of their composition. On the other hand, new comedies amounted to only one-third of the total number of comedies acted. In other words, there was a greater amount of dramatic activity by contemporary playwrights in the tragic vein than in the comic—at least as that activity was reflected in what the theater companies were willing to accept for performance. And conversely, there was necessarily a greater dependence upon older comedy than upon older tragedy, since the output of acceptable new comedy was smaller. But if the average number of performances is considered, it will be seen that new comedy had a better record of survival than tragedy, the average number of performances for new comedy being twenty-two, in contrast to fifteen for new tragedy. Both new comedies and new tragedies were more numerous than new musical pieces, which made up only 10 per cent of the total in the repertory. Nor did a new musical piece succeed as well in holding the stage as did a new comedy or tragedy. With a few notable exceptions—such as *The Duenna*, acted seventy-five times during its first season, and the popular comic operas of Bickerstaffe—musical entertainments rarely survived long as first pieces. Their substance was often too slight to fill up the required number of acts; if they later succeeded, it was usually in an abridged form, in which they appeared as fashionable afterpieces.

There are several significant implications. The composition of tragedy was more frequently undertaken than that of comedy, suggesting both that a serious-minded age looked at the former as a more congenial channel for its artistic expression and that the individual playwrights regarded tragedy as a surer road to authorial fame.[5] Only one-fourth of the resulting tragedies had as many as twenty performances, and an equal number did not survive for even the customary nine nights—indicating the universal inability of the contemporary playwright to make his composition measure up to his intention. The comedies, however, fared somewhat better. Although as many comedies as tragedies expired before the ninth performance—and consequently did not remain on the acting list beyond their first season—a larger proportion of new comedies (40 per cent) was revived during later seasons, and these had at least twenty performances each; moreover a half-dozen new comedies were acted fifty nights or more during the period. Nor is there anything comparable among the tragedies to the tenacity with which *The Suspicious Husband*, *The Clandestine Marriage*, and *The Jealous Wife* held the stage.

If the body of plays is classified on the basis of authorship, a notable situation at once becomes apparent. There is a definitely marked cleavage between those who wrote comedy and those who tried their hand at tragedy. Only six authors—Edward Moore, Arthur Murphy, Hugh Kelly, Charles Macklin, Thomas Hull, and William Whitehead—succeeded in reaching the stage in both genres. The remaining sixty-one who furnished the stage with full-length plays restricted their efforts to one or the other. Aside from this self-imposed specialization of dramatic effort, the number of authors is itself significant; for it cannot be said that original drama in the mid-eighteenth century was the work of a small group of writers. It is true that few succeeded; but many tried. More than a score of authors furnished only a single tragedy; and almost as many, a single comedy. Among these single contributions were some of the most successful plays of the day, for example Hoadly's *The Suspicious Husband,* Dodsley's *Cleone,* and Miller's *Mahomet;* but a far greater number were lifeless or ill-conceived attempts. On the other hand, a few authors were much more prolific, seven playwrights (Murphy, Cumberland, Colman, Mrs. Griffith, Kelly, Home, and Francklin) furnishing more than half the total number of tragedies and comedies that were acted. More than four hundred nights during the last sixteen years of the period were devoted to the plays of Murphy and Colman alone. Thus the repertory was the result of the combined efforts of a large group of writers. It was supplied in part by many amateurs who contributed relatively few plays to the repertory and soon abandoned dramatic composition. At the same time, most of the new plays were supplied by a relatively small group who, either because of their literary skill and reputation or because of their special knowledge of the stage's requirements, succeeded in maintaining their plays before mid-century audiences.

Besides the first pieces of various kinds, there was another important element in the repertory, a knowledge of which is necessary to an adequate understanding of theatrical history during the eighteenth century: namely, the afterpiece. These were of three principal kinds: pantomimes, farces, and musical entertainments. They share with the full-length drama one characteristic: they were also written by a large number of authors; yet only a few—particularly theater men like Garrick, Rich, Foote, and Colman—supplied most of the successful pieces.

Pantomime as a distinct type of performance was added to the repertory several years before the mid-century, the first such piece on the English stage—*The Tavern Bilkers*[6]—dating from the beginning of the century. It was John Rich, however, who popularized the species, first at Lincoln's Inn Fields and later at Covent Garden. These plays without dialogue depended heavily upon scenery, costume, machinery, and usually upon the acting of Rich himself, the unrivaled Harlequin of the century. Such pantomimes were attached to any play chosen for the night's performance. They not only constituted the chief attraction for audiences at Covent Garden, but also stimulated Drury Lane to follow suit. Famous pieces like *Harlequin Sorcerer, Harlequin Ranger, Queen Mab,* and *Harlequin Executed* continued to draw crowds to the theater through the mid-century, sometimes even when the best regular drama failed to do so.

Although the pantomimes must have formed a large part of the repertory during many years of the period, their very nature, depending rather upon the skill and ingenuity of the actor than upon established lines of poetry or prose, makes them elusive and ephemeral. They had apparently little influence on comedy, although it is possible that they helped to inspire the growing insistence upon greater realism in acting. Audiences familiar with the antics of "Lun" (Rich's stage name), who could successfully convey meaning without benefit of language, were prepared to receive with enthusiasm the carefully sympathetic representations of Garrick, whose acting approached reality more closely than did the older and more declamatory style of Cibber and Quin. But aside from this possible significance of the pantomime, and in spite of its considerable and persistent popularity, it can hardly be regarded as of enduring importance to the repertory. One contemporary wrote that "the business of Pantomimes is become a very serious concern," which, he explained, was caused by "the curiosity of mankind . . . perpetually thirsting after novelties," [7] and audiences were frequently satirized in the mid-century because of their taste for novel and "unnatural" forms of theatrical entertainment.[8] Although the popularity of pantomime might therefore be expected to furnish an important index to current taste and fashions, its effect on the rest of the repertory was relatively slight.

Farce held a position of greater significance. The term itself has a variety of meanings; but in the eighteenth century it had come to mean customarily a short piece, usually of not more than two acts, that made use of tricks and intrigue, the whole depending for its vitality upon humor and often descending to the low and coarse. Fielding had supplied many such pieces before the passage of the Licensing Act in 1737, and several of them continued to hold their place in the repertory. Such plays were regularly used as afterpieces, and eventually the term "farce" came to be applied to any short play used for that purpose. Thus a sentimentalized afterpiece like Dodsley's *The King and the Miller of Mansfield* or even a comic opera was sometimes called a farce.[9]

Besides Fielding and Dodsley, whose farces were popular during the early years of the period, other important authors in this genre were Foote, Garrick, Colman, Macklin, and Murphy, who together supplied the stage with nearly forty farces between 1737 and 1777. Many of them—for example, Garrick's *Miss in Her Teens*, Foote's *The Author*, and Murphy's *The Apprentice* —were acted many times and retained their popularity for several years. The production of farces was by no means limited, however, to a small group of writers. There were at least forty authors who tried their hand at this kind of writing, and together they furnished about one hundred farces that were given performance.

The difficulties of writing farce were not so great as those confronting the playwright who undertook regular comedy or tragedy. The shorter length, the concentration by the audience upon actor rather than upon lines, even the position the farce held in the evening's program—as a humorous relief after the more serious entertainment that preceded—all combined to lessen the demands made upon the playwright by spectators who required only that the piece amuse. Nor did authors ordinarily exert great ingenuity in contriving their plots or delineating their characters; rather they drew heavily upon full-length drama—abridging, lifting out scenes and acts, or merely translating episodes out of French comedies.

Yet, in spite of these advantages, fewer farces than five-act comedies and tragedies were produced during the forty-year period, even though the longer plays ordinarily required greater skill and effort in their composition. This situation is, however, readily explained. Three or four older farces that had proved stageworthy in preceding seasons, with perhaps a new piece or two, were alternated throughout the season; and, because a farce that had caught the public fancy could be added to any evening's program regardless of the nature of the full-length play that preceded it, few new farces were required during the season. A new farce, moreover, often meant an effort of memorizing and rehearsing not consonant with the probable contribution to the actor's reputation. It also meant considerable expense to the manager, whereas an older farce could continue to make use of settings, machinery, and costumes provided for previous seasons. Hence, the financial interests of the theater were best served by restricting the number; and because the reputation of a theater rested traditionally upon the quality of its full-length plays rather than upon its afterpieces—even though, paradoxically, the vitality of its new offerings was often to be found in the latter rather than in the former—most managers (Rich is, of course, a notable exception) chose to expend their time and money on comedy and tragedy.

A third type of afterpiece was the musical entertainment. There were several varieties, but the best known were the ballad opera, the masque, and the comic opera. The vogue of the first had been established by *The Beggar's Opera*, which continued to be given frequent performance throughout the period. The extraordinary reception accorded Gay's "Newgate pastoral" inspired a host of imitations, none of which had anything like comparable success. Since the original type depended upon the association of new words with old and familiar tunes, the material from which ballad operas could be made was soon exhausted. Although the term itself continued to be used late into the mid-century—when it had become synonymous with comic opera—the type in the manner of Gay had almost become extinct after about 1740. Consequently, except for the frequent revivals of *The Beggar's Opera* itself, little ballad opera is to be found in the repertory of the period. Masques also are few in number and, except for Dalton's and Colman's versions of *Comus*, which together were performed in twenty-two different seasons, they are of little significance in the repertory.[10]

Comic opera was of much greater importance than either of these types. The first to achieve success with this kind of composition was Isaac Bickerstaffe, whose *Love in a Village* was performed forty times in its first season (1762-1763) and was revived in fourteen of the next fifteen seasons. This play, however, like his almost equally popular *The Maid of the Mill* and *Lionel and Clarissa*, was acted as a first piece. But *The Padlock* (also by Bickerstaffe), Bate's *The Rival Candidates,*

Arne's *The Rose,* Sheridan's *St. Patrick's Day,* and numerous other comic operas served as afterpieces. The stage history of Lloyd's *The Capricious Lovers* (1764) illustrates how musical pieces might serve in either capacity. This opera was first acted early in the season, but after nine performances it was withdrawn. When it appeared three months later, it had been reduced to an afterpiece and was successively added to performances for several nights, including those of such diverse plays as *The Rival Queens, The Orphan of China, The Fair Penitent, Venice Preserved,* and *King Lear.*

Other types of musical entertainment, which were of fairly frequent occurrence, are closely akin to comic opera. Some of these were the operatic farce, used as an afterpiece exclusively, represented by such pieces as O'Hara's *The Two Misers* and King's *Love at First Sight* (called a ballad farce by the subtitle); the interlude (Garrick's *Linco's Travels*); the burletta (O'Hara's *Midas* and *The Golden Pippin*); the pastoral (Gentleman's *Cupid's Revenge*); and even more loosely defined types. The variety of names used to designate the type—comic opera, operatic farce, ballad farce, musical interlude, musical entertainment, burletta, as well as several others—indicates both an absence of a clearly understood distinction among them (frequently there was no real distinction) and an awareness of the need for novelty on the stage. That all the musical types except ballad opera and masque belong to the years following 1760 suggests the growing importance of music in the theater as well as the declining state of the drama that depended so largely on novelty.

The repertory was thus composed of several types of new plays, which, according to their position on the evening's program, may be divided into first pieces and afterpieces; and each of these may be further classified—the former into comedy, tragedy, and operatic piece, and the latter into pantomime, farce, and musical entertainment. The plays in the latter group, which for the most part followed well-established and time-tested practices within their respective types (even though the names used to describe them show a lack of uniformity), are of little importance at this point. The first pieces, however, because they show great variety in both subject matter and method of treatment and because the complexion of the repertory was determined chiefly by them, require further consideration.

The most frequently acted new comedies were, in the order of their popularity, *The Suspicious Husband, The Jealous Wife, The Way to Keep Him, The Clandestine Marriage, All in the Wrong, The West Indian,* and *The School for Lovers.* Their very titles are significant—the proper theme for comedy was love and marriage. And upon this theme the playwrights rang the changes, placing their husbands, wives, and lovers in almost every conceivable situation. In this respect mid-century comedy hardly differs from that of the Restoration period. But in attitude, and particularly in the various denouements, there is a vast difference. In most of these new comedies marriage is no longer a mask for adultery, and nuptial fidelity has become a desirable ideal.

The Suspicious Husband, the earliest of these plays (1747), shows a compromise between the lascivious and the moral, although the latter is finally triumphant. But in the later plays the tone is largely moral throughout. In *The Way to Keep Him* (1760), for example, although the plot provides the elements that a Vanbrugh might have made into another *Provok'd Wife,* the philanderers repent and the ladies triumph, and in *The West Indian* (1771) a spirit of morality and benevolence prevails. The new comedies are not all equally sentimental, although sentimentalism is an important element in most of them; and several seem to be efforts to capture some of the brilliance and wit that had reached its peak at the beginning of the century. Thus, the new comedies most frequently performed during the mid-century carry on the traditions made famous by both Congreve and Steele. An examination of the other comedies performed with considerable frequency—such as *The Foundling, The English Merchant, The Fashionable Lover, False Delicacy,* and *The School for Wives*—bears out this conclusion. The tradition of sentiment was so well established in comedy that even those who would break with the tradition—Goldsmith, for example—found it almost impossible to do so. At the same time, by returning to the older pattern of the comedy of manners, playwrights were attempting to infuse into the drama of their day a greater element of wit and humor and at least to restore the balance between the *dulce* and the *utile,* which for some time had been upset in favor of the latter.

Although not among the most often performed, two other types of comedy are found in the mid-century repertory. The comedy of "humours" was still popular, as is shown by the frequent performance of Jonson's plays, and numerous "humourous" characters are to be found in all types of new comedies, from the sentimental to the farcical. Few new plays appeared, however, that might be regarded as in the Jonsonian tradition, although Foote, whose *The Minor* and *The Lyar* were acted as regular comedies at the patent theaters, the former with considerable frequency, is perhaps best considered as a latter-day satirist of the tribe of Ben. Nor should it be overlooked that titles like *The Choleric Man, The Dupe,* and *The Hypocrite,* as well as names of characters like Lydia Languish and Sir Archy MacSarcasm, indicate that the influence of Jonson was still felt by the writers of comedy. The other type, called by Goldsmith "laughing comedy," is found chiefly near the end of the period. By that time a reaction against sentimentalism had set in,[11] which, although not entirely successful, helped the plays of Goldsmith and Sheridan as well as some of the comedies of Foote, Colman, and even Cumberland to gain an audience. Eighteenth-century comedy had never been completely devoid of humor, even in the Steelean depths of morality, and humor and satire form an important element in several comedies before *The Good-Natured Man;* but it was not until the last years of the period that audiences were content merely to be amused by a new comedy.

The new tragedies most often acted were *Tancred and Sigismunda, Merope,* Jones' *The Earl of Essex, Douglas, The Roman Father, Mahomet,* and *The Earl of Warwick,* each of which was acted twenty times or more in the course of several seasons. This group is fairly typical of all the new tragedies performed in the period. Many were drawn from Roman or Greek sources, such as *The Roman Father* and *Merope;* several, such as *Mahomet,* made use of Asiatic themes; English history supplied the setting and often the plot for a large number; and almost all, including the seven listed above, emphasize the love element, even at the expense of probability or historical accuracy. Most of them, in keeping with this greater emphasis on the love element, provide for a distressed female who—whether mother, wife, sister, or mistress—had almost become a *sine qua non* according to contemporary ideas of tragic character. Consequently pathetic tragedy, often inspired by the plays of Otway and Rowe, formed a large part of the theatrical repertory, and few tragedies that did not have a strong infusion of pathos survived their first performance.

In contrast to pathetic tragedy, heroic tragedy proved much less popular. Its rant and bombast, so much applauded in the seventeenth century, influenced many contemporary authors, who seem to have felt that heroic utterance was necessary to heighten the tone in the interests of morality. But there were few attempts to write entire tragedies in this vein. Heroic utterance had been appropriate to Cibber and Quin, who relished such parts, but hardly for the diminutive Garrick or for those actors who modeled their delivery upon his. It is also significant that at a time when most of the older drama was being ransacked to supply entertainment for the stage, the heroic drama of Dryden and his contemporaries was almost completely ignored. Pathos, not heroics, was the fashionable sentiment of the time. There is little matter for wonder, then, in the relative neglect of the heroic tragedy by both the playwrights and the theater companies of the eighteenth century; and the few new plays of the species that reached the stage received little encouragement. Johnson's *Irene* (1749) will serve to illustrate. In spite of the author's growing reputation and the best efforts of Garrick and a strong cast, the play was endured for only the nine performances granted a new tragedy and was never revived thereafter. Boswell's comment seems to represent accurately the contemporary judgment:

Irene, considered as a poem, is entitled to the praise of superiour excellence. Analysed into parts, it will furnish a rich store of noble sentiments, fine imagery, and beautiful language; but it is deficient in pathos, in that delicate power of touching the human feelings, which is the principal end of the drama.[12]

Domestic tragedy also had a relatively unimportant place in the repertory, the only new plays of this type that were successful being Moore's *The Gamester* and Dodsley's *Cleone*. It should be remembered, however, that Lillo's *The London Merchant* (1731) continued to be acted with considerable frequency, and several still older dramas owed at least part of their continuing popularity to their treatment of domestic affairs. Prose, employed by both Lillo and Moore—and, it would seem, appropriate where tragedy leaves the realm of the monarchical and lofty—was still not regarded as an adequate medium for serious drama. Moreover, Shakespeare had employed blank verse in his tragedies, and his example was enough to determine the practice in the eighteenth century. The result was that few dared to adopt the innovation. The tragedies that made use of domestic settings and situations in either verse or prose, except for a few plays such as those of Lillo and Moore, are indistinguishable from pathetic tragedies. Without an acceptable linguistic medium or the daring to depart completely from the Aristotelian dicta on greatness, the time was far from being ready for an Ibsen or a Shaw.

More popular than the domestic was a kind of tragedy written with such frequency that its consideration as a special type seems almost to be warranted. It was not actually a distinct species, however, as is shown by a comparison with the typical pathetic tragedies of the time. With them it shares the pathetic female, the heart-rending scenes of separation and reunion, the ultimate triumph of virtue over villainy, and the didactic morality. Its peculiarity as a type lies in its propensity to draw upon England's past for its plot, setting, and characters. Such tragedies—for example, Home's *Alfred,* Glover's *Boadicia,* Francklin's *The Earl of Warwick* and *Matilda,* Hull's *Henry the Second,* and Woodfall's *Sir Thomas Overbury*—portray actual historical characters and events on the stage or proclaim patriotic sentiments against a pseudo-historical or semihistorical background, and depend upon history or accepted legend instead of verisimilitude for their effect. Although occasionally reminiscent of Shakespeare's chronicle plays, they are not so much conditioned by renascent enthusiasm as by imperial vindication —there is no *joie de vivre,* but only a sense of the *fait accompli.*

Although dramatic activity was quantitatively great during the forty years of the mid-century, and plays of all kinds were written and produced, this dramatic activity was not uniform throughout the period; nor did comedy and tragedy attain their high points of composition at the same time. Whereas new tragedies were acted between 1737 and 1750 on the average of one a year, far fewer new comedies were produced, their total number being less than half that of the tragedies. In the next decade the disparity between the two types is even greater: only two new comedies were acted, but new tragedies were mounted at the rate of two each season. However, after 1760 the situation is reversed. Although the number of new tragedies diminished, two dozen new comedies reached the stage during the following decade—a greater number than in the whole preceding forty years—and for the first time since 1737 new comedies appeared at shorter intervals than did new tragedies. In the remaining years of the period, dramatic composition continued to flourish in both genres, with a notable increase in the number of tragedies, so that the attention given the two types by the theaters was equally divided. It is noteworthy that the writing and producing of tragedies were continually attempted but that comedy did not come into its own until after 1760. This "long gothic night" of comedy was frequently remarked by early historians of the theater,[13] and its end was welcomed when two successful comedies, *The Jealous Wife* and *All in the Wrong*, appeared in 1761. Musical pieces of various kinds also became more numerous after 1760. Consequently, it is strikingly clear that the complexion of the later repertory differed from the earlier, especially in its greater proportion of new works and in the necessary reduction in the number of nights that could be devoted to older drama.

CHAPTER FOUR

Revived Non-Shakespearean Drama

Of the three groups of plays to be considered here—Elizabethan and Jacobean (exclusive of Shakespeare's), Restoration, and early eighteenth-century drama—the plays of the last group were revived between 1737 and 1777 both in greater numbers and with greater frequency, and were outranked in number of plays only by new drama. Early eighteenth-century plays constituted one-fifth of all first pieces acted during the period, and accounted for almost one-fourth of the total number of performances. Of this number, almost 60 per cent are comedies, and there was approximately the same ratio of comedy to tragedy for relative frequency of performance.

In spite of the considerable attention given to early eighteenth-century plays in the mid-century repertory, as indicated both by the number of plays revived and by the number of performances, this attention was focused largely upon the work of a small number of playwrights. Of the fourteen writers of comedy whose plays were brought to the stage, Cibber is represented by ten plays, Steele and Mrs. Centlivre by four each, and Miller and Charles Shadwell each by three. The comedies of Miller received scant attention, however; and except for *The Fair Quaker of Deal*, a favorite piece of George II, Shadwell's also were infrequently acted. But several of Cibber's plays, especially *The Provok'd Husband, The Careless Husband, The Double Gallant, She Would and She Would Not, Love Makes a Man*, and *Love's Last Shift;* Steele's *The Conscious Lovers* and *The Funeral;* and Mrs. Centlivre's *The Busy Body, The Wonder*, and *A Bold Stroke for a Wife* were acted at least fifty times each in the period. Indeed, *The Provok'd Husband* was acted on a greater number of nights than any other play except *Hamlet, Romeo and Juliet*, and *The Beggar's Opera;* and *Hamlet* alone was revived in a greater number of seasons. Of other early eighteenth-century comic dramatists, only Fielding and Addison could compete with Cibber, Centlivre, and Steele during the mid-

36

century, and the popularity of each rested upon a single play. Fielding's *The Miser* was acted almost a hundred nights, and Addison's *The Drummer* was also frequently on the stage.

Few comedies of any significance first acted between 1700 and 1737 were not revived, although some only briefly, during the following forty years; and even the works of such unimportant writers as Taverner and Bullock were given a short life on the stage. Therefore it is notable that, except for *The Miser,* none of Fielding's full-length comedies was revived. It must be remembered, however, that many of his shorter plays, particularly *The Lottery, The Intriguing Chambermaid, The Mock Doctor, Tom Thumb,* and *The Virgin Unmask'd,* were frequently used as afterpieces. It has been suggested that Fielding's comic formula, depending upon "extravagance of plot and exuberances of fun," was no longer suitable for anything longer than a farce or a burlesque.[1] It should also be noted that Fielding himself recognized the shortcomings of the form in which he was working and soon after abandoned it for the novel. But with this one exception, mid-century theater audiences were able to see nearly all the comedies produced earlier in the century.

The shorter pieces of writers other than Fielding were similarly used as afterpieces. Henry Carey's *Chrononhotonthologos* and *The Dragon of Wantley,* Gay's *The What D'Ye Call It,* and Dodsley's *The King and the Miller of Mansfield* and *The Toy Shop* were among the most popular afterpieces of the mid-century until they were replaced by the farces of Garrick, Colman, and Foote. Longer comedies of the early part of the century were occasionally reduced to afterpieces. Thus, for example, Woodward drew upon Mrs. Centlivre's *The Busy Body* for a farce, *Marplot in Lisbon,* first acted in 1755.

Musical pieces were also revived as afterpieces. Ramsay's *The Gentle Shepherd* (in Theophilus Cibber's alteration) and Addison's *Rosamond* were both produced at Drury Lane in the 1760's to compete with Beard, the music-conscious manager of Covent Garden, and Coffey's ballad farce *The Devil to Pay* was acted nearly every season. Most pieces of this kind, however, survived only until the time of Bickerstaffe's introduction of a new type of musical entertainment; then that writer's comic operas became the most popular musical afterpieces. Even as

[1] For notes to chap. 4, see pp. 312-314.

early as 1737 the day of the ballad opera had largely passed, and such imitations of *The Beggar's Opera* as *The Lover His Own Rival, Love in a Riddle,* and *Love and Revenge*[2] were unable to survive. *The Beggar's Opera* itself, however, continued to hold the stage, being performed in thirty-seven seasons at Drury Lane and in twenty-nine at Covent Garden on a total of more than two hundred nights. Few plays of any kind could compete with it, and it is occasionally referred to by contemporaries as if it furnished a kind of measuring stick by which the popularity of new plays could be gauged.[3] Although it was sometimes attacked as morally corrupting, it never failed to find defenders.[4] Its sequel, *Polly,* prohibited in Gay's own time, was produced by Colman in 1777 at the Little Theatre in the Haymarket.

Fewer tragedies than comedies from the early part of the century were restored to the stage. Although the early eighteenth-century comedies revived with any frequency were restricted to those of a few authors, even fewer writers of tragedy during that period received attention on the mid-century stage. Of the twenty-eight tragedies revived after 1737, one-fourth are by Nicholas Rowe, inventor of the term "she-tragedy," who was regarded during the mid-century as excelling in the pathetic vein. Three of his tragedies, *The Fair Penitent, Jane Shore,* and *Tamerlane,* were more frequently revived than any other tragedies of the period; his *Lady Jane Grey* and *The Royal Convert* were acted in several seasons, and *Ulysses* and *The Ambitious Step-Mother* were each performed in a single season. Altogether the plays of Rowe were acted so frequently that the number of their performances amount to 10 per cent of the nights devoted to tragic drama of all types and to nearly half as many nights as were devoted to the tragedies of Shakespeare. So far had tragedy become synonymous with pathos.

Besides the dramas of Rowe, the most popular early eighteenth-century tragedies between 1737 and 1777 were, in order of popularity, Philips' *The Distrest Mother,* Hill's *Zara,* Lillo's *The London Merchant,* Addison's *Cato,* Hughes' *The Siege of Damascus,* and Young's *The Revenge,* each of which had fifty or more performances and was revived in ten or more seasons at each theater. It will be noted that in many of these plays the pathetic note is dominant, a characteristic common to almost all the tragedies thought suitable for revival during the mid-century. They share certain other traits as well. Several

draw upon English historical themes; for example, *Jane Shore,
Lady Jane Grey, The Royal Convert,* Dennis' *Liberty Asserted,*
Savage's *Sir Thomas Overbury,* and Sewell's *Sir Walter Raleigh.*
Several, including Trapp's *Abra-Mule,* Rowe's *The Ambitious
Step-Mother* and *Tamerlane,* Fenton's *Mariamne,* and Hughes'
The Siege of Damascus, employ Eastern legend; and Greek and
Roman history or myth furnishes the settings of Rowe's *Ulysses,*
Philips' *The Distrest Mother,* Mallet's *Eurydice,* and Smith's
Phaedra and Hippolytus. Thus, it would seem that the plays
were selected for revival in conformity with certain tendencies
of the mid-century: the antiquarian and philosophical interest
in English history, the growing awareness of England's imperial-
istic destiny, and the tenacious classical interest. That many
of them had been acknowledged by their authors as taken from
French originals was probably also to their advantage, for the
popularity of plays that could claim French influence was at its
height in the mid-eighteenth century.

Not only were early eighteenth-century plays of all types revived, but what passed for new plays in the mid-century were
often based upon the works of the preceding generation. Some
of these were merely alterations, undertaken in the interests of
the improved morality of the time—for example, Edward
Thompson's reworking of *The Fair Quaker of Deal.* In others
the revision was more far-reaching, as in Bickerstaffe's *The
Hypocrite* made from Cibber's *The Non-Juror,* where the allusions were made to apply to a later age. The reason for alteration is not always apparent, as in Swiney's *The Quacks,* acted
in 1705 after being twice prohibited and then brought to the
stage with alterations in 1745; but Thomas Arne seems to have
been seeking for a libretto when he adapted Fielding's *Don
Quixote in England* as *The Sot.* Hughes' *The Siege of Damascus,* according to Dr. Johnson,[5] established the fashion for
"Siege" titles, which persisted through most of the century. A
popular tragedy like *Jane Shore* naturally inspired many imitations, which similarly attempted to combine history and pathos;
and *The Conscious Lovers,* probably the most significant contribution of the age to drama, influenced plays as dissimilar as
Moore's *The Foundling,*[6] Cumberland's *The Fashionable Lover,*
Bickerstaffe's *Lionel and Clarissa,* and Hill's *Zara* (by way of
Voltaire's *Zaire*).[7] A reasonable conclusion, therefore, is that
the dramatic activity of the first four decades of the eighteenth

century was of considerable importance in the theatrical history of the later period; not only did the earlier years supply the mid-century theater with almost one-fourth its repertory, but these same years exerted significant influence upon many of the new dramas expressly written for the later stage.

Restoration drama[8] provided one-sixth of the plays in the mid-century repertory and accounted for about one-fifth of the total number of performances. Unlike the revived drama of the early eighteenth century, however, whose influence extended with considerable strength into the last quarter of the century, the popularity of many of the Restoration plays waned in the later years of the period. By that time most of the tragedies had disappeared from the boards, and with certain notable exceptions—particularly *The Beaux' Stratagem, The Provok'd Wife, The Recruiting Officer,* and *Love for Love*—Restoration comedy had also given way to newer plays.

Among the writers of tragedy, Otway was by far the most popular during the eighteenth century, although his fame rested entirely upon two plays, *The Orphan* and *Venice Preserved.* His other tragedies, including the rhymed *Don Carlos,* seem not to have been given a single performance. The strongly pathetic quality of both the revived tragedies explains why they were particularly congenial to the century after their composition. Next to Otway in popularity was Nathaniel Lee, whose *Rival Queens* and *Theodosius* were frequently performed. His *Massacre of Paris* was revived only once during the period—significantly, during the Jacobite Rebellion. *Oedipus,* the work of both Lee and Dryden, was revived during several seasons, although it did not have many performances. In spite of the objections raised against the bombastic quality of Lee's language and the improbability of his plots, the eighteenth century found his tragedies acceptable because of their ability to appeal to the emotions; Garrick, for example, said of *Theodosius:* "I am studying Veranes, . . . there is something very moving in ye Character, but such a Mixture of Madness & Absurdity was never Serv'd up, upon ye Stage before, except by ye same incomprehensible Nat Lee." [9] Almost equally popular as a writer of tragedy was Southerne. Although his comedies fared even worse than did those of Otway, his two tragedies, *Oroonoko* and *The Fatal Marriage,* were highly regarded for their pathos and were often acted. Dryden's tragedies suffered a worse fate. Besides the *Oedipus* already mentioned, only his *All for Love* and *Don Sebastian* were revived during the mid-century, the former with moderate success and the latter with less frequency. It is noteworthy that Dryden's play on the Antony and Cleopatra theme succeeded better on the mid-century stage than did Shakespeare's. Another Restoration dramatist, who was well known as a writer of comedies, wrote only a single tragedy, but it was performed more frequently than even his most popular comedies. The writer is Congreve; his tragedy, *The Mourning Bride,* was revived more often than any other Restoration tragedy except the two plays of Otway. Three plays by Banks, all on English historical themes, were given occasional performance; one of these, *The Unhappy Favourite,* was sometimes revived even after the plays of Jones and Brooke, also based on the story of the Earl of Essex, had become stock pieces in the later repertory.

There are several significant omissions among the Restoration tragedians. Left entirely unacted were the historical tragedies of Boyle and Bancroft, as were also the numerous serious dramas of Crowne, Gildon, Settle, Tate, and of many lesser playwrights such as Mrs. Pix, Mrs. Trotter, and Sir Robert Howard, at least seven of Dryden's tragedies (including all the rhymed plays) and an equal number of Lee's.

On the other hand, fewer Restoration comedies than tragedies were neglected after 1737. The most frequently revived author was Vanbrugh, whose *The Mistake, The Confederacy, The False Friend, Aesop, The Provok'd Wife,* and *The Relapse* were acted, the last two being among the most popular plays of the period. Five of Farquhar's comedies were revived—*The Constant Couple, The Recruiting Officer, The Beaux' Stratagem, The Twin Rivals,* and *The Inconstant*—and for a greater number of performances than even those of Vanbrugh. Indeed, so frequently acted were the plays of these two writers that 15 per cent of the evenings devoted to comedy were given over to one or another of these eleven plays, and together they account for almost one-twelfth of the entire theatrical repertory.

Following these two authors in popularity was Congreve, whose *The Double Dealer, The Old Bachelor, Love for Love,* and *The Way of the World* had frequent performance, the last two being revived at each theater during more than twenty seasons.[10] Two of Wycherley's comedies had moderate success when revived, but those of Etherege were less fortunate. Only three of Dryden's comedies were acted, and only *The Spanish Fryar* held the boards with much persistence. Howard's *The Committee* was revived during a greater number of seasons than all but the most popular of the comedies of Vanbrugh, Farquhar, and Congreve; and Ravenscroft's *The London Cuckolds,* in spite of its licentiousness, was often acted, chiefly because it was traditionally performed on Lord Mayor's Day. *The Rehearsal,* Villiers' famous burlesque, continued to be called for as long as Garrick was on the stage. As it was later performed, the play seems to have had little in common with the original except the title and the name of the chief character, the topical allusions whose significance was forgotten having been replaced with others that applied to fashions and politics of the eighteenth century.

The most notable omissions from the repertory were several of the comedies of Mrs. Behn and Durfey, and all but one of Thomas Shadwell's numerous plays. All the important comic writers of the Restoration period, however, were represented by at least a play or two, and all a writer's pieces were often revived. Even the comedies of Otway, which were thought to be "totally unworthy of him," [11] were acted, although they met with no encouragement and each succumbed after a single performance. Even where a play was not revived as a full-length comedy, it sometimes served as an afterpiece in shorter form. Thus Ravenscroft's *The Anatomist* and Tate's *A Duke and No Duke* were frequently performed as farces during the eighteenth century, the latter, for example, being acted at Drury Lane during every season from 1749-1750 to 1758-1759 for a total of sixty-six nights.

Besides providing an important segment of the mid-century repertory, Restoration comedy and tragedy also furnished later playwrights with plots, situations, and characters to be reworked into new dramas. Some of the latter were hardly more than alterations; for example, Gentleman's *The Royal Slave,* altered from *Oroonoko;* Hawkesworth's revisions of the same play and of Dryden's *Amphitryon;* Lee's alteration of *The Country Wife;* and Bickerstaffe's alteration of *The Plain Dealer.* Such pieces were regarded as revivals of older plays rather than as new dramas. Their alteration was considered necessary because of their licentiousness, and therefore they were expurgated in keeping with the stricter moral code of the time. Dryden was sometimes plundered to provide material for such pieces, and Vanbrugh's plays were favorite sources for later writers. Thus, Bickerstaffe's *The Captive* is based upon Dryden's *Don Sebastian;* Kelly's *The Prince of Agra* (often attributed to Sir William Addington) is reworked from *Aureng-Zebe; The Spanish Fryar* provided a three-act farce, *The Jealous Husband;* Cibber's *The Comical Lovers* used both *Secret Love* and *Marriage A-la-Mode;* and Dell drew upon both Dryden and Cibber for his *The Frenchified Lady Never in Paris.* Vanbrugh's *The Mistake* was used by Thomas Ryder in *Like Master, Like Man,* as well as for Lyon's unacted *The Wrangling Lovers;* Vanbrugh's *The Relapse* was drawn upon by Lee for *The Man of Quality* and by Sheridan for *A Trip to Scarborough.* Several of the most frequently acted alterations of Restoration drama were the work of Garrick. His *Isabella* (a revision of Southerne's *The Fatal Marriage*), *The Country Girl* (taken from Wycherley's *The Country Wife*), and *King Arthur* (altered from Dryden's masque) were successful experiments in three different dramatic genres—tragedy, comedy, and opera—and all had a longer-than-average stage life.

Thus Restoration drama continued to be important in the theater during the eighteenth century. It provided the mid-century stage with as many individual plays as did Shakespeare and all his contemporaries and immediate successors combined, and this in spite of the antiquarian movement that encouraged the return to the stage of many old and forgotten plays from the late sixteenth and early seventeenth centuries. Such a situation may seem all the more surprising when it is remembered that Restoration drama was written for a small, sophisticated, libertine audience, and that the most licentious drama could hardly have been more than a slightly exaggerated account of the average spectator's customary activity.[12] On the other hand, mid-eighteenth-century audiences were larger and more democratic, belonged to no single social group, and for the most part felt the need for a sterner moral code than had once prevailed. Such a paradox may seem insoluble; however, the solution is to be found, I believe, in the gradually changing moral temperament of the age. This development will be discussed later at length. At any rate a noticeable change occurs about 1760, and the later repertory reflects the replacement of the earlier moral uncertainty by certainty, of instability by the acceptance of a new sense of direction. With this change, most of the ribald dramas from the Restoration period were dropped from the repertory, and the few remaining were cleansed of the situations and dialogue that the eighteenth century found objectionable.

The Elizabethan and Jacobean dramas that were revived in the mid-eighteenth century are, to a greater degree than any previously considered, the work of a small number of authors. The traveling player in *The Vicar of Wakefield* told Dr. Primrose that the plays of Shakespeare, Fletcher, and Jonson were "the only things that go down," a declaration that an examination of the repertory of the period shows to be extremely accurate. Aside from Shakespeare, whose plays will be discussed separately, the early playwright who contributed the greatest number of dramas to the mid-century stage was Fletcher. Writing in 1783 of Beaumont and Fletcher, Davies remarks, "Of the fifty-four dramatic pieces, written by these great poets, two only at present preserve their rank on the stage, the Chances and Rule a Wife and have a Wife. No writers, sure, ever experienced such a reverse of fortune!" [13] Their fortune was quite different, however, during the preceding half-century. At least nine comedies (*The Chances, The Humorous Lieutenant, The Pilgrim, Rule a Wife and Have a Wife, The Sea Voyage, The Scornful Lady, Women Pleased, The Wild Goose Chase,* and *Wit Without Money*) were produced as first pieces, as were two tragedies (*The Prophetess* and *The Maid's Tragedy*) and the tragicomic *Philaster. The Beggar's Bush* also appeared as a full-length comedy in Hull's alteration under the title *The Royal Merchant;* and there is some indication that *The Faithful Shepherdess* was acted, only to meet with the same fate it had in 1610.[14] Cibber's *Love Makes a Man,* revived during numerous seasons in the middle of the century, may also be mentioned here, as it was based upon two of Fletcher's plays, *The Elder Brother* and *The Custom of the Country,*[15] although it was undoubtedly not regarded as anything else than Cibberian. In addition, several comedies, including *The Little French Lawyer, The Maid in the Mill,* and *The Tamer Tam'd,* were shortened to serve as afterpieces. Thus nineteen of the plays Davies mentioned are accounted for, and the number could be increased to twenty by including *The Loyal Subject,* altered by Thomas Sheridan for the Dublin stage but apparently unacted in London.

But in spite of the number actually performed, which itself might indicate that Fletcher's plays were highly regarded in the eighteenth century, few were maintained long as stock pieces, and several did not survive the season during which they were revived. Only *Rule a Wife and Have a Wife,* which was acted in more than twenty seasons at each patent theater, can be said to have competed successfully with the most popular plays of Jonson or many of Shakespeare's dramas. Nor is it difficult to conjecture why this play should have been singled out for retention on the boards. The part of Leon gave Garrick the opportunity to display his particular talent—the rapid transition from one emotion to another—and Woodward and Mrs. Pritchard were successful as Perez and Estifania. It is also significant that the play was thought to contain "an admirable lesson for proper conduct in the married state." [16] Thus, both because it was skillfully acted and because it flattered the audience's sense of moral rectitude, it had the opportunity to succeed where other plays by Fletcher did not.

Contemporary comment on the less successful plays is also enlightening. The criticism makes two principal charges: that Fletcher's plays are full of "indecencies," and that they are improbable. The mid-century world of the theater was nothing if not insistent upon decency and probability. Consequently, Garrick found it necessary that *The Chances* be "pruned . . . of all its indecencies," [17] a course that Colman also adopted in altering *Philaster.*[18] One of the most instructive comments on the second charge—that Fletcher's plays were too improbable for successful representation—is found in a letter written by Lord Orford. When asked by "Lady C-----n" to give his opinion of *The Scornful Lady,* he wrote:

It is like all the rest of the pieces of Beaumont and Fletcher; they had good ideas, but never made the most of them; and seem to me to have finished their plays when they were drunk, so very improbable are the means by which they produce their *denouement.* To produce a good play from one of theirs, I believe the only way would be, to take their plan, draw the characters from nature, omit all that is improbable, and entirely re-write the dialogue; for their language is at once hard and pert, vulgar and incorrect, and has neither the pathos of the preceding age nor the elegance of this. They are grossly indelicate, and yet have no simplicity. There is a wide difference between unrefined and vicious indecency; the first would not invent fig-leaves; the latter tears holes in them after they are invented.[19]

After such a gem of contemporary criticism, it is perhaps anti-climactic to note that Genest found *The Beggar's Bush* "unnatural and absurd." [20]

Although fewer plays by Ben Jonson than by Fletcher and his collaborators were given performance during this period, they constitute a larger part of the repertory because of their greater success in maintaining their places on the acting list. Three of his comedies, *Volpone, Epicœne,* and *The Alchemist,* had held the stage with some continuity since the Restoration.[21] During the earlier years, the stage history of *Volpone* depended upon the skill of James Quin in the title role, and consequently the play was performed almost exclusively at Covent Garden. The few performances of *Volpone* at Drury Lane coincided with Quin's membership in that company and with that of Delane, his chief competitor in the role.[22] The play fell into neglect after Quin's retirement and remained unacted from 1754 to 1771. Garrick had intended to revive the play; he once went so far as to put it in rehearsal, but for some unrecorded reason it was withdrawn.[23] It was finally revived at Covent Garden in 1771 with Smith as Volpone and Bensley as Mosca.

Epicœne, frequently announced as *The Silent Woman,* was less successful than *Volpone,* having only two-thirds as many performances and being revived in a much smaller number of seasons. The play was acted once or twice a year from 1737 until 1742 and was revived for a few performances at Covent Garden between 1745 and 1748, after which it almost disappeared from the boards. Garrick attempted a revival at Drury Lane in 1752, where "with perseverance it was dragged on for a few nights. The managers acquired neither profit nor reputation by the exhibition of it." [24] After almost twenty-five years of complete neglect it was again revived, this time in an alteration made by Colman, but was acted only four times. Of this revival in 1776, Davies remarks, "Mr. Colman, after all the pains and skill he could bestow on this comedy, found that it was labour lost; there was no reviving the dead." [25]

The Alchemist was much more successful than either of the preceding plays. It was acted almost every year throughout the period although with less frequency after *The Tobacconist* (an abridgment by Gentleman) appeared in 1770. Most of the famous actors of the time had parts in the play during its various revivals; but after 1743, when Garrick first appeared as Abel Drugger, the success of the play rested almost solely upon his popularity in that role, or, in the words of Davies, "these last forty years, it has been supported by the action of a favourite Abel Drugger." [26] It is interesting to note that the name had become well known by the mid-century and that John Hardham, a minor dramatist who wrote about 1750, chose Abel Drugger as his pseudonym.[27] There was one important alteration made during the period, but little was done to the play except to prune it of indecent passages and to reduce its acting time in conformity with contemporary theater practice. Altogether, more than nine hundred lines were removed from the play.[28]

Every Man in his Humour, however, had the most remarkable career of any of Jonson's plays between 1737 and 1777; in fact, it had one of the most remarkable careers in the history of English drama. Here again Garrick was largely responsible. Murphy notes of Garrick, "Zealous at all times for the honour of the English drama, he turned his thoughts to Ben Jonson. Having by his performance of *Abel Drugger,* made the *Alchymist* a favourite play, he chose to bring forward the comedy of *Every Man in His Humour.*" [29] He made some alterations in the original, expunged all passages that were thought to retard the plot or were obsolete,[30] added a scene between Kitely and his wife in Act IV,[31] gave it a strong cast (including Woodward, Yates, Ross, Shuter, Berry, as well as himself), and brought it to the stage in 1751. Whitehead, who wrote the prologue for the revived play, asked that the audience

> Kindly forget the hundred years between;
> Become old Britons, and admire old Ben.

Spectators quickly accepted that advice, for the play had more than 150 performances in the next quarter-century; and its announcement for a night at a theater—usually Drury Lane— was almost certain to bring an audience, even when the rival theater was at its strongest. The play had sixteen performances in its first season (1751-1752), and was acted every season thereafter until Garrick retired from the stage. It was acted only at

Drury Lane until 1762, when, with Woodward as Bobadil, a part in which he had played to Garrick's Kitely, it was revived at Covent Garden under the management of Beard. At this revival the play also had sixteen performances. Thereafter it continued as a stock piece at both theaters.

The other performances of Jonson's works can be recorded quickly. *The Tobacconist,* a farce made from *The Alchemist,* survived for only a short period, having fourteen performances between 1770 and 1776. It seems to have been an attempt to exploit, in an afterpiece that could be acted with other drama, the popularity achieved by Garrick as Abel Drugger in the longer play. *The Coxcombs,* a farce taken from *Epicœne* and, like *The Tobacconist,* the work of Francis Gentleman, had only one performance—at the Haymarket in 1771. *Abel Drugger's Return,* a burlesque interlude, had three performances at the same theater in 1774. And this completes the record of performances of Jonsonian comedy during the period. It should be noted however that Colman's *The Fairy Prince,* performed in 1771, made use of *Oberon;* and *The Druids,* an anonymous masque performed at Covent Garden in 1774, was, according to the title page of the printed edition, "chiefly taken from Ben Jonson." [32] But the eighteenth-century conception of the masque was far different from that held by Jonson,[33] and it is hardly surprising that the poet's numerous works of that type had disappeared long before 1737.

Of the remaining plays, *Bartholomew Fair* had been performed as recently as 1735 at Lincoln's Inn Fields, but was not brought to the stage during the period. *Every Man out of his Humour* was neglected after about 1675, and the lesser comedies were apparently never revived after the reopening of the theaters in 1660. The same fate was met by *Sejanus,* although Gentleman, the ubiquitous alterer of Jonson, offered a version of the tragedy to Garrick, who did not accept it. The author then published the alteration and stated in the preface the objections raised by Garrick, which were chiefly to the excessive declamation and the insufficient incident of the piece.[34] Several years later (1770) another alteration of *Sejanus* was published (perhaps the work of James Scott) under the title *The Favourite.* It was unacted; nor is it clear whether it was intended as a stage play. Jonson's other tragedy, *Catiline,* met with better success after the Restoration, but it apparently dropped out of sight about 1690 and had no revivals by 1777.

It was said that Garrick's friends urged him "not to confine his labour of love to Shakespeare, but to extend his plan, and to open the rich treasures of Fletcher, Jonson, and Massinger." [35] One of his early biographers stated that he "scorned to rummage the Continent of Europe for new fangled plays, and sooterkins of tragedy and comedy from Germany," preferring to resort to the "old school." [36] Many of the revivals of the plays of Fletcher and Jonson were brought about by his efforts; but Fletcher's plays proved unsuitable for the most part, and Jonson's, although remarkably successful in several instances, hardly fared better on the whole. As a contemporary pointed out,[37] the frequent allusions to "local customs and temporary follies" had become largely unintelligible with the passage of time, so that to preserve them required "a kind of stage learning" as well as a knowledge of the "satirical history of the age" in which Jonson lived.

The time was ripe, however, for such a revival. As early as 1733 Theobald had made extensive use of the lesser Elizabethan playwrights to explain Shakespeare's meaning, and this naturally directed some attention to them. The editorial work of Johnson and Warfurton later contributed to the same end.[38] At the same time many private libraries were being collected, including those of the queen, Lady Mary Montagu, and the Countess of Pomfret, which contained volumes of older drama; there is, of course, Garrick's extensive library of plays, to which Johnson had access—sometimes to the owner's discomfiture. Also collections, selections, and books of quotations were appearing—for example, *The British Muse* (1738); Dodsley's *Old Plays* (1744); an edition of Beaumont and Fletcher by Theobald, Seward, and Sympson (1750); and Coxeter's edition of Massinger (1759).[39] A better understanding of the Elizabethan and Jacobean stages must certainly have resulted, and presumably the better understanding should have contributed to the greater success of the older plays in the contemporary theater.

That their success was on the whole a very modest one, in spite of the antiquarian spirit in the air, is to be explained in the same terms that account for the decline of drama of all types; literary drama was preparing to leave the stage for the closet, and the rediscovered plays came to be more frequently read than acted. Even relatively early in the century it had become fashionable in some circles to read rather than to attend plays—even completely new plays. This new practice spread for various reasons, including the widening circle of literacy, the growing practice of novel reading, and the increasing preoccupation of the stage with novelties of "sound and shew"— an emphasis some contemporaries found objectionable. Shakespeare's plays as stage pieces survived for the most part the various vicissitudes of the time—but his greatest contemporaries met a harsher fate, and consequently the lack of success attending the revivals of other early drama is not surprising.

Few indeed of these revivals were attempted, and still fewer met with any encouragement. Massinger's *A New Way to Pay Old Debts* was revived at Drury Lane in 1748 with a new actor, Thomas King, making his first appearance as Allworth. The comedy was acted four times that season and revived again for one performance in the 1758-1759 season and one in the following year. After another ten-year interval it was given three performances in 1769-1770, thus ending its stage career. Massinger's *The Fatal Dowry* provided Aaron Hill with more than he acknowledged for *The Insolvent, or Filial Piety,* acted at the Haymarket in 1758, which, according to the title page, was based "Partly on a Plan of Sir William Davenant's and Mr. Massinger's." Genest thought, however, that "the far greater part . . . is stolen from Massinger." [40] This play apparently had a brief life, as no record of a second performance has come to light. *The Fatal Dowry* also seems to have provided Rowe with a situation he used in *The Fair Penitent,* but the original or a recognizable alteration of Massinger's play apparently did not reach the mid-century stage. Similarly Lee had borrowed from *The Emperour of the East* for his *Theodosius.* None of these plays, however, even though they might be given frequent performances, as was true of *The Fair Penitent* and *Theodosius,* could hardly have been regarded as a revival of Massinger's drama. Of his other plays, *The Virgin Martyr* had been altered by Benjamin Griffin as *Injured Virtue* (1715); *The Bondman* was acted under the title *Love and Liberty* (1719); and *The Roman Actor,* a favorite play of Betterton's, was acted as recently as 1722; but none of these seem to have been revived during the mid-century. Of

The City Madam, an early theatrical historian remarked that
it "would need very little Alteration to bring it on the List of
our most pleasing acting Plays";[41] but its only revival, at Richmond in 1771 as altered by James Dance, did not encourage the
managers of the London patent theaters to put it in rehearsal.

Albumazar, a comedy by the little-known Jacobean playwright
Thomas Tomkis, was acted briefly in James Ralph's altered
version, *The Astrologer,* in 1744. The original was revived by
Garrick in 1747 with moderate success and again in 1773.[42]
The City Match, by another minor author—Jasper Mayne—
provided the basis for Bromfield's *The Schemers,* acted twice at
Drury Lane in 1755, the first time as a benefit for Lock Hos-
pital.[43] Richard Brome, Jonson's servant and imitator in drama,
is represented in the repertory of the eighteenth century by
The Ladies Frolick; by James Dance's alteration of *The Jovial
Crew,* acted in 1770; and by *The Northern Lass,* performed
early in the period at Covent Garden. The first of these was
apparently transformed into a ballad opera by a Mr. Roome
and performed at Drury Lane about 1760.[44] The anonymous
Arden of Feversham was adapted for the stage by Lillo and
acted in 1759. *Eastward Hoe,* by Marston, Chapman, and
Jonson, was acted only one night, as a substitute for *The
London Cuckolds* on Lord Mayor's Day, but was then driven
from the stage. Altered by Mrs. Lennox as *Old City Manners,*
it survived through seven performances at Drury Lane during
the 1775-1776 season. No other plays by Chapman seem to
have been acted in any form, and the only other performance
of a play by Marston in the eighteenth century was apparently
Bullock's alteration of Betterton's version of *The Dutch Cour-
tezan,* acted as *Woman's Revenge* in 1715 but not revived thereafter. Only *The Lover's Melancholy* of Ford's plays was revived
at the patent theaters (for three performances at Drury Lane
in 1748), but his historical play, *Perkin Warbeck,* was acted at
Goodman's Fields in 1745 to take advantage of the popular
sentiment at the time of the Jacobite Rebellion. Macklin's
Henry VII, which deals with the same theme, is apparently not
indebted to Ford.[45] Ford's masterpiece, *'Tis Pity she's a Whore,*
did not reach the stage, a not surprising circumstance when
it is remembered that incest as a dramatic theme was quite
rigorously excluded from the theater. Baker wrote of this play,
in 1764, "In Consequence of this incestuous Passion . . . on

which the whole Plot of the Play turns, the Catastrophe of it is too shocking for an audience to bear. . . ." [46]

Finally—and the last is the only Jacobean play besides those written by Shakespeare, Fletcher, and Jonson that can be called successful—*The Gamester* by Shirley, altered by Garrick as *The Gamesters,* was performed seven times during the 1757-1758 season with a strong cast including Garrick, Woodward, Palmer, Yates, and Mrs. Cibber; thirteen times in 1772-1773; three times the following season; and once in 1774-1775 and 1776-1777. Moore's original tragedy *The Gamester* (1753) and Mrs. Centlivre's play of the same name, written in 1705 and occasionally acted during the mid-century, although hardly indebted to Shirley, attest to the popularity of plays about gaming. The vice, to be sure, was alarmingly prevalent at the time.[47] Garrick recognized the applicability of Shirley's play to his own day, as is apparent from the prologue he wrote for the 1757 revival. After making an appeal to the patriotic sentiment of his audience, he continues:

> Would you rekindle all your ancient fires,
> Extinguish first your modern vain desires.
> Still it is yours, your glories to retrieve;
> Lop but the branches, and the tree shall live.
> With these erect a pile for sacrifice,
> And in the midst—throw all your cards and dice;
> Then fire the heap, and, as it sinks to earth,
> The British genius shall have second birth.

Although Milton is not ordinarily considered as a dramatist who wrote for the theater, one of his works did have a notable stage history in the mid-century. The piece is *Comus,* performed in thirteen seasons at Drury Lane and fourteen at Covent Garden, on at least eighty nights. It was twice adapted for the stage—once by Dalton in 1738, and later by Colman in 1773. Dalton's version was arranged in three acts and furnished with additional songs, many of which were drawn from *L'Allegro* and other poems of Milton. This revival, apparently the first on a public stage, was strongly supported by Quin, Theophilus Cibber, Mills, Mrs. Cibber, Mrs. Clive, and Mrs. Arne. There was so much dancing and other stage business that, contrary to the custom at that time, the gentlemen were requested not to seek admittance behind the scenes, so that they would not interrupt the performance. The masque was acted on eleven nights during its first season, once as a benefit for Milton's daughter, who received more than £120 from Dalton.[48] Its revival in 1740 caused an incident that is both significant and amusing. A song had been written—apparently by Dalton—to be included in the masque and to be sung by "an Amazon." This little-known song is noteworthy both as a faint foreshadowing of the "noble savage" of a later date (in spite of its cavalier denouement!) and as an intended Miltonic encrustation.

> Swains I scorn, who nice and fair,
> Shudder at the morning air;
> Rough and hardy, bold and free,
> Be the man that's made for me.
>
> Slaves of fashion, slaves to dress,
> Fops *themselves alone* caress:
> Let them without rival be—
> They are not the men for me.
>
> He whose nervous arm can dart
> The jav'lin to the tiger's heart,
> From all sense of danger free;
> He's the man that's made for me.
>
> If undaunted he can lie,
> With no curtain but the sky,
> From cold damps and vapours free;
> He's the man that's made for me.
>
> While his speed outstrips the wind,
> Loosely wave his locks behind,
> From fantastic foppery free:
> He's the man that's made for me.
>
> Nor simp'ring smile, nor dimple sleek,
> Spoil his manly sun-burnt cheek;
> By weather let him painted be;
> He's the man that's made for me.
>
> If false he prove, my jav'lin can
> Revenge the perjury of man;
> And soon another, brave as he,
> Shall be found the man for me.[49]

Eventually the song had to be omitted because no actress could be found willing to sing it. But that a song of such a nature could be considered suitable to *Comus* suggests how much the original spirit of the masque had suffered at the hands of its alterers. A better-known revival is the one recorded by Boswell.[50] This was a benefit performance in 1751 for the poet's granddaughter, Elizabeth Foster, which Johnson urged the public to attend to pay tribute to Milton's memory and to rectify the neglect of his only living descendant. In 1778 Colman produced his alteration of *Comus,* compressed into two acts and supplied with music by Arne. In this new form it became an afterpiece at a time when musical entertainments of all kinds were commonly attached to full-length drama to satisfy the prevalent taste. Besides *Comus,* Milton supplied one other stage piece in the period, although it was acted only once. On the night after the Duke of York's funeral in 1767 an interlude titled *Lycidas* was performed; according to Victor,[51] it was adapted for the occasion as a condolence on the death of the duke. The music was written by William Jackson and the words were altered from Milton. Because it was also November 4th, *Tamerlane* was the advertised play, to which the interlude was attached as an afterpiece.

Thus it can be seen that hardly more than a dozen pre-Restoration authors were represented in the mid-century repertory. To complete this account of the later stage history of early drama, it is instructive to note which authors were not represented. Not only such lesser dramatists as Chettle, Daniel, Day,[52] Field, Greville, Kyd, Lodge, Munday, Nash, and Peele were completely ignored; but also unrepresented were such major writers as Dekker, Greene, Heywood, Lyly, Middleton, Tourneur, and Webster. Why some were omitted is not difficult to conjecture. The artificial style and lack of "business" in *Endymion,* the lack of unity in *The Shoemaker's Holiday,* the horrendous quality of *The White Devil* and *The Spanish Tragedy*—such characteristics perhaps explain why much early drama would have been uncongenial to eighteenth-century audiences. But why such plays as *Friar Bacon and Friar Bungay,* with its "fair maid of Fressingfield" as well as the opportunity it provided for amusing stage business, or *A Woman Killed with Kindness,*[53] which might have been readily altered to please a moral age, were not revived would be more difficult to

54

determine. Perhaps their revival had to wait for another Garrick whom years of acting had not exhausted.

More noteworthy than these omissions is the complete neglect of Marlowe. There is some resemblance between *Tamburlaine the Great* and Rowe's *Tamerlane,* but the political implications of the latter play were perhaps sufficient to conceal any debt the later dramatist owed to his predecessor. Likewise, Nathaniel Lee wrote a play with the same theme and title as Marlowe's *The Massacre at Paris.* Lee's play was briefly revived in 1745, when almost every piece that might be construed as anti-Jacobite in spirit was brought to the stage, but there is no indication that it was regarded as indebted to Marlow. The title character of Lansdowne's *The Jew of Venice,* which survived briefly during the early years of the period, has perhaps more in common with Barabas in *The Jew of Malta* than with Shylock in *The Merchant of Venice;* there was undoubtedly no thought, however, of an indebtedness beyond Shakespeare. Not even by a circuitous route can a connection be traced between Marlowe and the mid-eighteenth-century stage. Davies declared, "To place Marlowe as a competitor to Shakespeare would revolt the mind of any reader. . . ."[54] It is significant that he is speaking here of the *reader,* for Davies is almost exclusively concerned with drama as it was *acted* during the days when he was spectator and player. At a time when Marlowe's plays were hardly good enough for the closet, they could not be expected to receive the additional advantage of performance. Moreover, their strongly heroic quality would have prevented them from gaining a place in the repertory when *The Conquest of Granada* and plays of its kind had gone out of fashion.

In this examination of the repertory a recognizable pattern has emerged, for the age of the various plays amounts almost to a test of their right to admission among the revivals of the period from 1737 to 1777. The largest number of plays acted were those written by contemporaries, followed in order by early eighteenth-century pieces, by Restoration drama, and by still earlier plays. The frequency of performance is also in general agreement with this situation. And there is no drama at all in the repertory to represent pre-Marlovian times. A noteworthy announcement, which has been overlooked by students of the period, should be mentioned, however: the *London Chronicle* once advertised a revival of *Gammer Gurton's Needle,* promised for twenty successive performances[55]—a promise that was apparently never fulfilled. But the pattern is broken by the one remaining author to be considered, for eighteenth-century audiences might have applied approvingly to Shakespeare's plays the words Enobarbus spoke of Cleopatra:

> Age cannot wither her, nor custom stale
> Her infinite variety.

CHAPTER FIVE

The Shakespearean Heritage of the Mid-Century Stage

Thirty[1] of the thirty-seven plays accepted as Shakespeare's appeared on the stage as first pieces between 1737 and 1777, and two others (*The Taming of the Shrew* and *Pericles*) in shorter versions. As many as twenty-one separate plays were produced at the two patent theaters in a single season (1757-1758), although immediately after Garrick's retirement the number fell to ten, the smallest number acted during the period. On the average it was possible for the London theatergoer to see fifteen or sixteen of Shakespeare's plays during a single season. On the basis of frequency of revival, the popularity of the individual plays ranged from that of *Hamlet,* which was acted during every season at Drury Lane and all but one at Covent Garden, to that of *Henry VI,* which was performed on a single night. The total number of nights devoted to the performance of Shakespeare's plays in the forty years—record of approximately 2,500 has come to light—constitutes almost one-fourth of the entire theatrical program for the period.

When it is considered that, exclusive of Shakespearean drama, there were about 150 plays that may with justice be called stock pieces, and that it was against this large body of new and revived drama that Shakespeare's plays had to compete, their remarkable achievement in maintaining such a dominant place on the mid-century stage becomes apparent. This record is all the more remarkable when it is noted that a greater number of performances was given the thirty Shakespearean plays than was devoted to almost twice that number of Restoration dramas or to four times that number of new pieces. But the importance of Shakespeare to the mid-century repertory can perhaps best be seen when it is realized that it was possible for audiences to see, on the average, two performances of Shake-

[1] For notes to chap. 5, see pp. 314-317.

speare's work each week throughout the nine-month theatrical season. Although the managers of the patent houses were quite chary of undertaking the risks involved in adding plays to the acting list, they frequently restored even the lesser-known Shakespearean plays to the stage. The notable success of the great actors of the day in Shakespearean roles, the prevailing antiquarianism, the popularity and at least the nominal veneration of Shakespeare during the mid-century all tended to compliment the managers' judgment.

Of the thirty plays that were acted, nine were tragedies (*Hamlet, Macbeth, Othello, Romeo and Juliet, King Lear, Julius Caesar, Coriolanus, Timon of Athens,* and *Antony and Cleopatra*); eight were histories (*Richard III, Henry IV, Part I, Henry IV, Part II, Henry V, Henry VIII, King John, Richard II,* and *Henry VI, Part I*); and thirteen were comedies (*The Merchant of Venice, The Merry Wives of Windsor, As You Like It, Much Ado About Nothing, The Tempest, Cymbeline,*[2] *Measure for Measure, Twelfth Night, All's Well That Ends Well, The Winter's Tale, The Comedy of Errors, The Two Gentlemen of Verona,* and *A Midsummer Night's Dream.*) In addition, *Pericles,* a play not then generally regarded as Shakespeare's, was altered by Lillo into the three-act *Marina,* which was performed briefly by the summer company at Covent Garden in 1738. *The Taming of the Shrew,* although not acted as a full-length play, provided Garrick with the substance for one of the most popular afterpieces of the time. Of the five remaining dramas, two (*Love's Labour's Lost* and *Troilus and Cressida*) were considered for revival but were left unacted, and the other three (*Henry VI, Part II, Henry VI, Part III* and *Titus Andronicus*), often regarded as the least Shakespearean of all, were completely neglected. Consequently, in a sense it is true that, in the words of Garrick's boast, almost "no drop of that immortal man" was completely lost during the mid-century period.

On the basis of the number of performances, the tragedies received the greatest attention. Of the total number of nights devoted to Shakespeare in the forty years, 993, or 40 per cent, were given to tragedy, followed by the comedies (862, or 35 per cent), and the histories (628, or 25 per cent). The most frequently revived play—not only among Shakespeare's, but of all first pieces presented between 1737 and 1777—was *Hamlet;* but it was surpassed in number of performances by *Romeo and*

Juliet, which was revived by Theophilus Cibber at the Haymarket in 1744 after its absence from the stage for nearly a century.[3] It was revived at Drury Lane four years later in a form closer to the original than Cibber's had been, and thereafter it enjoyed long runs at both patent houses. Of the comedies, *The Merchant of Venice* was revived most frequently; and *Richard III,* of course in Colley Cibber's version, of the histories.

With this brief statistical survey in mind, we may turn to the stage history of Shakespearean drama. At once, however, a difficulty arises. Shall a play altered almost out of all resemblance to the original, but yet advertised and popularly thought of as Shakespeare's, be considered Elizabethan or later drama? The answer lies in the distinction between the two terms constantly recurring in every account of the stage history of Shakespeare's plays: "alteration" and "adaptation." The words, to be sure, are loosely used—are in fact sometimes regarded as synonymous. But in general the former should apply to those pieces which reflect the reviser's—or his sponsor's—dissatisfaction with the original. In such reworked plays there may be rewritten lines, new lines, omission of characters and situations (made not solely in the interests of shortening the original for a two-hour performance), even new characters, and denouements changed from tragic to comic or the reverse. Such alterations were often spoken of as "improvements," made in the interests of morality or decorum. Adaptations, on the other hand, are those shortened versions which, by omissions—of secondary characters and expository scenes or by the reduction of the longer speeches— were cut to make their performance possible within the time limits customary for first pieces. The line between alterations and adaptations is, obviously, a difficult one to draw. Although the intention of the reviser is usually apparent in the changes he makes, in some instances he was altering the play in some important regard while ostensibly shortening its acting time. The resulting play may be difficult to class as either a definite alteration or a mere adaptation. Similarly, a play that is almost certainly a shortened stage version may contain minor additions or transpositions that might be classed as alterations but that do not violate the spirit of the original. Such, for example, is the Capell-Garrick version of *Antony and Cleopatra,* one of the best (that is, because not un-Shake-

59

spearean) stage adaptations made during the eighteenth century. Most of the changes in this play are omissions; yet the
famous description of Cleopatra is moved forward to the first
act, and the bacchanalian song is provided with another stanza.
The relative purity of this adaptation is in striking contrast to
such deliberate alterations as: James Miller's *The Universal
Passion* (1737), a reworking of *Much Ado About Nothing* with
additions drawn from Molière; Cibber's *Papal Tyranny in the
Reign of King John* (1744), a short-lived mutilation given
topical additions to heighten its political significance; Cumberland's *Timon of Athens* (1771), an alteration of an alteration
(Shadwell's), to which non-Shakespearean characters are added;
and the "improved" versions surviving from the Restoration
period.

Between the two extremes of the relatively reverent handling
of Shakespeare's originals shortened for stage performance and
the unscrupulous mutilation of text and spirit are more than a
hundred different acting versions of the plays—some newly
made and others inherited from an earlier day, some maintaining their places in the repertory season after season and
others sinking into oblivion after a single performance. But
regardless of their date or their popularity, no version that was
given performance can be overlooked in a history of Shakespeare
on the stage in the eighteenth century, whether it is the original
or the vilest alteration.

From this point of view, Shakespeare's plays may be placed in
three groups and several subgroups: those which were revived
before 1737 but continued to be acted between 1737 and 1777;
those which were revived in the forty years of the mid-century
period; and those which remained unacted before 1777. Within
the first group, a distinction can be made between those revived
during the Restoration period and those restored to the stage
for the changing audience of the early eighteenth century, or
between those revived in a form close to the original and such
operatized versions as Dryden and Davenant's *The Tempest*
(1667) or such mutilations as Tate's *King Lear* (1681). Within
the second group it is also possible to distinguish between
revivals of the originals and revivals of plays in altered form. If
the plays are fitted into the above-described categories, the
record of Shakespearean performance during the mid-century
can be represented as in the accompanying tabulation.

I. Plays revived before 1737 and acted between 1737 and 1777
  A. Plays revived during the Restoration period
    1. In a form close to the original: *Hamlet, Henry VIII, The Merry Wives of Windsor, Henry IV, Part I, Othello, Julius Caesar*
    2. In a considerably altered form: *King Lear, Macbeth,* Cymbeline,* Romeo and Juliet* (Otway's *Caius Marius*),* *The Tempest,* Timon of Athens, Coriolanus,* Antony and Cleopatra* (Dryden's *All for Love*),* *The Taming of the Shrew* (Lacy's *Sauny the Scot*)*
  B. Plays revived between 1700 and 1737
    1. In a form close to the original: *Henry IV, Part II, Measure for Measure, Much Ado About Nothing, Henry V*
    2. In a considerably altered form: *Richard III, The Merchant of Venice* (Granville's *Jew of Venice*)*
II. Plays revived between 1737 and 1777
  A. In a form close to the original: *King John, Richard II, Henry VI, Part I, As You Like It, Twelfth Night, The Merchant of Venice, All's Well That Ends Well, The Comedy of Errors, Coriolanus, Antony and Cleopatra, Cymbeline*
  B. In a considerably altered form: *The Winter's Tale, Romeo and Juliet, Macbeth, The Taming of the Shrew, A Midsummer Night's Dream, The Two Gentlemen of Verona, Pericles, The Tempest*
III. Plays unacted between 1737 and 1777
  A. Considered for performance but unacted: *Love's Labour's Lost, Troilus and Cressida*
  B. Completely neglected: *Titus Andronicus, Henry VI, Part II, Henry VI, Part III.*

Obviously, no system of classification is completely adequate to represent the fate of Shakespeare's plays on the eighteenth-century stage. Because of the tremendous energy expended by poets and poetasters in their enthusiasm for reworking Shakespeare, innumerable adaptations and alterations were produced.

---

* Acted in the altered form after 1737 but displaced by a version closer to the original by 1777.

Sometimes two different versions of the same play reached the patent theaters at about the same time. After fierce competition one version might gain a place as a stock piece in the repertory while the other disappeared completely; and it is notable that not always was it the better version or the one closer to the original that succeeded. Often an original play was revived and then dropped after a few seasons, to be eventually supplanted by an alteration that was either a new version contrived by a contemporary or a reworking of an alteration dating from the Restoration period or from the early part of the century. Those whose duty it was to furnish the stage with dramas that would attract audiences had found in Shakespeare a veritable storehouse of characters, situations, plots, and dialogue; and for the most part they were not hesitant to lay hands upon whatever might serve their purpose. The stage history of Shakespearean drama in the mid-eighteenth century is not, therefore, to be easily recounted or simply tabulated.

Neither can it be considered entirely apart from its fortunes on the Restoration and early eighteenth-century stages, for it was the Restoration theater that took the initiative in reëstablishing Shakespeare's continuity on the stage, which had been broken during the Commonwealth period. Moreover, Shakespearean acting traditions, many of which went back to Shakespeare's own time, came to the eighteenth century by way of Davenant and Betterton; and many of the altered versions of Shakespeare's plays that were used in the later period were compiled between 1660 and 1700, and thus, unless restored or subjected to further alteration, they reflect the temperament of the Restoration period rather than that of the mid-eighteenth century. The mid-century stage cannot, therefore, be considered completely in isolation from the earlier stages, upon which it depended in such important ways, even though it had strongly marked characteristics of its own.

1. Plays and "Improvements" Inherited from the Restoration Period

In referring to the half-century following the Restoration, Downes, the most voluble theatrical annalist of the time, says, ". . . it is astonishing to see how few plays [of Shakespeare] were acted during so long a period." [4] Actually, only six

Shakespearean pieces can be said to have had sufficient appeal to the Restoration audiences to compete successfully with the plays of Dryden and his contemporaries: *Hamlet, Othello,* and *Julius Caesar* of the tragedies; two of the Falstaff plays, *Henry IV, Part I* and *The Merry Wives of Windsor;* and *Henry VIII.* These six plays seem to have been performed in not greatly altered versions. *King Lear* and *Macbeth,* which were acted briefly in their original forms, fell into complete neglect after the mutilations of Tate (1681) and Davenant (1663) appeared. *The Tempest, Timon of Athens,* and *Coriolanus* were also seen with varying degrees of frequency but in forms much changed from those given them by their author. *The Tempest* was altered by Dryden and Davenant in 1667, *Timon of Athens* by Shadwell in 1678, *Coriolanus* by Tate in 1681. Less frequently acted, but also to the exclusion of the originals, were Dryden's *Troilus and Cressida* (1679), Durfey's *Cymbeline* (1682), and Lacy's *Sauny the Scot* (1667), altered from *The Taming of the Shrew.* The remaining plays of the Restoration stage that have some connection with Shakespeare are better regarded as independent compositions than as alterations, so greatly do they differ from the originals: Otway's *Caius Marius* (1680), a reworking of the Romeo and Juliet story; and Dryden's *All for Love* (1678), which employs the Antony and Cleopatra theme.

Of the fourteen Shakespearean plays represented here, all but one—*Troilus and Cressida*—reached the mid-eighteenth-century stage; however, their stage histories are not altogether similar. For example, *The Tempest* was subjected to many further reworkings during the intervening years; Tate's *Coriolanus* was displaced by Dennis' alteration before it was restored, in 1720, in a form closer to the original; and *King Lear* was not supplanted by the original until the nineteenth century. On the other hand, *Othello* reached the mid-century stage without ever having been subjected to serious alteration. Moreover, their stage histories differ in the matter of continuity as well as in that of textual condition. At one extreme are such sporadically revived plays as *Cymbeline* and *Timon of Athens,* and at the other is *Hamlet,* which was virtually never off the acting list.

The first Shakespearean play to be revived after 1660 was *Hamlet.*[5] Its success thereafter was both considerable and continuous. Writing almost 120 years later, Thomas Davies declared that "no dramatic piece whatever has laid hold on the public affection so strongly and been acted so frequently." [6] Every actor of any consequence aspired to the leading role, including Betterton, Wilks, Milward, Garrick, Sheridan, Barry, Smith, and Henderson, the most famous Hamlets between 1662 and 1777. Although each attempted to bring something new to the part, Betterton's conception more or less determined the outlines of later interpretations. How near Betterton's idea of the part may have been to the author's is suggested by Downes: "Mr. Betterton took every particle of Hamlet from Sir William Davenant, who had seen Mr. Taylor, who was taught by Mr. Shakespeare himself." [7] How accurately the conception of Hamlet was transmitted cannot, of course, be determined, but there is adequate evidence that Davenant served in numerous plays as the connecting link in the continuity of acting tradition. Another example in this same play is the part of Ophelia, in which Davenant instructed Mrs. Betterton "as he could catch [the idea of the role] from the boy-Ophelias he had seen before the civil wars." [8] Since Garrick, the greatest Hamlet of the eighteenth century, and perhaps the actor who appeared most frequently in the part, was a careful student of the theater and its traditions, it is not surprising that he based his interpretation on that of Betterton. Consequently, the play most often seen by mid-century audiences was perhaps as faithful to the author's intention, in its stage representation if not in its text, as it is possible for a 150-year-old drama to be.

Garrick portrayed a sane Hamlet assuming madness, thus following Betterton, but he placed greater emphasis on the prince's filial love.[9] His costume was that of his own day, the court garb of George II, in which he was painted by the artist Benjamin Wilson. Historical accuracy in costuming was still at this time little regarded, and Ramillies wigs and orders instituted centuries after the days of the Danish King Hamlet were not yet considered unsuitable. Nor would the fastidious stage economy of Garrick allow anyone to appear on the Drury Lane stage unless he was carefully attired. Thus, even when the situation might require it, as Ophelia's description of the distracted Hamlet certainly does (II, i, 77-84), he appeared throughout the play as "the glass of fashion and the mould of form."

Spranger Barry, Garrick's chief rival among English actors, sometimes alternated with him in the title role when they were both members of the same company, and competed with him when at the rival house. But he was less successful in Hamlet, a part in which he had little scope for his particular excellence as a stage lover. Smith and Henderson were close imitators of Garrick when they undertook the part. In fact, the only notable variation from the Betterton-Garrick conception of the role was that of Thomas Sheridan. His innovations, in spite of the generally conservative attitude toward acting traditions, seem to have been well received.

Less is known of the representation of other characters in the play, although Ophelia, Gertrude, Polonius, and the Second Grave-digger are occasionally mentioned. Mrs. Cibber was apparently the first actress to interpret Ophelia adequately. She portrayed the part by applying to herself the girl's description of Hamlet as "sweet bells jangled, out of tune and harsh" (III, i, 166).[10] Before Mrs. Cibber had made the role her own, Mrs. Booth had been content to portray Ophelia as an "innocent, unhappy maid: but she went no farther." [11] Mrs. Baddeley, who bridges the lapse of time between Mrs. Cibber and Mrs. Siddons, kept alive the Cibber characterization, although in the meantime others, including Mrs. Clive, the reigning comedy queen, undertook the role. The part of Gertrude was unpopular with actresses for a time, although Mrs. Pritchard, a worthy rival of Mrs. Cibber, succeeded so well that it was regarded as "one of her prime characters." She was thought particularly effective in the closet scene.

Opinion among the critics was divided about the character of Polonius, some believing with Warburton that he was "a prating, pedantick, busy, obsequious statesman; a fool with a dash of the knave," and others with Johnson that he was a wise man in his dotage. The actors and the theatergoing public were not, however, in doubt. To them Polonius was a knave and a fool, and was best represented by a low comedian. That the public was justified, on the basis of stage tradition, can be shown by reciting the names of the actors who had earlier played the part: Lovell, Nokes, and Cross, followed by Griffin, Hippisley, Taswell, and Shuter, and later by Wilson, Baddeley, and Edwin —all low comedians. Garrick was dissatisfied, however, with the traditional interpretation, and, probably under the influence of his friend Dr. Johnson, determined to show **Polonius** as an astute statesman whose faculties were decaying. He assigned Woodward to the part. The result and its effect upon the audience have been preserved: "The character, divested of his ridiculous vivacity, appeared to the audience flat and insipid. . . . So little was the audience pleased with Woodward, or Woodward with himself, that he never after attempted Polonius." [12] The Second Grave-digger had long entertained the galleries by holding up the digging while he peeled off a series of waistcoats, but there is some doubt that this practice was continued during Garrick's reign. The entire scene was frequently omitted from the performance, on the grounds that it both unnecessarily lengthened an already overlong play and was indecorous in serious drama. [13] Of the other parts, that of the Ghost is occasionally singled out by annalists for comment. It was regarded as an extremely difficult role, one in which no one had greatly succeeded after the retirement of Booth except Quin, who copied "the manner of his old master as closely as he possibly could." [14]

Hamlet was acted more than two hundred times at the two theaters between 1737 and 1777, but the text of the play was not always the same. The alterations made in the text were of two kinds: those traditional excisions made in the interest of shortening the play and inherited chiefly from Wilks' acting version; and those made by Garrick when he altered the play in 1772, resulting in important changes in the final scene. Brownsmith, prompter at the Haymarket, records that the acted version of *Hamlet* required three hours and three minutes, one minute less than *King Lear* and only thirteen minutes more than *Macbeth*. [15] As *Hamlet* is longer than the latter play by more than 1,800 lines, it is obvious that large quantities of the poet's work must have been omitted. Excised entirely were Hamlet's long speech on his country's vice (I, iv), even though its sentiment must have appealed to the moralizing eighteenth century, and the scene between Polonius and Reynaldo (II, i), which was regarded as unessential and had been omitted for more than a century. Hamlet's advice to the Players (III, ii) may have been restored before 1737, although earlier it was generally omitted. [16] All the scene between Hamlet, Rosencrantz, and the Norwegian Captain (IV, iv), including the soliloquy "How all occasions do inform against me," was long omitted until restored by Sheridan late in the century. There were also numerous smaller excisions.

Alterations of another kind were those made by the actors themselves, sometimes without premeditation. Davies remarks that Hamlet's admonition, "Let those that play your clowns speak no more than is set down for them," could have been profitably directed to low comedians like Shuter and Hippisley, who were often "too guilty of adding to the author's text." [17] And Ryan, fearful that the audience would mistake Hamlet's meaning because of the changes in language, substituted "direst" for "dearest" in the line "Would I had met my dearest foe in heaven" (I, ii, 182).[18]

Garrick's alteration of *Hamlet*, first acted in 1772, has long been an incentive for the severest kind of condemnation of the actor, who claimed to have great veneration for Shakespeare's work. The acting copy was, however, never printed, and it had disappeared from sight completely until the present century. Consequently, those who censured Garrick were doing so without having seen his adaptation of the play. George W. Stone, Jr., who recently discovered the unique copy among the Folger Library's Garrick manuscripts, defends the play, which he calls "fast-moving" and "effective." [19] Twenty lines previously altered were restored to their original versions, 117 lines long entirely omitted were completely restored, eleven lines were altered, and thirty-five of the adapter's were added. The effect of these changes was to make the minor characters more important than they had been in the acting versions of Betterton and Wilks and to restore expository material that assisted in giving point to the action. In rearranging the play, Garrick made two acts of Act I and extended some of Act III into Act IV. Laertes, traditionally unpopular with audiences, was made "more estimable";[20] the spectators were not informed of Ophelia's fate; and the Queen was not poisoned but led from the stage, after which it is reported that her sense of guilt had driven her mad. The King defended himself with his sword against Hamlet and was killed in the encounter. The result was that Claudius emerged much less despicable than in the original. Although the Shakespearean representation of the King's death was more congenial to the eighteenth century in that it stigmatized his wickedness, Garrick made this change probably to achieve greater decorum. He is quoted as having said that before his alteration of *Hamlet* "the King used to be stuck like a pig on the stage." [21] Other omissions were the voyage to England, the return of Fortinbras, and the character of Osric. Laertes, who was kept alive at the end of the play, was to have the control of Denmark.

Tate Wilkinson wrote to Benjamin Victor, the treasurer of Drury Lane, for a copy of Garrick's alteration; but Victor replied that it was impossible to comply with his request and that furthermore, since the version was not meeting with general favor, it probably would never be printed. Wilkinson, who had seen Garrick's play, then made an adaptation modeled upon Garrick's[22] for his own use, and printed it in 1795 in *The Wandering Patentee*. The stage history of Garrick's *Hamlet* illustrates, however, that it did not lack the power to draw audiences to the theater. It was acted fourteen times between 1772 and 1776 and brought into the treasury more than 3,400 pounds. Altogether it was acted thirty-seven times over an eight-year period, until Bannister returned to Wilks' *Hamlet* in 1780.[23] But it may have been Garrick rather than *Hamlet* that audiences came to see. He was nearing the time when he would retire from the stage, and people of all ranks came to London, not only from all parts of England but from the Continent as well, to see the English Roscius in his greatest roles for the last time. Garrick's friend Davies said a few years later that the public "received" the alteration "out of respect for Garrick . . . but they did not approve what they barely endured. . . . The people soon [that is, after Garrick's death] called for Hamlet as it had been acted from time immemorial." [24] And so succumbed the only serious attempt to alter considerably Shakespeare's most popular play.[25]

Another play revived soon after the Restoration was *Henry VIII.* It was performed early at the Theatre-Royal, and at Lincoln's Inn Fields in 1664. It continued to hold the stage and could be frequently seen throughout most of the eighteenth century. Because of its possibilities as spectacle, and particularly because of its coronation scene (IV, i), it was popular for occasions of state ceremony. It had been performed at Hampton Court before George I in 1717, at the time of the coronation of George II in 1727, and was acted frequently in 1761-1762, following the accession of George III. In the mid-eighteenth century it was revived in seventeen seasons at Drury Lane and ten at Covent Garden, and was given nearly a hundred performances.[26] Rich, the proprietor of Covent Garden, who excelled in lavish spectacles and pageants, crowded his house for almost two months during 1741 by staging a highly decorative representation of Anne Boleyn's coronation, and Drury Lane in self-defense was forced to run the coronation almost forty nights in a row. That the play taxed the stage with its supernumeraries and machinery is suggested by the announcement on the playbill for April 27, 1739, at Drury Lane. Although *Henry VIII* was being shown that night as a benefit performance, when it was customary to construct boxes on the stage in order to increase the actor's revenue, on that occasion it was announced: "To prevent the interruption in the performance there will be no seats built on the stage." [27]

As for *Hamlet,* there had been handed down for *Henry VIII* a set of acting traditions that can be traced from 1613 to the middle of the eighteenth century. Sir William Davenant, from his remembrance of the performance of Lowin as the King, had instructed Betterton in the part. Booth exerted himself to emulate Betterton; and Quin, "who had the good sense to admire and imitate Booth, and the honesty to own it, kept as near as possible to his great exemplar's portrait." [28] It is also noted, however, that Quin sometimes "mixed in it a little of Falstaff's style." [29] Although Garrick seems not to have acted in this play, most of the leading actors of the day were at one time or another cast in the roles of the King, Wolsey, Gardiner, and Katharine. The part of Wolsey was particularly difficult to portray, and although Cibber, Ryan, Mossop, Digges, and Bensley all tried their hands at it, none was very successful.

Low comedy crept in where it could not have been intended by the authors, especially in the part of Bishop Gardiner. The actor Ben Johnson represented the part with "critical exactness," [30] but his successors did not maintain the same decorum: Hippisley "added some strokes of humour, which approached grimace," and Taswell's Gardiner was debased to a buffoon. For example, at the end of V, iii, as Gardiner follows Cranmer off the stage, Taswell held his crutch over Cranmer's head in order to arouse laughter in the galleries. Although he succeeded in his mirth-provoking efforts, it is also recorded that he was violently hissed from the pit.[31]

There seems to have been no considerable alteration of this

play, and none significant enough to bear its alterer's name found its way into print. There were traditional excisions for the stage, however, one such being the omission of III, i, as "tedious and unnecessary." [32] The modern reader of the play will wonder at such a comment, for the scene is essential to the character portrayal of the Queen. Davies notes also that, contrary to the authors' intention, in the trial scene Queen Katharine is made "to wait like a common suitor or culprit till she is summoned into the court." [33] But otherwise, little is recorded of the stage management except that which pertains to the extensive lists of personages who participated in the coronation march.

The Merry Wives of Windsor, which Pepys saw at the Theatre-Royal on August 15, 1667, but which had been revived somewhat earlier, was another of Shakespeare's plays to be acted soon after the Restoration. Between 1737 and 1777 it was acted in seventeen seasons at Drury Lane and twenty-seven at Covent Garden for a total of fifty-seven performances. Although outranked in popularity in the mid-century by *The Merchant of Venice, The Merry Wives of Windsor* was the only Shakespearean comedy to receive much attention before 1737. In 1702 it had been altered by Dennis, who produced it at Drury Lane under the title of *The Comical Gallant, or the Amours of Sir John Falstaff.* But except for this unsuccessful alteration, the play escaped the mutilation that many of Shakespeare's plays suffered. This fact is not surprising, for the eighteenth century inherited much of its critical attitude toward dramatic composition from Dryden and his contemporaries, and Dryden had pointed out in *The Grounds of Criticism in Tragedy* that *The Merry Wives of Windsor* is regular in respect to the unities. Dennis professed, however, to see three distinct plots in it and several unnecessary scenes. As a result he made Fenton's marriage the central action, enlarged the parts of Fenton and Anne Page, and diminished the roles of Caius and Evans. Dennis' uncertainty is shown in his changing the title, so that the part of Falstaff seemed to be the principal action, yet stating that he was replacing the original main plot with the secondary plot. The alteration did not survive, however, and was supplanted by the original, acted at court in 1704 and at Lincoln's Inn Fields the same year. Beginning in 1720, it was frequently acted there, and was revived at Covent Garden in 1733 and at Drury Lane in 1734.

Betterton, the Falstaff of the 1704 revival, was succeeded in that role by Quin, Delane, Shuter, and Henderson among others, of whom Quin was the most famous. Mrs. Butler, Mrs. Woffington, and Mrs. Barrington successfully portrayed the "wives" at various times during the mid-century. Garrick included Dr. Caius among his roles, although he seems not to have taken part in this play often. The frequency with which the play was acted depended largely upon the availability of a Falstaff in the acting company; and since Quin was usually a member of the Covent Garden troupe, the performances at that theater outnumber those at Drury Lane. In the period following Quin's retirement and that after Shuter, also a popular Falstaff, left the stage, there was a space of years in which the play was revived with less frequency. This point may be further illustrated by the fortunes of a Shakespearean imitation called *Falstaff's Wedding.* It was well received and highly regarded as a good imitation, but it did not continue on the stage for long because there was then no actor competent as Falstaff. Davies, who was familiar with this play, expressed the hope that since the stage then (that is, 1780) had Henderson, who also succeeded as Shakespeare's Falstaff, it would be restored to the stage.[34]

The first part of *Henry IV* had been revived at the Theatre-Royal at least by November 2, 1667, and succeeded in holding the stage with moderate success after that time. The success of this play, like that of *The Merry Wives of Windsor,* depended largely upon the availability of a competent Falstaff, whom one stage historian has called the play's "Lebenselixir." [35]

The most famous Falstaffs during the mid-century were Quin (who tried the part in *The Merry Wives of Windsor* at Lincoln's Inn Fields before essaying the more difficult character in the histories), Berry, Love, Shuter, and Henderson. For a time it was regarded as heresy to prefer another Falstaff to Quin's.[36] He continued to act the part occasionally, even after his retirement from the stage, and came to London once each year to play Falstaff for the benefit of Ryan, his actor friend and bottle companion, until the loss of his teeth prevented him. After that catastrophe he stayed in retirement at Bath, for, he said, he "would never whistle Falstaff." [37] Quin had also tried the part of King Henry, but more famous in this role were Milward, Barry, and Powell. These were preferred because of their greater ability to express the pathos of the part, a desirable quality at a time when the pathetic plays of Rowe were revived year after year and the expression of pathos was often the key to theatrical success.

Wilks seems not to have had a worthy successor in the part of Hal until Palmer appeared in that role in 1762. Hotspur was represented by Milward, Garrick, Barry, Holland, and Smith; and Mrs. Woffington was a famous Lady Percy. Garrick modeled his Hotspur on that of Booth, but found the part not to his liking and gave it up after five performances. If it had been possible to alter *Henry IV, Part I,* as he altered *Macbeth,* so that his dying speech ended the play, he might have appeared more frequently as Hotspur and the play might then have appeared more often at Drury Lane. Barry was favorably received as Hotspur, although a fellow actor remarked "there is a military pride, and camp-humour, if I may be indulged in the expression, to which Barry was a stranger." [38]

There is a record of one important change in the stage business of this play. Quin had no difficulty in getting Garrick up on his back in the scene at Shrewsbury, but the heavier Barry gave him much more trouble. At an earlier day Harper had had the same difficulty with Booth. The galleries, as well as the actor playing Hotspur, were greatly amused by Falstaff's efforts. It seemed apparent that a change in the traditional manner of acting the scene was necessary, especially after Henderson found it almost impossible to get Smith, a large man, on his shoulder. Davies notes: "So much time was consumed in this pick-a-back business, that the spectators grew tired, or rather disgusted. It was thought best, for the future, that some of Falstaff's ragamuffins should bear out the dead body." [39]

The early (that is, Restoration) performances had perhaps presented the play entire, but later versions omitted III, i, not permanently restored until 1853 (by William Creswick), and IV, iv. The former scene includes the conversation with the Welsh lady, and in the latter the Archbishop is seen dispatching letters to the Lord Marshal and Scroop. Glendower seems at one time to have been banished from the play, but was retained in the Betterton version of 1700. The retention of II, iv, allowed early eighteenth-century audiences to hear the speeches of Hal and Falstaff as they assume in turn the character of the King, but it was generally omitted during the mid-century as "an incumbrance to the action." [40] Although the scene was occasionally revived, it did not produce the effect expected, as it was not "stuffed with that high jocularity which throws an audience into fits of laughter." [41] When Garrick played Hotspur, he restored III, i, which was customarily omitted, as he thought that its omission detracted from Hotspur's part; however, after a performance or two he agreed to omit it again when he found that it "produced no effect." [42] One other recorded alteration that is representative of contemporary stage practice is the one the player who acted the Second Carrier made in order to draw a laugh from the gallery. In the line "Lend me thy lantern, quoth he? Marry, I'll see thee hang'd first," the actor substituted "damn'd" for "hang'd"—as Davies notes, "from the pitiful ambition of pleasing the upper gallery and getting their hands." [43] But aside from changes of the kinds illustrated, *Henry IV* was as fortunate in escaping wholesale alteration as it was in holding a place in the repertory for an entire century, from its first revival to the end of the mid-century period.

Othello, almost the only Shakespearean play to escape serious alteration of any kind, was revived at the Cockpit in 1660 (when Pepys saw it) and at the Theatre-Royal in 1669. Its continued popularity is indicated not only by its frequency of performance, but also by the fact that eight separate editions of the play appeared by 1705 and thirty-five more in the eighteenth century.[44] The title role was acted by Burt and Hart just after the Restoration, and then in turn by Betterton, Booth, Quin, Garrick, and Barry, so that it is obvious that it could not have long been absent from the stage. It was one of the three Shakespearean tragedies maintaining their places in the repertories of both patent houses in 1737 (the others were *Hamlet* and *Macbeth,* the latter in a much altered version). During the next forty years it was revived in thirty-one seasons at Drury Lane and thirty-two at Covent Garden for a total of 140 performances, ranking behind only *Hamlet, Macbeth,* and *Richard III* in popularity.

Of the leading Othellos between 1737 and 1777, Barry was universally regarded as the best.[45] His stately figure, combined with his ability to represent both the lover and the general, made him superior in this role to his chief rival, Garrick. The latter acted less frequently in this play than he did in most of the great tragedies, probably because his short stature could not represent the imposing figure expected in Othello and because the blackening masked the expressiveness of his face, upon which much of his reputation as an actor depended.

Although there are no known alterations of this play, David Baker, writing in 1764, thought the design of Young's tragedy *The Revenge* "seems to have been borrowed partly" from *Othello,* and he regards Young's villain Zanga superior to Iago.[46] It is hardly necessary to add that the original long outlived Young's dramatic attempt.

Julius Caesar, according to Genest, was first revived at the Theatre-Royal in 1682. There is some indication, however, that it had been acted by the King's Company as early as 1665.[47] The history of this play on the stage is somewhat unusual, for its earlier popularity faded and during the last half of the eighteenth century it was almost completely neglected. It had often been acted by Hart and Mohun after the Restoration, and during the reign of Queen Anne it was one of the three plays staged at court by royal command and given the advantage of the combined strength of the two companies.[48] Just before the time of Garrick it was acted with Quin as Brutus, Mills, Sr., as Cassius, and Milward as Antony. It was performed in five consecutive seasons at Drury Lane between 1737 and 1742, and again in 1746-1747. But it was never acted during Garrick's management. Similarly, at Covent Garden it was acted in ten seasons between 1742 and 1755, but had only three performances between the latter year and 1777. In only one season— 1746-1747—was it acted at both theaters. Davies' remark in 1784 well sums up its stage history: "Julius Caesar, though now laid aside and almost forgotten, was long the favourite of an English audience." [49] Garrick assisted in the decline of *Julius Caesar;* he would "never willingly put on the Roman habit," [50] because he lacked the imposing figure that suited the toga.[51]

The acting version of the play was apparently not greatly changed from the original. The scene in which Casca and Cicero meet (I, iii) was traditionally omitted, because, it was suggested, a man of Cicero's importance should not be introduced in "a scene of such inconsequence";[52] and the role of Casca was enlarged by giving him the part of Titinius. As Casca does not appear after Act III in the original, and because the companies were not usually numerous enough to fit out the whole dramatis personae, this alteration was apparently made of necessity.

There had been, however, various attempts to make more important changes in the play. The first of such alterations had been acted in Drury Lane in 1719 and was printed in the same year; but this may be only a "marked play-house copy" which furnished the basis for both the performance and the edition. It has been generally attributed to Dryden and Davenant.[53] The second alteration was made by John Sheffield, Duke of Buckingham, and printed in 1722. It was never acted, although it had been prepared for the stage in 1729 but was laid aside when the Italian singers, who were to make up the chorus, demanded more than the receipts of the theater were likely to be.[54] Although Sheffield altered almost every scene in the original, Antony's oration was kept intact. The poetaster's forbearance here demonstrates the high regard that even the "improvers" of Shakespeare had for the speech. The third attempt at alteration, Aaron Hill's *Roman Revenge*, acted at Bath and published in 1753, should perhaps be called an independent play although it is greatly indebted to Shakespeare's. Hill's effort had been praised by both Pope and Bolingbroke; but as neither Garrick nor Quin would consent to act the part of Caesar, it was never staged at the patent theaters.[55] It is not surprising that as long as the original play was on the boards, none of these alterations succeeded; but it is noteworthy that after the original was neglected, neither alterations nor new plays based on the old theme could gain a place in the repertory.

Thus, the six plays revived between 1660 and 1700 in approximately their original form continued on the stage well into the eighteenth century with relatively few mutilations in spite of the efforts of the "improvers." But such is to be expected. Those plays most congenial to the temper of the time were the ones most likely to be revived first and to be left unchanged. But along with these was performed a series of versions that had a much slighter resemblance to their originals. *King Lear* had been revived for a brief period after the theaters were reopened, only to be displaced by Tate's alteration in 1681; and *Macbeth* was supplanted even earlier by Davenant's alteration. But the other alterations were added to the repertory in the complete absence of their Shakespearean counterparts.

Such plays as Dryden's *All for Love,* Otway's *Caius Marius,* Dryden's *Troilus and Cressida,* Tate's *Coriolanus,* Davenant's *Macbeth,* Durfey's *Cymbeline,* and Lacy's *Sauny the Scot* may safely be excluded from consideration here. Although some of these maintained their positions as stock pieces into the eighteenth century, they were ultimately dropped from the repertory and were supplanted in the mid-century period by the originals, or at least by versions closer to Shakespeare's. Their influence was sometimes to be seen in the plays that supplanted them; but because the replacements reflect the eighteenth-century theater better than do the Restoration versions, it is the former that chiefly merit attention. Consequently, these plays will be considered later—as mid-century revivals. Dryden and Davenant's *The Tempest,* however, presents a special problem. It survived, with numerous further alterations to be sure, at least until 1777; and it is not clearly certain that the original was the one revived then. However, since the little existing evidence points in that direction, *The Tempest* also will be considered along with the mid-century revivals. But two versions dating from the Restoration period cannot be ignored here: Tate's *King Lear* and Shadwell's *Timon of Athens.* The former survived not only beyond 1777 but well into the next century; and the latter, although further altered by Richard Cumberland in 1771—in a version that had only a brief stage life—not only was the basis for Cumberland's alteration but survived it, and hence may be said to have maintained its appeal throughout the mid-century period.

King Lear, when revived briefly at the Duke's Theatre shortly after the Restoration, was soon neglected as "unprofitable to the players." [56] A few years later (1681) appeared the famous alteration by Nahum Tate, at once one of the most violent and one of the most long-lived. Tate's version could be seen on the London stage as late as 1823, when the original was restored by Elliston.[57] This *Lear* was successively portrayed by Betterton, Booth, Quin, and, for more than fifteen years, by Garrick. Even after the latter's alteration appeared in 1756, the influence of Tate was still strongly felt, for Garrick's version was heavily indebted to him, as were the later alterations of Colman (1768), Kemble (1809), and Kean (1824). When Elliston revived the original, Shakespeare's tragedy at last emerged, freed of the accumulated mutilations of a century and a half. Thus, *King Lear* meant to audiences throughout the mid-century Tate's play or a version based upon Tate.

Why the actors at the Duke's Theatre had found the play unprofitable is not clear, but it was apparently because of the terrible nature of the catastrophe.[58] It is not surprising then that the principal change made by Tate was in the nature of the ending, which leaves the virtuous happy and brings to a successful conclusion the love theme centering on Edgar and Cordelia. The King of France was necessarily omitted, and the Fool also disappeared. At the beginning of the play, Gloucester is already convinced of Edgar's treachery. Edmund's illicit affairs with Regan and Goneril are enlarged, and he is shown as lusting after Cordelia also. In order to carry out his evil designs, he has Cordelia and Arante seized (the latter is Cordelia's maid, gratuitously supplied by Tate), but Edgar arrives just in time to rescue them. The fifth act is largely new, and at the end Cordelia and Edgar are left to reign over the kingdom, whereas Lear, Kent, and Gloucester plan to retire to a cell for reflection. Tate thought he was motivating Cordelia's curt reply to her father's question by showing her in love; but he does not stop there. Cordelia appears in several love scenes and is on the stage much more than in the original. For a time she appears in the role of coquette and makes use of feigned coldness to test the ardor of her lover, in the manner approved by the ladies of Charles II's day.

This play was approved by Dr. Johnson, who said that he could not bear even to read the last act of the original.[59] And if we may concede Johnson's knowledge of popular taste, "In the present case the public has decided. Cordelia, from the time of Tate, has always retired with victory and felicity."

When Garrick adapted *King Lear* for the stage, he restored many lines that Tate had omitted, but retained the love scenes and the happy ending. He, like Tate, rejected the Fool, and he kept Tate's melodrama of the seizure and rescue of Cordelia. Colman, who altered the play twelve years later, rejected the love scenes, considered keeping the Fool but eventually rejected him also, and retained the happy ending, although Cordelia does not marry Edgar as in Tate and Garrick. It is obvious that both Garrick and Colman drew heavily upon Tate, but the contrasting fate of their plays is enlightening. Garrick's alteration, like its predecessor, was successful; but Colman's met with little applause and had few performances. Success, if it can be judged on the basis of the reception of the three alterations, depended upon the inclusion of the love plot, for only the version that had omitted this element proved unsuccessful.

The disagreement between the views of the critics and the audience is particularly apparent in the reception of Colman's play. Benjamin Victor, who was well acquainted with contemporary theatrical affairs and was one of their chief annalists, points to this disparity: "The Intent of this Alteration was, to clear this celebrated Tragedy from the Love Scenes of *Edgar* and *Cordelia*. . . . This Love Business had been ever ridiculed by the Connoisseurs and Admirers of Shakespear; and yet, when the above Alteration was performed, the Play-going People, in general, seemed to lament the Loss of those Lovers in the representation." [60] Colman himself, as the preface to his play indicates, apparently felt that he had correctly gauged public opinion—which he believed had changed since the days of Tate, when, he thought, "*love* was the soul of tragedy." [61] But he had misjudged his public; love was still the "soul of tragedy" in the mid-century. Davies, who had seen *King Lear* acted twenty or thirty times in the various alterations, comments: "I can truly affirm that the spectators always dismissed the two lovers with the most rapturous applause." [62]

Decorum, as well as the desire for a love plot, was in part responsible for the alterations. Tate had given the play greater unity and had furnished it with an ending that satisfied the demands of poetic justice. In both respects he was followed by Garrick and Colman. Although the latter saw no further need for the love element, he also allowed Cordelia to retire "with victory and felicity." Like Garrick, he rejected the Fool, because he was afraid that the audience might laugh during the representation of the tragedy,[63] and he rejected Gloucester's leap from the cliff as too improbable.[64] The desire for proper decorum is also indicated by Colman's manner of representing the blinding of Gloucester. Colman found this episode, which had previously been omitted, essential to the plot. But in the performance the deed was performed off stage, so that "the ears of the audience are more hurt by [Gloucester's] cries than their eyes can be when he is afterwards led on the stage." [65]

Quin, Davies, and Berry, the latter playing to Garrick's Lear, were the most successful Gloucesters of the period; Walker was successful as Edmund, and Spranger Barry was the most popular Edgar. The role of Edgar required an actor who not only could play the feigned madman but was also talented as a stage lover. It was undoubtedly the latter qualification that made Barry succeed. Mrs. Cibber, "the most pathetic of all actresses," Davies said, was "the only Cordelia of excellence." [66] But it was Garrick as the old King whom the public never tired of seeing. Many regarded this his greatest role, whether in Tate's version or his own. His ability to express rage, madness, and recovery caused him to surpass less versatile actors in the part. When he appeared, many of the scenes caused "a kind of momentary petrefaction through the house, which he soon dissolved as universally into tears." [67]

King Lear was acted on 146 nights in the forty-year period, and was revived at Drury Lane in thirty-one seasons and at Covent Garden in twenty-one. The record of the play's performances suggests that its popularity, whatever the version used, was to a considerable extent dependent upon a single actor. More than two-thirds of the performances were at Garrick's theater. Its frequency of appearance at Drury Lane immediately increased when he first joined the company, and when he went to Ireland it was no longer acted. It was again added to the repertory when he returned, and missed only one season thereafter until 1769—and during that season Garrick was in Italy. Although Garrick, in portraying Lear, kept the old king alive at the end of the play, and seems never to have understood Kent's injunction,

> Vex not his ghost; O, let him pass! He hates him
> That would upon the rack of this tough world
> Stretch him out longer,

nevertheless he must be credited with preserving for his time one of Shakespeare's greatest tragedies, even if in a mutilated version.

79

Shadwell, in altering *Timon of Athens,* had announced that he had "made it into a play," [68] by which boast he seems to have meant that by adding several love scenes and spectacular effects he had made it more suitable for the stage of his day. Ventidius is omitted, but two female characters are added: Evandra, an abandoned but still loyal mistress of Timon; and Melissa, whom Timon is about to marry but who leaves him in his adversity. A masque is added at one point for the entertainment of the characters and the audience, and the water at the banquet is replaced with toads and snakes. The part of Apemantus is made more important than it is in the original. In this play the eighteenth-century stage inherited not so much a Shakespearean drama as an example of a type familiar during the later seventeenth century—the story of faithful and faithless love, supplied with balance and counterbalance.

Cumberland's alteration was based upon Shadwell's, but he restored several passages from the original and added to the plot from his own invention. Evanthe, the daughter of Timon, is added; thereby the source of pity for Timon is removed, for he is shown squandering his wealth on his friends when he should have provided for his daughter.[69] She is wooed by both Lucius and Alcibiades, but the ardor of the former cools when the money is gone. In the last act, which is largely Cumberland's, the city is surrendered to Alcibiades; the citizens are spared through the intercession of Evanthe; Timon throws off his misanthropy, gives his daughter to Alcibiades, and dies. The treasure discovered in the woods turns out to be that of Lucullus, who had buried it there; and during the sack of the city the house of Lucius is pillaged. Thus, on both counts, the ends of poetic justice are served.

Davies preferred the earlier alteration to Cumberland's, and suggested that the 1771 play was given performance only on the strength of the author's reputation as the writer of the successful original play, *The West Indian,* which had appeared earlier in the same year.[70] Walley Oulton, the annalist who continued Victor's account of the London stage, makes a comment on this play that suggests that the critics and the public were divided in their opinion as to its merit. Although the public was apparently willing to let it die after its first season, "in the opinion of the critics," Oulton remarks, the play "with alterations and additions by Mr. Cumberland [was] rendered

. . . more fit for the stage." [71] But popular taste prevailed, and the alteration disappeared from the boards. A third alteration, brought out by Love in 1768, was acted at Richmond, but apparently had no influence on the Drury Lane revival, except perhaps to suggest to Cumberland the possibility of altering the play. Love's version is closer to the original than is either of the others, but he still retained much of Shadwell.[72]

Timon of Athens had been frequently acted at Drury Lane for several years. It appeared there in 1740 with Milward as Timon, Quin as Apemantus, Mrs. Butler as Evandra, and Mrs. Pritchard as Melissa. This was, of course, Shadwell's alteration. It was advertised as unacted for three years.[73] With Marshall and Yates in the cast, it was revived the following season at Goodman's Fields, the same season that saw at that theater the revivals of *The Winter's Tale* and *All's Well That Ends Well*. In 1745, when Quin was at Covent Garden, the play was revived there for the first time in eleven seasons. Quin again played Apemantus, and other parts were taken by Woodward, Theophilus Cibber, and Mrs. Pritchard. After two more performances at that theater in the following season, the play disappeared from the boards for almost thirty years. When it was revived in 1771, the new alteration by Cumberland was used, with Barry as Timon and Mrs. Barry as Evanthe. There were eleven performances in that season, after which the Cumberland version disappeared. In both versions the play had, however, only a fitful existence on the stage during the forty-year period, and its very moderate success owed much to the early popularity of Quin as Apemantus, as that role had been expanded and heightened by Shadwell.

2. SHAKESPEAREAN CONTRIBUTIONS OF THE EARLY EIGHTEENTH CENTURY

During the early years of the eighteenth century the London stage continued to be dominated by Betterton until his death in 1710. Throughout Betterton's career the Shakespearean repertory already described was the one that prevailed, and the great actor played no other *Lear* than Tate's and no other *Macbeth* than Davenant's. The repertory was even further restricted between 1710 and 1737, for only ten of Shakespeare's plays, including the alterations, maintained their positions as stock pieces. During this quarter-century *Hamlet* and *Othello* were acted every season but two, *The Tempest* missed three seasons, *Henry IV, Part I,* three, *Macbeth* and *King Lear* six each, *Julius Caesar* and *Timon of Athens* eight each. *Richard III* missed seven seasons between 1712 and 1737, and *Henry VIII* missed two between 1716 and 1737. *Caius Marius* could be seen occasionally until 1727; Granville's *The Jew of Venice,* based upon *The Merchant of Venice,* survived until 1741; and alterations of other plays appeared now and then. Such limitation of the repertory in this period was caused principally by the personnel of the leading company of the time, a company headed by the celebrated "triumvirate," Barton Booth, Colley Cibber, and Robert Wilks, who became joint managers of Drury Lane in 1724. These three actors, who could form various combinations in the major roles of Shakespeare's most popular plays, ably assisted by Booth's wife, dominated the legitimate theater for a time; and they seem to have made little effort to bring new plays or innovation of any sort to the stage, even when they were often severely challenged by the opera, which had recently become fashionable. Odell asks: "With such casts in the poet's greatest plays, why risk failure in reviving his less worthy work, for an apathetic public?" [74] It is in this period, nevertheless, even though it seems rather stagnant theatrically, that must be dated the revivals of four Shakespearean pieces in forms quite close to the originals: *Henry IV, Part II, Measure for Measure, Much Ado About Nothing,* and *Henry V.*

The first to be revived was *Henry IV, Part II,* performed at Drury in 1720[75] with Mills as Falstaff, Cibber as Shallow, Wilks as Hal, and Booth as the King. Although this play is actually an adaptation by Betterton, it differs from those mentioned above in that the whole text is Shakespeare's, the changes consisting chiefly of omissions.[76] The principal changes are the addition of lines from *Henry V* in Act V, the omission of Northumberland, and the excision of several comic scenes. This version continued to hold the stage at Drury Lane for many years, until the original was revived there in 1736 and at Covent Garden in 1738.[77] There seems to have been no further attempt at altering this play for the stage; an octavo edition appeared in 1766, however, in which the king and the courtiers are omitted.[78] Perhaps the unities were thus preserved, even though it meant leaving out the title character! This anonymous version was apparently unacted. A farce, *The Stage Mutineers,* acted at Covent Garden in 1734,[79] has only a tenuous connection with Shakespeare's play through the character of Pistol, who also appears in the farce.

Between 1737 and 1777 the play was performed, either in the original or in Betterton's adaptation, in twelve seasons at Drury Lane and fifteen at Covent Garden on a total of seventy-four nights. It was less frequently revived than the first part, although, judging from the number of performances, it was just as popular in the seasons when it was brought to the stage. Like the first part, its career as a stock piece depended upon the availability of an actor to play Falstaff. The most famous performers in this role were Quin, Love, and Shuter. Colley Cibber and, later, Ben Johnson were famous Shallows, the former coming back from retirement in 1737 to play the part for his son's benefit,[80] and the latter assuming the role when he was more than seventy years old.[81] The only liberty the actors took with the original text after it was revived seems to have been the omission of the first scene in the Forest of Gaultree (IV, i), which was never warmly approved and which was usually dismissed "with indifference" by the audience.[82]

Measure for Measure had been revived at Lincoln's Inn Fields in 1720, with Quin as the Duke, Boheme as Angelo, and Mrs. Seymour as Isabella. It had been revived twice previously, but each time in a much altered version. Davenant's alteration, called *Law Against Lovers,* had been acted in 1662 but did not long keep the stage. It included additions from *Much Ado About Nothing* as well as large borrowings from *Measure for Measure.* The second alteration, Gildon's *Measure for Measure, or Beauty the Best Advocate,* was acted in 1700 and printed the same year but was soon displaced. After the revival of the original in 1720, the play held the stage sporadically throughout the mid-century, although it never rivaled in popularity the great romantic comedies. It had forty-one performances in nine seasons at Drury Lane and eleven at Covent Garden. While Quin remained on the stage he continued to act the part of the Duke; and Mrs. Cibber became the most popular Isabella of the day. Mrs. Woffington played the heroine's role at Covent Garden at the same time and later was succeeded by Mrs. Bellamy. In the last years of the period the favorites in the leading roles were Henderson and Mrs. Yates, although they were soon to be surpassed by Kemble and Mrs. Siddons. Garrick maintained the play on the boards during his management of Drury Lane but apparently took no part in it himself.

No mention is made of *Much Ado About Nothing* by either Pepys or Downes, the most articulate playgoers after the Restoration; except for Davenant's use of some lines in his alteration of *Measure for Measure,* it seems not only to have escaped alteration but to have been neglected in its original form until the 1721 performances at Lincoln's Inn Fields. In that revival Quin, Ryan, Mrs. Cross, and Mrs. Seymour took the leading parts. Thereafter it was acted infrequently at Covent Garden and apparently not at all at Drury Lane until Garrick made his first appearance as Benedick during the 1748-1749 season. The play immediately became popular—Garrick acted Benedick sixteen times that season and seven the next—and held the stage until Garrick's retirement in 1776. The stage history of this play is closely related to the career of Garrick. Of its 115 performances between 1737 and 1777, all but nine were at Drury Lane when he was acting there; in the only season when it was unacted between 1748 and 1776 he was in Italy; and it was unacted in the season following his retirement. It was the first play in which he appeared following his marriage, when it was doubly attractive because of the aptness with which many of Shakespeare's lines could be applied by the audience to the actor's new situation.[83] Upon his return from Italy in 1765 he appeared first as Benedick, this time at the king's command, and the applause on that occasion was overwhelming.[84] Mrs. Pritchard early made the role of Beatrice her own, and later Mrs. Abington succeeded in that part.

Although the original play, after its revival in 1721, had gone almost unchallenged, in 1737 James Miller brought out his play *The Universal Passion* at Drury Lane. It was altered from *Much Ado*—a debt which he acknowledged—and from Molière's *Princess of Elis*—a fact he does not mention.[85] It was acted ten times in that season and then set aside. The change from Shakespeare's jesting title to the self-conscious label given it by Miller and the omission of those "good men and true" Dogberry and Verges indicate how the alterer was attempting both to moralize and to regularize Shakespeare's play. Miller's version was given a great advantage by a strong cast: Quin as

Protheus (Benedick), Mrs. Clive as Liberia (Beatrice), Mrs. Butler as Lucilia (Hero), and Mrs. Pritchard as Delia (Margaret). But in spite of this advantage it did not long survive, and the original easily prevailed.

A rhymed play by the Earl of Orrery entitled *Henry V* had been performed at Lincoln's Inn Fields in 1664, and Aaron Hill's play of the same title appeared at Drury Lane in 1723; but Shakespeare's history did not come to the stage after the time of Charles I until its revival at Goodman's Fields in 1735.[86] Orrery's play bears only a historical resemblance to Shakespeare's and therefore can hardly be called an alteration. Hill's is also independent in large part, although he is indebted to Shakespeare for his plan and for some lines as well as to Orrery.[87] But neither of these was included in the repertory of the 1737-1777 period. A farce, *Half-pay Officers*, acted in the first part of the century at Lincoln's Inn Fields is somewhat indebted to Shakespeare; it contains a Fluellen whose part is much the same as that in *Henry V*, and another character, Culverin, is drawn from Pistol. But the resemblance went generally unrecognized, for, as Genest remarks, "Fluellin [*sic*] was a new character to a considerable part of the audience, as Shakespeare was not very much read, and his Henry the 5th had not been acted since the Restoration." [88] This lack was not remedied until the 1735 revival.[89] The play was added to the acting list at Covent Garden three years later. Thereafter it became a popular stock piece, so that Baker, writing in 1764, could say, "The Original still stands its Ground, and is constantly performed with universal Applause." [90]

Between 1737 and 1777 it was acted eighty-one times, ten times in three seasons at Drury Lane while Garrick and Lacy were the new proprietors, and seventy-one nights ranging over twenty-four seasons at the rival house. The Drury Lane performances depended upon Barry as Henry, Macklin as Fluellen, Yates as Pistol, and Garrick as Prologue and Chorus. It is noteworthy, in view of its relative infrequency at Drury Lane, that the play provided no part ideally suited to Garrick's special powers. The Covent Garden revival prospered with Delane as Henry, Hippisley as Fluellen, and Ryan as the Chorus; later Smith and Shuter were favorite actors in the play. The banners of the English and French armies at Agincourt and the full panoply of war offered possibilities that the pageant-loving

Rich at Covent Garden did not overlook, and in his last year as patentee, which was also coronation year, he produced *Henry V* with the coronation pageant no less than twenty-six times.[91]

Six plays revived in the Restoration period and four others revived in the eighteenth century before 1737 were thus available to the mid-century repertory in forms relatively close to the originals. To these ten plays must be added the alterations of *King Lear* and *Timon of Athens* contrived in the late seventeenth century, since these were not supplanted by the originals. There must also be added one other alteration, Cibber's version of *Richard III*, first acted in the early eighteenth century and, like Tate's and Shadwell's alterations, not displaced until long after 1777. Other plays, either in original or in altered versions, had, of course, been acted between 1660 and 1737, as has already been noted; but they can hardly be regarded as stock pieces, as a regular part of the repertory immediately available to the mid-century stage of Macklin, Garrick, and their fellow actors. The play now to be considered may therefore be regarded as rounding out the "established" Shakespearean repertory before 1737.

Cibber's *Richard III*, the longest-lived of all Shakespearean alterations, was first acted in 1700. It began its career, however, under a cloud, for the licenser at first would not allow the whole of the first act to be performed, as it "would too much remind weak persons of James II, then in exile at St. Germain's." [92] It was little acted, therefore, during the first decade of the century. The first act was later restored; and the play proved highly successful, especially following its revival in 1710. Thereafter it maintained its popularity, and Malone, writing in 1790, remarked that it "has been represented, I believe, more frequently than any of our author's dramas, except *Hamlet*." [93]

In Cibber's version most of the original first act is omitted, and in the new Act I are inserted passages from *Richard II*, *Henry VI, Part II*, and *Henry VI, Part III*. This change became necessary when Cibber determined to begin his play with Henry VI still alive. Other changes include the reduction in the number of characters, the introduction of a scene in which the Queen is shown visiting the children and attempting to take them from the Tower, and the insertion of love scenes between Richard and Anne. Cibber's respect for his neoclassical heritage and his wholehearted sympathy with the growing sentimentalism—the same spirit that led him, along with Steele, to father a new breed of comic drama—are clearly apparent in such changes. Although the pathetic scene between Elizabeth and her sons must now be regarded as a mawkish encrustation, and the expanded love element an incongruity,[94] they delighted eighteenth-century audiences and went far to keep the play on the acting list. But the greatest change made by Cibber was in the character of Richard himself. The tyrant becomes more vulgar, and coarser in his cruelty—the blackest of villains. Hazlitt felt that the key to Richard's character is to be found in the lines[95]

> But I was born too high:
> Our aery buildeth in the cedar's top,
> And dallies with the wind, and scornes the sun.

It is significant that Cibber omitted these lines as well as similar passages that in the original play helped to make the evil king believable as a human being. Cibber's Richard is, in contrast, merely animal.

But this *Richard* proved extremely successful on the mid-century stage, and Steevens the editor, who likely would have credited Shakespeare with his just dues, attributes the success of *Richard III* partly to the revision made by Cibber.[96] It is also noteworthy that Garrick, who influenced most later actors in the role, found the justification for his interpretation of Richard's character in Cibber rather than in Shakespeare. It was the Cibberian role in which Garrick appeared at Goodman's Fields on October 19, 1741, his first performance on a London stage and a historic occurrence in the annals of the English theater. He continued to act the part until his retirement thirty-five years later, always to an enthusiastic audience. For a time he also contemplated making his farewell to the theater in the role, but finally substituted that of Don Felix in *The Wonder* as less exhausting.[97]

Richard III was performed on 220 nights in the mid-century period, more frequently than any other Shakespearean play except *Hamlet* and *Romeo and Juliet,* and was surpassed in the number of seasons during which it was acted only by *Hamlet, The Provok'd Husband,* and *The Beaux' Stratagem* among dramas of all types that reached the stage between 1737 and

1777. Garrick's excellence in the role was, of course, the chief factor contributing to its popularity. In a day when managers found it necessary to advertise the afterpieces—comic operas, pantomimes, and farces—in order to fill their theaters, no other attraction was necessary when Garrick acted Richard.[98] Several other reasons have also been advanced to account for its perennial favor. Davies, for example, thought it was popular because of "its comprehending such variety of historical and domestick facts, with such affecting scenes of exalted misery and royal distress." [99] Hazlitt remarked of the love scenes that they were designed to "gratify this favourite propensity." [100] Some recent critics, however, have tried to explain its popularity on quite different and, I think, untenable grounds: that, because of the generally low level of dramatic composition during the time when Cibber's *Richard III* was holding the stage, in contrast it "must have seemed vital and even in spots realistic." [101] Such an explanation can hardly be accepted. Twenty-five per cent of all tragedy on the mid-century stage was Shakespearean, and thus much of the competition that this play faced was from better, not worse, drama. Moreover, Cibber removed much of the contrast between *Richard III* and the newer tragedies by making it more like an eighteenth-century play than he found it in Shakespeare. Probably the greatest reason why it kept the stage was that it afforded the actor an opportunity to delineate strongly marked passions in situations that he could make deeply moving. Such, for example, was Garrick's "joyous chuckle of sardonic delight" when he cried, "Off with his head! So much for Buckingham." [102]

CHAPTER SIX

The Shakespearean Revival

The thirteen plays considered in the preceding chapter may be regarded as constituting the solid core of Shakespearean stage drama before 1737. But that number was to be more than doubled during the next forty years, so industrious were those responsible for determining the theatrical repertory in bringing the neglected plays of Shakespeare to the stage. Some of the added plays were never completely purified, and even in the later eighteenth century they still retained much of the dross added in an earlier day. But several others at last emerged in adaptations, which, except for omissions made to bring the plays within a two-hour acting time, were faithful to the originals in both text and spirit.

During the mid-century period several events of considerable significance to theatrical history occurred that help to account for the great upsurge in interest in Shakespeare's plays. In order of time, the first was the creation, in the 1737-1738 season, of the "Shakespeare Club" at Covent Garden. The club included as members some of the most intelligent and most fashionable ladies of the time. It was not entirely unlike the "party," a group of persons who banded together to praise or, more frequently, to "damn" a play and who were usually able to exert enough influence on the theater manager so that he acceded to their demands. The Shakespeare Club had, however, an organization that was longer-lived than the temporarily formed party, and had also a membership of higher social station. But it seems to have been at least equally influential, even though not so violent, for it succeeded in 1737-1738, the season of its greatest influence, in causing the manager of Covent Garden to revive three of Shakespeare's plays that had not been performed since the closing of the theaters and two others that had remained unacted for a half-century. In the next three seasons seven additional plays, some of them neglected for many years, were performed at the two patent theaters and at Goodman's Fields.

Although Drury Lane and Goodman's Fields had no such cohorts organized among their audiences, and although an actor like Macklin and a manager like Giffard must be given some credit for the renewed interest in Shakespeare's plays, undoubtedly the original momentum set up by the ladies of the Shakespeare Club at Covent Garden was an important factor in bringing about the remarkable series of revivals between 1737 and 1741.

A second event that encouraged the Shakespeare revival occurred in the latter year, for it was then that Garrick made his first appearance on a London stage. Contemporaries, both spectators and actors, agreed that his advent marked a change in the style of acting. This new style was highly suitable to the great Shakespearean roles; and during the next thirty-five years, while Garrick was taking leading parts in almost all the plays of Shakespeare that reached the stage, hardly a week went by when at least one of the great Elizabethan's dramas could not be seen. It may be debated whether audiences continued throughout the mid-century to come to the theater in order to see a Shakespearean play or to see a "star" actor in a role that gave him adequate scope for his peculiar powers; but it is hardly open to question that Garrick contributed greatly to the Shakespeare revival. It should also be noted that before 1769, the date of the Shakespeare Jubilee at Stratford-on-Avon, for which Garrick was chiefly responsible, Shakespeare had existed in the minds of the people only as an "old" dramatist; but during the festival, and of course in all the years since that time, thousands of Britons made pilgrimages to Shakespeare's birthplace. So Garrick must be credited, not only for much of the playwright's new vitality on the stage, but also for his recognition as a historical individual and a flesh-and-blood Englishman, one with "a local habitation and a name."

It is also highly probable that the considerable interest shown by publishers and editors in printing Shakespeare's plays ultimately encouraged their revivals in the theater. The complete works had been edited by Rowe and Pope earlier in the century, and Theobald had brought out his first edition of all the plays in 1733. Between 1737 and 1777 seven other editions of the complete works appeared. Moreover, beginning with Tonson, a publisher immortalized in *The Dunciad* as "left-legged Jacob," and continuing on to the time of John Bell at the end of the century, there appeared numerous editions of the individual plays, at prices that many could pay who were unable to afford the imposing sets of volumes edited by, for example, Warburton and Johnson. As the text of Shakespeare became more and more accessible and the reading public expanded with the increase of literacy among the middle classes, a greater familiarity with the plays naturally resulted. Although there were few among the typical mid-century spectators who should be regarded as dramatic critics, there were many who were connoisseurs of acting; and it is at least highly probable that they derived increased pleasure from seeing the actors portray roles and read lines with which they were familiar. Furthermore, critics began, about 1750, to mention the *reading* of plays while discussing their performance on the stage, which suggests a significant relationship between the theatergoer as reader and as spectator.

The factors that coöperated in encouraging the Shakespeare revival on the stage are of course not limited to the three mentioned above, although these were among the most important. National pride, antiquarianism, and expanding interests of various kinds often must have contributed. Also, special elements in the individual plays, such as the romance and pathos of *Romeo and Juliet* and the topicality detected in *King John* and *Richard II*, added their influence in determining the repertory. But whatever the causes, the incontrovertible fact that Shakespeare's plays bulked large among all stage drama of the mid-century adds an element of interest as well as of contrast in a period during which original dramatic activity moved on a uniformly mediocre plane, and supplies a further justification for regarding the time as one of theatrical importance.

The first long-unacted play to be revived in the period was *King John*, acted at Covent Garden on February 26, 1737. This was the first of the plays performed at the request of the Shakespeare Club. Delane played the King, Walker acted Faulconbridge, and Mrs. Hallam appeared as Constance. Although Delane failed as John, Walker became the most famous Faulconbridge of the time.[1] Thereafter it was performed thirty-seven times in fourteen seasons at Covent Garden, although it gave way briefly in 1744-1745 to Colley Cibber's *Papal Tyranny in the Reign of King John*. In 1745 the original was revived at

[1] For notes to chap. 6, see pp. 317-320.

Drury Lane, in competition with Cibber's alteration, with Garrick as John, Delane as Faulconbridge, and Mrs. Cibber as Constance; but it was revived there in only six later seasons while Garrick was patentee. Garrick did not excel in the role of the King, but Mrs. Cibber's Constance was thought to be her "most perfect character." [2] In other revivals Barry and Sheridan tried the part of John, and Macklin that of Pandulph.

Two notices for this play throw interesting light on Shakespearean performances in general during the eighteenth century. When *King John* was revived at Covent Garden in 1824, it was announced as having "propriety of costume, &c. *never before attempted,*" [3] suggesting the earlier lack of attention to realistic or historically accurate costume. Davies, when remarking on Garrick's production of *King John,* notes that it was customary for actors to slight scenes that, though necessary for exposition, were not highly applauded. He refers to the short scenes in Act V, and adds that it was the "great excellence of Garrick to hold in remembrance the character he played, through all its various stages. No situation whatever was neglected by him." [4]

The one alteration—that by Cibber—was produced to take advantage of contemporary interest in the Jacobite question, and the changes indicate how he attempted to give the play a topical application. He says in his prologue that he has increased the rivalry between Pope and King, an opportunity that he felt Shakespeare had overlooked. Actually it was Cibber who overlooked the fact that Shakespeare, in constructing *King John* on the basis of an older play, had rejected the very element he had set out to emphasize. Cibber's play was soon discarded in favor of the original. One of the bitterest comments that the usually polite Davies allows himself to make suggests that it was not highly regarded; Cibber, he said, "has not only mixed his cold crudities and prosaic offals with the rich food of Shakespeare, but has presumed to alter the oeconomy of the scene by superfluous incident." [5]

Richard II was revived at Covent Garden on February 6, 1738, also at the request of the Shakespeare Club. It had previously undergone alteration, by Tate in 1680, and by Theobald in 1719; and later in the century it was further altered by Goodhall (printed in 1772, but unacted). Tate's alteration, renamed *The Sicilian Usurper,* was acted twice, after which it was suppressed for political reasons; it did not reach the stage in the mid-century period. Theobald's purpose was to "regularize" the play, a goal he attained by omitting much of the first two acts and by centering the action in the Tower. These changes together with the added love element—supplied by creating Lady Percy as the beloved of Aumerle—succeeded in removing almost all resemblance to Shakespeare. This play had also succumbed by 1737. Goodhall's version was made up of 2,206 lines, of which 1,159 were his own. Besides transposing Shakespeare's scenes to bring together those occurring in the same setting, he managed to make eight scenes from Shakespeare's second and third scenes of Act II. The original nineteen scenes became in Goodhall's hands—to be sure, with much addition of his own— no less than forty-one.[6] The play was offered to Garrick, who refused it; thereupon it was printed at Manchester.[7] Thus, none of the recorded alterations made between 1660 and 1777 reached the mid-century stage.

Although the original, when revived in 1738, seems to have been mounted with considerable expense and effort, it did not hold the stage for long. It was acted ten times in its first season, on four nights in 1738-1739, and once the following season, after which it was laid aside until the nineteenth century. Richard Wroughton, a nineteenth-century alterer, remarked: "The Play of Richard the Second, has been hitherto neglected by the Managers of the London Theaters, being considered too heavy for representation."[8] Steevens had earlier held a similar opinion: *"the successive audiences of more than a century have respectively slumbered over it, as often as it has appeared on the stage."*[9] Its heaviness, however, was not the sole reason for its lack of success; for *Richard II* seems to have been destined from the beginning to stir up political feelings whenever it was performed.[10] Garrick never acted in the play, nor was it performed at Drury Lane during his management. But late in his career he was thinking of reviving it, as is apparent from an exchange of letters with Steevens. Garrick had asked the editor to suggest a Shakespearean play for revival and had inquired specifically about his opinion of *Richard II*. Steevens replied that it was "surely the most uninteresting and flattest," and that "a few splendid passages will not maintain a play on the stage."[11] Garrick apparently accepted Steevens' advice.

Since the Covent Garden revival was the only one in the

period, its stage management is deserving of special note. Although not much has been recorded, Davies says that the scene in which Hereford and Norfolk prepare to meet in single combat was completely fitted out with "armor and other decorations" invented by Adam Hallam, a relative of the proprietor. This spectacular scene was thought to have been appropriately staged with due attention to historical accuracy.[12] The seriousness of the scene was marred, however, when Walker, who acted Norfolk, found that his helmet was laced so tightly that he was unable to make himself heard. The cause of the misfortune was soon removed and the scene continued, with the great approval of the audience. Also in this revival the management found that it was unable to fill out the cast with the regular members of the company, and one "honest Michael Stoppelaer, of blundering memory" acted the Abbot of Westminster, much to the amusement of the spectators.[13] The actor of the time best qualified for the title role was Spranger Barry, but he seems never to have acted the part. Delane, who was cast as Richard, was unable to express the emotions that were the particular delight of Barry, although he was applauded in the scene with Gaunt. The latter role was taken by Johnson, the seven-foot son-in-law of Hill.[14] Its dramatis personae never strongly cast and its poetic beauty largely ignored, *Richard II* enjoyed hardly more success than it did during the preceding century, when it had remained almost entirely unacted.

The third play revived at the request of the Shakespeare Club, *Henry VI, Part I*, met with even less success than did *Richard II*. It was acted one night, March 13, 1738, apparently the only revival since Shakespeare's own day. It seems to have escaped alteration, although lines were borrowed from it on occasion to fill out the altered versions of other plays. Crowne's first play on Henry VI (1681) is sometimes regarded as an alteration of Shakespeare's *Part I*, but it is actually based on *Henry VI, Part II*.[15] Nor was Theophilus Cibber's *Henry VI*, acted in 1723, indebted to this play. Not only was *Henry VI, Part I*, neglected by actor and alterer; it also fared badly at the hands of the reading public. The first separate edition was published by Tonson in 1735, and only two other editions appeared in the entire century.[16] In the 1738 revival Talbot was acted by Delane, Gloucester by Ryan, Henry by A. Ryan, Suffolk by Walker, Margaret by Mrs. Ware, and Joan la Pucelle by

94

Mrs. Hallam. Although the playbill announced that it was acted "by desire of several Ladies of Quality"—a reference to the Shakespeare Club—even those energetic patronesses of Shakespeare could not prolong the stage life of the play.

These three plays are the only Shakespearean dramas unacted in their original forms since Jacobean times that are certainly known to have been revived through the direct influence of the Shakespeare Club; many others, some of which had been absent from the stage for a considerable time, were acted, however, while the club was in existence. In all, twelve Shakespearean plays were performed in the 1737-1738 season at Covent Garden, a much greater number than had been presented in earlier years. And, as was suggested earlier, the continued upsurge of interest in Shakespeare that resulted in performances of his forgotten plays, not only at Covent Garden, but at other theaters also, may have been at least partly owing to the influence of the club. The period of greatest activity in this upsurge came in the 1740-1741 season. In rapid succession, sometimes not more than a few days apart, *As You Like It, The Winter's Tale, Twelfth Night, The Merchant of Venice,* and *All's Well That Ends Well* were brought to the stage; and in the following season *The Comedy of Errors* was added to the repertory. It is obvious that none of these revivals can be credited to Garrick, who had recently come to London but had not yet appeared on the stage. Some credit, however, must be given to Charles Macklin, a worthy predecessor of Garrick as an actor who took part in several of the newly revived plays and whose perception of Shakespeare's genius led him to revive *The Merchant of Venice* even against the advice of his friends.

There is no record of a performance of *As You Like It* after Shakespeare's own day until that of the Drury Lane revival on December 20, 1740. It was then acted twenty-five times in that season and eight in the next. In the latter season it was also added to the repertory at Covent Garden, and continued thereafter as a popular comedy at both theaters through 1777. In this thirty-seven-year period it was performed twenty-six seasons at Drury Lane and seventeen at Covent Garden for a total of at least 130 performances—as many performances as were given *The Merchant of Venice,* the comedy acted in the greatest number of seasons, and more than were given any other Shakespearean comedy. The play had previously been altered—first by Charles Johnson, and then by a "J.C." [17] The former alteration, which was titled *Love in a Forest,* was acted six times in 1723 and then laid aside. The latter, called *The Modern Receipt, or a Cure for Love,* was published in 1739, but there is no record of its performance. That Johnson's play was given performance seventeen years before the Drury Lane revival does not detract from the assertion made that the 1740 appearance was the first since Shakespeare's time; not only had the title been changed, with the resulting loss of identity for all except readers of Shakespeare, but lines from other plays were added, especially from *A Midsummer Night's Dream.* Moreover, a play in which the erstwhile "melancholy Jaques" woos Celia and from which, among others, Touchstone, Audrey, and William have disappeared could hardly be regarded as more than remotely related to the original.

The playbills, which show that Shakespeare's entire dramatis personae had been restored, suggest that it was the original that was revived in 1740.[18] There was, however, one change. To the songs of Amiens, which had been newly set to music by Dr. Arne, was added "When daisies pied," borrowed from *Love's Labour's Lost* and inserted in the play.[19] In the first run Mrs. Clive and Quin, the leading actors of the time, were among those who acted in the comedy; but it was Mrs. Pritchard, hitherto relatively obscure, who gained the greatest popularity. Although she later turned to tragedy, she established her reputation in the part of Rosalind.

Less than a month later *The Winter's Tale* was performed at Goodman's Fields. It was advertised as "not acted 100 years." [20] Because the play appeared first at a minor theater, it may have attracted little attention; but it was added to the repertory of Covent Garden in the following season. The principal parts were performed at Goodman's Fields by Giffard, Yates, Mrs. Giffard, and Miss Hippisley. It was acted there at least seven times that season. After it reached the patent theaters it continued to be performed sporadically, although in its entirety it cannot be called a popular play. *The Winter's Tale,* with a lack of unity on which even the poet remarked, could not long escape the hands of the alterer. On March 25, 1754, Morgan's two-act afterpiece, made from Acts IV and V, was acted at Covent Garden. This play was built around the sheep-shearing scene, and a great deal of the original was entirely omitted. Two years later (January 21, 1756) Garrick's three-act version, derived largely from the last two acts of the original with additions from the first three, was staged at Drury Lane. It was in this form, shortened and pastoralized, that the theatergoing public knew—or, perhaps we should say, partly knew—*The Winter's Tale* through most of the mid-century, for Garrick's version, titled *Florizel and Perdita,* was commonly performed. Much later Colman brought out an alteration of the play at the Haymarket, but it was little more than an abridgment of Garrick's version, embellished with several additional songs.[21]

Pepys saw *Twelfth Night* three times, he says, but the play was soon dropped from the Restoration repertory. Charles Burnaby had produced his *Love Betrayed, or the Agreeable Disappointment* at Lincoln's Inn Fields in 1703. The outlines for his plot and about fifty lines of verse were borrowed from *Twelfth Night.* Some of his other lines were taken from *All's Well That Ends Well.* This was apparently the only attempt to alter the play for the stage; and thus, when the original was revived at Drury Lane on January 15, 1741, the audience was witnessing a play absent from the boards for almost eighty years. The comedy had a strong cast that included Macklin, Woodward, Mrs. Pritchard, and Mrs. Clive. It was acted eight times in the first season, but there is no record of a later performance until 1745-1746. Thereafter it missed only one season at Drury Lane until 1755, after which date it was again neglected until it was revived late in the period with Mrs. Abington as Olivia and Miss Younge as Viola. Although Garrick supervised the production, he seems never to have acted in it. There are records of only three performances of *Twelfth Night* at Covent Garden: two in the 1771-1772 season, which were in competition with Mrs. Abington's revival at Drury Lane, and one in the 1776-1777 season. In all, there were sixty-one performances in seventeen seasons at Drury Lane and two at Covent Garden. Thus the play that is often regarded as Shakespeare's comic masterpiece was outranked in popularity by no less than seven of his other comedies.

The most frequently revived of Shakespeare's comedies was *The Merchant of Venice,* first restored by Macklin at Drury Lane on February 14, 1741. It is noteworthy that this was the third revival of a long-neglected Shakespearean comedy at Drury Lane in about six weeks. After the Drury Lane revival the comedy was not long absent from the prompter's list at either patent theater. Macklin himself played Shylock, Antonio was acted by Quin, Portia by Mrs. Clive, and Nerissa by Mrs. Pritchard. The chatty Tate Wilkinson informs us that Mrs. Clive's Portia was "truly bad," [22] but Macklin was never challenged as Shylock. In fact it was not until his retirement that another actor (Henderson) could succeed in the role.

On the third night of the revival in 1741 Pope is said to have exclaimed, "This is the Jew that Shakespeare drew." [23] He was, of course, comparing the play he was then witnessing with Granville's *The Jew of Venice,* which had entirely supplanted the original from the time of its first appearance in 1701 until 1741. Even after Macklin's revival the alteration did not at once disappear, but for a time continued to compete with Shakespeare's play. Although there are many changes in Granville's play, the most important difference between it and the original as restored by Macklin is in the character of Shylock. Granville's Jew was a low comic figure, whereas Macklin played Shylock as a heavy villain. Also, Granville had made Bassanio more important than he is in the original, and his whole play borders on farce. Macklin determined to compete against this play by restoring the original, a hazardous undertaking from which the other members of the company tried to dissuade him. For a brief period during the first act on the night of its first performance there was some doubt that Macklin's restoration would be accepted. But the spectators soon expressed their approval with thunderous applause. Genest remarks of this historic event, "Never was a performer's triumph more complete, never were enemies more confounded and abashed, never was a Manager more agreeably surprised." [24]

Although Macklin's play has long been regarded as the original, it is apparent from an edition of 1777 based upon Macklin's acting version that there were several minor alterations. Morocco and Arragon were omitted, Jessica fled in woman's instead of boy's clothing, and Lord Falconbridge and the Scottish lord were not mentioned among Portia's suitors.[25] Decorum and patriotism were obviously the motives that dictated these changes. Moreover, the growing taste for music in drama is apparent, for Portia was given a song, which Arne set to music in 1742, and Jessica and Lorenzo were also made to sing.

Jessica's song, inserted in II, ii (Shakespeare's II, iii), might more appropriately be expected in *The Beggar's Opera:*

> Haste Lorenzo, haste away.
> To my longing arms repair,
> With impatience I shall die;
> Come, and ease thy Jessica's care,
> Let me then wanton play
> Sigh and gaze my soul away.

All's Well That Ends Well was revived on March 7, 1741, at Goodman's Fields, with Giffard as Bertram, Peterson as Parolles, Mrs. Giffard as Helena, and Mrs. Yates as the widow. It was advertised as "written by Shakespeare, and not acted since his time." [26] After nine performances at Goodman's Fields it was revived at Drury Lane, with Mills, Theophilus Cibber, Mrs. Woffington, Mrs. Butler, and Mrs. Ridout in the leading parts. Cibber succeeded as Parolles, but Mrs. Woffington was taken ill and her part had to be read at the first performance. The play was then deferred, but on the date announced for its resumption Milward, who played the King, was ill, and postponement was again necessary. The fortunes of the play were further complicated by the illness of Mrs. Butler and Mrs. Ridout. As a result the play soon was regarded as a bad omen.[27] Nevertheless it was acted ten times in its first season at Drury Lane, although it was not performed there again until the 1755-1756 season. But apparently it was barely maintaining a place in the repertory, for in 1757, "with the help of a pantomime, it was acted several nights";[28] it had also been revived at Covent Garden in 1746, but was infrequently acted. It is surprising that this comedy, which has never been a popular stage piece from Shakespeare's day to this, had as many as thirty-four performances between 1737 and 1777 (in eight seasons at Drury Lane and eight at Covent Garden). *All's Well That Ends Well* seems to have escaped serious alteration until Pilon reduced it to three acts in 1785,[29] although, as has already been noted, Burnaby had borrowed lines from it for his alteration of *Twelfth Night*.

In the year following that whose astonishing activity had brought no less than five neglected plays to the stage, one other comedy was added to the repertory—*The Comedy of Errors*. It was acted five times at Drury Lane in the 1741-1742 season but was not, however, revived there again. *Twins, or Comedy of Errors* was acted at Covent Garden, on April 24, 1762, but whether this is the original or an alteration is unrecorded. Shakespeare's play was apparently little known before Hull's version appeared in 1779,[30] but it then became a stock piece. Nothing is known of the various alterations of this play. Taverner's *Everybody Mistaken,* acted in 1716 but unprinted, has left no indication as to its relation to its source and was not alive as late as 1737; and William Shirley's *All Mistaken,* neither acted nor printed, had no connection with the theater.

The plays in the next group to be considered were revived after Garrick came to the stage, and most of them were restored to the theater through his efforts. Almost all of them supplanted alterations that had been acted in the Restoration period. Several, however, were still suffering from their earlier maltreatment. *The Tempest* and *A Midsummer Night's Dream,* for example, had not yet entirely thrown off their operatic accretions, and two plays—*The Taming of the Shrew* and *Pericles*—reached the stage only in shortened versions.

Romeo and Juliet, one of the two plays of this group not first revived through the efforts of Garrick, was staged at the Haymarket Theatre in 1744. The version used was the work of Theophilus Cibber, who is generally credited with driving Otway's alteration from the stage by restoring the original.[31] But Cibber's play was also an alteration, which in fact borrowed several features from Otway's tragedy. Indeed, the Otway version long exerted considerable influence, for Garrick's version, produced at Drury Lane in 1748, was also indebted to Otway. Later alterers were Charles Marsh, Thomas Sheridan, and John Lee, all of whom attempted to adapt the play for the stage between 1748 and 1777; but none of their versions was printed, nor did these later alterations influence the London repertory, for Sheridan's was acted only at Dublin, Lee's perhaps only at Edinburgh, and Marsh's play was unacted.

The original had been revived some time after the reopening of the theaters in 1660, and the actor Harris was famous as Romeo as late as 1682. But in 1680 Otway had brought out his *Caius Marius,* which soon displaced the original and held the boards for more than sixty years. Even earlier, alterations had been attempted, notably that of James Howard in 1662, which kept the lovers alive at the end; but this alteration soon disappeared. Otway did not follow Howard's lead in making the play into a tragicomedy, but he did make several important changes; and the Montague-Capulet feud was transferred to the partisans of Marius and Sylla. The most significant change in the plot occurs in the ending: Lavinia (Juliet) awakes before Marius (Romeo) dies. This alteration provided the opportunity for a pathetic scene, the probable reason for the change, and influenced Cibber, Garrick, and even Kemble much later when they came to adapt the play. Cibber's play, among other changes, omits the mention of Rosaline and keeps Otway's ending, although it does restore the Montague-Capulet framework. In Garrick's version also Rosaline is omitted, and when the play opens, Romeo and Juliet are already acquainted. Although Garrick removed much of the rhyme and added to the fifth act a scene showing Juliet's funeral—which has a dirge but no dialogue—his alteration is closer to the original than is Cibber's.[32] As these two versions were the only ones acted with any frequency in the mid-century period, audiences were unacquainted with the real nature of the Shakespearean ending. And, of course, the little-understood final scene, in which Friar Lawrence recounts what he knows of the circumstances that brought on the tragedy, was omitted in stage presentations, as it often has been to the present day.[33]

Romeo and Juliet had a remarkable stage history after its 1748 revival. It was performed twenty times at Drury Lane that season; two years later it was again revived, this time for nineteen performances. Between 1750 and 1777 it missed only one season at that theater. The Covent Garden managers also found it a popular addition to the repertory. First acted there in the season after the Drury Lane revival, it fared equally well throughout the rest of the period. For a time it served as a test of strength between the two companies. The most famous of such contests occurred in 1750. In that season *Romeo and Juliet* was acted on twelve nights by both theaters simultaneously and for a time the public found pleasure in comparing the parts of Garrick and Mrs. Bellamy with those of Barry and Mrs. Cibber. Although the spectators were quite evenly divided as to the respective merits of the two performances, Garrick, by holding out for one more performance and by adding a "diverting epilogue" on the last night, won a technical victory. Actually, however, Garrick was no match for

Barry, the greatest stage lover of the time, and he later changed to the role of Mercutio. Even if the real victors in this mid-century war of the theaters cannot now be determined, it is significant that Shakespeare's romantic tragedy was chosen as the vehicle for the rival actors.

In spite of the play's relatively late return to the stage, *Romeo and Juliet* was the most frequently performed of all Shakespeare's plays in the mid-century and, after *Hamlet, Richard III, Macbeth,* and *Othello,* the most often revived from season to season. Acted at each theater in twenty-seven of the forty seasons, on a total of almost 250 nights, it surpassed even *Hamlet* in frequency of performance, even though the latter play was already on the boards in 1737. It is not difficult to determine why it succeeded. The ever popular love story, portrayed by some of the greatest English actors, is enough to account for its tremendous success. But it is significant that the beginning of its modern period of popularity dates from the years that gave the world, for example, the odes of Collins and Gray and Warton's *Pleasures of Melancholy.* But besides the spirit that made *Romeo and Juliet* congenial to the time, its great illusional power must not be overlooked, for, in the words of a contemporary, "the process of the action is carried on with such probability, at least with such congruity to popular opinions, as tragedy requires." [34]

Macbeth, one of the most frequently revived of Shakespeare's plays between 1737 and 1777, had been brought to the stage soon after the Restoration in a version much like the original, but this was soon replaced by Davenant's mutilation, first acted in 1665. Davenant's play, among other changes, heightened the parts of Macduff and Lady Macduff to afford a parallel with Macbeth and Lady Macbeth, included a triple prophecy to Macduff as well as to Macbeth, omitted Ross, enlarged the part of Seyton, and made the ghost of Duncan appear to Lady Macbeth. But there were numerous other changes as well that, because of their special nature, made of *Macbeth,* as it was known to theatergoers for three-quarters of a century, an opera, fitted out with a fifty-voice chorus of witches. This operatized version held the stage to the complete exclusion of the original until 1744. Nor did its influence stop there, for Garrick did not venture to do away entirely with the operatic trimmings.

When Garrick revived the play, it was thought that the principal character could not hold the audience beyond the first two acts.[35] But the critics were wrong, for his imaginative interpretation of the role held his audiences spellbound, and contemporaries commented particularly on the "indescribable excellence" of Garrick in the banquet scene.[36]

The surviving records of the stage management of this play are illuminating, not only because they shed interesting light on the actors' treatment of *Macbeth* and of Shakespeare's plays in general, but also because they reveal two important contemporary attitudes toward drama. One of these concerns the matter of tragic decorum. It was expected throughout most of the century that the witches would furnish comic interludes in the plot, and so they did until at least as late as 1784[37]—a situation to which audiences did not object, no matter what the critics might say as to the inappropriateness of such a mixture of moods. Even the banquet scene was not without its touch of comedy. It was then customary for the actor playing Banquo to come on the stage in this scene as Banquo's ghost and, while the distraught Macbeth looked in horror, to point to his bloody head and slashed throat. This piece of business was not abolished until Kemble decided to play the scene with an empty stool; but there is no indication that the change was made to please an audience that objected to a "mixed type" of drama. Eighteenth-century audiences were indeed often notoriously "unorthodox" when they had to choose between the critics' rules and their own entertainment.[38]

The other attitude concerns may be called the trend toward visual realism on the stage. Whereas earlier actors had paid no attention to historical accuracy in costuming—Garrick, for example, played Macbeth dressed in a scarlet and gold coat and powdered wig—Macklin, in 1772, introduced Scottish costume, an innovation that was well received by the audience and imitated by his successors in the role. Similarly, in the sleepwalking scene, much of the traditional stage business for which Mrs. Pritchard is credited,[39] that actress kept hold of the taper so that the hand-washing motions, which later came to be an expected piece of business, had necessarily to be curtailed or even omitted. It might be inferred that mid-century actors must often have relied heavily upon the imaginative power of the spectator—a reliance that was frequently misplaced.[40]

The version of *Macbeth* that audiences saw and heard after

1744 has recently been described as "the most accurate stage version of a Shakespearean play which has appeared since 1671," [41] and Garrick was praised by contemporaries for having broken through "the fetters of foolish custom and arbitrary imposition" [42] by rejecting Davenant's play. This version is not, however, entirely Shakespeare's. In addition to the operatic trimmings, Garrick kept a dozen readings from the earlier alteration, substituted "Heaven" for "God" in the original text (a change made in almost all eighteenth-century alterations), omitted the porter, and removed Lady Macbeth from the conference after Duncan's murder. He made a few emendations of his own and added a dying speech that suited his particular talent of portraying a man in the throes of death. That he was seriously attempting to restore Shakespeare is certain, however, by his inclusion of many imaginatively poetic lines that Davenant had excised and by his request for advice on his alteration from both Johnson and Warburton. He seems to have chosen judiciously between the suggestions made by the two editors when they were in conflict.[43] But he retained the chorus of witches. This play was acted almost 150 times between 1744 and 1777 and was revived at one or other of the patent theaters every season.

The next Shakespearean play to be brought to the stage was *The Taming of the Shrew,* although in a much shortened version. In Garrick's alteration, titled *Katharine and Petruchio,* it was first acted in 1754. This is generally regarded as one of his most successful reworkings of Shakespeare,[44] and it was one of the longest-lived of all Shakespearean alterations. In its original form, the play seems to have been performed neither during the Restoration nor in the eighteenth century. Its stage history since 1660 had been the history of its numerous adaptations, dating from Lacy's *Sauny the Scot,* acted at the Theatre-Royal in 1667. The next recorded alterations were those of Charles Johnson and Christopher Bullock in 1716. Each produced a farce in that year with identical titles—*The Cobbler of Preston*—based upon the Induction. Johnson included political allusions directed against the Jacobites, who were active at the time. Bullock's was written to compete with Johnson's, but he omitted the political references. Worsdale drew largely upon Lacy's play for a ballad opera, *A Cure for a Scold,* acted at Drury Lane in 1735 and revived at Covent Garden in 1750.

The vogue of musical afterpieces was then nearing its height, and the levying upon older full-length drama to supply the framework for such pieces as well as to make up for the lack of inventiveness that plagued mid-century playwrights had by then become frequent. The alteration made by Garrick was, therefore, in the tradition of such adaptations of *The Taming of the Shrew,* extending back to Lacy.

His version was regarded as "regular," [45] "judicious," and "necessary," [46] and it pleased the audience. Woodward and Mrs. Pritchard acted the principal parts, with Yates as Grumio, when it was first performed, although it was Mrs. Clive who popularized the heroine's role. Garrick's alteration was acted forty-eight times in fifteen seasons at Drury Lane, where it proved to be a popular afterpiece. Its most successful season was 1756, when it shared the bill on twelve nights with Garrick's *Florizel and Perdita.* Contemporaries suggest that part of its success at that time was owing to the known antipathy that existed between the two chief actors, which was so strong as to make itself apparent on the stage.[47] A certain similarity between the stage life of Katharine and Petruchio and the private life of Kitty Clive and Woodward appealed to audiences who found in the stage and the greenroom their chief interests. By such petty circumstances was the destiny of the world's greatest dramatist sometimes determined!

Although Thomson's *Coriolanus* was acted at Covent Garden, January 13, 1749, for the benefit of the late poet's family, yet, because it was really a new play rather than an adaptation, the first revival of Shakespeare's tragedy after 1737 must be said to have been the one brought out in 1754 at Drury Lane. This version, later printed by Bell, may have been substantially the original.[48] It was acted on nine nights in competition with Sheridan's alteration, which had eight performances in the same season at the rival theater. The reason for the revival at Drury Lane is suggested by Wilkinson:[49]

. . . it is probable that Mossop, who gained considerable reputation as Coriolanus would not have had the luck of having this play brought out with expense, but that Garrick, who was a quick general, was eager to get the start of the rival theatre, where it was in preparation with infinite pomp and splendour—the very idea of a triumphal procession at C. G. struck terror to the whole host of Drury, however big they looked and strutted on common occasions.

Volumnia was acted by Mrs. Pritchard, who had to compete with the popular Mrs. Bellamy, then acting the role at Covent Garden. At Covent Garden Sheridan himself played Coriolanus, and Shuter, Ridout, and Mrs. Woffington acted the parts of Menenius, Cominius, and Volumnia. The play drew several crowded houses. *Coriolanus* was revived at Covent Garden in five later seasons between 1757 and 1768, probably in the Sheridan alteration. In all, between 1737 and 1777 there were at least twenty-four performances of the versions of this play that were partly based on Shakespeare besides ten performances of Thomson's independent version.

Garrick, whose only Roman role was Antony, did not act in any of the alterations, but both Sheridan and Quin succeeded in the title role. The latter especially, who was popular in several Roman parts, was highly regarded as the Coriolanus of Thomson's play. The stately though frigid rhetoric of the play was undoubtedly well suited to his declamatory style of delivering his lines. Quin's costume, as shown in an old print, consisted of a richly embroidered tunic with a stiff, flaring skirt and a helmet with three tall plumes.[50] The same print shows two women, one of whom is presumably Volumnia, dressed in habits that are more medieval than Roman; but then, consistency and accuracy in costuming were still largely matters of indifference. But one actress, at least, sought for greater visual realism, for, as contemporaries mention with considerable surprise, Mrs. Woffington, the greatest beauty of her time, covered her face with wrinkles to play the part of Volumnia. Never very popular in any of its various versions, *Coriolanus* had, except for *Timon of Athens,* the briefest stage history of any of Shakespeare's tragedies during the eighteenth century.

A Midsummer Night's Dream fared badly in the mid-eighteenth century, and only once, and then for a single night, did it appear with its original title. As an operatic farce used as an afterpiece, however, it met with considerable success. This piece was the third in a series of versions for which Garrick was largely responsible. His first alteration appeared in 1755 as an opera—*The Fairies*—and, according to Cross, prompter at Drury Lane, was spectacular enough to succeed without an afterpiece.[51] It appeared in February and was played eleven times in the remainder of that season and the following, bringing in 1,700 pounds. In 1763 another version was acted, again as an opera, but this time entitled *A Midsummer Night's Dream*. It failed, however, after one night. This play had been variously credited to Garrick and to Colman; it is apparent, however, from a copy of Tonson's 1734 edition marked in the hand of Garrick, that Garrick had planned to bring almost the whole of the original play on the stage, but that Colman, during Garrick's trip on the Continent, had further altered the play and presented it in a version not so close to Shakespeare's as Garrick had intended.[52] Three nights after the failure of this play, Colman introduced *A Fairy Tale* as an afterpiece. This was an abridgment of the opera, apparently designed to make use of the machinery and costumes provided for the longer version.[53] This shortened play held the stage well into the next century, when one critic referred to it as "the first of that series of Shakespeare's Dramas which were with happier effect converted into Musical plays by the addition of songs, &c. from the Author's own works." [54] By 1777 it had had about fifty performances. The alterations of this play in all three forms were undoubtedly attempts at Drury Lane to challenge the supremacy of the rival theater, where musical pieces had long been successful.

Long before the mid-century there had been several alterations of *A Midsummer Night's Dream*, but they had quickly disappeared. The play had been made into a popular droll, called *The Humours of Bottom the Weaver*, even before the Restoration. An anonymous opera, called *The Fairy Queen*, was performed in 1692; and a comic masque ridiculing Italian opera, the work of Leveridge, was acted at Lincoln's Inn Fields in 1716. A later alteration was the mock opera, with music by Lampe, staged at Covent Garden in 1745.[55] But none of these apparently influenced Garrick's or Colman's alterations, and they differ from the versions of the 'fifties and 'sixties in a significant respect—each chose for representation only one set of characters from the original play. One later play based upon *A Midsummer Night's Dream* that dates from the mid-eighteenth century has recently come to light. It is Thomas Hull's *The Fairy Favour, A Masque,* published in a slender octavo in 1766. The title page asserts that it is taken from Shakespeare's play, but except for the use of some of Shakespeare's names for the characters the reader will find little resemblance. It was apparently performed at Covent Garden, for the author states that the play was written for the entertainment of the Prince of Wales on the occasion of his first visit to that theater.

Although both Dryden and Sedley had written plays based on the story of Antony and Cleopatra, neither was an alteration of Shakespeare's play. Nor did either influence Garrick's version. The latter, produced in 1759, was apparently the first attempt to revive the original since 1607.[56] But it had little success. Garrick had obtained the services of Capell in preparing the alteration for the stage; but when it reached the boards, it had only six performances, even though it had been prepared at great expense and more than the usual attention had been paid to scenery and costumes. Garrick himself acted Antony, and Mrs. Yates played Cleopatra. Garrick was not at his best in this part, as he lacked the imposing stature necessary for the "demi-Atlas of this earth," nor did the role provide sufficient opportunity for his special talent—the rapid transition of emotions. Mossop seems to have been entirely unsuited for the role of Enobarbus. When Garrick saw that the play did not live up to expectations, he withdrew it.[57]

Since Garrick's play is a superior stage version and not an "improvement," it is instructive to see what changes he thought it necessary to make in the original. The number of characters is reduced by eight, with the omission of Ventidius, Scarus, Philo, Gallus, Menecrates, Varrius, Taurus, and Euphronius. A total of 613 lines,[58] including ten entire scenes, is omitted in the interests of shortening the play. With the smaller cast it became necessary to redistribute the remaining speeches. Among the omitted passages are the accounts of Ventidius in Parthia and of Antony in Athens. The short introductory scenes are cut in Act IV, so that the arming scene begins the act. The parts of Pompey and Octavia are greatly reduced by omission of speeches; passages dealing with historical and political matters are frequently excised; some of the *double-entendre* is removed; and there are a few emendations, apparently as a matter of establishing suggestive phrasing for the contemplated stage business.[59] The result is a faster-moving play that concentrates on the love of Antony and Cleopatra, almost to the exclusion of every other element in the original. The part of Enobarbus, however, is retained almost in its entirety. The only addition is in the drinking song, which is given another verse, probably to prolong the Bacchanalian revels; and the only transposition of lines consists in moving the famous description of Cleopatra (II, ii, 218ff.) to Act I, Scene i. By the transposition her charm and regal luxury are established for the audience at the very beginning of the play. Compared to the usual kind of alteration, this play is a serious attempt to present Shakespeare unadulterated. In contrast, when Kemble revived the play in 1813, he found it necessary to insert passages from Dryden's *All for Love*.[60]

Victor credits Garrick with restoring *Cymbeline* to the stage.[61] The original had, however, been revived briefly as early as 1744. Although Garrick had demonstrated his interest in the play fifteen years earlier (see his letter to Hoadley quoted below), it was not until 1761 that he brought *Cymbeline* to Drury Lane, in a version he himself had prepared. When this alteration was later printed, he apologized for the changes he had made, but justified them as necessary in order to "bring it within the compass of a night's entertainment." This version of *Cymbeline* became quite popular and was acted in every season until Garrick's retirement, on a total of almost a hundred nights. The first performance of Garrick's play at Covent Garden took place in 1767, when it was staged with great expense,[62] and it was maintained in the repertory of that theater through the 1774-1775 season. Garrick's play was hardly the original, in spite of Victor's remark. Durfey had altered *Cymbeline* in 1682 as *The Injured Princess, or the Fatal Wager*. Although he called his alteration a comedy, it is more tragic than the original, which the folio editors placed with the tragedies. Some of the characters are given different names, and Clarinna, the confidante of Eugenia (Imogen), is added. Durfey's play was acted once in the period, at Covent Garden in 1738. John Hoadley was working on an alteration in 1746, for in September of that year Garrick wrote to him: "I am glad to hear you have dock'd & alter'd Cymbeline & beg you will send it up immediately directed for Me, at my Lodgings in James Street Covt Garden; You will give me great Pleasure & may do me Service by it. . . ."[63] The alteration was not staged, however; indeed, it was never completed, a circumstance suggesting that it did not meet with Garrick's favor. Charles Marsh was the next to try altering the play. He printed his version in 1753, which, however, was not acted. An alteration by Hawkins was acted for six nights in 1759, but was apparently never revived again. Hawkins made numerous changes in the original. Iachimo disappears completely, and Posthumus does not appear until Act III. The parts of Philario and Pisanio are curiously confused, and those of the King's sons are enlarged. The Queen has died before the action of the play begins. The unities of time and place are maintained, and the ends of poetic justice are fulfilled when Palador (Polydore) is the instrument of Pisanio's punishment. Genest remarks that it is no wonder Tate and Cibber dared to "mangle" Shakespeare during an age when he was out of fashion; for Hawkins, who was a professor of poetry at Oxford, made at least as violent changes in *Cymbeline* during an "enlightened" age of the theater.[64]

Some must have felt, however, that Hawkins had saved Shakespeare's play from neglect, for it was remarked that *Cymbeline* is "only fitted to the *English* Stage, by removing some Part of the Absurdities in Point of Time and Place, which the rigid Rules of dramatic Law do not now admit with so much Impunity as at the Time when the original Author of *Cymbeline* was living."[65] But Gentleman, writing in the *Dramatic Censor* in 1770,[66] although he agrees that alteration was necessary, found Hawkins' play unsatisfactory:

. . . we view Shakespeare between these two gentlemen as a stately tree, abounding with disproportionate superfluities, the former [Garrick] has been so very tender of pruning, that a number of luxuriances remain; and the latter [Hawkins] admired the vegetation of his own brain so much, that he has not only cut the noble plant into the stiffness of an yew hedge, but decked it like a maypole, with poetic garlands, which prove rather gaudy than useful ornaments.

The general opinion seems to have been that the play was worthy of revival because of its beauties and because of the challenge it offered to the actors—especially to Garrick as Posthumus; but there was also unanimity about its violation of the rules. In spite of the critics, the audiences must have liked it, for it was more frequently acted than any of the comedies except *The Merchant of Venice* and *As You Like It*.

One other Shakespearean play was altered for the stage during Garrick's management, but it was not the work of the manager. Benjamin Victor's adaptation of *The Two Gentlemen of*

Verona was brought out at Drury Lane in 1762 and was acted for six nights.[67] This was apparently the first attempt to revive the play since Shakespeare's time, and it furnished the basis for Kemble's revival of 1808, even though the original had been revived at Covent Garden in 1784. Victor's alteration was made largely by omission, with some transposition of scenes. The scene between Silvia and Eglamour in Act III was moved to Act IV, and Valentine's crucial remark, "All that was mine in Silvia I give to thee" (V, iv, 83), was omitted. Speed and Launce are brought on the stage in two new scenes, apparently to increase the comic element in the play.[68] Fitzpatrick, the belligerent leader of the "Town," chose Victor's benefit night to contest with Garrick about the admission prices. To avoid further difficulty with the notorious bully, who had succeeded several times in exerting his will on the proprietors of both theaters, the play was not acted and the money was returned.[69] After one more performance Victor's alteration was dropped, and thus ended the only revival of *The Two Gentlemen* in the mid-century.

The Tempest was the last of Shakespeare's plays to be revived by 1777 as a first piece in a form close to the original.[70] Although it had more than a hundred performances in the forty-year period, perhaps all but the fifteen at Drury Lane in 1777 were in an operatized alteration. Dryden and Davenant had first given the play operatic form in 1667, and had provided new characters parallel to Ferdinand, Miranda, Ariel, and Caliban. Shadwell made it into a regular opera in 1673, and Downes reported "that not any succeeding Opera got more Money." [71] But the opera proved too expensive, and it was replaced in 1674 by his own version of the 1667 alteration. The 1674 version held the stage until Garrick produced a new alteration in 1756, still in operatic form. It was embellished with several new songs, which were taken from the plays of Jonson and Dryden, and even Prospero is made to sing. This version was acted eighteen times the first season and in all but two seasons thereafter while Garrick was in charge of the theater. It was of this play that Theophilus Cibber was speaking when he remarked that although Garrick claimed to venerate the work of Shakespeare, yet he had "castrated [*The Tempest*] into an opera." [72] It was finally revived as a play by Sheridan in 1777, with Bensley as Prospero, Bannister as Caliban, Mrs.

Cuyler as Miranda, and Miss Field as Ariel, but otherwise there seems to be nothing recorded of this performance.

To the thirty-one Shakespearean plays discussed in this and the preceding chapter, one more may be added as having performance in the mid-eighteenth century, although its position in an account of the repertory is somewhat anomalous; it appeared only in an abridged version, it was never staged in the regular season, and it never appeared under its original title. This play, a three-act piece by Lillo entitled *Marina,* for which the author admitted his indebtedness to Shakespeare's *Pericles,* was acted briefly at Covent Garden in 1738. In the prologue to this play, where Lillo speaks of his debt to Shakespeare, he also indicates that he recognized the generally low level of such alterations. But like many others, he did not allow the recognition to prevent him from trying his hand at the fascinating game. Lillo draws only upon the last two acts of the original for his alteration, and although what remains undergoes considerable change, the play was regarded as a better-than-average adaptation. There is considerable doubt, however, that Lillo's play was generally regarded as altered from Shakespeare; *Pericles* was not included in the First or Second Folio or in the first printing of the Third, and it had been rejected by several editors in the eighteenth century. But whether it was regarded as an original or an alteration, Lillo's play was not very successful and was quickly neglected. Indeed, in the nineteenth century a historian remarked, apparently unaware of Lillo's play: "Many old English authors mention it's [*sic*] [that is, *Pericles'*] very great popularity; yet it is the *only* drama by Shakespeare, which has never been once altered for the modern stage." [73]

The remaining plays have no direct connection with the history of the theater in the period. *Troilus and Cressida* had never been staged in its original form after the Restoration, and Dryden's alteration, subtitled *Truth Found Too Late* and first acted in 1679, disappeared from the stage in 1734. There was no other revival of the play in any form by 1777, although Steevens suggested to Garrick in 1773 that the original might be successfully revived "if it were well clipped and decorated." [74] Just three years before his retirement Garrick perhaps felt unable to undertake another extensive pruning of Shakespeare; but whatever the reason, the play was not revived.

More extended consideration was given to the addition to the repertory of *Love's Labour's Lost*. Although it was not revived in any form between the closing of the theaters and the 1839 revival by James Anderson and Eliza Vestris, it was altered by an anonymous playwright in 1762; the alteration was printed as *The Students, a comedy altered from Shakespeare's Love's Labour's Lost and adapted to the stage*. This play has no significance to stage history, however, since it had neither performances nor imitations. More important is an alteration by Captain Edward Thompson, which has recently been discovered.[75] It was undertaken in 1773, at the request of Garrick, and follows the original closely although it is given operatic form. It contains twenty-one songs, all taken from the original verbatim or put in close paraphrase. A total of 765 lines are cut, a third of which had previously been excised by Pope, upon whose edition this alteration is ultimately based. The longest single omission is that of the pageant of the Nine Worthies. Thompson said that he had omitted the pageant because he had "observed all plays, played on the stage are heavy."[76] Why the play was not acted is unknown. In this same year Garrick had written to Steevens in search of additional plays to revive, but, as Stone suggests,[77] he may have thought that the day of operatic alterations had passed.

Finally, there remain to be mentioned three plays that were not only left unacted, but also were apparently ignored completely—*Henry VI, Part II, Henry VI, Part III*, and *Titus Andronicus*. John Crowne had based two plays on the second and third parts of *Henry VI* (1681 and 1680), and Theophilus Cibber borrowed heavily from Crowne for his *Henry VI*, acted at Drury Lane in 1723. But none of these plays survived. The only remnants of *Henry VI, Part II*, and *Henry VI, Part III*, to be found on the mid-century stage are the occasional passages borrowed from them by uninventive mutilators of Shakespeare to fill up the gaps in their alterations of other plays, or occasionally by plunderers who inserted some of Shakespeare's lines into their own dramatic compositions.[78] *Titus Andronicus* had been made even more gruesome by Edward Ravenscroft in an alteration subtitled *The Rape of Lavinia,* acted at the Theatre-Royal in 1678. By 1724 this horror of horrors had disappeared, and the play was apparently unknown in any form in the mid-eighteenth-century theater.

Besides the debt the alterers owed to Shakespeare, there were numerous authors of "original" dramas who borrowed scenes, names, or lines for independent plays, or who proclaimed that they were writing in imitation of the master. Of the imitations, Kenrick's *Falstaff's Wedding*, first performed at Drury Lane in 1766, was regarded as one of the best. Havard's *King Charles the First,* acted at Drury Lane in 1740, was advertised as "an historical play, written in imitation of Shakespeare." Of this piece Genest remarks: "Havard was quite right to inform the public that King Charles the First was written in imitation of Shakespeare, as no one could otherwise have discovered the circumstance." [79] The same comment was made by a contemporary on Shirley's *Edward the Black Prince* (1750), which the author claimed to have written in imitation of Shakespeare.[80] Hawkins was attacked on similar grounds for his unacted *Henry and Rosamund.* Rowe not only was attempting to imitate Shakespeare in *Jane Shore,* which was still a popular tragedy in the mid-century, but in it he inserted a scene taken almost in its entirety from *Henry VI.*[81] On the other hand, plays like Jerningham's *Margaret of Anjou,* Francklin's *Earl of Warwick,* and Macklin's *Henry VII* are indebted only in a general way to Shakespeare.

It will be noted that all the plays just mentioned are either based upon Shakespeare's histories or are imitations of them. Although imitations of the tragedies and comedies, or evidence of borrowing from them, can be found, it is significant that the histories figure so largely here. Authors of the latter half of the eighteenth century were particularly fond of basing dramatic compositions on events and persons in English history. The Larpent Collection, for example, contains seventy or more such pieces.[82] The great storehouse of popular history to which these authors could conveniently turn was, of course, the chronicle plays of Shakespeare. And it is especially noteworthy that the number of such plays increased after about 1740, the approximate date when the Shakespeare revival got under way.

But both imitators and alterers must have found themselves in a difficult situation. If they announced that they had imitated the great Elizabethan's language, they were open to criticism by those who held that Shakespeare's diction was that of a barbarous age. Moreover, writers of all later ages, unable to detect anything that might be called a Shakespearean manner or a Shakespearean mannerism, have ultimately despaired of equaling his powerful conceptions or his expressive poetry. Yet his name and the names of his characters and plays had come to have a tangible value for one who hoped to gain fame or wealth by supplying the stage with actable drama. That this attitude had not been held earlier is indicated by a comparison between the situation in the later eighteenth century, when Shakespeare's fame was at its height in the theater, and that at the beginning of the century. A recently published analysis of the 1703-1704 theatrical season[83] shows that, although eight of Shakespeare's plays were acted, only once is his name mentioned in the announcements of performance. On the other hand, the three plays of Jonson acted that season are invariably announced as "by the famous Ben Johnson [*sic*]," and recently deceased authors, Dryden, Shadwell, and Etherege, are also fully credited. The theatergoing public presumably knew that the eight plays were by Shakespeare and hence did not need to be informed of that fact; but they presumably knew the authors of the other plays as well. Fifty years later, however, playwrights and managers knew that Shakespeare's name was a considerable asset, and it is highly likely that for this reason many a title page contained the words, "written in the manner of Shakespeare," and many a playbill announced the performance of a play "as written by Shakespeare."

PART II: THE CONDITIONS—
PROFESSIONAL

CHAPTER SEVEN

The Manager

The theatrical repertory of mid-century London assumed its special character for a number of reasons. These reasons, arising from what I have called the conditions of dramatic performance, can be traced to various types of influences, conveniently classified as professional and amateur. The latter, exerted chiefly by eighteenth-century audiences, will be discussed in later chapters. The former may be further classified as the influences exerted by the manager, the actor, and the playwright. Obviously there was a close relationship among these professional theater men, and the responsibility for such matters as the addition of a particular play to the repertory, its failure to survive there, and the length of its run or the frequency of its revival is not, therefore, always certainly assignable. There are, however, rather large spheres of influence where there is less uncertainty, and these can be profitably examined. There is also a considerable body of data concerning the stage histories of many of the plays that were performed, on the basis of which, if we may believe theatrically minded contemporaries, it is possible to assess the evidences of influence.

The manager was a peculiarly important functionary in the mid-century theater. Similar in some respects to the director-stockholder of the Elizabethan stage, he was later supplanted by the producer, who took over most of his duties. He was regularly the patentee or a joint patentee, if his theater was one of those holding a royal charter. All financial affairs were his concern, although he often delegated these to a lesser official; but where several held the patent jointly, financial matters were sometimes looked after by one of the patentees while another served as the manager. The manager was also the director, and normally attended preliminary readings in the greenroom and all the rehearsals. He was in sole charge of the repertory and, on his own responsibility, could add or withdraw plays. He dealt directly with playwrights who offered their compositions for performance, and sometimes had new plays written or older plays altered on order. He was in immediate charge of the acting company, cast new plays, settled disputes among the actors, and helped to maintain their priorities, especially as to the "possession of parts." He determined the costuming and stage *décor,* and employed seamstresses, wigmakers, carpenters, and painters to carry out his intentions. He was also his own press agent—or propagandist, as the case might be—who advertised his wares and defended his policies in the public prints—often anonymously. As time went on and the theater company became a homogeneous and closely knit group, he established, in some instances, a pension fund for retired actors and saw to it that the fund was maintained and properly disbursed. Moreover, in addition to all these duties, he was usually an actor as well; hence the title "acting-manager," which is sometimes used in contemporary accounts.

The men who held this important position in the various theaters of mid-century London were few in number, especially after the Licensing Act virtually suppressed all but the two royal theaters, and they were not, of course, equally important in determining the complexion of the repertory.

The patent of Drury Lane Theatre, which can be traced back to the seventeenth century, was bought by Charles Fleetwood in 1735 from Giffard, Highmore, and Mrs. Wilks, who had acquired the shares held earlier by the famous triumvirate of Cibber, Wilks, and Booth. Fleetwood served as the manager much of the time during which he was patentee, but occasionally many of the managerial duties were fulfilled by members of his company, notably by Charles Macklin. But Fleetwood was quite inept in matters of both play production and finance. Finally, in 1744, he was forced to relinquish his title to the brokers Green and Amber. James Lacy then became sole proprietor until he granted to Garrick in 1747 a half interest in the patent in return for his services as actor and manager. Garrick continued as manager until his retirement from the stage in 1776, whereupon he sold his share of the patent to James Ford, Thomas Linley, and Richard Brinsley Sheridan. The management of the stage was taken over by Sheridan. In the meantime the other half of the patent had passed, at the death of Lacy, into the hands of his son Willoughby, who had a brief and not very successful career as an actor in the Drury Lane company.

The rival patent theater, Covent Garden, was similarly under the management of a small group of men throughout the mid-century period. The patent under which it operated also had a long history, which goes back to the licensing of Davenant's company by Charles II soon after the Restoration. John Rich opened Covent Garden in 1732; he brought to his new theater, not only most of the acting company formerly at his playhouse in Lincoln's Inn Fields (opened by Rich in 1714), but also the charter privilege of that stage, which now made of Covent Garden a theater-royal. Rich was manager and sole proprietor until his death. In fact, the patent under which Covent Garden operated was a family possession for more than half a century; not only had Rich acquired it from his father (Christopher Rich, who had bought it in 1688), but upon his death in 1761 it passed to his son-in-law, John Beard, who had been an actor with the Drury Lane company from 1749 to 1759. Beard then served as manager until he was incapacitated by deafness. In 1767 the patent was finally sold to Colman, Powell, Harris, and Rutherford. Colman served as manager, not without considerable trouble and frequent disputes with the other patentees, until he acquired the Little Theatre in the Haymarket in 1777, whereupon he sold his share of the Covent Garden patent to Harris and Powell.

The most important of the "minors," the Little Theatre in the Haymarket (not to be confused with the older Haymarket theater, otherwise known as the Opera House, built by Vanbrugh in 1705) was first opened in 1720. It was generally on a precarious footing, for it was in direct—and illegal—competition with the patent theaters. The Little Theatre was open only sporadically and with varying degrees of success under the management of Theophilus Cibber, Henry Fielding, and Samuel Foote at various periods between 1733 and 1766, but was almost as frequently closed to any kind of performance. One of its most successful periods was that under Fielding's management from 1735 to 1737. After the passage of the Licensing Act of 1737, which prohibited dramatic performance except at the royal theaters, it was kept open by means of various subterfuges, the most famous being Foote's "Dish of Tea" (1747). Finally, in 1766, Foote built a new theater on its site and, through the influence of the Duke of York, was granted a patent for life in that year. Thereafter it was designated as "Theatre-Royal," and existed on the same basis as did the two major playhouses. It was, however, no longer in competition with the older patent houses, for the royal license allowed performances only between May 15 and September 15 of each year. Consequently it is properly regarded after 1766 as a "summer theatre," even though its irrepressible manager slyly lengthened the season whenever it was in his interest to do so. In 1777 Foote and Colman entered into an agreement by which the latter became the manager and sole owner. Foote died in the same year, and the patent expired. However, the theater remained open under Colman by virtue of an annual license granted by the Lord Chamberlain, and it continued to be called a theatre-royal in spite of the lapse of the charter.

Of the other theater managers of the period, Henry Giffard is the most important. It was chiefly owing to his daring that the theater in Goodman's Fields remained open between 1732 and 1737 and, after being closed as a result of the Licensing Act, during the 1740-1741 season. The effect of Garrick's popularity upon the receipts of the major houses in 1741-1742 brought about the closing of Goodman's Fields, and Giffard was thereafter associated with Drury Lane, except for a brief period in 1743 when he was at the theater in Lincoln's Inn Fields. Plays were produced also at Vanbrugh's Opera House in the Haymarket, at Sadler's Wells, and at Lincoln's Inn Fields at various times between 1737 and 1777, but those playhouses have little to contribute to the theatrical history of the time.

It will be seen from this brief account that the destinies of the London stage for almost half a century were in the hands of a small group of persons, and that the only managers who could have exerted any considerable influence on the theatrical repertory were Garrick, Rich, Beard, Foote, and Colman. It is with these men, therefore, that I shall be chiefly concerned in the following pages.[1]

The theater manager of the eighteenth century combined in himself several functions. As patentee, he was regarded as a royal servant who must make a public appearance at court on special occasions. If, for example, he was not present on a

[1] For notes to chap. 7, see pp. 320-324.

royal birthday, "it would be taken notice of, judged a remiss-
ness, and not respectful." [2] He was, therefore, a marked man,
one whose conduct, dress, and relationships with others were
fair game for gossip in private or comment in print. He could
be an influential friend or a powerful enemy. Moreover, his
theater and company had to be always in readiness to cater to
royal command or whim. But he was also a public servant
and, as such, was depended upon to maintain peaceful relations
between the theater and the public. It was his "positive duty,"
Victor tells us, "to oppose all Measures that cause Dissentions
in the Theatre" and to be "deaf to the Voice of Faction." [3] To
carry out this duty was not always easy. Thomas Wilkes regarded the position of manager extremely difficult to fill with
satisfaction to both the public and the company. He remarks,

Often it happens that when he has done his utmost to serve the
public in preparing an entertainment to their taste, and adapting it
to the different geniusses [sic] of his performers, his most sanguine
hopes are frustrated by the inconsiderate behaviour of some, who,
void of all manners and decorum, and out of a particular pique to
some poor author, or actor, or for some other trifle of that nature,
disturb the public entertainment, and turn the Theatre, which is, or
ought to be the School of Manners, into a Beargarden. [4]

But in his own sphere he was usually more successful, and
he had almost dictatorial powers. He could, in fact, become
an arbiter of taste, for the selecting and casting of plays was in
his care, and he had it in his power to reject or accept the
pieces offered for performance by contemporary playwrights.
The initiative in reviving older dramas, as well as determining
the order for presenting stock plays, generally came from him. [5]
Murphy, for example, felt that "the public taste, the honour
of old English authors, and the state of dramatic poetry in
general, are all committed to his care," [6] and Wilkes called
him "the trustee or conductor of the most rational amusements
of the public." [7] There were, to be sure, those who tried to
belittle managerial power. An editor of Garrick's correspondence, for example, exclaimed, "The power of a manager indeed! what is it to an actress of powerful talent, backed by half
the women of fashion in the metropolis?" [8] But the records
show that whatever might have been her individual hold on
the public, the most temperamental actress could do little in

the face of the manager's opposition. Such was the position of manager during the mid-eighteenth century—a position that can best be appreciated by realizing that it was filled by some of the most important professional figures in the theatrical history of the time.

The first of these, chronologically, was John Rich, who had inherited the Covent Garden patent from his father. More than any other theater manager, Rich is singled out by his contemporaries for attack. Murphy accuses him of having debauched public taste;[9] Davies, of taking delight in "thwarting the inclinations of his actors";[10] and Wilkinson, of adopting a policy that made new plays and revivals of long-unacted old plays almost impossible of performance.[11] The source of his harmful influence on public taste, according to writers of the day, was his predilection for pantomimes. An "admirable machinist," [12] he found it unnecessary to depend upon a strong acting company and a varied repertory of regular drama when he could fill his theater with those who came to be startled by the ingenious effects he produced on his stage and amused by the antics of Harlequin.

Rich was convinced—justly, it seems—that the success of a performance at Covent Garden was due to his own mechanical contrivances, and he was therefore unwilling to share his glory with either actor or playwright. Many persons who depended for their livelihood upon the theater, finding themselves relegated to a distinctly secondary position, took occasion to ridicule Rich's theatrical offerings. Thus, Foote delivered a "comic lecture" at the Haymarket theater in which he belittled Rich's fondness for "Roman triumphs, ovations, &c. also Italian burlettas; in one of which there was a sneezing duet." [13] But, in spite of all the scorn which Foote and others could muster, audiences found the fare offered at Covent Garden to their liking, and Drury Lane often found itself outrivaled even when its strongest actors and most popular pieces were listed in the playbill. Murphy's charge that he debauched public taste seems, therefore, to be well grounded.

But his influence on the theatrical history of the time goes even beyond this. Because he had little sympathy with the actors, they preferred to seek employment at the rival theater; and thus the Covent Garden company, except in a small number of seasons—for example, in 1750-1751—was much weaker than the Drury Lane company. This fact, together with Rich's well-known disparagement of additions to the repertory other than his own pantomimes, severely limited the opportunity for performing new plays to the Drury Lane stage.

Contemporary managers believed the nature of a single season was such as to make impossible the introduction of more than three or four new plays, together with a smaller number of revivals.[14] This fact demonstrates that the outlet for dramatic talent was very small; and it is somewhat surprising that such relatively large quantities of drama were written with so little encouragement or possibility of performance. To be sure, some new plays were first staged at Covent Garden, two of the most famous being Dodsley's *Cleone* and Home's *Douglas*. But both of these were first offered to Garrick, who, for reasons that are still debated,[15] rejected them. Had Rich, however, been as amenable to new drama as was Garrick, the theatrical history of the period might have been different; for, with two stages rather than one open to contemporary playwrights, the performances of new pieces might conceivably have been almost doubled, and the motifs briefly tried—for example, by Lillo and Moore—if they had been given greater opportunity for further experiment and exploitation, might ultimately have led to a type of serious drama both congenial to the age and inherently vital.

An obvious objection to such a conclusion is that dramatic genius was lacking—a charge frequently leveled at the age. But the other qualities usually regarded as necessary for a vital theater were present: an interested and heterogeneous audience, a talented and versatile acting company, an adequate stage, a body of capable and active critics, and a pervasive nationalism.[16] Had there also been sufficient outlet for its products, dramatic genius might also have been present.

To lay the blame entirely on Rich is to oversimplify the case; the Licensing Act, which had legislated out of existence all but two of London's theaters, must bear the larger share of blame. Yet, had the two remaining theaters been equally accessible to aspiring playwrights, a greater number of eighteenth-century plays might have survived with some vitality. Then too, largely owing to Rich's threatening competition, Garrick was forced to give over his theater to frequent performances of illegitimate drama. Thus the extent of Rich's influence—on the repertory at Drury Lane as well as on that of his own theater—can be seen in proper perspective.

Fortunately for theatrical history, Garrick had a view of the manager's responsibilities altogether different from that held by Rich. In no respect can this be seen more clearly than in his willingness to put new plays into rehearsal. In contrast to the relatively small number of plays introduced at Covent Garden, Garrick revived more than a score of long-unacted older dramas and brought almost eighty new plays to the stage during the thirty years of his management, more than twice as many as were performed at Covent Garden during the same period under both Rich and his successor, Beard. Included in this number are nearly all the tragedies of the age. There were those who felt that he should have been even more liberal in this respect, especially among authors whose plays he had rejected. Smollett, for example, who tried unsuccessfully to get his tragedy *The Regicide* on the stage, gave Garrick harsh treatment under the name of Marmozet in his novel *The Adventures of Roderick Random*.[17] But such charges are more than offset by the statements of others who thought, especially during the latter part of his career when he ceased to act parts in new plays, that he was too prone to accept new pieces, even some of little merit.[18] After considering both kinds of opinion, we may safely conclude that Garrick, as a manager whose financial stake in the theater might well have caused him to rely more heavily than he did upon stock pieces—which ordinarily involved a negligible outlay of money—was extraordinarily receptive to new drama. Indeed, he became thereby a symbol of encouragement to contemporary playwrights. This encouragement often took the form of active participation in the new play (if it contained an appropriate role); and Garrick's support of the play on the stage was certain to benefit the author, for it was thereby assured of at least temporary success. Even after the manager ceased to take new parts, he gave the new piece the advantage of his direction during rehearsal and the sanction of his attendance in the audience during its performance.[19]

The actors as well as the playwrights also received, on the whole, liberal treatment during Garrick's management. Although Dr. Johnson said that he ruled them "with a high hand,"[20] contemporary accounts of his dealing with the members of his company show him willing to provide opportunities in the repertory for their special talents. This was true even with temperamental actresses like Mrs. Cibber, who was often on unfriendly terms with Garrick, and with rival actors like Spranger Barry, to whom he readily ceded roles, such as those of Othello and Romeo, in which Barry was recognized as superior. In this respect, therefore, Garrick's influence upon the repertory was of a constructive, though passive, kind; for he did not allow himself as manager to stand between actor and audience, a state of affairs in considerable contrast to that prevailing at Covent Garden, where Rich's eccentricity sometimes resulted in the curious miscasting of plays.[21]

A further influence upon the repertory resulted from Garrick's views of his responsibility to English poetry. Murphy noted this attitude of the manager, and commented that he was "zealous at all times for the honour of English drama." [22] His zeal led him to revive many of Shakespeare's plays.[23] It also caused him to explore almost the entire field of English drama and to bring to the eighteenth-century stage several Elizabethan, Jacobean, and Restoration plays that had fallen out of use. The amazing representativeness of all English drama in the Drury Lane repertory during the years of his management, and whatever result such a situation may have had upon the taste of contemporary audiences, are almost solely owing to Garrick's opinion of the duties of a theater manager.

But the greatest influence he had upon the repertory—that is, as manager, and apart from the tremendous influence he had as the favorite actor—was probably that which was exerted in direct contact with the audience, as the acknowledged arbiter of theatrical taste. Whitehead wrote in his "Ode to Mr. Garrick": "A nation's taste depends on you," a sentiment expressed frequently and variously.[24] Not everyone willingly conceded his beneficial influence, but everyone was forced to admit his power. Theophilus Cibber, for example, acknowledged that "his Houses were crowded," but added that it was "Hobson's Choice with the Town." [25] Likewise the author of *D—ry–L—ne P—yh—se Broke Open, in a Letter to Mr. G———*, quotes a "young Gentleman" who accused Garrick of trying to *"cram down our Throats the old damn'd Plays, damnably acted."* [26] And there were undoubtedly many like these two who, moved by jealousy or disappointment, asserted that he took into account only his own preferences and whims. But more disinterested writers picture him as constantly deferring to the public's wishes. The compiler of *Theatrical Biography,* writing while Garrick was still on the stage, said that "he had, from year to year, added to the entertainment of the public; whose taste he had, with every becoming judgment and assiduity, invariably consulted . . . ," [27] an opinion that is readily substantiated by an examination of his career, for perhaps never in the history of the theater has there been a manager so sensitive to the wishes of his audience. Finally, there was an occurrence that, although apart from the repertory, shows clearly how his position caused him to be regarded as an authority in matters of literary taste. At least on one occasion, when John Walker, the lexicographer whose dictionary has determined the pronunciations of numerous words to the present day, wished to consult the best contemporary practice, he went to Garrick to settle a disputed pronunciation.[28]

But even if it is conceded with Davies that "the more advanced state of the stage" [29] was the result of Garrick's wise management of theatrical affairs, it must also be concluded that not even he could always guide the audience's taste in drama. Rich's successes with pantomime sometimes caused Garrick to cater to the popular demand for spectacle and to bring *Queen Mab,* a pantomime, on the stage "sacred to Shakespeare." Likewise, the coronation pageant was an attempt by Garrick to forestall the rival house in much the same way that Covent Garden tried to anticipate Garrick with a pageant at the time of the Shakespeare Jubilee. The rivalry between the two patent houses was, in fact, sometimes the chief factor in determining the theatrical repertory, a notable example being the famous *"Romeo and Juliet* war,"* the history of which plainly indicates that competition between the theaters was the sole motive for its prolongation; for if popular wishes had been consulted, the rivalry would have ended much earlier than it did.[30] The effect of this managerial competition was not, however, always detrimental. Garrick, for example, sometimes met Rich's challenge by offering a revival or a new play, the novelty of which he hoped would offset the spectacular nature of the program at Covent Garden. Thus the revival of *The Mourning Bride* was an attempt by Garrick to offset the greater strength of Covent Garden during the 1750-1751 season by offering a long-unacted piece to the public,[31] and Mallet's *Alfred* was produced "with splendid scenery and much vocal and instrumental music" for the same reason.[32]

Without doubt the greatest influence exerted by a single individual on the theatrical history of the time was that of Garrick, so much so that the period is often called the "Age of Garrick." Fired by a genuine love for older English drama, admired by all theatergoers for his complete mastery of his art and for the efficiency with which he conducted the affairs of his theater, respected—occasionally revered—by the members of his profession, and skilled in perceiving the tides of taste, he was the ideal manager in an age of great actors and acting. It is not surprising that such a figure should have played a considerable part in determining the theatrical repertory of the time. Of the other managers, only Rich came anywhere near rivaling him in influence, and, as has been shown, Rich's influence can hardly be regarded as benign.

The remaining managers of the mid-century are of much less importance. Lacy, Garrick's partner at Drury Lane, limited his activities largely to the physical arrangements of the theater, although during the interval when Garrick was on the Continent he, along with George Garrick, took over the active management. During this brief period his chief concern seems to have been to rival Covent Garden, which he regarded as an English opera house. For that purpose he added serious operas to the repertory, mounted with "splendid scenes, and all the decorations of grand machinery."[33] But his chief importance in theatrical history is the result of his perspicacity in securing the services of Garrick as acting manager of Drury Lane in 1747.

John Beard, Rich's successor at Covent Garden, exerted a considerable influence on the repertory of that theater for the short time of his management. Victor says that he "very naturally and judiciously exerted his Powers to distinguish that Theater by musical Performances, as his Predecessor had done by Pantomime."[34] The move was natural because Beard was himself a singer, and judicious because all the best actors were then (1761) at Drury Lane. He engaged a number of excellent musicians for his company, and between 1761 and 1767 he produced many new musical pieces, including *The Accomplished Maid, The Guardian Out-witted, Love in a Village, Love in the City, The Maid of the Mill, Midas, The*

Shepherd's Artifice, The Summer's Tale, and *Artaxerxes,* as well as frequently reviving such older favorites as *The Beggar's Opera, Comus,* and *The Jovial Crew.* Beard's musical program proved highly successful for four seasons, but in the fifth, interest began to wane; and as Beard himself was growing deaf, a grievous affliction for a manager who depended so largely upon musical pieces, he soon sold the patent.[35] But before that calamity occurred, Beard's successes had made themselves felt at Drury Lane, which attempted to compete for popular favor by staging such operatic pieces as *Almena, The Capricious Lovers, Cymon,* and *The Royal Shepherd,* and *The Beggar's Opera* was given more than thirty performances.[36]

As a manager Samuel Foote exerted less influence on the repertory than he did as author and actor, although the fact that the patent theaters' only successful competitive house was in the hands of a man whose caustic wit and boisterous satire made him a force to be considered had some influence on Drury Lane. As noted above, Foote sometimes ridiculed Rich's offerings at Covent Garden; but Rich seems to have been impervious to criticism. Garrick, however, was notoriously thin-skinned, and to protect himself he reached a working agreement with Foote that prevented such attack. The result to the repertory of Drury Lane was that satirical pieces that might provoke a reply from Foote were carefully avoided. George Colman, Sr., who succeeded Beard at Covent Garden, proved to be a capable manager, but his importance as an influence on the repertory dates largely from his acquisition of the Haymarket in 1777. Oulton praised him highly as a manager, and especially remarked on his liberality to young authors.[37] Finally, it may be noted that Harris and Sheridan, whose terms as managers come at the very end of the period, and who were respectively directing the affairs of the two patent theaters when Davies was writing, are lauded by that author because they "give the town more novelty than any of their predecessors." [38]

These, then, were the men who, by virtue of their managerial position in the theater, had it in their power to determine the character of the mid-century stage and, to a lesser extent, of mid-century drama. But it is apparent from what has been said that they were not consistently successful in exerting that power. What contemporaries regarded as the mark of a successful manager, we can now see, was largely his ability to supply plays that conformed to temporary fashion, and few managers displayed any desire to look further than the popular taste of the hour. Garrick, as was said, is an apparent exception; but then it must be remembered that his superb support of a play on the stage contributed greatly to his success as a manager and that he was better known as an actor than as the chief patentee of Drury Lane. It is true that, unlike the other managers of the period, he as frequently established as followed public taste in drama, but it is doubtful whether he would have done so if he had not been endowed with the histrionic gifts that enabled him to give powerful representation of his ideas upon the stage. It may reasonably be maintained that the manager of the mid-eighteenth century, in spite of his extensive powers, was of less influence upon the repertory than was the audience, from which the shrewd manager found it profitable to take his cue.

Yet in one field of managerial activity his word might be the sole authority. He could accept or reject new plays that were offered for performance; and although he was wise if he took into account the temper of his audience, he did not need to consult anything but his own preference. But to accept a new piece, to put it in rehearsal, where—in addition to the hours of practice required—conflicting interests and views of ambitious actors and actresses often had to be patiently reconciled, to provide it with the necessary costumes and scenery, only to have it irrevocably damned because of the "Funn of the First Night," [39] was a sequence of events all too frequent to permit managers to undertake new plays lightly. Nevertheless, more than a hundred new five-act dramas and a fairly large number of new afterpieces did reach the stage between 1737 and 1777. It is therefore important to discover wherever possible the motives upon which managers acted when they accepted the works of contemporary playwrights for performance—and equally important to learn why they rejected others.

Obviously, a manager was willing to accept a new play that he deemed of sufficient merit to succeed on the stage. Or, if he were also the author of the piece, as was quite often the case, he might add it to the acting list in order to further his own interests. That, in the former, he was sometimes wrong in his judgment, and, in the latter, that he was blinded to his play's defects by his ambition for fame as an author, is copiously indicated by the number of plays that failed before they had attained the normal run for a new piece. But plays were occasionally brought to the stage which were neither meritorious in the judgment of the manager nor conducive to his interest. One of the chief causes of this situation was the pressure brought to bear upon the manager by persons not otherwise associated with the theater, often by persons of political importance.

A few examples will serve to indicate how common was the practice. In 1743, through the influence of Pitt and Lyttelton, their friend Thomson's tragedy *Tancred and Sigismunda* was brought to the stage at Drury Lane.[40] The play met with considerable success, especially because it was strongly supported by Garrick and Mrs. Cibber; but had it not been for the efforts of the author's powerful friends, the play might never have been given performance. Two plays by Murphy—*The Orphan of China,* a tragedy, and *The Upholsterer,* a farce—had in turn been rejected by Garrick. But Fox and Walpole convinced him that he should reconsider the tragedy, and he finally promised to bring it out the following year. Later, when Garrick reverted to his original intention not to stage the tragedy, Whitehead prevailed upon him again to change his mind.[41] Fox alone forced Garrick to stage Murphy's farce, and he did so by resorting to a trick. Fox, who was a friend of Murphy, invited Garrick to dinner at his house. He had previously taken the trouble to memorize various lines from Murphy's play, which he recited at the table. During the naturally ensuing discussion of the play, Fox referred to it as if it were in rehearsal, and added that soon the whole town would be quoting those lines from it. Garrick, of course, was wise enough to take the hint.[42] In fairness to Garrick it should be added that once he saw that a play must be mounted, he spared no expense in doing so and gave it the advantage of a strong cast. At about the same time Garrick was subjected to pressure from another political quarter. It is sometimes said that he accepted Home's *Agis,* a play decidedly inferior to the same author's *Douglas,* in order to exploit the fame of the author, who was then at the height of his popularity. Such an explanation sounds reasonable, especially when it is recalled that Garrick had lost a valuable attraction by rejecting *Douglas* shortly before. A letter written at the time by James Grainger shows, however, that Garrick accepted the play against his will, and only because Home's powerful friend Lord Bute had taken up the cause.[43]

The patron was not always a political figure. We are told, for example, that the Countess of Coventry "compelled the unfortunate Garrick to accept the tragedy of her friend Crisp. . . ." [44] Similarly, Mrs. Montagu's polite insistence that the efforts of her friends be acted is well known. In 1770 she sent Garrick the play *Bon Ton,* written by a friend whom she kept anonymous. Garrick's reply indicates how much he felt compelled to acquiesce to such requests from persons of fashion or noble birth:

I shall not read it in ye Common way, but think twice, before I speak my mind—if I can see a Merit in it proper for ye Stage, You may depend upon it, that I will shew my regard for you, by my zeal in promoting its success.[45]

But even noblemen as influential as Chesterfield and Lyttelton were occasionally unsuccessful. Although both lords supported the efforts of Jane Marishal to get her comedy *Sir Harry Gaylove; or Comedy in Embryo* accepted by one of the managers, she met with nothing but promises and delays, and finally had to be content with printing the lords' commendatory letters with her play when it was later published by subscription.[46] Eighteenth-century managers, because of their power in theatrical affairs and their prominence as royal patentees who moved in aristocratic society, must often have felt as Garrick did when he wrote to John Hoadley for advice:

I have a Play now with Me, sent to me by My Lord Chesterfield & wrote by one Smollett. it is a Scotch Story, but it won't do, & yet recommended by his Lordship & patroniz'd by Ladies of Quality: what can I say or do? Must I belye my Judgment or run the risque of being thought impertinent, & disobliging ye great Folks? [47]

Various other motives sometimes led managers to accept plays. Mme Celisia's *Almida* was given performance as an expression of gratitude. When Garrick had been at Genoa the author, who made her home there, introduced him into Genoese society and otherwise treated him kindly. Later, when she sent him her tragedy, Garrick produced it to repay her kindness to him.[48] He did not lose by accepting it, however, for Mrs. Barry's brilliant acting in the title role kept it on the stage for twelve nights. Mrs. Sheridan's comedy *The Discovery* was given performance for quite a different reason. Even though the manager and the playwright's husband were at the time on unfriendly terms, Garrick accepted her play because of his high opinion of her talents—not as a dramatist, but as the author of the novel *Sidney Biddulph*.[49] *Elvira* and *Alfred,* both the work of Mallet, were said to have reached the stage by a curious combination of circumstances. Mallet had been left a thousand pounds by the Duchess of Marlborough to write the life of her famous husband. Mallet told Garrick that in the book he was writing the manager was to be given a special niche in the hall of fame. Although Mallet never wrote a line of the biography, Garrick, moved by both gratitude and vanity, produced the author's *Elvira*[50] or, according to Dr. Johnson, *Alfred*.[51]

Friendship, political pressure, a desire for the perpetuation of fame—such were often the factors that influenced the manager and, through him, the repertory. But there were also other influences upon the manager, of a kind more professionally commendable. Of these the most important is the manager's recognition of the particular strength or special talents of his company and their suitability for the play in question. This point will be discussed later, but it may be noted here that a manager like Rich, whose genius did not lie in his ability to judge actors, relied on the advice of others on occasion, and that the repertory at Covent Garden sometimes depended, therefore, upon the nature of such counsel. He was told, for example, that Spranger Barry, whom he had just acquired, was well suited for the hero's part in Lee's *Alexander,* and that he had the rival queens in Mrs. Woffington and Mrs. Bellamy. As a result he determined to revive the play.[52] Likewise, when he acquired the most successful Romeo of the time to play to Mrs. Bellamy's Juliet, he naturally gave Shakespeare's romantic tragedy a run. When a "concourse of people . . . crowded for seats," the actress commented on the play's success; but Rich stubbornly insisted, "Yes, Mistress! but it is owing to the *procession*."[53] Rich could hardly have been unaware of Barry's popularity as a stage lover; but his disregard of the importance of actors and of the necessity of casting a play properly, together with his slight acquaintance with earlier drama, prevented him from exploiting to the full on his own initiative the special talents of his company.

An examination of the histories of rejected plays demonstrates also how various, and sometimes how petty, were the managerial influences upon the repertory. One of the most practical motives for rejecting a play was that its performance would be too costly. Any new piece entailed considerable expense, especially as the arts of the stage carpenter and costumer were gradually becoming as important as the work of the actor and the poet. Managers no doubt expected to take risks with some plays. At any rate, we know that Rich lavished money on many of his pantomimes and that *The Chinese Festival* cost Garrick four thousand pounds. But in each of these the manager thought he was providing a kind of entertaining novelty that would be certain to succeed. Rich's shows did succeed, and the failure of *The Chinese Festival* is to be blamed on political causes rather than on the poor judgment of the manager. But expensive failures were certain to make the patentees cautious in accepting new plays, and such caution, of course, frequently influenced the repertory. Glover's *Jason*, for example, required scenery "of the most expensive kind." Although it was a sequel to his *Medea*, which had met with considerable success when it was produced in 1767, it was rejected by the manager as a too costly undertaking.[54] In this instance not even the rather widespread fame of the playwright was sufficient to offset the cost of bringing the play on the stage. For the same reason, Garrick was unwilling to undertake the performance of Dr. Hawkesworth's three-act play, *Almoran and Hamet*, which was intended for the stage but later reached the public as a novel.[55] Garrick's refusal of this mediocre piece is readily understandable, for his great loss in *The Chinese Festival* fiasco was then recent.

It is noteworthy that a great many of the rejected plays of the time, whatever the cause for their rejection, found their way into print, either by subscription among the friends of the playwright, by the author's single efforts, or in the collected works when they later appeared. That the authors and publishers concerned felt that there was a sufficient demand for printed plays, especially when we consider how many hundreds of such works appeared during the eighteenth century, is indicative of the rapid growth of the reading public. This attitude toward drama on the part of the public is clearly seen in its extreme development in the early nineteenth century, when large quantities of literary or "closet" drama were published with no thought of performance upon the stage. We are concerned here, however, with plays that were written for stage presentation and were printed later, and with rejected plays printed in lieu of performance. Of the latter group, the published play was ordinarily accompanied by a preface that recounted the author's attempts to get the play accepted, sometimes listed the manager's reasons for refusing it, and often attacked the manager for his refusal. From these prefaces we can learn two matters of importance to theatrical history: that the refusal might be based upon any one of dozens of possible reasons, ranging from the lack of time to bring out the play to objections to its diction or plot; and that the most frequent cause for rejection was that a play had too much declamation and too little incident—perhaps considerable literary merit but no adaptability to the stage. For example, when Garrick returned Gentleman's *Sejanus,* he complimented "its merits" but added that "it had too much Declamation in it to succeed on the Stage." [56] This point is especially significant. Gentleman (and there were many like him) felt that he was writing a stage play. What he had actually produced was, in every respect except the author's intention, a closet drama. And when Garrick commented on it, he was expressing a view that might have been repeated with increasing frequency by managers of the later eighteenth and early nineteenth centuries. But it was also a view that managers ultimately found it virtually unnecessary to express. Such plays were submitted to the managers with increasing rarity; for the men who followed in the footsteps of the author of *Sejanus* gradually turned away from the stage and regarded the printed page as their proper means of expression. Lord Byron eventually gave this view its ultimate expression. In the preface to *Marino Faliero* he says:

I have had no view to the stage; in its present state it is, perhaps, not a very exalted object of ambition; besides, I have been too much behind the scenes to have thought it so at any time. And I cannot conceive any man of irritable feeling putting himself at the mercies of an audience. The sneering reader, and the loud critic, and the tart review, are scattered and distant calamities; but the trampling of an intelligent or of an ignorant audience on a production which, be it good or bad, has been a mental labour to the writer, is a palpable and immediate grievance, heightened by a man's doubt of their competency to judge, and his certainty of his own imprudence in electing them his judges.

The rise of what Allardyce Nicoll has called "still-born drama," [57] was, then, along with the costliness of production for some plays, an important factor in bringing about the managerial veto.

Because they were more limited in their application, other causes for rejection will be noted only briefly. Occasionally a play was rejected because it was anticipated by another. Garrick rejected, for example, Goodhall's *Richard II*, probably not only because it was a bad alteration, but because he had in mind either bringing the original to the stage or altering it himself.[58] Likewise, when Charles Marsh offered to Garrick his alteration of *The Winter's Tale*, it was rejected because the manager was at work on his own three-act version of that play, which he soon brought to the stage as *Florizel and Perdita*. Similarity of a different kind was also the cause for the rejection of the tragedies of Meilan; but in this instance both Garrick and Colman, to whom they had been offered, declined them because they contained too many reminiscences of Shakespeare and Rowe.[59] This was not, however, a customary objection; in fact numerous plays were reaching the stage which deliberately emphasized their imitation of older drama, especially of Shakespeare.

Finally, it should be mentioned that rejection of a play was sometimes based upon factors that not only are not clear to the student today but were not always understood by the manager himself.[60] Of all the men of the age, Garrick was doubtlessly the one who could most readily determine whether a new play was suitable for the stage. Yet even he was not always certain what was necessary to make a play succeed, as his rejection of the tragedy *Timoleon* demonstrates. When that play was offered to the manager by its author, Dr. George Butt, Garrick told him that it needed alteration. Butt asked for advice on its revision, whereupon Garrick "read it several times, and at last (we are told) confessed his inability to discover a fault in it." [61] The play was thought to be "abounding in beauty and pathos, . . . regular in the plot, interesting in the progress, and affecting in the catastrophe"; in short, it had all the qualities believed necessary. But it apparently lacked an essential quality that not even Garrick could either name or explain.

Thus the mid-century managers helped to determine the repertory in a variety of ways, some commendable and some blameworthy, and for a variety of reasons, both selfish and disinterested; but in many respects the manager's influence did not originate with him at all—he merely executed in terms of the repertory what his audiences commanded. Before turning from the manager to the acting company, I shall mention at least one other sphere of managerial activity because of its possible effect on theatrical history—the manager's knowledge of his actor's special talents, his ability to cast his plays to the best advantage, and the result in terms of success or failure in the opinion of the audience.

Adequate casting of a new or newly revived play is, of course, a matter of importance in any age, and the mid-eighteenth century is no exception. Plays might succeed or fail then as now if sufficient care were not given to the assignment of suitable parts to the available members of the company. A manager like Rich, who was both unappreciative of and indifferent to actors' special talents, would hardly be expected to expend much care in the assignment of roles; that function seems to have been performed frequently by a principal actor in the Covent Garden company, particularly Quin until his retirement. But, except in a few instances, Rich's miscasting was probably not of primary importance during his regime, for his theater depended largely upon the pantomimes in which the manager himself played the leading part and upon the spectacular effects he introduced into stock plays.

On the other hand, there is evidence that at the rival theater the success or failure of a play, and hence its vitality in the repertory, was often directly dependent upon the skill with which the roles had been assigned by the manager. The respective fates of three plays—a revival, a new farce, and a new full-length play—will serve to illustrate. Because the revived *Every Man in his Humour* was so perfectly cast, it was highly successful—much more so than its earlier revival; and this good fortune, we are told, must be attributed "to this care of the manager. . . ." [62] *The Upholsterers,* Murphy's farce that Garrick had at first rejected, "met with great success," said its author; he modestly added, "A farce, so completely acted, was never seen before or since." [63] The new full-length play, Moore's *Gil Blas,* met with a different reception. Mrs. Bellamy thought that it was "condemned to oblivion" on the second night of performance because it was miscast. As specific examples of miscasting, she mentions that the roles of Garrick and Woodward should have been reversed and that the young lady should have been played by a juvenile.[64] It is noteworthy that Moore's play is a comedy, for rarely were new tragedies— apparently considered of greater consequence, if we may believe contemporary statements—so cavalierly treated. But occasionally even the serious plays "did not go with the applause that was expected" because the actors were unsuited to the roles. Such, for example, was true of Murphy's *Alzuma,* a tragedy acted at Covent Garden during the management of Colman and Harris.[65] It may be safely concluded that an important influence exerted by the manager on the repertory depended upon his skill in assigning roles, for this factor frequently determined how long a play might continue on the stage.

It should be added here, however, that the attitude toward the casting of plays in the mid-eighteenth century was different from that held in the Restoration period, and even from that of the earlier decades of the eighteenth century. Speaking of the 1682 revival of *Julius Caesar,* Davies remarks that then "very eminent actors thought it no diminution of their consequence to play the inferior parts." [66] The same writer, comparing the days of Booth and Wilks with his own time, states that in the early eighteenth century leading players undertook parts that "would scarcely be accepted now by third-rate actors." [67] A revival of *All for Love,* in which Booth and Mrs. Oldfield took the leading roles, had, for example, the famous Wilks in the "trifling part" of Dolabella, and Cibber and Mrs. Porter in the minor roles of Alexas and Octavia. After the decline of the triumvirate, however, audiences rarely came to see a play "well acted all round," as it was termed, but rather to see one or two actors in favorite parts.[68] In other words, the conception of a play as a vehicle for a "star" actor had come into being, consequently diminishing the importance of complete casting.

This changed attitude is particularly noticeable after the advent of Garrick in 1741, although some earlier indication of it can be seen in the reception of such favorite actors as Quin and Macklin, and it helps to mark off the mid-century quite sharply from the ages of Betterton and Booth. Any conclusion as to the influence of the manager upon the repertory through his assignment of roles must necessarily take this shift into account.

The most noticeable effect this changed attitude had upon theatrical history is that, by placing increased emphasis upon the principal actor, plays that furnished strong roles for the "star" came to bulk larger in the repertory; and, conversely, plays that had no such parts were neglected by a company that had a Barry or a Garrick. Moreover, a highly detrimental effect upon the theater accompanied the new practice. With the decline of complete castings, actors and actresses, especially those in lesser roles, were all too frequently prone to remain "in character" only during those lines or scenes in which they had an important part in the action and dialogue. Ben Johnson (namesake of the playwright) and Thomas Weston were among the lesser actors who were "so truly absorbed in character, that they never lost sight of it," [69] and the greatness of Garrick and Macklin depended to a considerable extent upon their ability to continue the illusion of their parts even when not in the center of attention. But these are among the exceptions. The references to the listlessness of many actors when they were not taking part in the dialogue are numerous in the contemporary records of performances. Mrs. Ward, for example, spent her time adjusting the knot on her glove during one of the most pathetic scenes in a performance of *The Fair Penitent;*[70] Mrs. Pritchard, said Dr. Johnson, "no more thought of the play out of which her part was taken, than a shoemaker thinks of the skin, out of which the piece of leather, of which he is making a pair of shoes, is cut";[71] and Davies asserted that he had seen "very great players . . . when on the stage laugh at a blunder of a performer or some accidental impropriety of the scene." [72] But the same plays in which such improprieties occurred might continue to be favorite stock pieces, without even a change in the cast, as long as the leading part was played by an excellent actor. Hence, the introduction of the "star" onto the eighteenth-century stage had far-reaching consequences upon the repertory and upon the extent of the manager's influence in determining its nature through his function as assigner of roles.

The mid-century theater manager held, indeed, an important position. His awareness of the interests of his audiences, his skill in holding together a company of actors and supplying them with suitable plays, his relations with the playwrights and the critics, and his knowledge of the drama and the theater—all make him a figure of importance in any study of theatrical history. If he possessed these qualities and combined with them unfailing good taste, he could be a powerful force in improving the state of the stage. If not, he could be an equally powerful force to its detriment. The number of eulogies and caustic invectives that appeared in pamphlet and periodical indicate that he was popularly regarded as a force, of one kind or the other. But if there is a question as to whether his influence in determining what the public could see at the theaters was as great as that exerted by the audience itself, the answer must be that the greater influence came from the boxes, the pit, and the galleries. Garrick, the ablest manager of the time, himself recognized where the actual control over the repertory originated when, at the outset of his career as manager, he spoke with approval these lines from Dr. Johnson's prologue:

> The drama's laws, the drama's patrons give,
> For we that live to please, must please, to live.

CHAPTER EIGHT

The Actor

In the middle of the eighteenth century the acting company was a relatively stable body of professionals who were jealous of their prerogatives but were limited to a rather narrowly circumscribed sphere in which those prerogatives could be enjoyed. An actor might come to the London stage from one of the Dublin theaters or from a provincial troupe, or occasionally he might make his first appearance at one of the London patent houses; but once he was accepted by the audiences in London, he usually remained attached to the Drury Lane or Covent Garden company until he retired from the stage. He might move from one of the patent theaters to the other, or he might even go to Ireland for a season or two; but, so small was the world of the theater in eighteenth-century Britain, that he had virtually no other opportunity to display his talents.

During the early years of the period—until about 1742—he might find employment at the Haymarket or Goodman's Fields if he became discontented under the management of Rich or Fleetwood, but the attachment was for the most part quite temporary. Later, a few actors, chiefly those who had not yet established themselves, joined Foote's company at the Haymarket; but the almost complete domination of that stage by the manager did not provide suitable conditions for the formation of a stable company. After Foote was granted a patent, however, his theater provided employment for members of the other patent companies during the summer but did not disturb their membership in the regular season. The number of stages that could furnish employment to the actors of the day was, therefore, exceedingly small. Moreover, the prestige and compensation that the actor enjoyed as a member of the Drury Lane or Covent Garden company tended to keep him there.

Such a state of affairs was naturally conducive to the establishment and maintenance of stable, closely knit acting companies
in which competition was potentially so keen that strict rules,
especially in regard to seniority and what came to be called the
"possession of parts," were an inevitable development.

The number of regular actors was also relatively small
during the period, even in proportion to the small number of
theaters. In fact, the size of the companies was sometimes
inadequate to support the entire dramatis personae of some of
the plays. *Richard II,* for example, at the time of its revival at
Covent Garden in 1738, called for more actors than the company afforded,[1] and the manager had to go outside his regular
company to fill out the parts. *Julius Caesar* presented the same
difficulty, which in this instance was sometimes overcome by
altering the play.[2] The Drury Lane company seems to have
been, during most of the period, larger than the rival company, but neither could it provide enough actors on occasion.
Prompter Hopkins indicates the practice when a large cast was
needed, when he states in his diary that *The Royal Shepherd,*
revived in 1764, could not be acted on Tuesdays and Saturdays
because on those nights it was impossible to recruit additional
actors from the Opera House.[3] Recruiting of a different kind
was done by Garrick for his farce based upon *Gulliver's Travels.*
This entertainment, which appeared in 1756 as *Lilliput,* was
acted by more than a hundred boys and girls whom the
manager had especially trained for the performance.[4] But
usually the theater depended upon those actors who were
members of its company at the time, and the practice of recruiting, either from other companies or from the general
public, seems to have been of rare occurrence.

The result was that audiences soon became familiar with
the faces of the same actors and actresses, which they saw night
after night in a variety of roles and in plays of all types. They
came to know the personnel thoroughly, almost intimately—
not only their peculiar manner of playing the various parts,
their fortes and their failures, but even the details of their
private lives. Indeed, so stable was the membership of the
acting company that the novelty of a new actor or actress was
rare—so rare that such an innovation was exploited in the

[1] For notes to chap. 8, see pp. 324-329.

playbills, usually met with a large and receptive audience, and was deemed sufficiently important by contemporary theatrical historians to receive mention in their annals.

Within this fairly small group an even smaller number had much influence in determining the repertory of the theater. Leading—or, as the term was then, "capital"—actors, like Macklin, Quin, Barry, Garrick, Powell, Henderson, Yates, and Woodward, and actresses like Mrs. Cibber, Mrs. Clive, Mrs. Bellamy, Mrs. Woffington, Mrs. Pritchard, Mrs. Barry, Mrs. Yates, and Mrs. Abington, were almost the only ones who were in a position to exert such an influence. Lesser actors and actresses, although some were regarded as having certain excellences in special minor roles, if they were not effective enough to be allowed the "possession of parts," could have little influence in determining what plays should be acted. The whole question of determining the nature and the extent of the influence exerted by the acting company upon the repertory is, therefore, one that must be treated in terms of the special acting abilities of a limited number of important actors, and, to a lesser extent, in terms of the rather infrequent occasions when an actor made his first appearance on the stage.

The possession of parts was chiefly the result of the actors' peculiar talents in certain roles, although it depended sometimes merely on seniority. Quin, for example, who was probably the favorite actor after the death of Booth and before the advent of Garrick, progressed very slowly as a new actor because of the jealousy with which "the seniority of the green-room" was guarded.[5] Similarly, Mrs. Abington, although acknowledged as excellent in comedy roles, had to wait until the death of Mrs. Pritchard and the retirement of Mrs. Clive before she could play their parts.[6]

This situation led not only to disputes among the members of the company, but—more important to my purpose—to the identification of actor with character in the minds of the audience. There are numerous indications in contemporary accounts that this was true. Davies, for example, indicates time after time that there were very clearly drawn lines in acting roles, and that particular characters and types were popularly associated with particular actors and actresses.[7] The line between tragedy and comedy was particularly rigid, and only a few actors of the time were regarded as equally capable in both

144

types of plays. Garrick was such an exception, and a contemporary biographer remarks that he "united the *universality* of acting in one person, and left the superiority of his excellencies to this hour undecided in the very contrasted walks of Richard and Dorilas, Lear and Drugger, Hamlet and Fribble." [8] But such actors were extremely rare. Mrs. Cibber, regarded as the greatest tragic actress of her day, tried Estifania in *Rule a Wife and Have a Wife,* but soon resigned the part to Mrs. Pritchard when she found that "Melpomene could not transfer herself into Thalia." [9] Leading comic actors also frequently tried their hand at tragedy, but almost without exception met with little encouragement from the audience.[10]

The distinctions insisted upon by the audience were not limited, however, to such general traits as those characterizing tragedy and comedy. Within each type was a further identification of a particular actor with a special kind of character. Thus, Mrs. Pritchard's reputation as a comedian rested upon her ability to represent characters of "a middle path between high life and the humor of the lower class," such as Lady Townly, Lady Betty Modish, and Maria (in *The Nonjuror*), and in "situations of intrigue, gayety, and mirth," like Beatrice, Berinthia, and Mrs. Sullen.[11] Mrs. Clive was thought to be "*beyond* compare" as Mrs. Heidelburg or Widow Blackacre, "yet her Portia was . . . truly bad." [12] Ross was especially approved by the audience because he gave promise of restoring "the long lost character of the real fine gentleman," [13] a type of comedy role that was a favorite with the public but that not even the best of the comic actors was thought to portray with success. Similar distinctions were made in tragedy. Barry succeeded as Othello because he was highly esteemed as a tragic lover, but Garrick was a relative failure in the part in spite of his great popularity in almost every other play.[14] An actor, greatly inferior to these two, succeeded so well in the "impassioned-declamatory parts of tragedy" that he was called by his colleagues "Tyrant" Aickin although his private life belied the epithet.[15] Examples could be multiplied readily, but these are perhaps sufficient to indicate to what extent specialization existed in the acting company.

The typical audience of the time was made up of frequent theatergoers who were capable critics of the actors and their methods of portraying character. Such an audience, in combination with the restricted number of theaters and the relatively small number of actors—many of whom had in their possession a considerable number of parts—made for a highly professionalized stage with, to use the economist's term, a recognized division of labor. Under such conditions, the presence or absence of a particular actor or of a particular combination of actors was bound to have an important influence upon the repertory.

This influence was exerted in several ways. The continued membership of an actor in the company resulted in the retention in the repertory of the stock pieces that provided roles for his particular forte. Thus, the success during the 1740's and 1750's of *The Orphan,* long a popular tragedy in the eighteenth century, was largely owing to Mrs. Bellamy's portrayal of the heroine, and it was most frequently acted when she was a member of the company.[16] The popularity of *Much Ado About Nothing* was dependent upon the acting of Garrick and Mrs. Pritchard and, after the death of the actress, was less frequently brought to the stage until much later when Mrs. Abington undertook the part.[17] *The Merchant of Venice* was most frequently acted when Macklin and Mrs. Clive were available to play the parts of Shylock and Portia. It is a strange and at the same time characteristic paradox that Mrs. Clive was popularly identified with the heroine even though, according to the traditional view of the eighteenth-century audience, she misinterpreted the character.[18] *The Rehearsal,* one of the most frequently revived plays in the entire period, depended almost solely upon the special genius of Garrick as Bayes. "Theatricus," writing in the *London Chronicle,* noted that that burlesque had lost much of its effect because the allusions were no longer understood; but, he added, we "must own, notwithstanding its great merit, nothing but the pleasure of having a favourite actor constantly playing before our eyes, could keep it up in great vogue."[19]

Garrick's acting, of course, was the sole support of many plays that without him, at least after their initial runs, would no doubt have had far fewer performances. *Macbeth,*[20] *The Alchemist,*[21] and *The Wonder,*[22] to name but a few, represent various types of plays that largely owed their continued existence on the stage during the mid-century to his presence in the company to support the leading roles.[23] *Othello* and *Romeo*

and Juliet were often included in the Drury Lane repertory
while Barry was a member of the company, but when he moved
to Covent Garden the plays virtually moved along with him.[24]
It is natural that leading actors in major roles should exert
such influence. But even lesser actors in minor roles often had
the same effect upon the repertory. As an extreme example
there is Hippisley, who "kept alive an indifferent comedy of
Durfey, now absolutely forgotten, called The Plotting Sisters,
by his incomparable representation of Fumble, a ridiculous
old dotard." [25] But the instance that shows most clearly how
the repertory was influenced by the inclusion of an actor in
the company is the destiny of *The Constant Couple.* The part
of Sir Harry Wildair in that comedy had been one of Wilks'
greatest roles, and after his death in 1733 the play had "for the
most part lain dormant." [26] Seven years later Mrs. Woffington
undertook the role. The audience came out of curiosity to see
her in a male part; but they stayed to applaud and the comedy
had twenty performances in that season.[27] When she left the
company soon after, the play was unattempted until she returned in 1743, when again it was frequently acted. She continued to act the role until her death in 1760, and so completely was she identified with the part of the fine gentleman
that the presence of the play in the repertory of a theater is a
certain indication that Mrs. Woffington was a member of the
company at the time. The play was felt so entirely to be dependent upon the actress that the *London Chronicle,* three
years before her death, notes that she is to be thanked for "preserving the play." [28]

New plays as well as revivals were also affected by the personnel of the acting company. Murphy attributed the success
and continued popularity of three of his plays, *The Way to
Keep Him, All in the Wrong,* and *Three Weeks after Marriage,*
to the ability of Mrs. Abington.[29] The popularity of *The Jealous Wife,* according to a contemporary statement, was in part
owing to the success of Moody as Captain O'Cutter, whose
"humorous manner of supporting this character, assisted the
run of the piece." [30] Mrs. Clive's success as Nell in *Devil to
Pay* not only

established her own reputation [but] fixed the piece itself on the
constant list of acting farces; an honour which, perhaps, it would

never have arrived at, had she not performed the capital character in it, nor may long maintain, when her support in it is lost.[31]

New tragedies as well as comedies were thus affected. For example, Victor asserts that the limited success that came to Home's *Fatal Discovery* was "greatly owing to the Persons who acted in it, particularly Mr. and Mrs. Barry, late Mrs. Dancer." [32] Similarly, the applause accorded Hoole's *Cyrus* was chiefly for Mrs. Yates and Powell, who took the leading parts.[33] Mrs. Yates, who became the favorite tragic actress after the death of Mrs. Cibber in 1766, was a chief contributor to the success of *The Orphan of China*.[34] Francklin acknowledged his debt to Miss Younge, Reddish, Smith, and Palmer when he published his *Matilda,* a tragedy they had supported during its brief stage life.[35] Garrick and Mrs. Cibber gave powerful assistance to Brown's *Barbarossa,* without which that play would have had slight success.[36] Murphy says of Cibber as Pandolph in his own *Papal Tyranny in the Reign of King John,* "Curiosity was excited, and numbers flocked to the house to see a veteran performer." [37] Victor notes that Cibber had just lost his teeth, so that "his Auditors could only be entertained with his Attitudes and Conduct, which were truly graceful." [38] But it is significant that they were willing to be thus entertained.

Even plays superior to those just mentioned often depended to a considerable extent upon the actors who were first cast in the principal roles. The long first-season run of Cumberland's *West Indian,* for example, was attributed to Mrs. Abington's origination of the part of Charlotte Rusport, and to Moody, famous as a stage Irishman, who brought his special talents to the role of Major O'Flaherty.[39] Genest found even the later popularity of *Douglas,* the most famous tragedy of the mid-century, owing to Mrs. Crawford and Mrs. Siddons, "one of whom brought it into repute and the other who kept it so." [40] The same historian remarks of the 1776 revival of *Douglas* that because Webster, who made his first stage appearance as Norval in that year, was well received, "this play was acted several times during the season." [41]

It is unnecessary to multiply instances; and of course it is obvious that in any age a play's success on the stage depends, at least in part, upon the ability of the actors who support it.

Rather, the point is that in the eighteenth century, when crea-
tive ability in the dramatic form was perhaps at its lowest ebb,
histrionic ability had to supply the vitality in stage representation that contemporary dramatists were unable to infuse into
their plays; for dramas, aside from the ever vital and favorite
stock plays from earlier times, then depended almost entirely
upon the ability of the actors to give them life. Eventually,
when plays came to be read more often than seen, they acquired
a new kind of vitality, but this existed apart from the theater.
As long as audiences continued to think of dramas as acted
plays, and critics continued to regard them as intended primarily for representation rather than study, what success the work
of mid-century playwrights achieved was far more often less
attributable to the authors than to the actors.

I have shown how the special talents of actors contributed
to the success of both new and revived plays; but so far, in the
instances examined, the prolonged runs and the frequency of
revivals were owing to the fortunate coincidence of actor and
role. Further to demonstrate the extent of influence upon repertory exerted by the acting company, it may be noted that
deliberate attempts were also made, either by authors who supplied new plays for the stage or by those who altered older
pieces, to provide vehicles for particular members of the company. Because the alteration or the new play was often necessary to avoid infringing on the rights of the other members
of the company, the "possession of parts" was thus actually instrumental in broadening the repertory. The actor, through
the playwright, was therefore of considerable and direct influence in determining what the public might see on the stage.

Among notable revivals purposely arranged for particular
actors, those of *Every Man in his Humour, Philaster,* and *Isabella* are representative. Jonson's comedy was altered by Garrick purposely to provide an adequate part for Shuter, an actor
whom Garrick had just discovered and in whom he saw considerable promise. Shuter played Master Stephen, a role of
less consequence than Kitely and Bobadil, which parts were
taken by Garrick and Woodward, but he "carried off equal
honours." [42] Thereafter, the play was frequently acted, often
without Shuter in the cast, but its original inclusion in the
repertory of the time was nevertheless due to him. Beaumont
and Fletcher's play was revived in an alteration prepared by

Colman. This revival benefited Powell, an actor who took the leading parts at Drury Lane while Garrick was on the Continent. We are told that "the play, but particularly the Actor, met with universal applause." [43] *Philaster* was chosen, not only because it provided a role especially suited to Powell's talents, but also because critics could not then compare him with "any former actor" (Garrick?).[44] *Isabella,* Garrick's alteration of Southerne's *The Fatal Marriage,* was first acted in 1757, when it was "revived and altered to shew Mrs. Cibber to advantage." [45] Among less successful plays, Davenant's *The Man's the Master* was revived in 1775 as a suitable vehicle for "a young lady" making her first appearance on the stage,[46] and Young's *Busiris* was revived at Covent Garden to give Miss Nossiter an advantageous role.[47]

New plays were likewise written with a particular actor or actress in mind. Thus Thomas Sheridan wrote his *Captain O'Blunder* for Isaac Sparks, who played the title role with "powerful effect." [48] Goldsmith, in gratitude for Quick's excellence as Tony Lumpkin in *She Stoops to Conquer,* wrote for the actor his farce *The Grumbler,* in which Quick acted for his own benefit.[49] Bickerstaffe's *Daphne and Amintor,* little more than an alteration of Mrs. Cibber's translation of the French *Oracle,* was brought out with added songs to provide a suitable part for Miss Wright, who was both singer and actress.[50] Hopkins records in his diary that Garrick's operatic farce *May Day,* with music by Arne, "was wrote on Purpose to introduce Miss Abrams, a Jew Girl, upon the stage." [51]

As is suggested by some of these illustrations, often the play was brought to the stage purposely to introduce a new actor or actress. Such, for example, was the motive behind Foote's *The Englishman in Paris,* acted for Macklin's benefit but written "to introduce Miss Macklin to advantage, and prove to the town that Mr. Macklin had not spared any expense to render the education and accomplishments of his daughter worthy the notice of the public." [52] But the new play might also be used as a vehicle for an old acquaintance, often for one who had been absent from a theater for some years. Thus the English adaptation of Voltaire's *Electra,* produced in 1774, was performed "purposely to introduce Mrs. Yates to the audience of Drury-Lane, before whom she had not appeared these eight years." [53] Oulton's comment on this performance is indicative of the influence of the actress: "It therefore met with temporary applause."

The special talents of the actors, or at least the popular interpretation of their talents, were therefore important factors in determining the repertory, whether by prolonging the life of new and revived plays to which their powers were especially suited or by inspiring playwrights to provide vehicles that would exploit those powers. Important confirmatory evidence of a kind that may be regarded as negative is also readily available to indicate the actor's importance to the repertory. If an actor was taken ill, if he moved to another theater, or if he withdrew from the stage entirely, the effect was immediate. Likewise, if he refused to undertake a role or if he failed in one he did undertake, his influence was apparent.

Illness of the actors became at times the bane of a manager's existence and resulted in a change of program, even when a certain play had been "given out" for the evening. In the winter of 1750-1751 at Covent Garden, for example, Mrs. Cibber and Spranger Barry, the principal tragic actors, were frequently ill. Mrs. Woffington's comedies were often substituted, and instead of Mrs. Cibber as Jane Shore the audience might see Mrs. Woffington as Sir Harry Wildair.[54] Thus the complexion of a season's theatrical fare might on occasion reflect nothing more profound than the indisposition of important members of the company. Of Shakespeare's plays none was more influenced by the actors' illnesses than *All's Well That Ends Well*. When this play was revived for the first time at Drury Lane in 1742, Mrs. Woffington was taken ill and the part of Helena had to be read at its first performance. Deferment because of illness was necessary on several later occasions also, to such an extent, as shown earlier, that the play came to be regarded as a bad omen and was infrequently acted.[55]

New plays were similarly affected. Although Dodsley's *Cleone* had an uncommonly long run for the time, Mrs. Bellamy believed that it would have had even greater success in its first season if her health had permitted her to act more often.[56] The run of Murphy's *Grecian Daughter*, although promising to continue for some time, was cut short for a similar reason, this time the illness of Barry.[57] Occasionally the illness seems to have been feigned. Mrs. Yates, for example, after the first performance of Cradock's *Zobeide*, "fell into a *political indis-*

position; and the piece, which was in a languishing state, consequently perished." [58] Garrick was also believed to feign illness when it was convenient to do so. One contemporary saw in this trait of Garrick's an influence on the repertory that extended even to the rival theater.[59] Mrs. Cibber was also suspected of using illness as an excuse to refuse a role or even to kill a play. Murphy, who was wise to the ways of the temperamental actress, would have had only the labor of writing his *Orphan of China* for his reward if he had not secretly requested Mrs. Yates to understudy Mrs. Cibber as Mandane. As Murphy had expected, shortly after the play was put in rehearsal, Mrs. Cibber was announced as too ill to undertake the role; and when Garrick was about to put the play over until the following season, the author brought forward Mrs. Yates, who was of course then prepared to play the part.[60]

The desertion of a theater by an actor also influenced the repertory. Thus when Barry left the Covent Garden company in 1754 and went to Ireland, the plays in which he had excelled, especially those with difficult roles, were either struck from the acting list or revived less frequently than formerly. The undertaking by Murphy of the part of Othello at Covent Garden in that year was therefore particularly hazardous for the actor because of "the well known excellence of Barry in that character," [61] and was probably dared only because it was anticipated that the first appearance of an actor on the stage might offset the dangers of an unfavorable comparison with Barry. Mrs. Woffington's desertion of Drury Lane for Covent Garden in 1748, conjectured to have been the result of Garrick's marriage to Mlle Violette, affected the repertory of both patent theaters. At Drury Lane the comedies in which she excelled were less in evidence; and by joining Quin at the rival theater, she made possible the revival there of several plays, including some of Shakespeare's, in competition with Garrick's company.[62] Later, when she left Rich for Ireland, "her absence cast a damp on most of the comedies." [63] A similar event occurred ten years later. Woodward, upon whom Garrick chiefly depended for comedy and farce, left for Dublin when his demands for higher salary were refused. Garrick, "with something like a spirit of revenge," then attempted one of Woodward's most popular parts, Marplot in *The Busy Body;* but he met with his first failure.[64] The absence of the popular comedian was quickly felt; and, to fill up "this chasm in his theatrical army," Garrick was forced to come to terms with Foote.[65] The special talents of the new comic lead obviously played an important part in bringing about a change in the theater's offerings for the rest of the season.

The retirement or death of an important actor naturally produced a similar result. The death of Mrs. Woffington in 1760 and Mrs. Clive's retirement from the stage in 1769, for example, removed from the mid-century theater the two principal supports of high comedy; and when Mrs. Cibber died in 1766, Garrick, although he had not always found it easy to maintain harmony in his company while she was a principal member, nevertheless remarked on hearing the news, "Then tragedy has expired with her." [66] Lesser actors likewise might have their effect upon the repertory. Cumberland said that his *Choleric Man,* a popular comedy, had to be shelved after the death of Weston, who had created and often played the role of Jack Nightshade.[67] A clear example of this dependence of play upon actor is seen in the effect of the death of Palmer, a minor actor noted for his portrayal of fine gentlemen. Many years earlier, Wilks had been highly successful in such roles; but after his death, so rare were the actors who could act in those parts that, as Victor notes, "the Loss even of Mr. *Palmer* was not easily supplied." [68] It was noteworthy that when *Lethe* was revived after his death, the fine gentleman was excised and Tattoo was changed into a horse-grenadier.[69]

The refusal of an actor to undertake certain roles was sometimes an important factor in determining what the audience might see on the stage, especially when the actor was a principal member of the company. For example, *Julius Caesar,* long a favorite with audiences, fell into neglect in the mid-century largely because Garrick "would never willingly put on the Roman habit." [70] The same reason probably accounts for Garrick's refusal to undertake Aaron Hill's *Roman Revenge.* Both Murphy and Victor agree that Garrick refused Home's *Douglas* because it did not offer a strong male role for him.[71] If it had been acted first at Drury Lane, with Garrick and Mrs. Cibber in the leading parts, its success, extraordinary as it was, would no doubt have been much greater. Instead, its revival from season to season depended throughout most of the period on the strength of the Covent Garden company, for not until

1769 was it acted with any regularity at the other patent house. Dodsley's *Cleone,* it is generally believed, was rejected for a similar reason, but the play found adequate support in Mrs. Bellamy at Covent Garden, whose popularity in the role helped to keep it in the acting list.

Both these tragedies met with success in spite of a leading actor's refusal to undertake them, but others were less fortunate. Brown's *The Fatal Retirement,* for example, did not survive its initial performance because Quin, then the chief actor in the Drury Lane company (1739), refused to act in it.[72] Quin's influence with the other members was sufficient to encourage them to neglect the play in rehearsal, and consequently it was poorly performed. Although it was "deservedly damned," [73] Quin's refusal was apparently not based solely upon its lack of merit (for, as Genest remarks, he had acted in worse tragedies); rather, the play gave no opportunity for "that unnatural language to which he was used on the stage," the declamation and bombast of the tyrannic school of acting.[74] On the other hand, the actor's refusal might mean only a temporary change in the repertory. When Mrs. Clive, for example, was summoned to a rehearsal of *The Merchant of Venice* and learned that Foote was to play Shylock, she exclaimed, " 'What, you!' looking contemptuously on him: *'you* play *Shylock* to my *Portia!* Oh! then I'm off;' and she was as good as her word; for she instantly quitted the theater, and the play was obliged to be changed." [75] Not only dislike of a performer, but also the unwillingness to undertake difficult roles on successive nights sometimes led to an actor's refusal of a part and a substitution for the announced play. On one occasion Mrs. Bellamy had selected *The Distrest Mother* for her benefit and was to play the "very easy part" of Andromache herself. Mrs. Yates, cast as Hermione, which she considered a more difficult role, refused to take part because she was scheduled to act Medea and Mandane, both difficult parts, on the two following nights.[76]

Equally, perhaps more, influential in determining the repertory was the failure of an actor in a particular role. Several of Shakespeare's plays were thus affected. *Antony and Cleopatra,* although produced at great expense on the only occasion of its revival in the eighteenth century, did not live up to expectations because Garrick, Mrs. Yates, and Mossop, who took the leading parts, were not well suited for their representa-

tion.[77] As a result the play had a short run and was never revived thereafter. *Richard II* was another play that met with
misfortune. Garrick never took the part; Barry, who of all the
actors of the time might have best portrayed the poetical king,
was never called upon to undertake it; among the lesser actors,
Delane, to whom the part was entrusted at the play's revival
in 1738, could not "exhibit the tender feelings of the king's
distressful situation." [78] *Othello,* although often acted, was well
below the other great Shakespearean tragedies in frequency of
performance because Garrick was not well suited to the role,[79]
and the success of the play depended largely upon Barry. The
latter actor, on the other hand, was little regarded as Macbeth
and Richard III. Consequently the dramatic fare at the two
houses while Garrick and Barry were the principal actors reflected not only the strength but also the weaknesses of the
two tragedians in Shakespearean roles. A rather curious example of the influence of an actor upon the repertory is seen
in the fate of *King John.* It had met with great success at the
time of its earlier revivals, and promised to do the same in
1761.[80] Sheridan, who had just come to Drury Lane from the
Dublin stage, acted the King to Garrick's Faulconbridge and
Mrs. Cibber's Constance. The play was, however, denied the
run that might have been expected because Garrick became
jealous and thought that he was a relative failure compared
to Sheridan, whose portrayal of the King was regarded as excellent.[81]

But actors' failures in stock pieces, whether in Shakespearean
parts or in later plays (for example, Barry's acknowledged ineffectiveness as Bajazet and Horatio), were of less consequence
in determining the repertory as a whole than was an actor's
failure in a new play. In a Shakespearean revival, since the
play had already proved its merits as a stage piece, it was generally certain sooner or later to find an adequate cast, and the
individual actor's failure did not therefore "damn" the play,
only that particular revival of it. But in a new play, the success of the actors who originated the roles was of prime importance. Their failure meant the play's doom. Contemporary
records are full of the obituaries of plays that met such a fate.
In some instances it may have been merely the "Funn of the
First Night," [82] and in many others the play merited its sudden
demise. But frequently, some of Lillo's plays being unfortu-

nate examples, the failure was the result of the ineffectiveness of the acting, a matter in which the audience felt itself capable of judging. To indicate the effect that poor acting could have, even on a new play of high merit, a well-known example may be given. When *The Rivals* was brought to the stage, Lee was cast as O'Trigger. The play had only two performances and was then withdrawn. Several alterations were then made, and Lee was dropped from the cast. Shortly after, it was returned to the stage with Clinch in the part, and its success was immediate although it had previously been on the verge of failure.[83]

Of less persistent influence on the repertory, yet important on certain occasions as a determining factor, was the presence in a theater company of two rival actors. Perhaps the most famous rivalry of the century was that of Quin and Garrick soon after the latter's first appearance on the stage. Both actors were members of the Covent Garden company in the 1746-1747 season, and it was at first feared that the rivalry might prove detrimental to the theater. But, as Davies noted, "they had however too much sense to squabble about trifles—the difficulty lay in choosing such plays as they might both appear in to advantage." [84] That difficulty seems to have been met by reviving *The Fair Penitent,* a play with two male roles of virtually equal importance, which was acted at least thirteen times in the season and proved to be the theater's most effective competition against the opera.[85] Six years later Garrick welcomed to his Drury Lane company the actor Mossop, whose presence made possible the revival of the same play as well as others having two strong roles.[86] It is also notable that this was the season chosen by Young for the performance of his tragedy *The Brothers,* written almost thirty years earlier. Garrick and Mossop, by playing the title characters, offered the audience an effective study in contrast of their special powers.[87]

The presence of rival actors did not always have such a beneficial effect. The struggle between Mrs. Lessingham and Mrs. Yates for the part of Imogen in *Cymbeline* at Covent Garden during the management of Harris and Colman resulted, first, in the play's postponement, which might have stretched out indefinitely if a command performance had not brought the play to the stage two months later; a second result was a short run—only six performances even though it was "gotten up at considerable expense"—when the part was given to Mrs. Yates

over the objections of Harris and Rutherford. The rivalry between the actresses was regarded as directly responsible for the
play's untimely withdrawal from the acting list.[88]

It is also apparent that the "possession of parts" was both
an important characteristic of mid-century acting companies
and an important determinant of the repertory. The practice
was related to, and most probably had resulted from, the attitude toward acting that became current especially with the
advent of Garrick on the London stage in 1741. Thereafter
a play was regarded almost solely as the vehicle for a "star"
performer, in whom the entire interest of the audience usually
was centered. When an actor had attained sufficient skill and
popularity to feel that his presence in the company was indis-
pensable to the manager, he might lay claim to certain roles
in which he excelled—or perhaps only thought he excelled.
As a result the manager, striving to maintain peace within his
company but also keeping a watchful eye on the receipts of the
house on the nights when the actor performed his favorite
parts, was willing enough to support the actor's claim when
he found that it contributed to his own interests as patentee.
On the other hand, the acknowledged superiority of an actor
in a certain part was by itself often sufficient to discourage
other actors from attempting it. In either event the manager
stood to gain by adopting the policy, at least tacitly, of the
possession of parts, although that gain might be somewhat offset by the increased salary which the actor demanded.[89]

It is in terms of this "star" actor that the "possession of
parts" had its greatest significance in helping to determine the
repertory, although lesser actors also established claims to certain characters and might occasionally therefore exert the same
kind of influence. This influence, particularly when exerted
by a principal actor, made itself felt in several ways. The possession of parts tended to keep the repertory the same from
year to year; for as long as the personnel of the acting company
remained almost the same—and as I have shown, changes were
infrequent—each principal performer would continue to support on the stage those plays, relatively limited in number, in
which he was both popular and already proficient. A minimum
of effort was thereby required by the actor to maintain his
reputation. The result to the repertory was of course that
stock pieces were encouraged. It is not then surprising to dis-

cover that throughout the forty-year period a large but stable group of plays continued to supply from season to season the bulk of the theatrical offerings, and that most of such plays were tenaciously associated with particular actors in their well-tried roles.

Contemporary evidence proves how well established the practice of laying exclusive claim to important characters had become by the middle of the century. Murphy, for example, noted that "eminent actors, besides their general merit, made some favourite part their own, out of reach of any competitor," and cites as examples Quin's Falstaff, Barry's Othello, and King's Lord Ogleby in *The Clandestine Marriage*.[90] After Mrs. Woffington had undertaken the main role in *The Constant Couple*, "the actors," we are told, "even Garrick himself, made a voluntary resignation. . . . She was the only *Sir Harry Wildair* during the remainder of her life."[91] Mrs. Bellamy remarked that "Quin had been in possession of the character of Zanga [in Young's *The Revenge*], alone and unrivalled for years."[92] As is suggested by these illustrations, possession was the natural consequence of special excellence. But once the part came to be associated with the actor, an aggressive assertion of the exclusive right to the character seems to have been the usual result. Mrs. Bellamy, recalling later her first years on the stage, confirms this view: "The possession of parts at that time [about 1748] (except when permitted novices for a trial of their theatrical skill) [was] considered as much the property of performers, as their weekly salary."[93] How completely the practice was accepted is indicated by the fact that even the domineering Rich felt it necessary to ask Mrs. Bellamy's permission before giving the part of Juliet to Barry's protégée Miss Nossiter for her debut.[94]

One of the chief means by which the possession of parts influenced the repertory was thus in the maintenance of a stable body of stock pieces, but there were other ways in which the practice helped to determine theatrical fare. When Mrs. Bellamy, then a new actress without possession of parts or a following among audiences, found that she could not be "indulged with" the various principal roles on the London stage, she went to Dublin where she could play them, receiving at the same time the benefit of stage experience and the instruction of Sheridan at Smock Alley.[95] Her departure from London as a tyro actress had of course no immediate effect upon the repertory. But it is notable that her purpose in going to Dublin was to undertake the leading roles in the very same stock plays that were on the London stage throughout the mid-century period, and that when she returned, having in the meantime acquired a reputation as a tragic actress, she was acknowledged to have possession of certain parts, thereby helping to continue the already well-established practice—the same practice that had previously driven her from the London stage. Mrs. Bellamy's experience shows that, not only did the possession of parts help to maintain in quantity the stock plays of the time, but also that it tended to discourage new actors from undertaking favorite roles and to restrict the membership of the acting companies.

This discouragement had, in turn, a further effect. As already shown, new plays or alterations of long-unacted plays were often provided for a new actor. This practice was necessary for two reasons: first, the plays already on the acting list were in the possession of the older actors, who—unless they were willing to allow the inexperienced actor a limited number of trials of the part, as Mrs. Bellamy did for Miss Nossiter —would not risk a role, upon which they sometimes had built their reputations, in the hands of another actor for fear that he might outshine the acknowledged possessor; and second, new actors hesitated to try their strength in a part that would invite unfavorable comparison with an actor long a favorite in the same character.

Consequently, to this practice may be attributed the addition of several pieces to the repertory that otherwise might never have been mounted. For example, *Philaster* was revived as a vehicle for Powell, then new to the stage, so that his particular merits as an actor might not suffer by comparison with other actors. The revival of *Busiris* and the original performance of Morgan's *Philoclea* (1754) were specifically intended to provide for Miss Nossiter parts that neither infringed on the rights of the other actresses in the Covent Garden company nor handicapped her by requiring that she imitate previous performers in an identical role.[96]

Finally, the possession of parts operated in still another way in regulating the theatrical diet. So complete might be the identification of actor and character through long possession that upon the retirement or death of such an actor it was popularly thought that the play itself was doomed; a younger actor would naturally hesitate to undertake the role, knowing that he would more likely meet with the resentment of the audience than with its approval. Perhaps the most notable example of this situation in the period is the identification of Quin with Falstaff. The following lines from an *Epigram on Quin the Comedian* are representative of the popular attitude:

> . . . we never shall Falstaff behold so well done,
> With such character, humour, such spirit, such fun;
> So great that we knew not which most to admire,
> Glutton, parasite, pander, pimp, letcher or liar.
> He felt as he spoke, Nature's dictates are true,
> When he acted the part, his own picture he drew.[97]

Not only was Quin the best Falstaff on the stage; he was Falstaff. And so the audience viewed the matter at the time of Quin's death. The result could have been predicted: the Falstaff plays were much less frequently acted, until, many years later when the memory of Quin had considerably dimmed, Ned Shuter, famous for his ability to contort his face into laughable guises, succeeded in the part.

The actors influenced the repertory in a variety of ways: by their successes and failures in various roles; by their indisposition—real or feigned; by their jealousies and rivalries; by their refusal to undertake roles or their withdrawal from the company; by the possession of parts and the popular identification of actor with character. The results of such influence have so far been cited in terms of individual plays in the repertory. It is also instructive to see how the influence of the actors was exerted upon an important and considerable part of the repertory that may be considered as fairly homogeneous—the Shakespearean dramas that reached the stage in the period. For various reasons, many of which are discussed elsewhere, the time was congenial to the revival of many long-unacted plays by Shakespeare; at the same time those of his dramas that had previously held the stage, almost without exception, continued to do so. Of the thirty-seven plays in the Shakespeare canon, only five were not given performance in some form or other between 1737 and 1777. What was the actors' contribution to this notable movement?

Among the tragedies, audiences apparently never tired of seeing Mrs. Pritchard as Lady Macbeth, Garrick as Hamlet and Lear, Barry as Othello, Quin as Falstaff, and Mrs. Cibber as Juliet. Almost equally popular were Mrs. Pritchard as Beatrice, Mrs. Clive as Portia, and Theophilus Cibber as Pistol; Benedick, with Garrick as the reluctant lover, almost rivaled that actor's famous tragic parts.[98] As long as these actors were members of a company, the plays in which they had popular roles were acted over and over. When they were absent, the plays were acted with less frequency. It is reasonable to conclude, then, that an important part in the Shakespeare revival was played by the actors who portrayed his characters on the stage. One annalist of Shakespearean drama on the stage has even gone so far as to declare that "in every case the repertoire was regulated by the presence or absence in the company of actors capable of drawing the public in certain characters." [99] This is obviously an overstatement, for on numerous occasions actors undertook Shakespearean roles when they were not suited for them, particularly lesser actors on their benefit nights— and it must be remembered that benefit nights were many during the course of a season; and even "capital" actors might attempt parts in which they were relatively unknown, because of the illness of the actor who was famous in the role, because of his withdrawal from the company, or for a number of other reasons. It is, of course, true that Shakespearean plays succeeded best when the appropriate actors were available for the leading parts; but the records from season to season show that Shakespearean plays continued to be a large part of the total repertory, and that the demand for those famous dramas continued, even aside from the demand for actors in specific characters. A large part of the credit for maintaining Shakespeare on the stage during the mid-century may therefore be attributed to the actors without agreeing that they are to be regarded as responsible "in every case." [100]

The significance of certain contemporary statements must be assessed with this conclusion in mind. Thus, when Mrs. Montagu remarks that Shakespeare's "very spirit seems to come forth and to animate his characters, as often as Mr. Garrick, who acts with the same inspiration with which he wrote, assumes them on the stage," [101] she is reiterating the popular opinion—that the success of Shakespearean dramas on the stage was greatest when the greatest actor of the time supported them. Her statement so reduced becomes an obvious platitude. Yet when a large number of similar remarks are examined, many of which cast additional light on the subject—for example, Oulton's statement that Garrick and, after his death, Henderson were the only performers who could adequately support the characters of Shakespeare,[102] or Warburton's comment that Garrick was Shakespeare's greatest "living editor"—it must be concluded that the dependence of Shakespearean drama upon the actors was indeed great. And although it cannot be over-emphasized that the time, with its interest in antiquarianism, its growing preference for romantic drama, its tendency to inquire into national history, and its pride in England's earlier artistic achievements, was congenial for a Shakespeare revival, it must also be insisted with equal emphasis that the Elizabethan's dramas came to the stage and continued there partly—perhaps even chiefly—because they furnished the actors with strong characters, situations that could be profitably exploited, and dialogue that could be rendered captivating even by a lesser actor.

An examination of the destiny of Shakespeare on the mid-century stage thus makes it necessary to align side by side the influences from two important directions that coöperated to determine at least one-fifth of the entire theatrical repertory during the forty years. Shakespeare's plays were produced because the actors, capable of portraying the characters, found those characters eminently suited to their purpose, and because the audience, prepared to welcome the plays of a poet whose name they revered (actually or nominally), took delight in beholding the embodiment of the characters in those plays by their favorite actors. Beyond this, it must be added that the preparation of the audience to favor Shakespearean drama as well as the example inspiring the actors to undertake Shakespearean roles was in part owing to the fortunate coincidence that brought to the theatrical world at the proper moment a powerful figure whose veneration for the master poet caused him to be regarded as Shakespeare's "high Priest."

What has just been said is necessary in order to modify the erroneous opinion sometimes held that the choice of drama for stage presentation depended primarily or even solely upon the actors. In various ways they exerted an important influence and, in terms of Shakespearean drama regarded as a whole, they were influential, along with audience and manager, in placing and maintaining those plays in the repertory. If other segments of the repertory were similarly investigated, further evidence not only of the pervasive interrelation of actor, manager, and audience but also of the considerable influence of the acting company alone, would appear. But these considerations must be considered in proper perspective—the perspective that Wilkinson conveniently supplies in speaking of what he calls "a rule fixed in the theatrical corps": "most young actors think if it be a principal role, the business is done; for . . . parts make the actor—not the actor the parts." [103]

The actor influenced the repertory in at least one other important way—this time not in the selection or exclusion of plays for stage representation but in the determination of the form in which the play was seen by the audience. Actors were responsible for many alterations made in text or situation, some forced upon the author by the insistence of the actor, and others made by the actors themselves, who often took the liberty of making gratuitous additions or omissions during the actual performance. Such changes or additions were frequently made in order to get applause from the galleries, where sat those whose taste inclined to low comedy. Davies remarks that Hamlet's admonition to the players to "speak no more than is set down for them" might appropriately have been directed to actors like Hippisley and Shuter, who were but "too guilty of adding to the author's text." [104] He also notes a tendency for actors to slight those scenes that, although necessary for exposition, were not highly applauded—for example, the short scenes in *King John*, Act V.[105] But, whether it was an addition or an omission, the motivating force was the desire of the actor for applause.

The other kind of alteration—causing the author or reviser to alter his text—was of course more deliberate; and it is also more revealing. Thus, when Garrick rejected a soliloquy (III, iii, 73-96) from *Hamlet* (he was the first actor to do so), he was making the play more agreeable for his audiences, which found the passage "highly improbable," "shocking," "horrid," and "a poor contrivance to delay the catastrophe till the last act." [106] When he did not restore the Fool in *King Lear*, he was not only following the critical dictum that had influenced

Tate before him but he was also omitting a character whose interruptions in some of the play's most powerful scenes were deemed harmful to the role in which, with the possible exception of Hamlet and Richard, he was most famous.[107]

Additional examples will show how extensive and how various was this kind of influence by the actor. Mallet's *Alfred*, as it was originally acted, had as "the great part, though not the principal character, that of the Hermit, . . . adapted by the author to his friend Quin." But when the play was later revived at Drury Lane, the author made Alfred the most striking part, the character then played by Garrick.[108] Macklin, the author of *Henry VII*, who also acted the part of Huntley when his play was performed, made that character more important than even Perkin Warbeck.[109] Cumberland's *The West Indian*, one of the more successful plays in the later part of the period, had one less scene when it was originally offered to Garrick. The scene was added at the request of the actor, who told the author, "Never let me see a hero step upon the stage without his trumpeters of some sort or other." [110] The author took the actor's advice at once. Boswell records that Goldsmith's original design for Miss Hardcastle was not carried out because of the actress to whom the part was given. One evening at General Oglethorpe's, Goldsmith sang a song that he said he had written for Miss Hardcastle; but because Mrs. Bulkeley, who created the role, could not sing, it had to be omitted, and it was apparently never restored.[111] A song was also omitted from Dalton's alteration of *Comus* at its revival in 1740, again because of the actors, but this time on different grounds. The ballad, quoted earlier in its entirety, expresses scorn for egocentric fops, extols the virtues of the sunburned male who is at home in nature's wilds, but ends on a fickle note. Thomson was already celebrating the glories of nature and the simple life; but whether it was because such sentiments were felt to be too strong for the stage, or because the female of 1740 did not care to call attention to her fickleness, "none of the ladies of the theatre would undertake to sing it." [112] Female delicacy prevailed once at least even over the obdurate Young, who unexpectedly complied with Mrs. Bellamy's request that Irexine's line "I will speak to you in thunder" be omitted as inappropriate and ungraceful for a lady to speak.[113]

The actor's imposing his will upon the author was not, of

course, new in the mid-eighteenth century. Johnson records that Hughes, for example, in his *The Siege of Damascus* (1720) had originally made the hero "apostatize from his religion," and thereby gave reasonable motivation to the outcome; but when the actors demanded that the hero's guilt lead to his desertion to the enemy, the author, "unwilling that his relations should lose the benefit of his work, complied with the alteration" [114] even though the alteration made the plot improbable. A century earlier, Shakespeare was very likely subjected to the same pressure from the actors. It is rather that such alterations reflect special conditions in the theater of the mid-century, ranging from the concept of the "star" actor to the false delicacy of contemporary society—or merely the inability of an actor to portray the role as the author intended. It is obvious that the effects on the drama of the actor's requirements of the playwright were not always beneficial; in fact, if we judge all such alterations together, we may well agree with the youthful Edmund Burke, who complained that actors lacked taste; for, he said, having "the election of two pieces [that is, the original and the alteration], they chuse the worst. . . ." [115] But whatever the cause, the result was the same: the individual play, like the repertory as a whole, frequently reflected the predilections and powers of a small group of actors, many of whom were at once among the greatest and the most eccentric in the history of the English stage.

CHAPTER NINE

The Playwright

Tristram Shandy's father struck a pose and delivered for Uncle Toby's benefit a disquisition upon "Man"; whereupon Sterne commented: "O, Garrick! what a rich scene of this would thy exquisite powers make! and how gladly would I write such another to avail myself of thy immortality, and secure my own behind it." [1] Like Shandy, many writers of the time considered the possibility of gaining fame and fortune as dramatic authors by hanging onto the brocaded skirts of Garrick's stage coat, for the theater had indeed become a beckoning avenue to literary reputation. But for some, more immediate considerations than a posthumous fame provided the incentive to write for the stage.

Although the playwright was not necessarily a regular member of a theatrical company, he often had a professional connection with the stage; and as a furnisher of new plays and of alterations of older drama, he is an important figure in theatrical history. His talents (or lack of them), his theories of dramatic composition, and his particular interests and eccentricities—all helped to determine what mid-century audiences could see on the stage. Likewise, his education, the nature of his association with the theater, and the motives that induced him to attempt stage pieces often had an important bearing on the regulation of the theatrical repertory. The playwright, along with the manager and the actors, must therefore be considered a source of influence on the theatrical history of the time.

I have shown that the actor or manager sometimes exerted his will upon the author; moreover, when plays were revived, he might, by alteration and addition, virtually usurp the prerogatives of authorship to himself. Popular taste was likewise a force that served to limit the scope in which the author could

[1] For notes to chap. 9, see pp. 329-333.

function with any hope of success. Consequently, the interrelations of influence of playwright and audience and of playwright and manager or actor tend to qualify any conclusion that can be reached as to the importance of the author alone to the repertory. The playwright, like the manager and actor, could, on occasion or in special ways, exert an independent force; more often he was restricted in his influence by factors over which he had no immediate control. In short, those who were professionally concerned with theatrical affairs were to a considerable degree interdependent, and the success or failure of a stage offering depended upon the coöperation of manager, actors, and playwright in attaining a goal that was largely predetermined by the audience.

In many ways, however, the author was an important—and sometimes an independent—determinant of the repertory. There was no dearth of new plays. In 1739 the Countess of Hertford wrote to a friend that "Mr. Fleetwood has promised so many authors already, that it [Brooke's *Gustavus Vasa*] probably must be deferred to another year." [2] And almost forty years later Garrick wrote to Mrs. Montagu, who had acted as intermediary for the anonymous author of *Bon Ton* in offering that play to the manager, ". . . the Author should know that we are at this moment engaged to more plays & petites pieces than we can do for the two winters to come, unless any of the Authors of them should chuse to withdraw their performances." [3] The facts prove that these statements, made respectively at the beginning and at the end of the period, are not mere exaggerations; a count[4] of the plays performed between 1737 and 1777 reveals that about 450 plays—new pieces, revived plays, and new alterations of older plays[5]—actually reached the London stage. Since this number does not include the numerous pieces refused by the managers, those prohibited by the Lord Chamberlain's office, and those written with no intention of performance, it is apparent that there was no lack of dramatic activity during the period.

Responsible for these new and newly altered plays were approximately 140 different writers, ranging in education from that received by a ropemaker's apprentice to that represented by a Master of Arts degree from Cambridge, and pursuing vocations as various as fencing master and clergyman. Included in the number were many from Ireland and several from Scotland, among them some of the most influential and prolific playwrights of the time: Henry Brooke, Charles Macklin, Richard Glover, Paul Hiffernan, the Sheridans, Henry Jones, Hugh Kelly, Arthur Murphy, and Oliver Goldsmith from across the Irish Sea; and John Delap, Alexander Dow, David Mallet, John Home, John Moncrieff, and James Thomson from the north. Only a few (twelve) were women, for writing for the stage was still a man's profession. There are some indications, however, that the knowledge by the audience that the playwright was a woman sometimes influenced the play's success on the stage. Victor notes, for example, that Mrs. Celisia's *Almida* "was received by the Audience with universal Applause, and has escaped the Censure of the Critic, perhaps, as the Performance of a Lady." [6] But the sex of the author did not prevent Mrs. Griffith's *The Platonic Wife* from being damned the first night, even though the actors, out of friendship for the author, "laboured through groans and hissess . . . till they obtained a second benefit for Mrs. Griffith, and then laid down their arms." [7] Eighteenth-century audiences were often intensely aware of the author, and showed their favoritism sometimes quite apart from any consideration of the play's merits. But chivalrous forbearance because the author was a woman seems on the whole to have been a minor factor in influencing the repertory. Nor was the nationality of the playwright of great importance in this matter, although the interest in Irish affairs and the hatred of the Scots occasionally contributed to a play's success or failure.

More important as determinants were the education and the vocation of the playwrights. Of the 140 writers, the largest definable group, constituting one-fourth of the total number, was composed of those who were already connected with the theater in some professional capacity. Of these, many had been actors before trying their hand at drama, including relatively important playwrights like Thomas Hull, Arthur Murphy, and Henry Woodward; many had been both actors and managers, like Garrick, Samuel Foote, and George Colman, Sr. Others, although notable as actors, furnished only a play or two—for example, Mrs. Cibber, Mrs. Clive, and William Havard. Among those already associated with the theater, not only the actors and managers tried their hands at dramatic composition. Thomas Arne, for example, who supplied seven musical pieces and a burlesque to the stage of the period, apparently first considered the theater as an outlet for his talents while he was leader of the musicians at Drury Lane.[8] Theophilus Forrest, an attorney whose musical piece *The Weathercock* was brought to the Covent Garden stage in 1775, first came in contact with the theater as legal adviser in theatrical affairs.[9] Robert Hitchcock, whose comedies had moderate success at the Haymarket, was the prompter at that theater.[10] Massink, famous as a theatrical machinist in both Dublin and London, is credited with at least one piece of his own.[11] Benjamin Victor, who tried his hand at altering Shakespeare's *The Two Gentlemen of Verona,* was treasurer of the Drury Lane company.[12] It should also be noted that actors and managers not primarily connected with the London theaters—for example, John Jackson, the manager of the Edinburgh theater, and Thomas Sheridan of the Dublin stage—also wrote plays that became a part of the London repertory. But, as I shall show, the most important contributors to the dramatic fare of the London stage were the actors and managers directly connected with the two patent companies.

It is not surprising that such persons should try their hand at dramatic composition. Already established as actors or managers, they attempted a further means of establishing their fame —authorship. They must often have felt, as they rehearsed a new piece, that their own efforts to supply suitable dialogue for the performers might succeed at least as well as the play in rehearsal; and if they were sufficiently persistent (other qualifications for authorship seem often to have been disregarded), actors might readily become playwrights. Their acquaintance with the manager tended to encourage such an ambition, for they were less likely to meet with that greatest of authorial discouragements, the refusal of the manager to accept the piece. And the monetary incentives were considerable. According to the practice of the time, every third performance of a play in its first season was a benefit night for the author; and the proceeds from such performances were frequently quite large, particularly when the playwright, as actor, was a favorite with the public.

Aside from material conditions conducive to authorship among the members of the company, the actor's or manager's acquaintance with the limitations of the stage and with the kind of scene or character most applauded by audiences qualified him in an especially effective manner to provide stage pieces that would meet with popular approval. Although no plays by such actors-turned-authors were among the thirty most frequently acted in the period, many of them were often brought to the stage: among the tragedies, Murphy's *The Grecian Daughter, The Orphan of China,* and *Zenobia;* among the comedies, Murphy's *The Way to Keep Him* and *All in the Wrong,* Colman's *The Clandestine Marriage,* and Kelly's *False Delicacy;* among the farces, Garrick's *Miss in Her Teens* and *Lethe;* and the pantomimes of Woodward. Contemporary records of performance show that these and similar plays were popular. These plays were written with an eye to furnishing effective roles, and hence reveal the experienced hand of the actor-author, as, for example, in such characters as Evander, Mrs. Heidelberg, and Flash. Garrick considered Evander in *The Grecian Daughter* such an effective role that, although he had then (1772) ceased to act new parts, he considered undertaking it.[13] It is also significant that this play remained long on the acting list as one "of those pieces which young actresses think necessary to go through before they consider their reputations established."[14] Mrs. Heidelberg, the old aunt in *The Clandestine Marriage* who is miserly and full of ancestral pride, although little more than a caricature, was obviously drawn by a writer who knew the stage well. A contemporary remark suggests that Flash and his fellow Fribble in *Miss in Her Teens* were created purely for their stage effect:

The inimitable Performances of the Author and Mr. Woodward in these Characters seem'd to overbear even the slightest Reflection of this Kind [that is, that the characters are "outré" and improbable] that might arise, since even in the Répresentation of what might itself exceed the Bounds of Nature, the enchanted Audience could scarcely perceive that they were not walking in her very straitest and most limited Paths.[15]

The plays produced by these playwrights show the same uncertainty of purpose that underlies the drama of the period as a whole, and any homogeneity that may exist within this group of authors is to be found in their professional attachment to the acting company rather than in their theories or practice of play writing. Yet there seems, as was suggested above, to have been one phase of dramatic composition in which the actor-author at least had the opportunity to excel—the delineation of characters (which are perhaps more accurately described as caricatures). To the examples from the works of Colman and Garrick may be added the creations of Foote, whose boast, in defending himself against the attack of Dr. Johnson, was that he was the "man who has added sixteen characters to the English drama of his country!" [16] But it will be seen at once that such characters, lacking as they do any large share of human nature, are effective only as they are portrayed by an accomplished actor and hardly bear closer scrutiny. Or, in the words of an observant Italian who lived in London during the mid-century, "The plays which appear alert, active, and entertaining to the eye on the stage, by dint of stage-trick, and win some applause in the first presentations, are damned in the closet, and never more revived on the theatre." [17]

It is not surprising then to find that the dramatic form most frequently exploited by the actor-author was the farce or other short afterpiece. Such pieces often met with tremendous success, and might accompany a wide variety of full-length plays in the course of the season. But they were relatively short-lived, seldom surviving for more than a season. During their life, however, they added to the author's fame; and if he were, as was frequently true, the principal actor in the farce as well as its author, his profits as well as his fame might be greatly increased.

From the accompanying table two significant conclusions can be drawn about the actor-playwrights. Of the seven dramatists here listed, who are the most prolific suppliers of the stage in the mid-century, six were members of acting companies; and these six produced 30 per cent of all the dramatic pieces of every kind appearing on the stage between 1737 and 1777. Furthermore, the fact that four of the six wrote many more afterpieces than full-length dramas indicates how congenial the actors found farce and caricature when they attempted dramatic composition.

Author	First pieces	Afterpieces	Total plays
David Garrick	15	24	39
Samuel Foote	18	6	24
George Colman, Sr.	8	14	22
Arthur Murphy	12	7	19
Isaac Bickerstaffe	4	14	18
Thomas Hull	4	7	11
Henry Woodward	1	10	11
Totals	62	82	144

But aside from the common propensity for farcical incident and character, the authors who were also actors and managers show the same disparateness as do other dramatists of the time. Arthur Murphy, for example, tried the same type of tragedy that many of the more classical-minded authors of the day were attempting, a kind of neoclassical hybrid indebted to both the tradition of *Cato* and that of *Jane Shore*. Murphy was, at least, no worse in this genre than the Francklins, Masons, and Browns of his day; and Dr. Johnson, although he refused to class Murphy with the great dramatists, remarked, "at present I doubt much whether we have any thing superiour to Arthur." [18] Few other actors tried their hands at original tragedy, and those who did met with less success than did Murphy. Macklin's *Henry VII* did not survive the occasion (the Jacobite rebellion) that give it temporary interest. John Jackson's *Eldred*, regarded even then as poorly contrived, although it was "loudly applauded" during its brief run at the Haymarket, seems indebted for its success to the author's stage portrayal of the title character.[19] Havard's *King Charles the First* was one of the numerous historical plays "written in imitation of Shakespeare," but met with no success; and Hull's *Henry II* fared only slightly better. The tragic mode was not the actor's forte when he turned playwright.

Nor was inventiveness a characteristic of these authors, and it is therefore readily understandable why they frequently turned to older dramas for their plots and characters. In fact it is probably as alterers of old plays rather than as original dramatists that these writers are most appropriately regarded. Almost all types of literature were used for the purpose, and nationality or age did not make a piece unsuitable for adaptation. French dramas furnished the framework for countless plays of the time,[20] some of which were little more than translations. Occasionally novels—for example, *Pamela* and *Longsword*—furnished the actor-authors with sources for plays, and Garrick dramatized part of *Gulliver's Travels* as *Lilliput*. Minor English drama of the early eighteenth century also served as source material; Woodfall's *Sir Thomas Overbury*, for example, was hardly more than a later revival of Savage's earlier tragedy.[21]

But it was to Elizabethan, and particularly to Shakespearean, drama that the members of the company turned in search of plays that they might adapt to their own stage. It is notable that a large proportion of such adaptations was the work of actors and managers. Hull, for example, who was long a highly regarded actor on the Covent Garden stage, altered *The Comedy of Errors*, a play by Beaumont and Fletcher, and, later in the century, another Shakespearean play and one of Massinger's. Colman, Sr., drew upon Beaumont and Fletcher for his *Philaster* and *Bonduca* and upon Shakespeare's *A Midsummer Night's Dream* and *The Winter's Tale* for shorter pieces. John Lee, an actor who tried to rival Garrick, altered *Macbeth, Romeo and Juliet,* and two Restoration comedies. Four of James Love's plays were based respectively upon Shakespeare's *Timon of Athens,* Brome's *The Jovial Crew,* Massinger's *The City Madam,* and Beaumont and Fletcher's *Rule a Wife and Have a Wife.* Thomas Sheridan's alteration of *Coriolanus* and Victor's alteration of *The Two Gentlemen of Verona* were other such plays that reached the London stage. Best known of all for drawing upon older drama is Garrick, who produced not less than nine alterations of Shakespeare and two of Jonson, and who drew upon the works of Fletcher, Tomkis, and Shirley, as well as upon several later authors, notably Dryden, Southerne, and Wycherley. This list is by no means exhaustive, but it will serve to indicate how prevalent among members of the company was the practice of turning to older drama for material that could be made useful on the contemporary stage.

The success of such alterations in maintaining their place in the repertory was no doubt often owing to the influence of the author, who in his capacity as actor or manager could see that his play was given favorable treatment. But, on some occasions at least, the nature of the alteration—because it was adapted to contemporary taste—was also responsible for its success. Since the playwright was conforming to the popular attitude toward drama, it is instructive to look briefly at examples of the work of these actor-authors who adapted older plays for stage presentation.

The best of such authors was Garrick, and it should be remembered that the alterations of the other writers in this group are as a whole quite inferior to his. Because the following works of Garrick are unrepresentative, they should not be considered here: *Antony and Cleopatra,* which was largely the work of Capell; *Macbeth,* which has been called "the most accurate stage version of a Shakespearean play which had appeared since 1671";[22] *Cymbeline,* which was rather an abridgment for the stage than an alteration; and other plays that were simply shortened acting versions. Such plays, because they do not show the imposition of eighteenth-century ideas upon the Elizabethan basis, are not typical of the efforts of the actor-author who went about altering older drama, but rather tend to confirm a frequently stated, but certainly not an entirely accurate, opinion—for example, that "Garrick's point of view . . . was solely that of the theater manager and actor." [23] To maintain the proper perspective, it should be added that, compared to other adapters, Garrick was highly conservative in this respect.

There is, however, another side to Garrick as alterer, which is represented by his treatment of *The Taming of the Shrew, The Winter's Tale,* and Southerne's *The Fatal Marriage.* The first play was completely changed in its total effect (even though almost all the lines are still Shakespeare's) because most of what was considered as its "wild, confused, and almost inexplicable fable" [24] was cut away, with the result that it became "the most regular" [25] of all the adaptations of *The Taming of the Shrew.* Southerne's play was regularized in another way. The original had had a considerable and vital comic element, which, though it increased the play's interest for the audience, violated a critical dictum at least nominally revered. When the play appeared as *Isabella* in Garrick's version, the objectionable element had been entirely excised.[26] But most instructive is his treatment of *The Winter's Tale.*[27] Here he strove for the closest possible unity of time and place; speeded up the action by shortening the play—wherever necessary introducing expositional material from the omitted scenes; left out archaisms, obscenity, puns, and verbal witticisms; made the diction more "correct"; and attempted to heighten the play's histrionic qualities, especially in striving for effective scene endings. It is apparent that he paid most attention to contemporary notions of decorum in making his alteration. It must be admitted that the result is a highly actable afterpiece; and if there is merit in bringing to the stage a Shakespearean play, even though in mutilated form, when it would not otherwise have reached the stage in any form, that merit cannot be denied Garrick.

But this alteration is an example of what often happened when an actor undertook to adapt Shakespeare to his stage. There is the same conflict between the practical requirements of the stage and the worship of certain critical theories that is to be found in numerous original tragedies and comedies of the period. Typically, such plays held the stage for a few nights or for a single season only because they provided the skillful actor with an opportunity to make the most of a pathetic scene or an eccentric character. But both the plays and the alterations (including those of Garrick, who was thoroughly familiar with contemporary dramatic theory), although written with an eye to stage effect, lacked a greater ingredient —the portrayal of intensely vital and consistently probable human beings. Thus, while pruning *The Winter's Tale* in the interests of actability and decorum, Garrick was shearing away many passages that, although they did not contribute directly to the elements that he considered the most important, provided the breadth and depth of characterization through which the dramatis personae emerged as more than mere stage figures. The result was a stage piece that, although often satisfying to critical theorists, depended almost entirely upon the opportunities it offered for stage business and for the histrionic ability of a principal actor in a role specifically retained, or even heightened, for that purpose.

Two conclusions from this consideration of the actor as author seem justified. The same lack of inventiveness and the same inability to create three-dimensional characters beset him that prevented professed poets and acknowledged literary masters from writing enduring drama. And in spite of, perhaps even because of, his greater acquaintance with the require-

ments of stage plays, his peculiar knowledge found a congenial and vital outlet only in caricature and farce. Moreover,
when he attempted full-length drama, since he was usually
aware of the critics' demands upon the theater, his regard for
critical theory often produced its baneful effect and congealed
the springs of dramatic composition. When it is considered
that one-fourth of the 140 playwrights who produced the
drama for the mid-century stage belong to this group, the
extent to which they influenced the repertory becomes apparent; and it becomes even more apparent when it is realized
that these writers produced almost one-half of the entire dramatic output between 1737 and 1777.

Although Garrick was the author most influential on the
contemporary repertory among the playwrights being considered, he cannot be called the most important to dramatic
history. His knowledge of the possibilities of the stage together with his dominant position as actor and manager make
him a force to be reckoned with in considering the influence
of the playwright upon the dramatic fare of the mid-century
theater. Yet, except for his alteration of *The Taming of the
Shrew*, the fate of his stage pieces, whether independent plays
or reworkings of older drama, depended upon his theatrical
career. The same is true to an even greater extent of the plays
of other actor-authors. The survival of these plays as vital
elements in the repertory depended either upon the initiative
of their authors, who, from their vantage ground as members
of the professional company, could secure for their plays the
advantages of stage presentation, or upon a favorite role that
the actor-author had provided for himself. But upon the
author's retirement from the stage—if not before—such plays
disappeared.

One playwright included in this group is, however, a notable
exception; some of his plays are of significance, not only to
the contemporary repertory, but also to the later history of
drama. In spite of the fact that his work comes at the very
end of the period and that his dramatic efforts did not have
the influence they deserved, he cannot be dismissed as sum-
marily as can the general run of professional theater men, most
of whom were merely dramatic hacks. This man is, of course,
Richard Brinsley Sheridan, a member of a family long associated
with the stage. His father was a famous actor and for several

years the manager of the royal theater in Dublin, and his mother had written several plays. He turned quite naturally to the stage, therefore, and, although unsuccessful as an actor, he was long associated with the theater as manager and royal patentee. But he made his most notable impression on the repertory as dramatist, especially by adding to it two superior full-length plays as well as several shorter works.

His first acted drama, *The Rivals,* appeared at Covent Garden in 1775 and, after an initial setback, met with more than ordinary success. Although Sheridan was to surpass other contemporary playwrights in his efforts to provide a suitable medium for the English comic muse, he was not altogether successful in doing so in his first attempt. *The Rivals* combines conventions of several types of comedy. The principal love plot satirizes the sentimental comedy of the day; yet the underplot is essentially sentimental, and Julia was regarded by a contemporary reviewer as "in the line of elegant and sentimental Comedy" and "an honour to the drama." [28] The dialogue is reminiscent of the comedy of manners of Congreve, and, as in that author's plays, the servants are able to compete on even terms with their masters in witty repartee. The comedy of humors makes its contribution also, and characters with names like Languish, Absolute, and O'Trigger are not only reminiscent of Jonson's practice in naming his own characters—for example, Dame Pliant, George Downright, and Tom Quarlous—but might be described with equal appropriateness by Jonson's famous definition:

> . . . when some one peculiar quality
> Doth so possess a man, that it doth draw
> All his affects, his spirits, and his powers,
> In their confluctions, all to run one way,
> This may be truly said to be a humour.

In this attempted fusion of comic elements Sheridan shows, not only his skill as a dramatist, but also his familiarity with the course and corpus of English comedy. In the latter he is not greatly different from the clerics and scholars who tried their hands at dramatic composition. But he resembles the actor-authors in a different respect—for the intrigue in *The Rivals* borders on farce, and the characters are almost caricatures. Moreover, the play has the kind of stage business in which audiences delighted—for example, the duel scene (V, ii), and shows the results of the same familiarity with the stage as that which made the farces of Garrick and the comedies of Colman maintain their positions in the repertory. Contemporary critics seem to have been unable to decide just how Sheridan's play was best regarded, whether as a sentimental or as a "laughing" comedy,[29] an indecision itself suggestive of Sheridan's inability in *The Rivals* to fuse with complete success the conventions of the various genres from which he had borrowed.

The fusion was more successful, although still not quite complete, in his next play, *The School for Scandal* (1777). The same conventions are again employed; nor can it be said that any single element in the play is notably original.[30] Again a dominant trait is announced in the names of characters, such as Teazle, Crabtree, Backbite, Sneerwell, whose "confluctions . . . run one way." Although sentimentalism is ridiculed in the person of Joseph Surface, it is a definite strain in the make-up of others—for example, Charles Surface and Lady Teazle, who are more amiably treated. The complete poetic justice of the denouement, demanding of the audience that issues of probability be not pressed too far, likewise relates it to the sentimental kind. On the other hand, the "manners" element, derived from Congreve and his contemporaries, furnishes the principal ingredient of the play, so much so that one of the most hackneyed critical observations on eighteenth-century drama is that *The School for Scandal* is the finest example of the comedy of manners after Congreve. It differs, however, from Congreve's comedies in that the *esprit gaulois* has been rigorously chastened and made inoffensive for a consciously moral age.

Yet in spite of the variousness of its elements, it succeeded where other plays had failed in finding the mean of theatrically effective high comedy between the extremes of farce and unnaturally refined sentimentalism. That the author was familiar with the stage made it possible for him to devise a situation like that of the famous screen scene (IV, iii), regarded as one of the most effective in all English drama. But stage effectiveness, although it might well cause the play to survive, does not account for the author's success in fusing into a satisfactorily unified whole the ingredients that he employed.

√ That success is to be sought in other directions. First, Sheri-

Interior of Drury Lane Theatre

For the Benefit of Mr. POWELL.

At the Theatre Royal in *Drury-Lane,* 1765

This prefent MONDAY, the 25th of MARCH,

KING *LEAR.*

[For the Laft Time This Seafon]

King *Lear* Mr. POWELL,

Glofter by Mr. BURTON,

Edgar by Mr. HAVARD,

The *Baftard* by Mr. LEE,

Kent by Mr. BRANSBY,

Gentleman-Ufher by Mr. GRIFFITH,

Albany by Mr. PACKER,

Cornwall by Mr. JACKSON,

Burgundy by Mr. ADCOCK,

Goneril by Mrs. LEE,

Regan by Mrs. HOPKINS,

Cordelia by Mrs. YATES

(Being her Firft Appearance in that Character.)

End of the Play, an Entertainment of Dancing call'd The MEDLEY,

By Mr. *Slingfby*, Mifs *Baker,* &c.

To which will be added a Mufical Entertainment, of two Acts, call'd

The CAPRICIOUS LOVERS,

The CHARACTERS by

Mr. Vernon, Mr. Yates, Mr. Baddeley,

Mr. Didier, Mr. Fox, Mifs Slack,

Mifs Plym, Mifs Wright, and Mrs. Clive.

Act I. of the Entertainment, a New Dance call'd The *Irifh Milkmaids*

By *Mafter Cape*, Mifs *Rogers,* &c.

† Part of the PIT will be laid into the Boxes.

† LADIES are defired to fend their Servants by Three o'Clock.

To-morrow, (Not Acted thefe three Years) The WINTER's TALE,

with a Comedy of two Acts (Acted but Once) call'd The CHOICE,

For the Benefit of Mr. YATES.

Playbill of the mid-eighteenth century

The Farmer's Return, by William Hogarth

Garrick as Richard III, by William Hogarth

Garrick and Mrs. Bellamy in *Romeo and Juliet*

The Universal Register Office
March 7, 1761

Sir
We intend performing this Farce
if it should meet with the approbation
of my Lord Chamberlain

Garrick
Lacy

Not thought fit to be acted.

The

Universal Register Office.

a Farce

of Two Acts.

not thought fit to be
acted

Title page of play, bearing mark of censor's disapproval

The Screen Scene from *The School for Scandal*

John Rich as Harlequin

dan was dealing with a society that he knew well, and he was acquainted with many actual Lady Sneerwells and Mrs. Candours at Bath.[31] Second, we have it on the authority of Sheridan's biographer that the play was written with conscientious care and was revised deliberately and in detail.[32] The playwright showed that he had learned well from his earlier experiment in comedy. Third, and perhaps most important, the author succeeded in giving the whole an air of universality, in subsuming the particular under the general—an accomplishment that was beyond the reach of most of his contemporaries. It has often been remarked that the title of this play is not appropriate because it refers to only a minor element. But from the beginning Sheridan never intended to relate the title to the main plot, even though he did consider more than one name for his play.[33] Rather than to question the appropriateness of the title, particularly when we know that it was a deliberate choice, it is more instructive to consider its significance. By calling the play *The School for Scandal,* Sheridan has indicated the functional importance of the scenes in which Lady Sneerwell and her sisters appear in giving the whole a more extensive background. The restricted society of the scandal club becomes society at large, and the ladies' wrong estimates of Joseph and Charles Surface have a counterpart in the calumny and backbiting of Sheridan's London.[34] If Sheridan had continued to cultivate the muse of pure comedy, or if he had found capable successors in that genre who were equally familiar with the requirements of the stage, undoubtedly the history of drama during the later eighteenth century would have been quite different.

Sheridan is therefore the exceptional dramatist among that large group of writers who had other connections with the theater. He shared with them the propensity for farcical situation and caricature; but he went beyond them in providing the stage with "literary" drama. Equally skillful in creating effective stage business, he surpassed them in that he was able, by gaining a detachment impossible in sentimental comedy, to open out his plays on larger horizons. Nevertheless, Sheridan supplied only two enduring dramas; and these, in spite of their merit, could do little more than point the way for other professional theater men. But the time was late. By 1777, the date of *The School for Scandal,* the professionals had largely turned to melodrama, musical farce, and comic opera. Actor-authors and manager-authors thereafter largely confined their efforts to the furnishing of bare scenarios, of mere outlines, which made possible the exploitation of maximum "sound and shew."

It is frequently said that Sheridan is the last "literary" dramatist until the later nineteenth century, and that after *The School for Scandal* new dramatic literature is to be found only in closet drama. But the effect of this decline was at least as important to the theatrical repertory as it was to dramatic history, and, in a study of the conditions of dramatic performance, is more relevant. Before 1777 the seasonal repertory had included—along with several Shakespearean dramas, a few other revived plays written before about 1730, and the new dramatic efforts of the year—quite a large number of plays of the year before or of ten or twenty years before. That is, dramas had been written throughout the mid-century that were substantial enough (even if mediocre in a literary sense) to maintain their places in the repertory. The repertory continued to be representative, therefore, of mid-century dramatic effort. But later in the century the situation changed. Besides the Shakespearean and other revivals from the sixteenth and seventeenth centuries, the repertory contained very little that was recent unless it was completely new. In other words, the repertory had become unrepresentative of all but current dramatic activity. The desire for novelty, the increasingly scornful attitude many writers had for the stage, the increased size of theaters—these and many other factors played a part in bringing about this change. But the fact that the new actable plays themselves had become little more than directions for the actors (and for scene painters, stage carpenters, musicians, and choreographers) tended to perpetuate the changed situation, so that repertories ever after—even during the recent dramatic renascence—have not been arranged along the well-established lines that were followed in the eighteenth century. In short, except for dramatists like Sheridan who combined literary skill with an effective knowledge of the theater, the actors and managers, instead of adding to their permanent fame by authorship, had, by composing new pieces only for immediate use on their stages, written themselves into dramatic oblivion.

A second group of authors, less numerous than the first but

nevertheless clearly definable, consists of university-trained men, widely read in the classics and for the most part destined for the church. Such writers were, for example, Dr. John Brown, Richard Cumberland, Dr. Thomas Francklin, William Hawkins, John Home, William Mason, and Edward Young. Brown, whose tragedies *Barbarossa* and *Athelstan* were acted on the Drury Lane stage a few years before insanity and suicide put an end to their learned author's existence, received Orders after graduation from Cambridge. Cumberland, the author of several tragedies, comedies, and musical pieces, was a bishop's son and also a graduate of Cambridge, where he had made a reputation as a Latin scholar. Dr. Francklin, author of two tragedies performed at the patent theaters, was Greek professor at Cambridge, the first chaplain of the Royal Academy, a famous preacher at St. Paul's, and a highly regarded translator of Cicero, Sophocles, and Lucian. William Hawkins, the perpetrator of one of the worst Shakespearean alterations of the time, was professor of poetry at Oxford. John Home, the author of the most famous tragedy of the mid-century, was a member of the Scottish clergy until expelled for writing drama. William Mason, whose tragedies *Elfrida* and *Caractacus* were written "in imitation of the antients," was a portrait painter, an accomplished musician (he also improved the pianoforte and invented the celestina), along with Gray and Hurd one of the "polite scholars" at Cambridge, and vicar of Aston. Young, several of whose tragedies were performed, was not only the distinguished author of *Night Thoughts* but also an Oxford graduate and rector of Welwyn. Here is indeed a polite and learned company.

With these may be grouped others, also for the most part university-trained, who, although primarily engaged in literary pursuits of other kinds, often or occasionally tried their hands at drama. This group may be represented by Richard Bentley, son of the famous critic and a literary friend of Walpole; Capell and Theobald, editors of Shakespeare; Thomas Cooke and Paul Hiffernan, translators; Mrs. Griffith and Tobias Smollett, novelists; Richard Glover, epic poet and patriot; William Whitehead, the laureate; and Edward Jerningham, James Thomson, Dr. Johnson, and Oliver Goldsmith, of varying degrees of literary fame.

These two groups—clergyman-playwrights and literary men

who turned on occasion to the theater—may be best treated as one, since the line distinguishing them is so faint as to be nearly invisible. Together they comprise a number almost as great as that of the actor-dramatists previously mentioned. But there is this noteworthy difference: whereas the actors produced approximately half of all dramas acted on the London stage between 1737 and 1777, the university men provided little more than one-sixth of the total. Their relative lack of dramatic productivity is perhaps explainable on several grounds. Other pursuits often left little time for the drama. Most of them did not have the same easy access to the theater enjoyed by the actor-playwrights. Occasionally an author with an already established reputation in another literary genre attempted to add to his fame by writing for the stage; but, disappointed in his attempt, he abandoned the dramatic form after one or two trials. A few tried writing for the stage to make money, but, finding unsuccessful plays unprofitable, they turned to other means of making a livelihood. Others approached the drama with the air of literary dilettanti, and their contributions could hardly be expected to be anything but infrequent and sporadic.

More important to the complexion of eighteenth-century drama and the theatrical repertory, though still related to the matter of their relative unproductivity, was the effect of their literary knowledge and classical predilections upon the plays they wrote. These plays, for the most part tragedies, reflect the learned interests of their authors in plot and setting, their reverence for critical authority in structure, and their lack of acquaintance with the theater in character and situation. They could do little else than fail, or at best live through the nine performances customarily granted to new plays. What success they did have was often owing to the author's reputation in some other capacity and not to his merit as a dramatist. Mrs. Bellamy notes, for example, of the ten performances accorded Young's *The Brothers,* "this arose more from the author's character being so universally revered, than from any intrinsic merit there was in it." [35] Francis' *Constantine* was expected to succeed because of the author's reputation, especially as a translator of Horace, but there was only "the melancholy prospect of empty benches." [36] Similarly, Jerningham's *Margaret of Anjou,* it was felt, would "afford the entertainment

which was expected from the author's abilities." [37] Johnson's
Irene is a better-known example. Contemporary records suggest that the public looked forward to a superior tragedy when
Irene was announced;[38] and several years earlier a Lichfield
acquaintance, Gilbert Walmsley, had made a similar assumption, that Johnson would "turn out a fine tragedy writer" because he was "a very good scholar and poet." [39] All four of
these plays failed to survive their initial runs; but the public
nevertheless thought it was justified in looking to its scholars
and poets to provide successful and enduring drama.

More informative than an exhaustive list of such pieces is a
consideration of the motives that impelled certain representative figures in this group to write for the stage, for such consideration should indicate some of the ways in which the
repertory was influenced by the learned playwrights.

William Mason, a man of considerable ability and cultivated
taste, has been called a "good specimen of the more cultivated
clergy of his day." [40] His classical interests became apparent
early, encouraged by his father and later by his studies and
acquaintances at St. John's College. Something of an aesthete,
he opposed the "philologists" as a student at Cambridge while
he continued his avid reading of the Greeks and Romans. He
submitted his writings to his correspondents Gray and Walpole
for their criticism. After some occasional poems in the Greek
manner—*Musaeus* in memory of Pope and an ode on the
installation of the Duke of Newcastle as Chancellor of Cambridge—his first dramatic effort, *Elfrida,* appeared in 1752,
which according to the title was "Written on the Model of the
Antient Greek Tragedy." This play, although it had only
limited success when it was finally brought to the stage twenty
years later, was by way of being "all things to all men." There
was the Sophoclean chorus of virgins chanting their dithyramb
in the Hellenic mode. For the proponents of the "rules," there
was strict adherence to the unities. The setting was Anglo-
Saxon England, in conformity with the popular practice of
representing the nation's past upon the stage. There was a
preponderant moral note in the treatment of the theme. There
was a thread of romance in both the portrayal of character
and the handling of the setting. And for those who came for
"sound and shew," there were music and spectacle. The
opinions of the public were divided. Davies thought Mason's

success would "deter all future writers from attempting a fable already so nobly executed";[41] and Boswell thought it "exquisite." [42] But Dr. Johnson saw only "some good imitations of Milton's bad manner." [43]

The division of opinion is significant; for Mason was obviously trying something new—what Draper calls "a rococo combination of what [were] regarded as the virtues of types and schools that were really in essential opposition . . . a new aesthetic synthesis." [44] It is easy to conjecture why Mason wrote such a play. His romantic propensities caused him to "play at republicanism" until much later, when the French Revolution frightened him out of sympathy with radical movements.[45] He once had a piece rejected by Hannah More's *Cheap Repository Tracts* because "it had too much love in it." [46] This side of his nature, combined with his strongly marked classical leanings, tended to make him a typical figure in the mid-century fashion that has been called "Romantic Hellenism." [47] *Elfrida* is the congenial effort of a cultured clergyman-poet writing under such a combination of influences.

Not many plays like *Elfrida* reached the stage—or indeed were written—and Mason as a determinant of the repertory must therefore be regarded only as one extreme within the group of authors under discussion. Yet his influence was considerable; or rather, the traits and tendencies of which he may be regarded as typical are of importance to theatrical history and exerted an influence on even a playwright like Richard Cumberland, who is at almost the opposite pole.

Cumberland first tried his hand at drama because of his admiration for *Elfrida,* and he produced a play on the Caractacus story that Mason had also used for a drama.[48] *The Banishment of Cicero* (his first five-act drama on a classical theme) and a verse translation of Seneca's *Troades,* neither of which was intended for the stage, indicate his classical leanings, which might have made him another Mason if he had followed them. Certainly his dramatic creed pointed in that direction:

I hold it a matter of conscience and duty in the dramatic poet to reserve his brightest colouring for the best characters, to give no false attractions to vice and immorality, but to endeavour, as far as is consistent with that contrast, which is the very essence of his art, to turn the fairer side of human nature to the public . . . to make worthy characters amiable but . . . not . . . insipid.[49]

But he soon turned to comic opera (*The Summer's Tale*) and comedy (*The Brothers, The West Indian, The Fashionable Lover*).

He was to return to the tragedy later, but not to the kind that Mason had written. That he had found such tragedy unsuited to his purpose is strongly suggested by his own statement that he came to choose his heroes from those who were the "butts for ridicule and abuse, and endeavoured to present them in such lights, as might tend to reconcile the world to them, and them to the world." [50] In carrying out this plan, he chose for his characters such victims of prejudice as the Irishman and the West Indian, a choice that led him infallibly into the realm of comedy. *The West Indian* (1771) met with great success, and on the strength of his reputation as its author his reworking of *Timon of Athens,* "indeed a miserable alteration," [51] was accepted by Garrick.

Cumberland's next play, *The Fashionable Lover* (1772), perhaps best illustrates how he, like Mason, was striving for a new dramatic synthesis but, unlike Mason, in the guise of comedy. The play has many hackneyed elements and long-familiar characters. In several respects it is reminiscent of *The Conscious Lovers.* A note of sensibility appears, especially in Mortimer, the disillusioned but kind-hearted cynic, and in Augusta, the distressed female. The wealthy middle class is represented by Aubrey and Bridgemore, who have amassed their riches through foreign trade. The characters, self-consciously decrying vice, talk at length about virtue and honor. A strong patriotic note asserts itself, particularly in the references to the French and Russian wars, and—more important— we find much sincere praise of nature, the "noble savage," and the simple life, as well as "humours" characters and scenes that descend almost to the level of farce. And the unmotivated reformation of the villain, though reminiscent of Elizabethan tragicomedy, is also prophetic of the melodramas that were to become popular in the next generation. The play may, therefore, be in one sense regarded as transitional; but it is perhaps more accurate to describe it as synthetic. The playwright, alert by heritage and education to the general level of mediocrity of English drama, and like most of the dramatists of his time desirous of restoring to the theater some of its former greatness, was consciously attempting, by drawing upon all his own resources and upon various dramatic traditions, to exert his influence for the improvement of the stage.[52]

The influence of the authors of this group upon the repertory may be seen further in other playwrights, whose work falls between the two extremes marked by the "Romantic Hellenism" of Mason's tragedies and the synthetic comedies of Cumberland. The work of Dr. Thomas Francklin, as might be expected of the translator of Sophocles and the author of a critical work on ancient drama, is closer to that of Mason than Cumberland. His tragedies show a similar interest in English history but also considerable distortion of historical fact—for example, in *The Earl of Warwick*—in order to make room for the dominant love element. In both that tragedy and in *Matilda* a distressed maiden is torn between conflicting duties; but unlike the Antigone of Francklin's obvious model, Margaret and Matilda never quite succeed in being alive and convincing. As in Mason's *Elfrida,* deeds of violence are carefully kept off stage, but in *The Earl of Warwick* the author keeps his hero alive long enough to arrive on the scene and expire for the delectation of an emotional audience. We must conclude that the modest success these tragedies had was principally owing to the excellence of the actresses who took the leading roles, especially Mrs. Yates and later Mrs. Siddons as Margaret in *The Earl of Warwick;*[53] and it is indeed wonderful that even a Yates or a Siddons could give a semblance of naturalness to the language with which many of these writers felt it necessary to ornament their dramas. Francklin was not the worst offender in this respect, but he shared with numerous other dramatists of the age the opinion that to write serious drama it was necessary to "imitate Shakespeare" and that to imitate Shakespeare necessitated the lavish use of high-flown language. This characteristic of these writers has been noted more than once by recent scholars, but an eighteenth-century observer perhaps best described the result as "verbage [*sic*] without imagery to sustain it, a cold altisonant, gigantesque shadow, inane and puerile." [54]

The Hellenic note is also found in the work of Whitehead, both in his nondramatic poetry and in his tragedies (*The Roman Father* and *Creusa, Queen of Athens*).[55] The former play retold the famous story of the Horatii and the Curiatii as the author found it in Corneille; the latter used the legend

that furnished the plot of Euripides' *Ion. The Roman Father*
met with more than average success, being performed in seven
seasons at Drury Lane and four at Covent Garden by 1777,
although its prolonged initial run (twelve performances) was
chiefly owing to the efforts of Garrick, Barry, and Mrs. Pritchard in the principal roles.[56] Whitehead, as a classicist, was
concerned with dramatic theory, and this tragedy illustrates his
regard for the rules. The English play has greater unity than
its French source, the number of scenes and characters is
reduced, and much of Corneille's ornamentation has been
shorn away. The poet's ideal was apparently to bring it as near
as possible to the form of Greek tragedy.

Another Hellenist among the playwrights was Richard Glover,
whose long poems *Leonidas* and the *Athenaid* as well as one of
his tragedies, *Medea,* were on Greek themes. He had established an enviable reputation as both poet and patriot by his
first poem, but his plays failed to live up to expectations. His
Boadicia, using Roman England for its setting, was thought
to be "unaffecting" and written in a "cold languid" manner.[57]
A strong cast, including Garrick, Mossop, Mrs. Cibber, and
Mrs. Pritchard, kept it on the stage for ten performances,[58]
after which it was never revived. His *Medea,* in spite of the
care he took with it,[59] met with an even worse fate.

Richard Bentley was also well read in classical literature, but
the only play of his to be produced in this period—a comedy,
The Wishes; or Harlequin's Mouth Opened—took a different
direction. It was a burlesque of Greek tragic drama, which
showed his knowledge of the ancient theater, but because it
lacked the qualities that audiences required—novelty, variety,
and wit—without providing situation and allusion that they
could readily understand, the play failed.[60] Here indeed the
playwright's learning was a genuine obstacle in the way of a
play's success, even though the play was a light comedy.

A final representative of this group is John Home. His great
success with *Douglas,* his first play, caused him to attempt
tragedy again and again. But none of the succeeding five
plays (*Agis, The Siege of Aquileia, The Fatal Discovery, Alonzo,*
and *Alfred*), acted between 1758 and 1778, met with anything
like comparable success. That some of them were acted at all
seems to have resulted from Home's fame as the author of
Douglas.[61] We find less of the classical note in these plays

than in most of those previously considered. Instead, there is a reedy romanticism—strongest in *Douglas,* barely perceptible in *Alfred*—that may have resulted from Home's efforts to bring to the drama a characteristic trait of his own nature. We are told that he was highly susceptible as a youth, full of romantic sentiments, and given to heroic utterances.[62] This tendency effectively modified the author's classical propensities, and resulted in such a play as *Douglas,* in contrast to the *Elfrida* of Mason, in which the romantic strain was present only experimentally, and to the *Boadicia* of Glover, in which it was entirely absent.[63]

Implicit in the plays of these educated clergymen and poets are the answers to several questions that might be asked about the theatrical repertory between 1737 and 1777. Such authors, possessed of wide knowledge of men and books but largely ignorant of the practical requirements of the stage, were able to produce only plays that almost without exception could not maintain themselves as stock pieces. Without playwrights like Garrick and the other theater men to supply new compositions for the stage, the plight of drama would have been grave indeed; for lacking a contemporary reservoir of plays, rehearsed and mounted in previous seasons, to draw upon, the repertory necessarily would have continued to rely entirely upon a large residuum of tested offerings—many of Shakespeare's plays, the comedies of Cibber and Steele, and the tragedies of Otway and Rowe. But since not even the theater men were much more successful, the stock plays, along with the few new pieces supplied from season to season—which were acted and then commonly laid on the shelf like their predecessors—continued to make up the repertory and to keep its complexion nearly the same throughout the period.

But, aside from this negative effect, these playwrights influenced the dramatic fare in other ways. The fact that many of them were clergymen tended to increase the number of plays that were deliberately "moral," which were written to instruct a public that was already self-conscious about its virtue. Consequently the type of drama that was given birth in the vicar's study only reinforced a trait that was prevalent in the mid-century audience. Such a piece was usually brought to the stage with considerable éclat (often out of respect for its author), the professed lovers of morality came to pay lip service, and after the customary number of performances the play was laid aside and forgotten.

Many of these playwrights were scholars who tended to add to the repertory plays that reflected the learning of their authors—learning that, whether understood or not by the audience, was either ill assimilated or not accompanied by compensatory theatrical qualities. Lacking the professional and technical knowledge of the stage, they failed to provide their plays with even the effective situation or the eccentric character that gave vitality to the comedies and farces of the actor-authors; and, inclined by education and heritage toward serious drama, the learned playwrights largely restricted their efforts to tragedy, a genre requiring an intensity and creativeness that knowledge alone could not supply.

But tragedy, still universally regarded as poetic drama (Lillo and Moore excepted), had not only to find suitable content but even an appropriate idiom. Its attempts at Shakespearean diction, as that was then understood, resulted only in verbosity and bombast. Consequently, any real vitality in eighteenth-century drama is to be expected in comedy rather than in tragedy, for comedy accepted the prose form cultivated by the Restoration playwrights, many of whom were still popular on the stage. Moreover, the early eighteenth-century writers of comedy, including the popular Steele and Cibber, had countenanced the practice by employing prose in their own comedies.

Among the scholars and literary men, only one—who found both a suitable prose style and a situation that he succeeded in giving stage effectiveness—produced an actable play that proved to be of enduring merit. That play was *She Stoops to Conquer,* and the man was Oliver Goldsmith. The son of an Irish clergyman, he tried his hand at law, medicine, and teaching school before he began to earn his living by his pen. After writing essays, poems, biography, and a novel, he offered his first play, *The Good-Natured Man,* to Garrick, who, however, refused to undertake it. It was then accepted by Colman and produced at Covent Garden in 1768. The preface to the printed play illustrates how Goldsmith, like many of his contemporaries, felt it necessary to lead comedy back to its proper function—"to delineate character"—and to warn his countrymen against the excesses of French comedy, which he said had become "so very elevated and sentimental, that it has not only banished humor and Moliere from the stage, but it has banished all spectators too." But I suspect, knowing Goldsmith's readiness to take umbrage when outdone, that the preface is a retaliatory afterthought, written when Kelly's *False Delicacy* continued to draw audiences at the rival theater after his own comedy had survived through only the usual nine performances. But whatever his purpose in the preface, the play itself shows how he had attempted to fuse several traditional comic patterns. The principal plot is that of a sentimental comedy, and the hero might with little change have appeared appropriately in Kelly's play. Lofty is a later version of Sir Fopling Flutter, whereas the title itself places the play in the tradition of sentimental comedy. At the same time an element of humor looms larger than that in other plays of the day, the author declaring that he was willing to descend "in pursuing humour . . . into the recesses of the mean." [64] As a result *The Good-Natured Man* is hardly more than a sentimental comedy with some infusion of humor from the "laughing" variety.

His next play, *She Stoops to Conquer* (1773), was a more successful attempt at true comedy. Although some felt that it bordered too nearly on farce,[65] the improbabilities in the plot are willingly passed over in the sustained bustle of merriment and gaiety. Tony Lumpkin's activities help to enliven the whole, and intrigue and practical jokes abound. Miss Hardcastle has nothing in common with the heroines of sentimental comedy; in fact she speaks satirically of the "man of *sentiment*," [66] and Mrs. Hardcastle later exclaims, "Pshaw, pshaw! this is all but the whining end of a modern novel." [67] The play was enthusiastically received,[68] even though it ridiculed the audience's long-cherished darlings—prudish sensibility and cultivated sentimentality.

For all his play's success, however, Goldsmith did not succeed in changing thereby the nature of comedy, for the plays that followed *She Stoops to Conquer* to the stage were largely written in the familiar vein,[69] a vein corrupted by the "poisonous drugs" that Garrick had also ridiculed in the prologue he furnished for Goldsmith's play. The "genteel" comedy supported by Kelly and Cumberland was too deeply embedded in the age to be suddenly uprooted. So deeply was it entrenched that Goldsmith himself did not entirely succeed in avoiding it in his most earnest attempt.[70] For example, Miss Neville,

urged by Hastings to elope with him, replies—just as many
of her dramatic predecessors might have done—"Prudence once
more comes to my relief, and I will obey its dictates. In the
moment of passion, fortune may be despised, but it ever pro-
duces a lasting repentance." [71]

Goldsmith among literary men, like Sheridan among those
professionally connected with the stage, was an exception
among playwrights. With the skill as author that he had demonstrated in *The Deserted Village* and *The Vicar of Wakefield,*
he brought together in one comedy plausible character, amusing situation, and satisfying dialogue. None of his contemporaries, despite their learning or their knowledge of what was
demanded by dramatic convention, had been able to do so.
And this happy union of qualities resulted in a play that succeeded in holding the stage where those of his fellow authors
failed. Although Goldsmith managed to give vitality to a single play, he failed, however, to do so for the repertory as a
whole—or even for comedy as a stage genre. Sheridan, who
had the advantage of following Goldsmith, and the support of
Foote and Colman, similarly was unable to change the course
of dramatic history. Individually, of course, Goldsmith, like
Sheridan, is important as a contributor to the eighteenth-century repertory. But if their comedies had been written before
the day when melodrama and operatic farce were about to
banish legitimate drama from the theater, their influence might
have been much greater.

The remaining dramatists to be considered are of much less
merit than either Goldsmith or Sheridan and are, with one
exception, of slight importance as influences on the repertory.
We might surmise that this lack of significance in theatrical
history even derives from lack of merit, except that the relative importance of such inconsequential writers as Foote and
Hull—or, more notably, later in the century, the German
Kotzebue—warns us against making such an inference.

Although the authors in this miscellaneous category equaled
in number the two groups previously discussed, their output
was relatively small and for the most part of less importance.
There are, however, some noteworthy exceptions. Among the
more prolific writers of the time were Isaac Bickerstaffe, John
Hawkesworth, Joseph Reed, and Edward Thompson, all of
whom may be placed in this group. And among those who

wrote plays that met with success or are notable for other reasons (although they contributed only a few pieces—sometimes only one—to the stage) are Robert Dodsley, Henry Jones, Henry Crisp, and General John Burgoyne. In many ways these playwrights show great variety, ranging in social station, for example, through the middle classes to the lowest rung of society.

The most influential of these was the Irishman Bickerstaffe. He was a military man by profession and was for a time an officer in the marines. When he turned to play writing, he found a congenial mode in the comic opera, which he made a fashionable and successful type of dramatic performance. In 1772 he fled from England charged with a serious crime, leaving behind him an unenviable reputation.[72] But between 1760 and 1772 almost a score of his pieces—comic operas, comedies, and farces—were produced on the London stage. He drew freely on Spanish and French as well as upon earlier English plays for his themes, and many of his plays had incidental music composed by T. A. Arne, Samuel Arnold, and Charles Dibdin. The result was often highly successful—for example, *Love in a Village,* performed every season after its first appearance in 1762 through the rest of the period; *The Padlock* (1768); the almost equally successful *Lionel and Clarissa* (1768); and *The Maid of the Mill* (1765). Some of his comic operas show clearly that they fell under the pervasive spell of sentimental comedy. A notable example is *Lionel and Clarissa,* of which the author was particularly proud, because, he asserted, he had not borrowed for it "an expression, a sentiment, or a character, from any dramatic writer extant." [73] Almost any scene might furnish passages and situations illustrative of the characters' extreme sensibility, but the following speech by the hero is typical:

Lion. Was ever such a wretch—I can't stay a moment in a place; where is my repose?—fled with my virtue. Was I then born for falsehood and dissimulation? I was, I was, and live to be conscious of it; to impose upon my friend; to betray my benefactor, and lie to hide my ingratitude—a monster in a moment—No, I may be the most unfortunate of men, but I will not be the most odious; while my heart is yet capable of dictating what is honest, I will obey its voice.[74]

And all the while Lionel is actually guiltless, and must have seemed so to the audience, who perhaps found vicarious pleasure in seeing him revel in his emotions.

Another minor playwright is Edward Thomson, a naval lieutenant before he wrote his first play. Encouraged by Garrick, who later helped him to obtain a captain's commission, he wrote for the stage. In the mid-century period three short pieces—*The Hobby Horse* (1766), a farce; *The Syrens* (1776), a masque; and *St. Helena* (1777), an interlude—were produced at the patent theaters, as were his two alterations *The Fair Quaker* (1773) and *The Beggar's Opera* (1777). Neither his original plays nor his alterations had much success.

A military man of considerably higher station than either of the preceding was General Burgoyne, whose comic opera *The Maid of the Oaks* (1774) came to the stage almost by accident. It had originally been written, in a somewhat different form, as an entertainment for the wedding of the author's nephew, but was produced at Drury Lane to take advantage of the popular interest in the *fête champêtre* at Banstead Downs, where the wedding had occurred.[75] The author, who was an amateur actor, a gambler, a member of all the fashionable clubs, as well as a dramatist and military leader,[76] serves to represent those among the gentry who were dabblers in literature and as such were almost infallibly led to try a play or two.

John Hawkesworth, a Presbyterian watchmaker, later turned to literature, although much of his energy was spent on his duties as a director of the East India Company.[77] He tried his hand at alteration, as did most of the authors and poetasters of the day; and his *Amphitryon* and *Oroonoko,* altered respectively from Dryden and Southerne, were both produced at Drury Lane. Turning to musical pieces, he produced *Edgar and Emeline* (1761), a "fairy tale" with music by Michael Arne, and two oratorios, *Zimri* (1760) and *The Fall of Egypt* (1774).[78]

Another artisan-author was Joseph Reed. He is invariably identified as "the rope-maker," which profession he followed at his native Stockton and later near London, until he turned to the writing of plays in 1758. He furnished the repertory with a burlesque, two farces, a comic opera, and a tragedy. Most of his efforts met with little success, and Murphy calls his tragedy *Dido* (1767) a "still-born Play." [79] His comic opera *Tom Jones* (1769) was, however, given a better reception, because in it he was exploiting the genre that Bickerstaffe had popularized.[80]

Henry Crisp and Henry Jones represent lower ranks of society. The former, a member of the Custom House, was the author of a single tragedy, *Virginia* (1754). The play, based on the familiar story of Appius and Virginia, was well received and had eleven performances in the season but was never revived thereafter. Jones was an Irish bricklayer who early showed poetic tendencies, composing, it was said, his verses while he worked, so that "his walls and poems rose in growth together." [81] His dramatic attempts were both in the tragic vein: *The Earl of Essex* (1753) and the unfinished *The Cave of Idra,* later revised and completed by Hiffernan, who produced it at Drury Lane as *The Heroine of the Cave* (1774).[82] *The Earl of Essex* was revived in several seasons.

Of a still lower rank was Robert Dodsley, a footman who wrote verses and became the most influential publisher in London. His first dramatic attempts, satires written under the influence of Fielding, were highly successful. Most popular was *The King and the Miller of Mansfield* (1737), which was frequently revived throughout the forty-year period. He also tried his hand at ballad opera, a type popularized shortly before by Gay, and produced *The Blind Beggar of Benthnal Green* in 1741. But perhaps Dodsley the dramatist should be remembered as the author of his one tragedy, *Cleone* (1758), even though it was less successful than some of his shorter pieces. Although *Cleone* met with much applause in its initial season, it was revived only fitfully thereafter and lingered to a slow death within a decade. But it promised, although with little effect upon the later repertory, to bring to the stage a type of tragedy with a greater vitality than had most other serious drama of its time. It appealed strongly to the emotions, and the last scenes, in which Cleone's madness is shown, were thought to be "wrought to the highest Pitch." [83] It produced an illusion of historical reality without being bound to actual legend or event, and it exploited interest in domestic tragedy.[84] If Dodsley had had a successor in this vein—one who brought to dramatic composition greater poetic gifts and a surer knowledge of the stage—he might have been a pioneer in an enduring and worthy dramatic genre instead of a lone experimenter.

Within this miscellaneous category of writers, then, were dilettanti and deliberate artists, writers who turned out many plays and others who tried the stage only once, men from a variety of professions and social strata. What justifies their treatment as a single group, and at the same time distinguishes them from the actor-authors or the clerical and literary dramatists, is a negative quality—their lack of technical understanding of the stage and, for the most part, of traditional learning and literary experience. They could hardly be expected, therefore, to innovate or even to excel. They were attracted to the stage for various reasons and, in trying their hands at drama, were largely content to follow, usually at some distance, a popular fashion—sentimental comedy, comic opera, or pathetic tragedy. Neither their vocation nor their education encouraged them to persist in an endeavor that did not promise success; consequently most of them wrote but little, unless, like Bickerstaffe, they found a congenial type of drama to exploit. Thus, although the dramatists in this group are numerous, they were influential in determining the theatrical repertory neither in furnishing a large quantity of actable drama nor in supplying plays of high quality.

Insofar as the repertory reflects the influence of contemporary playwrights, we must conclude that the nature of the repertory was determined primarily by those already connected with the theater who attempted to add to their laurels by writing plays, and to a much slighter extent by those others— scholars and poets for the most part—who brought to the drama their learning and literary power. The fact that on the whole the level of dramatic composition in the mid-eighteenth century does not rise above sterile mediocrity must, of course, also be charged principally to these two groups. If playwrights had succeeded in dressing the philosopher-historian's "man in general" [85] in suitable histrionic garments, they would have had an influence on theatrical history similar to that exerted in other ages by a Shakespeare, a Dryden, or a Shaw. But instead we must look to the actor for the source of the vitality that contemporary drama had, and to the spectators' innate (and perhaps to them, inexplicable) preference for tested stock pieces of an earlier day, retained in the repertory in spite of anachronism or rule.

PART III: THE CONDITIONS—
AMATEUR

CHAPTER TEN

The Audience

On a balmy May evening a certain "fashionable Baronet," whose attention was called to the fragrance of the countryside through which he was then walking, said: "This may be very well; but for my part, I prefer the smell of a flambeau at the play-house." [1] The baronet was hardly alone in his opinion, for contemporary records indicate that interest in the drama and the theater was remarkably high during the mid-eighteenth century. Arthur Murphy thought the theater "engrossed the minds of men to such a degree, that it may now be said, that there existed in England a *fourth estate,* King, Lords, and Commons, and Drury-Lane play-house," [2] and declared that "dramatic poetry was universally in vogue." [3] Nor was this interest in the theater limited to certain social classes or economic groups. The anonymous author of *Theatrical Biography* (1772), explaining why he undertook to edit the memoirs of the actors, felt that

in the whole catalogue of public professions, none have engaged curiosity so much as the theatre: ministers of state have indeed long been a favourite topic with many, but then this is confined to a certain set, whilst the stage, like a game of chance, engages the attention of all. [4]

Theatergoing, it was remarked, had indeed become the "favourite amusement of all degrees and ranks throughout the city of Westminster." [5] It was by no means even restricted to the residents of the metropolis. Visitors to London also regularly attended the theaters, which, along with Westminster Abbey and the Tower, were included in the countryman's usual round. [6] We can therefore expect to find that the typical audience was both large and heterogeneous.

[1] For notes to chap. 10, see pp. 333-334.

Throughout the mid-century period, securing a seat in the playhouses often necessitated waiting outside the theater for as much as an hour—sometimes longer. Or a more affluent person might send his footman to hold his seat from mid-afternoon until the hour of performance—usually six o'clock. The theaters were not, of course, always full. A weak company at one of the patent houses, current fashions of one kind or another, political issues of the moment—these and many other factors had a direct effect upon attendance. Even an excellent actor in a popular play might occasionally fail to fill the boxes and benches. But theaters did not usually lack a large body of spectators.

How consistently the theaters were frequented throughout the mid-century can best be seen by noting such comments of contemporary playgoers as the following, which, drawn at random from letters and diaries, may be regarded as representative. The journal of Mrs. Boscawen, the wife of a famous admiral and one of the "blues," contains this entry for 1748: "And, as to plays, Mr. Garrick is so crowded that I have no chance of seeing him, but when some charitable body provides a place and invites me to it." [7] George Dempster wrote to his friend in 1756: "In dirt and boots I flew there [Drury Lane theater] and found good fortune had just preserved one place in the whole house for me." [8] Two years later, John Baker wrote in his diary: "I went 'Provoked Husband' and 'Upholsterer'—Mr. Hardham's box, for came not till 2nd act and no other room." [9]

Later in the period the situation had not changed. Walpole wrote to Horace Mann in 1763: ". . . at present all the boxes are taken for a month." [10] In the following year Lord Bath wrote to Mrs. Montagu: "Last night I went to the play, it was as full as it could hold. . . ." [11] A letter from Mrs. Delany to Miss Dewes in 1768 mentions not only the size but also the appearance of the audience: ". . . such a crowd as was in the pit I never heard of. They were so close and so hot that every man pulled off his coat and sat in his waistcoat!—some had sleeves, more had none, and the various hues made a most surprising sight!" [12] Baker's diary contains this entry for 1772: "To Drury Lane—not a place anywhere." [13] Young Samuel Johnson of Devonshire describes the hardships of his Uncle Daniel in 1775, who ". . . after a fruitless attempt to get into the Pit, and infinite trouble to get into the Gallery . . . could at last get but room enough to stand, with 500 weight, Uncle says, all the time upon his back." [14] And several months later, George Cumberland wrote to his brother: ". . . the House was full so full you could not have thrust your little finger in, notwithstanding your Plague sweeps us away by dozens. . . ." [15] As is suggested by the various dates of these contemporary remarks, which it will be noted extend through the entire mid-century, the popularity of the theater as a place of entertainment was persistent. Although it cannot be doubted, in view of several of the above quotations, that Garrick, the favorite actor, had a great deal to do with upholding the position of the theater, Covent Garden—and Drury Lane when Garrick was not acting—also drew large and frequent crowds. To attribute the phenomenal popularity of the mid-century theater to the energy and genius of a single person—even though that person can justly be said to have dominated the London stage—is therefore a distortion of the picture.

Not only were mid-century audiences large, but they were also exceedingly heterogeneous, a situation far different from that which had prevailed in the later seventeenth century, when audiences were relatively small and were made up generally of members of the higher social ranks. In contrast, during the eighteenth century anyone from His Majesty to the "sallow Jews and the Gentry of *Wapping* and *Rag-Fair*" [16] might be found in the theater. Although the king himself was present only on occasion—and then most often at Covent Garden, where there was an easy passage from his box to the Green Room[17]—the nobility was well represented. Samuel Foote's biographer William Cooke speaks, for example, of the "crowded boxes of beauty and elegance" [18] at even an inferior play.

As is suggested by Cooke's remark, the persons of the higher ranks of society regularly occupied the boxes, which lined both sides of the eighteenth-century theater and extended beyond the proscenium on and above the stage itself. The part of the audience that sat in the boxes did not always attend primarily to see the play, however, as is more than once noted by contemporaries. Mrs. Boscawen wrote to Mrs. Delany in 1770:

on Thursday, when Garrick acted, [Mrs. Montagu] had Lord Chatham's children at dinner, and carried them to the play. His lordship *himself* was to have been of her party (Miss Mary Pitt told me), had not the gout intervened; but for this contretemps I think my friend's box would have been honoured *with the acclamations of the upper gallery.*[19]

Personal and political motives are also suggested by a letter from the Earl of Buckingham to the Dowager Countess of Suffolk in 1763. He had just read in the newspapers reaching him at St. Petersburg that Lord Cranby, Mr. Wilkes, and the Reverend Mr. Churchill had been seen together in a side box at Drury Lane, which occurrence, he thought, must have been "to the great satisfaction of the pit and gallery." [20] Sometimes the motive was merely personal vanity. A little-known novelist of the period remarks of one of his characters that "not any one came into the side-box at a playhouse with so graceful a negligence . . . ," [21] and William Hays exclaims in an epigram, "See the mix'd croud! how giddy, lewd, and vain." [22] Nor were the boxes always gracefully occupied. Lord Beauchamp ironically informed Lady Hartford in 1742 that he "can't help mentioning how well the two stage boxes were filled: in one there was Lady Delves, who drinks like a fish, and Mrs. Cavendish; in the other, the famous Mrs. Hamilton; so I think there was good company." [23]

Those who came rather to be seen than to see the play frequently invaded the stage itself, where they sat on temporarily erected benches which occupied much of the rear of the stage. At various times the managers had attempted to stop the practice, which many in the audience found annoying. One who called himself a "six-penny pamphleteer," for example, complained to Garrick in 1748:

this Seat of Decorum is once more over-run by the *Goths* and *Vandals:* At present the Beaux pop in and out with as little Opposition as Modesty; and have made so absolute a *Burrow* of the Stage, that unless they are *ferretted* out by some Means or other, we may bid farewel to Theatrical Entertainments.[24]

How detrimental to dramatic illusion the presence of spectators on the stage could be is shown by the many contemporary accounts of actors' difficulties in carrying on the necessary stage business. Mrs. Cibber, as Juliet, for example, found it possible to enter the tomb of the Capulets only by pushing her way

through crowds of people! It had long been customary to erect
seats on the stage for benefits to increase the beneficiaries' in-
come from the performances, thus making it difficult for the
managers to abolish the practice. But at last they succeeded—
Garrick seems to have been the one to take the courageous
step first—and the noisome custom, which had survived from
Elizabethan times, was finally and permanently ended. But
aside from those who preferred to sit on the stage whenever
possible, members of the aristocracy and those of considerable
wealth—a group that gradually came to include the rich merchants and their wives—were to be found in the boxes, where
they could see the performance well if they chose, and where,
because of their elevation above the pit, they could be clearly
seen by those sitting both above and below.

Above the boxes and occupying most of the rear of the theaters ranged the two galleries, to which admission could be had
for as little as one and two shillings. Here sat those at the
other end of the social scale. The uppermost gallery was regarded by the footmen of the nobility as their own special
province. This right was jealously guarded, as was shown on
one occasion when a great number of footmen threatened to
burn down the house "unless they were immediately admitted
into what they call *their* Gallery." [25] In the galleries might
also be found those "Gentry of *Wapping* and *Rag-Fair*," or
their counterparts of the City, who sometimes made theatergoing precarious for the more affluent. Young Johnson's Uncle
Daniel, besides his difficulties getting into the theater already
noted, "had His pocket pickt of a knife which he sot a great
value on . . .";[26] and in the dramatic interlude *New Brooms,*
which Colman wrote for the opening of his theater in 1777,
Mr. Furrow says: ". . . have a care of thy metal watch, Frank!
Mind your pockets, dame Furrow! A Plaguy pick-pocket place,
this same play-house, I promise you." [27]

It should not be thought, however, that those in the galleries
were merely noisy and riotous. They must have included a
large number of habitués whose approval managers and actors
alike sought to gain. Contemporary annalists furnish evidence
that those in the galleries were often influential members of
the audience, even when their wishes ran counter to those of
the spectators in the boxes.[28] Garrick, for example, often found
it expedient to address them directly, as in the prologues to

Desert Island and *Florizel and Perdita;* in the latter he calls them "my hearts of oak," and in the "Occasional Prologue," spoken when he retired from the stage, he says:

> To you, ye Gods! I make my last appeal
> You have a right to judge, as well as feel.

There was good reason for such managerial strategy. There was also theatrical precedent, for it seems clear that the galleryites of the eighteenth century were the successors to the groundlings of the sixteenth;[29] and it is well known that Shakespeare and his contemporaries were often careful to keep in mind that important segment of the audience. Whereas the gentlemen in the boxes might occasionally draw their swords if they felt that a favorite actress had been affronted or the privileges of their station had been slighted, these inhabitants of the galleries expressed themselves both more frequently and more vociferously, often with a shower of decaying fruit or dried peas. But they were equally ready to applaud a favorite actor or a well-delivered line. Although socially inferior to the other members of the audience, they too exerted power. Between these two extremes of the social order were the merchants, clerks, and professional men who made up most of the pit audience. It was this element that seems to have furnished the stabilizing force. The actor Charles Macklin, recalling the days of his triumph as Shylock in 1741, said: "We had few riots and disturbances, the gravity and good sense of the pit not only kept the house in order, but the players likewise." [30] The anonymous author of a letter to Caleb D'Anvers was describing the pit audience when he said that *"the Patrons of the Stage* . . . include most People of *Wit* and *Taste,* as well as Multitudes of *good Sense* and *exemplary Virtue."* [31] Not everyone, however, held such an opinion. Colley Cibber, angry at the bad reception given his *Love in a Riddle* when it was brought out at Drury Lane in 1729, remarked: "I had not considered, poor devil! that, from the security of a full pit, dunces might be critics, cowards valiant, and apprentices gentlemen!" [32] And later in the period George Steevens complained in a letter to Garrick: "One hour I was squeezed to death at the door in Bow Street; another spent I in the pit among half the blackguards about town. . . ." [33] But Cibber

was speaking as a disappointed author and Steevens as a patron
who, he felt, had been given less consideration than he deserved.
More important evidence of the pit's merits is the fact that
numerous prologues and epilogues were specifically directed
at the critical audience that sat there. From such a passage as
this from the epilogue to *The Lying Valet* it is apparent that
those in the pit were regularly regarded as judges whose approbation the professional stage must have:

> *The* poet, *willing to secure the pit,*
> *Gives out, his play has humour, taste, and wit:*
> *The cause comes on, and, while the judges try,*
> *Each groan and catcall gives the bard the lye.*

Scores of similar remarks can readily be found. That such
special attention was given the pit from the stage attests also
the recognition by the managers and their acting companies of
the growing influence and position of the middle class, since
it was largely members of that social rank who sat there.

Such in general was the nature of the mid-eighteenth-century theater audience, heterogeneous in its make-up but united
in its continuing interest in its "favourite amusement." On
occasion, however, special circumstances might temporarily
prevail. At the first performance of a new play, for example,
the theater was sometimes packed with the author's friends,
who came to insure the play's success. When Goldsmith's *She
Stoops to Conquer* was given its first performance, loyal friends
of the author, strategically placed among the crowd, applauded
heartily at opportune moments, taking their cue from Dr.
Johnson in the pit.[34] On the day after Hoole's tragedy *Cleonice*
had reached the stage, the *Morning Post* reported: "We cannot help remarking that the boxes were well-lined with the
author's friends, and resembled a levee of the late Lord Clive's;
India House had vomited up its directors, its proprietors, its
clerks." [35] But, on the whole, the impression we get of the
nightly audiences is that they were very much the same in composition throughout a season and from one season to the next.
The pit, the boxes, and the galleries might each have prejudices
and propensities of their own, but they were stable quantities
whose measure the efficient manager and the popular actor had
carefully taken.

It was for this audience that Dr. Johnson wrote the "Prologue Spoken by Mr. Garrick at the Opening of the Theatre in Drury-Lane, 1747," which contains the famous lines:

> Ah! let not Censure term our Fate our Choice,
> The Stage but echoes back the publick Voice.
> The Drama's Laws the Drama's Patrons give,
> For we that live to please, must please to live.

Undoubtedly Johnson overstated the case, and thereby flattered the audience—a wary, and probably a necessary, procedure to assure for his friend and former pupil a favorable reception as the new manager of one of London's two patent theaters. It was, however, not only the "publick Voice" that regulated the theater, but also the playwrights of the day, the actors with their particular fortes and preferences, as well as the managers themselves. But the audience, nevertheless, had great influence on the regulation of the repertory, and in various ways helped to determine the dramatic fare of the eighteenth century. Its emotional and moralistic tendencies, its patriotic fervor, its concern for what are usually termed "middle-class virtues" and for prudential ethics, its increasing preoccupation with the merely tuneful and spectacular, and the fascination that the theatrical "Chapter of Accidents" and the *causerie du théâtre* held for a large segment of the populace—all these are necessarily reflected in that repertory. The specific manifestations of these various prepossessions in terms of the repertory must be discovered, therefore, if we are to understand the precise role of the eighteenth-century audience.

The problem of determining the extent to which the repertory reflected the temper of the audience is inextricably involved with the question: why did people go to the theater? Dr. Johnson, in the famous "Preface" to his edition of Shakespeare, had a ready answer: "They came to hear a certain number of lines recited with just gesture and elegant modulation." The "six-penny pamphleteer" cited earlier seems to agree:

. . . provided you [he is addressing Garrick] entertain 'em well at the Theatre, and give 'em *Richard, Hamlet, Lear, Bayes,* &c, with Propriety and Decorum, and at the usual Price, they won't trouble their Heads whether Mr. *G-----k* has offended Authors, wrong'd his Actors, lain with the Actresses, or ev'n robb'd a Church.[36]

But the answer is not so simple; and the latter author himself admits later that what he has said applies to only a fraction of the audience. Many indeed might be the reasons why the spectator was in attendance; and, more important for our purpose, many were the ways in which his predilections helped to determine the theatrical repertory.

CHAPTER ELEVEN

Fashions and Fancies

In an age when taste was "the darling idol of the polite world," [1] fashion alone frequently determined the size of theater audiences; for, to be a virtuoso, a connoisseur, a man of taste (all coveted—and fashionable—appellations of the day), was also to know and follow the prevailing fashions, including those related to the theater. Nor was this attitude restricted to the "polite world" that came to the theater in crested coaches. The middle class, though it might despise the imprudence and impecuniosity of the nobility, emulated its betters in virtu. [2] So there were fashionable theaters, fashionable days for playgoing, fashionable actors, and fashionable plays. The fashion of the hour might rest on precedent qualities of a more tangible nature, but for the hour—or the season—fashion alone often sufficed.

As to fashionable theaters, a comment in the *London Chronicle* is both typical and significant. The writer notes that in 1758 the ladies were again attending Covent Garden, where they had not been accustomed to going for some time. [3] That Covent Garden was sometimes an unfashionable theater is also suggested by a letter from Mrs. Wilkinson to her actor-son, then in Dublin: "The house at Covent Garden is quite forsaken, and Rich gives away his box tickets by the Dozen." [4] Wilkinson himself refers frequently to fashionable nights. Speaking of Vanbrugh's *The Confederacy,* a play sufficiently popular to be revived sixty-four times at the two patent theaters during the mid-century, he remarks of the thin audience that it was "not an extra-ordinary circumstance to relate then of an unfashionable night at Covent-Garden Theatre." [5] Drury Lane apparently was never an unfashionable theater in the mid-eighteenth century; it is, however, admittedly difficult to distinguish here between the theater itself and its usually strong

[1] For notes to chap. 11, see pp. 334-337.

company—which included most of the fashionable actors of the time. Wilkinson's observations on operagoing are especially revealing. He says: "The prevalence of custom is astonishing—a Lady in London will go to a known bad opera on Saturday, and though she professes being an amateur in music will not go on the Tuesday, though a good opera, because it *is* Tuesday." [6] (In contrast, Saturday night was unfashionable at Dublin's Theatre-Royal.) What was true of the opera in London was also true of the play. Intrinsic merit was frequently of no consequence; for ". . . on fashionable nights . . . what the play is, does not signify the flirt of a fan." [7]

As to fashions in actors, Garrick was, of course, the favorite player of the time. His first appearance at Goodman's Fields, though a remote and unfashionable theater, brought there the "splendour of St. James's and Grosvenor-square; the coaches of the nobility filled up the space from Templebar to Whitechapel. . . . not to admire him would not only have argued an absence of taste, but the grossest stupidity." [8] Walpole, who had seen the acting of Garrick, said that although he saw "nothing wonderful in it . . . it is heresy to say so." [9] After Garrick began acting at the patent theaters, however, it was probably his histrionic ability alone rather than recurrent fashionableness that made him almost continuously popular. Two other actors of the time sometimes regarded in a similar light were James Quin and Samuel Foote. Quin, a comedian who had a strong following and was highly esteemed generally, at times was a fashionable actor as well. Then large crowds could be expected to see him in even his poorest roles. But fashions could also reverse themselves and become as detrimental to actors as they had previously been beneficial. In the 1750-1751 season at Covent Garden, for example, Quin fell out of favor, and it then became fashionable to hiss at his appearance even in his best parts.[10] Of Foote, another of Garrick's contemporaries, Wilkinson remarks, "It would have been much more unfashionable not to have laughed at Foote's jokes than even at Quin's." [11] Foote's "dish of tea" at the Little Theatre in the Haymarket, a ruse by which he circumvented the Licensing Act of 1737, became for a time a society craze.[12] Among the lesser actors, Ned Shuter stood for a while in the dazzling light of social favor and on one occasion is spoken of as having "brought the whole London world" to Covent Garden.[13] Actresses too enjoyed the same kind of transient glory. Mrs. Abington, who set styles in dress because of her popularity on the stage,[14] became one of the chief ornaments of the London theater, and Dr. Johnson admitted that he attended her benefit only "Because, Sir, she is a favourite of the public." [15] Managers were, of course, quick to exploit the members of their companies who came into such favor. For example, when it became fashionable to see Mrs. Woffington as Sir Harry Wildair in *The Constant Couple,* "the managers soon found it to be to their interest to announce her frequently for that favourite character; it proved a constant charm to fill their houses." [16]

Fashions in plays frequently depended upon fashions in actors, but there are many instances where this elusive quality is independently discernible. Bentley's *The Wishes; or, Harlequin's Mouth Open'd* had been so much discussed while it was being privately rehearsed that a large crowd turned out to see it.[17] Cumberland's *The West Indian* drew a large audience on its first night for a similar reason.[18] Foote's *The Author* became, in its second season, "so fashionable, that *Becky— my dear Becky,* was a constant phrase from all ranks of people both high and low, as they walked the streets of London." [19] The same author's *The Minor* became such a "rage astonishing [that] it is not describable the crowds of all degrees that crushed in to that little theatre in the Haymarket, night after night in the hottest months of the year." [20] Fashion likewise followed plays into print. Lady Luxborough, for example, adopts an apologetic tone when she writes to the Duchess of Somerset: "I am almost ashamed to own I have not read . . . *Boadicia,* nor *Philoclea.*" [21] And the Countess of Hertford wrote to the Countess of Pomfret about *Mustapha:* ". . . I hear it so much commended, that, as soon as it is printed, I will endeavour to find some means of conveying it to you";[22] and of *Edward and Eleanora:* "I hear it is the fashion to decry it extremely; but, I own, I am ungenteel enough to prefer it infinitely to *Agamemnon.*" [23] Again it is apparent that vogue rather than merit often determined the repertory.

Not only was theatergoing a favorite amusement, but anything concerning the theater and its company seems to have been of wide and popular interest. Garrick's prologue to *The Englishman in Paris* probably does not greatly overdraw the picture:

Sir *Peter Primrose,* smirking o'er his tea,
Sinks from himself and politicks, to me.
Papers, boy!—Here, Sir! Tam, what news to-day?
Foote, Sir, is advertised—what—run away!
No, Sir, he acts this week at Drury-Lane.
How's that! (cries *Feeble Grub*) Foote come again!
I thought that fool had done his devil's dance;
Was he not hang'd some months ago in France?

Letters from Londoners abroad to their friends in town were frequently devoted to inquiries about the theaters. The Earl of Buckinghamshire's letter quoted earlier is only one of many such; and Lord Orrery, writing from Dublin in 1750, makes a similar request of his friend Riley Towers: "Now let me inquire after the Garrick, the Quin, the Barry, and that sweet Syren, Mrs. Cibber? Have you any Harlequins? Any new Plays, or any old Dramas revived?" [24]

This interest, whether directed to matters as important to the public as changes in theater policy or to the trivia of stage gossip, naturally influenced the size of the audiences and consequently the repertory. On one occasion, for example, when Mrs. Bellamy was to make her first appearance on the London stage, a "splendid audience" turned out to see her, a not unusual occurrence when a new actress was announced. But here novelty was not the only lure; for Quin and Rich, both of whom had large—and sometimes contentious—followings, had recently, it was well known, rather violently disagreed about the probability of her success. This minor war of the green-room, which had been widely noised about town, was therefore instrumental in causing Mrs. Bellamy to attract such large crowds, which not only came to see the new actress but also to support the respective factions.[25] Another contention, this time between actresses, occurred when *The Rival Queens*—an appropriate play for the occasion—was revived at Covent Garden. Although Lee's play was not one of the most popular revivals of the mid-century, at this time it was more than usually successful, because the dramatic dispute between the queens was enhanced by the notorious personal dispute between Mrs. Bellamy and Mrs. Woffington, who played the title roles.[26] This episode became so famous that the following season Foote successfully exploited the popular interest with a dramatic entertainment titled *The Green-Room Squabble; or, a Battle*

Royal between the Queen of Babylon and the Daughter of Darius. Interest in the personal life of Garrick was also a determinant of the repertory. A notable example is the frequency with which *Much Ado About Nothing* was performed shortly after his marriage in 1749. Shakespeare's comedy was often called for at that time because the audience found great pleasure in identifying the newly married "Roscius" with Benedick, an identification that was made with "infinite mirth" and "the loudest applause." [27] Examples of these kinds could readily be multiplied. It is apparent that the theater held a highly important place in the average Londoner's life and that he was interested in anything that concerned the stage. A man like Nat Clarke, the original Filch in *The Beggar's Opera,* was popular because as a living storehouse of theatrical information he made himself "acceptable to busy enquirers after theatrical matters by communicating to them many a laughable anecdote." [28]

One of the results of such interest was a matter of considerable influence on the repertory. Popular curiosity about the theatrical "Chapter of Accidents" frequently resulted in creating for an individual actor a strong following, which could best show its loyalty to the player on his benefit night. The Duchess of Queensberry, for example, took 250 tickets and all but three of the boxes on the night of Mrs. Bellamy's benefit.[29] As benefit nights became more and more frequent (Drury Lane allowed benefits not only to the actors but also to the prompter, the doorkeeper, and other attendants), a steadily larger number of the plays performed in a season were selected for special, and usually personal, reasons; and benefit performances eventually came to bulk large in the total number of play nights, particularly in the latter part of each annual season. On such nights the manager's worries about the size of the house were temporarily put to rest. In fact the managers seem to have taken advantage of benefit nights occasionally in order to stimulate wearying theatergoers; for example, Wilkinson remarks of one season: ". . . the business was so bad, that we were obliged to begin the benefits, in hopes that what our good acting could not produce, yet regard for individuals would soften their hearts and fill the house." [30]

In at least three different ways this practice had an important effect on the repertory. When the beneficiary was one of the leading members of the company, the play chosen for the performance usually contained the role in which the benefiting actor was most admired by the audience. Thus, Barry frequently chose *Othello;* Quin, one of the *Henry IV* plays; Mrs. Woffington, *The Constant Couple;* Mrs. Bellamy, *The Distrest Mother;* and Mrs. Cibber, *Zara.* Such a tendency increased the proportion of stock plays in the total repertory. When the beneficiary was a lesser actor, he frequently selected one of the heaviest roles, such as Hamlet, Lear, Richard III, or Othello. Thereby he was at once satisfying an ambition to try his hand in the greatest parts the repertory had to offer (since the benefiting actor had the right to cast the performance) and setting himself up temporarily—often at the insistence of particular friends —as a rival to Garrick, Quin, Barry, or some other leading actor of the day for whatever advantage might accrue to him. This tendency also helped to increase the frequency of performing the stock pieces, especially the great tragedies of Shakespeare. Finally, as the number of nights devoted to benefits increased, and because that part of the season considered best for benefit nights was the same as that in which new pieces were regularly brought to the stage, the practice resulted in limiting the number of new plays that could conveniently be introduced in a season, since a new play was seldom performed as a benefit. The few exceptions were usually afterpieces. Sheridan, for example, gave to Laurence Clinch (the actor whose success as O'Trigger saved *The Rivals* from being damned) the newly written farce titled *St. Patrick's Day* for his benefit in gratitude for his acting.[31] The use of a new full-length play for a benefit was indeed exceptional. The expenses involved in mounting a new comedy or tragedy and the traditional obligation of the manager to make every third performance a benefit for the playwright made almost impossible the use of plays in their first season for actors' benefits. Thus the continuing practice of devoting many nights to benefit performances tended, on all three counts, to reinforce the effects of such other characteristics of theatrical history in the mid-eighteenth century as the audience's inclination to identify actor and character, the possession of parts, the relatively unchanging personnel of the theater companies, and the increased interest in older English drama—all of which resulted in the maintenance of an unusually large number of stock pieces throughout the forty-year period, at the expense of new drama.

It is therefore accurate to say that the practice also tended to produce a theatrical—as distinct from a dramatic, a critical, or a social—environment that was relatively uncongenial to new plays.

Fashions directly related to theatergoing and those concerning the actors themselves thus were obviously far-reaching in their influence upon the repertory, even though they may be regarded as extrinsic to the drama. Another kind of contemporary interest among many of the spectators also played an important part in determining what plays should reach the stage. These interests, which are more intrinsic in nature, may be called literary fashions.

One of the most important of these was the Shakespearean revival, which has already been discussed in some detail. A great share of the credit for this renewed interest in Shakespeare's plays as actable drama on the contemporary stage must be given, as has already been noted, to Garrick, whose personal tastes and special histrionic powers inevitably led him to the great Elizabethan's work. Other actors, especially Macklin and Quin, also contributed. Consequently not all the forces that brought about the Shakespearean revival can be attributed to the audience. There are, however, several indications that the audience did contribute to this movement in important ways. One of the most influential was that which received its stimulus from the "Shakespeare Club," a group of ladies that included "some of the first Quality, eminent likewise for their Beauty, Virtue, and just Taste," [32] who "bespoke, every week, some favourite play of this great writer." [33] Although the club limited its activity to Covent Garden, where, in the season of its greatest influence (1737-1738), three of Shakespeare's plays were revived for the first time since the closing of the theaters in 1642, and two others after a half-century or more of neglect, Drury Lane was perforce led to follow suit. The latter theater had no such cohorts in its audience, but the competition offered by the Shakespearean revivals at the rival house resulted in similar additions to the acting list. Within the next three years *As You Like It, Twelfth Night, Merchant of Venice,* and *The Comedy of Errors* were revived at Drury Lane after a long absence from the stage; *The Winter's Tale* and *All's Well That Ends Well* were restored to the stage at Goodman's Fields in the same period; and *Cymbeline* was later added to the Covent Garden repertory. All these plays, it should be noted, were revived before Garrick's first appearance on the London stage, and he cannot therefore be credited with their restoration.

Rather, the audience must be credited with an increasing interest in Shakespeare. Many of his plays, particularly the tragedies, provided sustenance for the sensibility of the time. Davies regarded this quality as highly important in maintaining Shakespeare's drama on the stage: "It is to such abundant moral and pathetic applications to our feelings, that he owes a great part of that preference we give him over all other dramatic writers." [34] Likewise, the opportunity that Shakespearean drama gave the skillful actor to portray subtleties and transitions of passion contributed to their popularity at a time when amateur and professional critic alike considered themselves capable judges of acting techniques.[35] Supporting evidence of the audience's importance to the Shakespearean revival can be drawn from such manifestations as the favorable reception of the many editions of both single plays and collected works, the popular interest in the Shakespeare jubilee at Stratford and the dramatic entertainments brought to the stage soon after in celebration of that event, the formation of private libraries of early English drama, and the appearance of such books as *Thesaurus Dramaticus* (1724) and Dodsley's *Collection of Old Plays* (1744). Here, of course, we come face to face with the phenomenon known as antiquarianism, which exerted a considerable influence on the theater as it did upon most other aspects of contemporary cultural activity.

A second literary fashion that affected the repertory is related to the rise of the novel. Characters, situations, and whole plots of one literary form were occasionally taken over by the other. This kind of influence, however, was rather that of playwright upon novelist or the reverse than that of audience upon repertory. But it should be mentioned that the popularization of a particular theme by one form might result in increased patronage for or interest in the other when the same theme was used. Thus, the audience recognized in Joseph and Charles Surface in *The School for Scandal* the theatrical counterparts of Blifil and the hero in *Tom Jones,* and Fielding's novel in turn was influenced by *The Foundling,* a play by Moore.[36] Likewise, novel readers had come to regard themselves as capable critics of new drama that exploited the same situations that the novelists were finding to be popular. A notable instance concerns the connection between sentimental comedy and novels in the Richardsonian tradition. Cooke says, for example:

The mass of the public saw the innovation [of the later sentimental comedy] with a kind of indolent pleasure not entirely devoid of self-gratification. It was so much like the light fantastic kind of novel writing which their wives and daughters read in the parlour, that they were thus far critics when they came to the theatre. Having a previous knowledge how a modern love-match should be commenced, entangled, disentangled, and concluded, they became umpires of the drama, instead of mere spectators. . . .[37]

This kind of critical—or perhaps pseudocritical—involvement at times must have been of first importance as an influence upon the repertory. In fact it is probably not claiming too much credit for the influence of the novel to assert that the popularity of Steele's and Cibber's plays would not have been so long-lasting, and their influence upon such later playwrights as Kelly, Cumberland, and Murphy so vital, if the mid-century novels had not contributed to the literary vitalization of sentimentalism. It is even more certain that the sentimental novel, which had opportunities of expression and technique impossible to the stage, contributed to the decline of a type of drama already attenuated by its superficial and dittographic practices. But if the growing popularity of novel reading was often influential in attracting spectators to the theater, it could have a directly opposite effect. Moore's *Gil Blas,* for example, met with little success, it was said, because not even a Garrick could represent to the audience's satisfaction the hero of the romance, which was then being widely read.[38] Here we have an example of the kind of dissatisfaction that has led modern authors and publishers to omit pictorial illustrations from their novels.

Another species of novel had a somewhat similar relationship to drama. Near the end of the mid-century period there was a growing interest in those elements of both drama and novel that are designated as "Gothic." It has customarily been held that the popularity of the Gothic novel, beginning with Walpole's *Castle of Otranto,* caused playwrights to exploit this interest by giving a similar coloring to their plays. Considerable evidence shows, however, that the influence may have operated in the opposite direction.[39] But in either event the original stimulus is to be found in the public itself. It was an age when architects designed buildings that were at the same time decorative as "ruined" abbeys and useful as sheepfolds. Horace Mann sent to Walpole what he considered a suitable gift, a "pretty altar-tomb," [40] which undoubtedly was given a suitable niche in Walpole's neo-Gothic castle at Strawberry Hill. Serpentine walks and broken "prospects" had become necessary for fashionable estates, an affectation that furnished matter for pleasant satire in *The Clandestine Marriage* (I, ii):

Lord Ogleby. A most excellent serpentine! It forms a perfect maze, and winds like a true-lover's knot.
Sterling. Ay—here's none of your strait lines here—but all taste— zig-zag—crinkum-crankum—in and out—right and left—to and again—twisting and turning like a worm, my Lord!
Lord Ogleby. Admirably laid out indeed, Mr. Sterling! one can hardly see an inch beyond one's nose anywhere in these walks. . . .

Lord Ogle. Ruins, did you say, Mr. Sterling?
Sterl. Ay, ruins, my Lord! and they are reckoned very fine ones too. You would think them ready to tumble on your head. It has just cost me a hundred and fifty pounds to put my ruins in thorough repair. —This way, if your Lordship pleases.
Lord Ogle. *Going, stops*. What steeple's that we see yonder? the parish-church, I suppose.
Sterl. Ha! ha! ha! that's admirable. It is no church at all, my Lord! it is a spire that I have built against a tree, a field or two off, to terminate the prospect. One must always have a church, or an obelisk, or a something, to terminate the prospect, you know. That's a rule in taste, my Lord!

If a medieval atmosphere was regarded as a congenial environment for living, it is hardly surprising that the same atmosphere should be demanded in drama and novel. Only the affluent, of course, could afford such Gothic luxury in their everyday lives. The less fortunate had to be content with its reflection in imaginary guise. But since the less fortunate were usually the less literate, and since the novel therefore demanded an ability for its enjoyment beyond the reach of the multitude, the Gothic drama was the only means by which a great number could respond to this literary fashion. Thus the current popularity of medievalism had a considerable influence upon the theatrical repertory.[41]

But undoubtedly the greatest effect the new literary genre had upon the repertory was one from which the theater has never completely recovered. As conditions among the middle classes improved—and, somewhat later, among the lower classes —opportunities for education likewise improved. The result was of course an increase in literacy, and hence an increase in the number of potential novel readers. The novel indicated early that it had many advantages over the drama, especially of the kind that appealed to middle-class tastes—such as the fuller exploitation of emotional scenes, the untrammeled opportunity for reader identification with characters of great wealth or power or beauty, and the idealistic provision for romantic escapism. For many, therefore, novel reading came to replace theatergoing as an amusement. Indeed it is clear that even when Garrick and Mrs. Cibber were at their greatest powers, there were some who read plays in preference to seeing them. The development of "closet drama" was of course a related manifestation—the auctorial counterpart of the read stage play —even though it is also to be accounted for both by the growing divergence between the drama and the theater and by the simple inability of the writers to create characters and incidents that would not wither in the severe light of stage performance. Nevertheless, the drama that did reach the stage in the later eighteenth century, unsubstantial though it was by literary standards, showed the continuing influence of the novel in its choice of sentimental, romantic, and impossible fictions and by its preference for melodrama and spectacle. From the effects of this situation the drama did not recover for a century, until, under the influence of Ibsen, Shaw, the Abbey Theatre playwrights, and others, it again immersed itself in the central currents of life. But from the greater effect—the very displacement of the drama by the novel as the most popular literary form— the drama has never recovered, so that from the dominant position it held from about 1580 to about 1780 it passed to its present place of distinctly secondary importance.

A third literary fashion affecting the dramatic fare of the mid-century is to be found in the popularity of foreign drama. Many of the plays of Corneille, Molière, and Voltaire, as well as those of several lesser French dramatists, were translated into English, in which form they were sometimes acted on the London stage. More often English playwrights drew heavily upon

French plays for pieces of their own, many of which were hardly more than English adaptations. The determining factor here was probably the playwright more often than the audience. The poets who lacked genius to invent situation and character for themselves found French drama a rich storehouse of theatrical material upon which to draw. But the audience's regard for such pieces was also a determining factor, and perhaps explains why playwrights freely acknowledged their debt to specific French plays and authors, in both prologue and preface. That more than mere literary honesty motivated the playwrights who made such acknowledgments is suggested by a passage in Reynolds' *The Dramatist:* "I'll tell you,—write a play, and bad as it may possibly be, say it's a translation from the French, and interweave a few compliments on the English, and my life on't, it does wonders." [42] Thomas Davies, who on more than one occasion shows that he was a shrewd judge of audiences, offers additional testimony: "Italy, in [Shakespeare's] time, gave the ton of fashion, as France does now, to all Europe." [43] It is only one more among the numerous paradoxes of eighteenth-century England that political and cultural sentiments relating to France and the French were often diametrically opposed. Although spectators might flock to see a French comedy on a London stage, they were equally disposed to make a shambles of the theater if they felt that French actors were being given precedence over the English, as they were at the time of *The Chinese Festival.* The drama of other countries had comparatively little influence on the repertory. The day of the German Kotzebue on the English stage had not yet arrived, and the Italian influence on the theater in England was largely confined to the opera house.

Thus it can be seen that fashions directly related to the theater, as well as preoccupations with various literary phenomena, had a considerable, although sometimes an indirect, influence in determining the repertory in the mid-century. A third kind of influence, although neither literary nor theatrical, also stemmed from what I have called fashions and fancies— the interest in social customs and personal idiosyncrasies. This kind of interest had an important and direct influence because it determined the very content of the plays that were acted. It manifested itself chiefly by means of allusions, often thinly veiled, to identifiable individuals or by means of satire of social groups and fashionable practices. As might be expected, it found its most congenial vehicle in farce and caricature.

Although most of the plays added to the repertory because of this kind of interest were new works especially written for the occasion, revived plays also were made to bear a burden of contemporary reference. One of the best-known instances is the revival of Addison's *The Drummer* in the 1761-1762 season. This play, which the author had subtitled *The Haunted House,* gained a temporary popularity at that time because of the general interest throughout London in the Cock Lane ghost.[44] The managers of both patent houses brought it to the stage to take advantage of the popular excitement—the only time it was revived at both theaters in the same season during the entire mid-century, although it seems to have been carried as a minor stock piece by the Covent Garden company for some years. The growing prestige of science in an age that prided itself in its rational outlook (even though such a view was somewhat inconsistently held) also may account for the popularity of several plays that deal with pseudo science—most notably, *The Alchemist, Albumazar,* and *The Astrologer.* The first two are revived Elizabethan dramas, and the third is an alteration of Tomkis' play. It has recently been conjectured that "the satirical hit at superstition" may have contributed to their success on the stage.[45] Similarly, Shirley's *The Gamester* and Mrs. Centlivre's play of the same name owed much of their success upon revival to the prevalence of gaming in London, a situation to which Garrick specifically directed attention in the prologue he wrote for his own alteration of the former play.[46] Here a further effect on the repertory is noticeable, since the popularity of the vice and of the plays that dealt with it contributed to the origin of a new tragic drama, Moore's *The Gamester,* which had a moderate success on the stage. But perhaps the most noteworthy example is *The Rehearsal* (1672), a burlesque of heroic tragedy written by the Duke of Buckingham. Bayes, originally a satirical portrayal of Davenant, became one of Garrick's most popular roles, and the play was frequently acted as long as he was on the stage. But the play, which even in its original state was little more than a hodgepodge of caricatures and satire, constantly underwent changes in content so that it served to ridicule with satisfying contemporaneity "the public transactions—the flying follies of the day

—the debates in parliament—the absurdities of playwriters, politicians, and players. . . ." [47]

But a greater effect on the repertory is to be seen in those plays especially written to capitalize on current interests and follies. Of this practice, Davies wrote: "That the English comedians often bring on the stage, for their emolument, public, and sometimes private, transactions, cannot be controverted. Let the Receipt-tax, a farce, be an instance." [48] A better example than the unidentified farce that Davies mentioned is Burgoyne's comic opera *The Maid of the Oaks*. Originally written to serve as an entertainment given at Banstead Downs by Lord Stanley for his betrothed, Lady Betty Hamilton, it was almost immediately expanded and brought to the stage. The reason is obvious. People from all over England had flocked to the much publicized *fête champêtre* at Banstead Downs, and, it was said, "for the rest of the year all England lived in an atmosphere" of that celebrated event. [49] Such a piece could hardly fail on the public stage where those of lesser wealth and social status could participate, even though at some distance, in the affairs of the great and the fashions of the hour—any more than could the Shakespeare Jubilee performance have failed when it was brought from Stratford to Drury Lane some years earlier. [50] But in another sense such pieces as the two just mentioned are atypical, for the mode in which plays based on current events found their most congenial expression was that of satire. Satirical comedy, it will be remembered, was compatible with the spirit of the later seventeenth and early eighteenth centuries. It attained its full growth in the plays of Fielding just at the beginning of the mid-century period. But Fielding's satire was largely directed against the government, and such attacks became dangerous—and almost impossible—after the passage of the Licensing Act in 1737. Although drama continued thereafter to be used for satirical ends, the objects of satire were matters of lesser importance—of personal, social, sometimes theatrical, but seldom of national, concern.

Of those who dealt in personal satire, Samuel Foote, one of the most extraordinary persons in mid-century theatrical history, is the most famous—or, as some thought, the most notorious. Of his more than a score of dramatic pieces, mostly comedies and farces, several were largely given over to caricature of actual individuals. *The Author*, for example, one of his earliest pieces, was in this vein. When the play was produced at Drury Lane in 1757, Foote, whose powers of mimicry were much relished by audiences, acted the part of Cadwallader, the principal caricature in the piece. This portrait was drawn from a gentleman of education and fortune named Aprice, a corpulent, boisterous, and clumsy friend of Foote who was ideally suited for caricature. He was pictured as ridiculously ambitious to be considered a patron of the arts. At first he regarded the whole matter as a joke, but after his friends began to avoid him and he became generally called by the name of the character instead of his own name, he finally had the play suppressed by the lord chamberlain.[51] One of Foote's last compositions, *The Trip to Calais*, produced twenty years after *The Author*, shows him still exploiting the same vein. This comedy was to contain, in the character of Lady Kitty Crocodile, a venomous portrait of the Duchess of Kingston. Foote did not keep his plans secret, however, and eventually the duchess learned of them. Again the lord chamberlain was asked to interfere, and Foote was obliged to remove the objectionable scenes. But to give vent to his peculiar genius he altered the play to *The Capuchin,* in which Jackson, a newspaper editor and adviser to the duchess, portrayed as Dr. Viper, was the target of an attack as bitter as the one originally intended for Lady Kingston.[52] Although the affair resulted in a legal action against Foote, it also brought him crowded houses, not only on those nights when one of his controversial pieces was performed, but also on other occasions; for Foote had a large number of friends as well as enemies, and, moved either by curiosity or by admiration of his boldness, they made his theater in the Haymarket a thriving establishment. A similar effect upon the repertory is seen in Fielding's *Miss Lucy in Town* (1742). The popularity of this piece depended chiefly upon its being regarded as including a caricature of a "particular Man of Quality." [53] Here also the lord chamberlain's power of prohibiting performances was invoked, although the prohibition seems to have been shortly withdrawn.

The reception of such pieces illustrates two quite different characteristics of contemporary audiences. Because the power of censoring plays was often exerted to prohibit their performance, their support by the audience was a means of expressing its enmity to the unpopular Licensing Act of 1737; and in an age when liberty not only was a frequently used watchword but was also a cry often raised in the theaters by that large element of the population who seemed to regard the pit or the galleries as ideal vantage grounds for its utterance, crossing swords with the lord chamberlain or other officials with restrictive powers was both a popular and a patriotic pastime. A second characteristic, one of less serious import although equally revealing, is suggested by Foote's biographer in commenting on the actor's preparations before presenting one of his satires: "The name of the person intended to be mimicked, and the plot, being previously insinuated into the boxes, they were prepared for the likeness. . . ." [54] The spectators, in the author's or actor's confidence, felt complimented, and were gratified to find themselves in a position to judge the degree of likeness;[55] at the same time they could enjoy the amazement, the dismay, or perhaps even the wrath of the ignorant victim, sometimes actually present at the performance.

Fashionable follies and social classes were other favorite targets for dramatic satire. One of the most productive playwrights in this genre was Garrick, to such an extent that the *London Chronicle* called social satire "his favourite game." [56] One of his earliest pieces, *Miss in Her Teens* (1747), was directed against two classes: the swaggering young officers then frequenting coffeehouses, represented by Captain Flash; and the delicate, "pretty gentlemen," represented by Fribble. This farce was extremely popular, and Flash and Fribble were repeatedly acted by Woodward and Garrick. The play succeeded, it was said, in laughing "out of society" the two types.[57] *The Male-Coquette* (1757) had a similar purpose, ridiculing under the name of Daffodil, the hermaphroditic anomalies then frequenting Bath and other popular resorts,[58] "a set of people, whom the author thinks more prejudicial to the community, than the various characters of Bucks, Bloods, Flashes and Fribbles, which have by turns infected the town, and been justly ridiculed upon the stage." [59] Townley was another writer who tried social satire. His farce *High Life Below Stairs* (1759) was highly successful in this vein, satirizing both the "vanity of servants and the manners of the fashionable world, which are rendered completely ridiculous, when they descend from the parlour to the kitchen." [60] Thus each element in the audience had the opportunity to laugh at the expense of the other, although on occasion the footmen in the upper gallery showed their resentment rather than their sense of humor.[61]

Fashion in dress was a particularly fruitful subject for satirical purposes in the eighteenth century.[62] *Lilliput,* Garrick's farce drawn from *Gulliver's Travels,* as originally acted in 1756 at Drury Lane, was produced so that at "the sight of such diminutive creatures, adapting the follies of real life, the fashionable world might learn to lower their pride, and the dignity of vice would be lost." [63] But as it was revised by the author and acted at the opening of the Haymarket Theatre under Colman (1777), it was designed to ridicule women's extreme fashions. Included in the procession, which made up much of the performance, was "a mock profile of a fine lady, with an enormous high head, stuffed with wool, and a large cork rump, and a real lady with a tête stuck full of feathers, riding on an ostrich with a bare rump, [which] had an astonishing effect." [64] *Taste,* a farce by Foote, brought out at the Haymarket in 1776, had a similar purpose. The author appeared as Mrs. Pentweazle with an exaggerated headdress full of enormous feathers, the whole being a yard wide, which fell off as the actor left the stage. This play was reputed to have started the reform of the extravagant fashion.[65] Sheridan, writing at the same time as Foote, also seemed to think that reform was necessary. In the prologue to *A Trip to Scarborough* (1777) he remarks of the ladies:

> Were they design'd to be, when put together,
> Made up, like shuttlecocks, of cork and feather?

and in *St. Patrick's Day* (1775) he has the scheming lieutenant declare:

> Upon my word, doctor, you are right; the London ladies were always too handsome for me; then they are so defended, such a circumballation of hoop, with a breastwork of whalebone that would turn a pistol-bullet, much less Cupid's arrows—then turret on turret on top, with stores of concealed weapons, under pretence of black pins—and above all, a standard of feathers that would do honour to a knight of the Bath. Upon my conscience, I could as soon embrace an Amazon, armed at all points.

The records of theatrical performance prove that such pieces as those of Garrick, Townley, Sheridan, and Foote just mentioned were highly successful. This success can be explained in part at least by the perennial desire of audiences to laugh at the absurd, particularly when absurdity can be identified as the exclusive possession, not of themselves, but of their acquaintances or enemies.

In this group of plays may be included those directed against an element of society differing from the norm in religious conviction rather than in fashionable folly. Of this type, those attacking the Methodists created the greatest furor. Foote's *The Minor,* altered from Cibber's *The Nonjuror* in such a way as to ridicule the followers of Whitfield, caused a flurry of pamphlets to be written,[66] and inspired Israel Pottinger to write *The Methodist,* a continuation of Foote's play, printed in 1761 but unacted. *The Minor* at first met with little success. Foote was then at the Crow Street Theatre in Dublin but, upon returning to England, he altered the play and added an epilogue, "spoken by *Dr. Squintum* in the true cant of Whitfield," with the result that he enjoyed thirty-eight "full houses." [67] The tremendous success of this piece, not only in its first run but also in later seasons, was caused not only by Foote's renowned powers as a mimic but also by its satire of the Methodists.[68] But in general little dramatic satire was directed at religion, whether that of the Establishment or that of the Dissent; and it should be remembered that when *The Provok'd Wife* was "improved" for the mid-century stage, Brute appeared in the night scene disguised as a woman—no longer as an inebriated parson!

Finally, one group of plays directed their satirical thrusts at literary and theatrical practices. In *The Patron* (1764) Foote satirized in the character of Sir Thomas Lofty, the patron, the favorite subject of ridicule that had called forth attacks on Lyttelton by the progovernment periodicals in the days of Fielding. The particular object of satire in Foote's play was said to be George Bubb Dodington.[69] An earlier farce, *Taste* (1752), by the same author was directed at a larger segment of the audience. This farce ridiculed "the fashionable folly of what is called *virtu,* which in general is a pretended enthusiastic passion for the arts, without any skill or knowledge." [70] The play was little appreciated, however, except by the boxes, and had only a short run. Here is a clear indication that as early as the middle of the century the middle class had become a force sufficiently strong to determine the success or failure of a piece on purely social grounds, for within the middle class were those members of the *nouveau riche* who aspired to be connoisseurs.

In Jackman's *All the World's a Stage* (1777) we have the curious situation of a satire on a practice that owed its existence to the theater itself. This farce, in the words of a contemporary reviewer,

is aimed at the prevalent phrenzy for spouting and acting, which has not only shown itself in the parlours of private houses, but even descended into the kitchen and stables, the very footmen and grooms becoming Romeos and Alexanders, while cooks and scullions have left their fire-sides and their dripping pans to love like Juliet and die like Statira.[71]

The play was obviously directed at the current rage for amateur theatricals; this form of entertainment was affected by the wealthy and cultivated to such an extent that often huge sums were spent on scenery and costumes, and the advice and assistance of such professionals as Garrick, Quin, and Mrs. Bellamy were eagerly sought.[72] It has previously been noted that one of the most frequently revived Restoration plays in the mid-eighteenth century was *The Rehearsal,* itself a theatrical satire. Several imitations of this play were written in the mid-century, including Mrs. Clive's *The Rehearsal; or, Bays in Petticoats* (1750), Garrick's *A Peep Behind the Curtain; or, The New Rehearsal* (1767), and—surpassing the rest—Sheridan's *The Critic; or, A Tragedy Rehearsed* (1779), a burlesque with sufficient vitality to be given a professional revival as recently as 1946. It is not surprising that plays were written with the theater itself as their setting and with their situations and characters drawn from practices and persons immediately concerned with the theater, for these plays were for the most part written by playwrights who were also actors. The almost unanimous success of such pieces shows that eighteenth-century audiences were both consistently and intensely interested in anything that concerned their favorite amusement—and that they regarded the theater as peculiarly their own. That the number of such plays was relatively large also suggests the sad plight of eighteenth-century drama generally; for, suffering from mediocrity and declining as a literary form, the drama had begun to gnaw at its own vitals.

To devote an entire chapter to such a matter as fashions as

they concern the theater may perhaps seem to be merely the repeating of platitudes or the belaboring of the obvious; for theatergoing is—and has been at least since the Renaissance—an amusement, a form of entertainment. And the motives that impel those who seek recreation to choose this kind of amusement instead of that, or to choose now this kind and now that, are notoriously unpredictable and irrational, because mere entertainment, except in the case of self-conscious avocationists, for whom it ceases to be mere entertainment, is based upon nothing more profound than whim and temporary desires. In this area of human activity, uncontrolled as it is by any consistent or thoroughly reasoned behavior, fashion provides not only convenience and accessibility but also the path of least resistance. More important, it provides the opportunity to enhance the intended pleasure by a kind of social participation that at least for the moment is considered desirable. Hence, fashion is implicit in theatergoing—even inseparable from it.

Yet certain pieces of knowledge have been acquired by this consideration. Examination of the really widespread and intense interest in anything concerning the theater not only indicates certain predilections of the mid-eighteenth century but also establishes the necessary premises for drawing conclusions about more significant aspects of the time. For only when it is demonstrated that the theater was a genuine center of gravity, as it were, for a large, representative, and thoroughly implicated segment of society can the nature of the repertory and the customs of the theater serve to throw light on such larger topics as morals and manners. Again, the examination of what I have called literary fashions has indicated certain areas of contiguity —for example, between the novel and the drama—where further exploration would be profitable. It is precisely in such areas that the interrelations of audience, professional theater, and critic are operative; and this triangular structure of theatrical history has never been adequately described for the eighteenth century. Finally, our concern with the influence on the repertory of the audience's interest in various contemporary affairs has explained something of the nature of author-spectator relationship.

CHAPTER TWELVE

Novelty and Variety

Fashions, which often had a powerful influence on the theatrical repertory in the eighteenth century, come into being ordinarily when something new is introduced. Those whose taste is thought dependable and perceptive—or, as it would have been said then, those who have virtu—may accept the innovation, and the public soon follows. Thus a new fashion is born. It soon became the fashion, for example, to attend the theater in Goodman's Fields to see Garrick—a new actor; or to witness the performance of a play by Hugh Kelly—a new playwright; or to patronize the theaters when a comic opera was being presented —a new dramatic species. But the fashion often continued long after there ceased to be any novelty. It might do so for any of a number of reasons. The intrinsic merit of Garrick's acting made it fashionable to see his performances when they were no longer something new; indeed, in this instance at least, popularity survived even the fashion. Similarly, comic operas continued to be well attended when there could have been no thought of them as constituting a new genre. On the other hand, Kelly, while still a relatively new playwright, went out of fashion; so that even when he produced a new play, *A Word to the Wise*, it was not well received—but for reasons that have nothing to do with the merit of the play, or in fact with anything related to the theater (he had become a ministerial hackwriter and had received a pension from Lord North). But novelty alone often sufficed to attract audiences, when there was little or no consideration on the spectator's part of the fashionableness of his attending a certain performance or of his being present at a certain theater.

Novelty, of course, in one form or another has always been sought by those who strive to please the public, for the love of novelty is a permanent human trait. And in the eighteenth century, those who wrote about the theater recognized its importance. Arthur Murphy, for example, noted that "variety is the ruling passion, the *primum mobile* of the public mind," [1] where it is clear from the context that he meant novelty as well as variety. A writer in *The Adventurer* who signed himself "Lun Tertius" concluded that "the business of Pantomimes is become a very serious concern" because "the curiosity of mankind is perpetually thirsting after novelties. . . ." [2] Some thought that Garrick's success as a manager was largely owing to his ability to provide the stage with an endless string of novelties. The audience's demand for novelty was obviously a potent factor in the determination of the repertory. But some qualifications should be made at once, for innovation in all departments of theatrical activity was not equally well received.

Novelty in plot was usually welcomed in new plays. Thus Macklin's *Love à la Mode* was for a time "in high rage of fashion with the public" because, it was said, it provided novelty of situation.[3] Similarly it was thought that *The Guardian* succeeded because the author, by introducing "new conjectures, new doubts, and new discoveries," had been able to keep the audience "in suspense and eager expectation." [4] But both these pieces, it will be noted, are comedies. In more serious drama the situation was somewhat different, for decorum was there more actively operative and tended to inhibit innovation. For example, in Johnson's tragedy the strangling of Irene with a bowstring was objected to by the audience to such an extent that the unfortunate actress was unable to make her dying speech and was forced to retire from the stage still alive.[5] Before the second performance the offending part was excised, and Irene was thereafter carried from the stage to be murdered behind the scenes. Rowe, however, had provided a stage murder in *Tamerlane* that was brought about by the same means, to which eighteenth-century audiences did not object. Edmond Malone comments on the distinction that "this shews, how ready modern audiences are to condemn in a new play what they have frequently endured very quietly in an old one." [6] Thus novelty in plot and situation, although ordinarily welcomed, might also work to the detriment of a play; and it is always necessary, therefore, to discriminate carefully among the types of plays —new and old, comic and tragic—before the nature of the effects of novelty in terms of the repertory can be correctly as-

[1] For notes to chap. 12, see pp. 337-338.

sessed. But obviously the repertory was influenced in one way or other whatever the kind of play.

The audience sometimes welcomed novelty in the techniques of the actors, although the welcome was often granted reluctantly, particularly in older drama that was well known. There was no reluctance in the general approval of Garrick as Richard III when he first appeared at Goodman's Fields in 1741, even though the great difference between his methods and those of Quin and other earlier favorites was immediately recognized; and Macklin's novel representation of Shylock, after a few moments of deliberation on the part of the audience, was highly applauded. But in general, actors were hesitant about breaking with long-established acting traditions. In new plays, however, new methods of character portrayal were usually successful. Mrs. Bellamy, for example, against the advice of Lyttelton and Johnson, elected to play the title role in Dodsley's *Cleone* with simplicity, although "the public had been accustomed to noise and violence in their *mad* stage ladies"—and she was well received. Her success, she modestly records in her autobiography, was due to the audience's love of novelty.[7] On another occasion, Mrs. Cibber, cast as Mandane in *The Orphan of China*, was taken ill before its first performance, and Mrs. Yates took her part. After hearing the latter read her lines in rehearsal, Garrick, who was always quick to sense what would appeal to audiences, remarked to the author: "This is the best thing that could happen; Mrs. Cibbers' [*sic*] acting would be no novelty, but Mrs. Yates will excite the general admiration";[8] and so it turned out. Here we see the audience's love of novelty influencing both actor and manager—and, through them, the repertory of the period. But in general, innovations by actors entailed far greater risks than did those introduced by playwrights, a situation that strongly suggests that the typical eighteenth-century audience was made up of histrionic rather than dramatic critics.[9]

Numerous other effects of the audience's interest in novelty on the stage are easily found. This predilection for novelty influenced every aspect of theatrical activity from the content of new plays to the determination of the theater's economy. It was responsible for the movement of actors and actresses between Dublin and London; for the casting of women in male parts; for the importation of Continental players; for the employment of acting dogs, foreign singers, and magicians who promised to put themselves in small bottles (a promise that was not fulfilled); and for the reviving of a large number of old plays. Although we may dismiss many of these novelties as of little importance to the repertory, the last-named was of much greater consequence. Garrick, for example, who was constantly on the watch for successful means of drawing crowded houses, brought many long-unacted plays to the stage, including several of Shakespeare's lesser-known dramas. The rival theater was of necessity compelled to follow his example. By means of these revivals both the popular demand for novelty and the growing antiquarian interest of the time were satisfied,[10] with the result that some of the greatest masterpieces of English dramatic art were once again restored to the stage.

Some of these effects were obviously owing to a combination of causes. The revival of Shakespeare's plays, for example, if explained completely, will be seen to have bearings not only upon the desire for novelty and the interest in antiquity but also upon such other matters as national pride and the interest in England's history, sensibility and the romantic temperament, managerial preferences and whims, the availability of strong acting roles, the impotence of contemporary playwrights, and even lesser manifestations. On the other hand, certain changes in theatrical practice came about wholly or largely because of the thirst for novelty. Three of the most important of these— because they were innovations with a far-reaching influence upon the repertory—are the increased use of the spectacular, the addition of the afterpiece, and the greater employment of music. Not all of these are necessarily to be thought of as originating in the mid-eighteenth century, but they all reached a point of development then that makes their consideration essential.

One of the greatest effects of the audience's interest in novelty on the stage was the increased emphasis upon the spectacular in the theater. Spectacle is of course by its very nature a necessary ingredient of any stage performance, regardless of time or type; but an illuminating indication of the widening split in the eighteenth century between the views of the audience and those of the critics, between dramatic practice and dramatic theory, is the fact that spectacle should become an overwhelming determinant of theatrical success in an age in which at least the critics still regarded Aristotle with considerable reverence; for Aristotle had said: "The Spectacle . . . of all the parts . . . is the least artistic, and connected least with the art of poetry." [11] This critical dictum is indeed borne out by that most popular embodiment of spectacle in the eighteenth century, the pantomime.

This theatrical type, influenced by various comic and farcical traditions, though leaning most heavily upon the Italian *commedia dell'arte,* was not an innovation of the mid-century. Some years earlier, John Rich, then manager of the theater in Lincoln's Inn Fields, had tried his hand at acting. Tragedy, which first attracted him, he found uncongenial, and he ultimately turned to pantomime. He immediately became the most famous Harlequin of his time, and he continued to play the part in a long series of pantomimes almost until the day of his death in 1761. The special qualities of the typical eighteenth-century pantomime were thus largely determined by Rich. Because he was unable to speak effectively on the stage, he made the part of Harlequin and the other traditional characters taken over from the Italian theater into silent roles that depended upon expressive dumb show. Facial expression and quick gesticulation with the entire body were the principal ingredients of this kind of acting. At the same time, there was a considerable use of music and—especially—of all kinds of spectacular and surprising effects obtained by means of ingenious machinery. The whole was usually held together tenuously by a hyperbolic plot based upon a classical myth. This heterogeneous combination of farce, ballet, opera, spectacle, and dumb show provided excellent opportunities for the introduction of all kinds of novelties.

Drury Lane early discovered in "Lun," as Rich called himself, a rival who could hardly be overcome, even by the best efforts of Booth, Wilks, Cibber, and Mrs. Oldfield. Whereas they could bring in five hundred pounds in a week, Rich's pantomime drew twice that amount.[12] And this popular interest in pantomimes by no means abated in the mid-century. In 1737 a writer in *The Craftsman* noted not only their great popularity but also their influence upon a part of the population:

I can impute it to nothing else than the influence of "dumb Shews, Pantomimes, &c." that so many fine Gentlemen, now-a-days, look more like *Harlequins* and *Scaramouches* than Persons of Fortune and Distinction, [even to their] light *tripping Pumps,* and large *Harness Buckles,* their short *Mop Wigs, black Bags,* and *Windmill Sweeps.* . . .[13]

Ten years later, when Garrick became manager of Drury Lane, he declared his intention to bring Shakespeare to the stage more frequently; but at the opening of the 1750-1751 season he had already found it necessary to proclaim, in the prologue written especially for the occasion:

> Sacred to Shakespeare was this spot design'd
> To pierce the heart, and humanize the mind,
> But if an empty house, the actor's curse,
> Shows us our Lears and Hamlets lose their force,
> Unwilling we must change the nobler scene,
> And, in our turn, present you Harlequin;
> Quit poets, and set carpenters to work,
> Shew gawdy scenes, or mount the vaulting Turk.

In 1753 *The Adventurer,* in the form of a fable, satirized the taste of the ill-favored son (the "Town") of the Great Man (the Public), whose demands had brought the Necromancer (Harlequin) into the palace (the theater).[14] Numerous other satirical attacks on the practice appeared in poetry and periodicals, which attest to the great popularity of pantomime. In 1763, pantomimes had gained even greater influence over the theater. In that year the half-price riots took place, led by the bully Fitzpatrick, with the result that only on nights when new pantomimes were shown could the managers refuse to reduce the price of admission after the third act. Murphy says of this action: "And thus, according to these critics [that is, the rioters], Harlequin was to frisk, and frolick, and leap over the heads of the best writers of the age." [15] Francis Gentleman, in the *Dramatic Censor* (1770), concluded: "It is certain, that three-fourths of every audience are more capable of enjoying sound and shew, than solid sense and poetical imagination." [16] Others too objected to pantomime because they thought it debauched public taste. An anonymous writer in the *London Magazine,* for example, had complained as early as 1737 that "Dumb

233

shows, with their ingenious tricks and machines," were contributing to the degeneracy of the stage.[17] But such objectors
were in the minority, for it is readily apparent that this kind
of theatrical entertainment continued its hold upon the audience throughout the mid-century period.

A notable stand against pantomime was made by Garrick at
Drury Lane, by introducing a long series of new plays and
revivals of older dramas in which he usually acted the principal role, thereby succeeding in drawing large audiences. So
powerful was his hold over public opinion, both as actor and
manager, that he seems to have temporarily succeeded in improving the popular taste in drama. Because of his taste and
influence, says Murphy, "the pleasure of the eye was transferred to the ear";[18] and Whitehead hailed Garrick's management with an ode that promised

> No more the poor polluted scene
> Shall teem with births of Harlequin.

But even Garrick could not long hold out single-handed against
a popular fashion. Wilkinson has left a graphic record of his
difficulty:[19]

Indeed I have known even in London, when Mr. Rich has revived
an old pantomime tagged to a vile-acted play, that Garrick has
trembled; and I have heard him remark, that if they came to a
tragedy at Drury-Lane from want of admittance by an overflow of
Covent-Garden, they were not in humour the whole night, as the
grown masters and misses were disappointed of seeing the puppet-
shew, and were deprived of their rattle. . . . to Harlequin Sorcerer,
the doors were obliged to be opened at three o'clock, and were at
times broken open, so eager were the million of admittance.

Garrick soon retaliated by staging Woodward's *Queen Mab*
(1750). The author himself played Harlequin, and the piece
succeeded so well that "people crowded for above forty nights
to see this exhibition," [20] and its success made Rich in turn
"tremble on his throne." [21] But this was one of the few pantomimes that met with encouragement at Drury Lane,[22] and
Garrick attempted to exploit the popular taste for the spectacular in other ways. One of his most famous attempts was
The Chinese Festival, upon which he expended tremendous

amounts of money and labor. He hoped that "such an exhibition would most probably have the attraction of novelty, and supersede the necessity of introducing those monstrous pantomimes, with which Mr. Lun [Rich] hoped he could silence Shakespeare, Jonson, Otway, and Rowe." [23] The failure of *The Chinese Festival* was brought about not because of its lack of appeal but because of popular hatred against the French, who were believed to make up much of the cast. That he was still attempting to appease the public taste for spectacle late in his career is shown by a passage in one of Mrs. Montagu's letters. She wrote to Mrs. Vesey in 1773:

Mr. Garrick has just produced a fine spectacle on the stage. As Melpomene will not tread, nor trip the stage, he has hired certain necromancers who sail on seas of milk in ships of amber and beseige castles built of cards, and the Town stares, and Dr. Young says, "Wonder is involuntary praise." [24]

But a later passage in her letter also indicates that some were tiring of the fashion: "Some people think five acts of mere spectacle is too much." Garrick's farce *Lilliput* (1756) as altered by him for the opening of the little theater in the Haymarket under Colman's management (1777) was partly intended to ridicule the rage for mere spectacle on the stage.[25]

Garrick's career as manager, in terms of his attitude toward pantomime, shows how strong was the interest of the audience in that theatrical type. Boldly opposing popular taste with serious drama, he was able at first to influence the public by the novelty of new or long-unacted plays. But when he could no longer succeed solely by this means, he tried in turn staging pantomimes in competition with those at Covent Garden, ridiculing the species in short burlesque pieces, and introducing spectacular effects in other types of drama. Each of the three attempts was an admission that the popular demand for spectacle had become a powerful force in determining the theatrical repertory. Fleetwood, Garrick's predecessor as manager of Drury Lane, had perhaps a more practical view of the exigencies of the time:

However distasteful such pieces may be to the delicacy of some judgments, yet there are others, to whose taste they are suited; and as the Playhouse may be considered as the general mart of pleasure, it is only from the variety of entertainment, the different tastes of the publick can be supplied—of this the receipts of the house are a sufficient evidence, it being notorious, how necessary the addition of such pieces is towards procuring the *best play* a *numerous audience.*[26]

But whoever the manager, the demand for spectacle was much too strong to be ignored.

The pantomimes of Rich had placed a heavy emphasis upon spectacular scenery and machinery of marvelous ingenuity. The poet's art had indeed been eclipsed by that of the carpenter and scene painter. But Rich's interest in spectacular effect was not confined entirely to his favorite genre. In 1757, after having a succession of thin houses, he resolved to revive Beaumont and Fletcher's *The Prophetess* in an attempt to draw larger audiences. The play was chosen "because he could introduce a good deal of machinery in it." [27] How well he succeeded is suggested by the fact that the play was given thirteen performances in the season. On another occasion he revived Lee's *Rival Queens,* which, in spite of the strong cast that included Barry, Mrs. Woffington, and Mrs. Bellamy, would have had only a moderate success if Rich had not added a triumphal entry. Mrs. Bellamy remarks that it was the most magnificent thing of its kind that she had ever seen, and that although it was an expensive addition it reimbursed the manager handsomely. Rich, who had always merely tolerated actors, confident that his pantomimes and other spectacles were the offerings that drew audiences, might in this instance, Mrs. Bellamy concludes, "with great justice have produced his snuff-box, and cried, 'It is my triumph.' " [28]

Shakespeare's plays were also affected by the audience's interest in the spectacular. *Henry VIII* provided sufficient opportunity for magnificent processions and coronation scenes, even in its unaltered form,[29] and was frequently performed. The operatized versions of *The Tempest* and *Macbeth* likewise were given various scenic additions and had considerable success in this hybrid form. An interesting example of the effect of the popularity of spectacle is the revival of *Antony and Cleopatra* in 1759, its first performance after its original appearance in 1607. Garrick seems to have decided to restore the play to the stage in order to rival Covent Garden, then enjoying a series of successful pantomimes, by offering the public a new Shakespearean tragedy. He was in particular distress because Woodward, his main support in farce and pantomime, had gone to the Dublin theater two years before and because his additions to the repertory during the interval had met with but little success.[30] Thus, the very existence of this tragedy on the eighteenth-century stage is due to the public preoccupation with the spectacular. But the play itself, as it reached the stage, also showed the influence of the same interests. Although a superior adaptation in that there was little tampering with the poet's lines, it was lavishly mounted and equipped with new scenery and costumes. The revival was a relative failure, as it was performed only six nights; but the nature of its appeal to at least some in the audience is indicated by the anonymous author of a pamphlet that appeared shortly after its first performance: "Upon the whole, we think this play is now better suited for the stage than the closet, as scenery, dresses, and parade strike the eye, and divert one's attention from the poet." [31] So far had spectacle invaded the theater! *Richard II,* a play almost entirely neglected during the mid-century, was once intended for revival by Garrick, whose "chief expectations from it, as he himself confessed, would have been founded on scenery displaying the magnificence of our ancient barriers." [32] It is readily apparent that the audience's desire for novelty chiefly affected regular drama in one of two ways: either by causing the addition of spectacular ornamentation, or by placing drama directly in competition with pantomime and other slight but popular entertainment.

A still greater influence on the repertory—one less destructive to the integrity of dramatic pieces but nevertheless often equally detrimental to public taste—was the practice of adding an afterpiece to the theatrical fare. Here the love of both variety and novelty is operative. The afterpiece was sometimes a pantomime, particularly at Covent Garden under Rich's management; but it might also be a farce, an operatized abridgment of an older play, a burlesque, a masque, or—later in the period—a comic opera or operatic farce. The practice of adding an afterpiece to the evening's entertainment began early in the century, and may have developed as an answer to an understandable demand by the audience for something less serious than the sentimental comedies and pathetic tragedies that then constituted much of the dramatic fare. As the afterpiece often became a greater attraction for the audience than the regular drama it accompanied, its selection became a serious concern of managers or of actors on their benefit nights, knowing that the difference between a thin and a crowded house was frequently a new or popular farce or musical piece. Indeed, the afterpiece became so popular that the choice of the longer drama sometimes depended upon it. Wilkinson, for example, told Mrs. Abington: "My reason for taking a tragedy was solely that its gravity might aid and give spirit when the new farce came on. . . ." [33]

The account of Garrick's successful farce *Miss in Her Teens* in its first season is indicative of the treatment of the afterpiece in the repertory. The farce was added to various plays, in some of which Quin acted; but he, growing tired of acting in serious dramas before audiences that came chiefly to see the afterpiece, at last "surlily swore he would not hold up the tail of any farce." Thereupon Garrick selected from the prompter's list those plays that could be acted without Quin and

were not supposed to have any internal strength to draw company of themselves. To these Miss in her Teens was tacked every night for above a month, or five weeks. Quin would sometimes, during the run of the farce, pay a visit to the theatre; but on being told that the house was crowded, he would give a significant growl and withdraw.[34]

An even longer run was enjoyed by *The Jubilee,* originally produced at Stratford in tribute to Shakespeare and later brought to the Drury Lane stage, where it was acted ninety-one times in the 1769-1770 season, twenty-seven times the following season, and revived in 1775-1776 for thirty-five performances. As long as such pieces were included on the playbill, it seemed to matter little what was offered as the first piece.

Both new and old dramas were given the support of afterpieces. Even Shakespeare's plays sometimes needed to be thus bolstered. When Garrick revived *All's Well that Ends Well* in 1757, we are told, "with the help of a pantomime, it was acted several nights." [35] His more popular plays, however, such as *Hamlet* and *Richard III,* apparently needed no such aid.[36] It had been customary also not to supply with an afterpiece any new play, regardless of its merits. But Garrick changed the practice in 1767, because, he thought, it was "highly detrimental to the author as well as the manager." He decreed:

> If a play was strong enough to run its course without additional aid, the weakest farce on the list might furnish the after-piece: and, on the other hand, if the play wanted support, the best two-act comedies might be added.[37]

His decree not only indicates how well entrenched was the practice of adding an afterpiece by the later eighteenth century, but it also suggests that many such pieces had become much more substantial than the one-act farces of an earlier day. Examples of this trend, all of which appeared as afterpieces, are: Lee's *The Man of Quality* (1774), altered from Vanbrugh's *The Relapse;* Gentleman's *The Tobacconist* (1772), condensed from *The Alchemist;* Colman's two-act version of *Comus* (1775); as well as the various plays of Shakespeare that were similarly treated—*The Winter's Tale, A Midsummer Night's Dream,* and *The Taming of the Shrew.* Such irreverent treatment in reducing the regular comedies of older dramatic masters to mere divertissements is hardly surprising in an age that saw violent hands laid on *Hamlet* and *King Lear,* but it also shows that the theaters pressed every kind of drama into service to satiate the audience's voracious thirst for novelty and variety. It suggests too that often the afterpiece had become a genuinely substantial offering.

A third kind of influence that the desire for variety and novelty exerted upon the repertory, particularly in the later years of the century, depended primarily upon what the *London Chronicle* approvingly called "the fashionable Goût for music." [38] Because of this "goût," musical entertainments of all types reached the stage in greater and greater numbers. Actually the types were so anomalous that they had a variety of names, and adequate classification is impossible. Serious opera, comic opera, ballad opera, burletta, and masque are, however, reasonably distinguishable. Of these, all but the first were often used as afterpieces, and the burletta was most frequent at the minor theaters. It should also be noted that regular dramas were often given a larger proportion of musical content.

Music was not, of course, a theatrical innovation of the mid-eighteenth century. Shakespeare's company certainly employed musicians, as did the Restoration theater. And Richard Steele provided no fewer than thirteen songs for his first three plays (1701-1705) "to please an audience that loved music as a decorative accessory to their bill of fare." [39] But, with the single exception of *The Beggar's Opera,* which not only was frequently performed but inspired numerous imitations, never had musical entertainment bulked so large in the theaters as it did after 1760.

This state of theatrical affairs is hardly exaggerated in an occasional prelude spoken at Drury Lane in 1766-1767. Mrs. Woffington has just asked what entertainment the town has been having.

Mrs. Cibber. They have been mostly amused with comic Operas, consisting of very indifferent poetry put to old tunes, without character, and scarcely any sentiment.
Mrs. Woffington. Astonishing!
Mrs. Cibber. And more so, when you consider that these harmonious pieces would fill houses, when Garrick and myself, in Shakespeare's best plays, could scarce pay expenses—this indeed was the principal reason of the manager's going abroad, and I think he would not have done wrong, if he had never acted till the vicious taste of the town had been entirely corrected.[40]

Ironically perhaps, but certainly prudently, Lacy and Garrick's brother, in whose hands Garrick had left the management of the theater when he left for the Continent, depended to a considerable extent upon musical pieces to compete with Covent Garden.

The latter theater had come under the management of John Beard in 1762, who

very naturally and judiciously exerted his Powers to distinguish that Theatre by musical Performances, as his Predecessor had done by Pantomime . . . and therefore the best Singers and musical Performers were engaged.[41]

The history of musical performances on the eighteenth-century London stage is, in fact, to a large extent the story of the competition between the two patent theaters. But the impetus was largely derived from the activities of two men—Beard and

Isaac Bickerstaffe. Beard, who was both a musician of considerable virtuosity and the manager of Covent Garden after the death of John Rich, his father-in-law, had both the special talent and the authority that made possible the inclusion of a large number of musical entertainments at that theater. Bickerstaffe was the most important writer—and almost singlehandedly the inventor —of a new dramatic type, the comic opera. His most successful experiments in this genre were *Love in a Village* (1762), *The Maid of the Mill* (1765), *The Padlock* (1768), and *Lionel and Clarissa* (1768). He had many imitators who soon found it profitable to supply the stage with similar pieces. It is noteworthy that both Beard and Bickerstaffe became active as influences on the repertory in the same year—1762—and that the increased use of spectacle on the stage also dates from approximately the same time. Music and spectacle—or "sound and shew"—joined forces thereafter in furnishing audiences with various novelties; and, significantly, they prepared the way thereby for the series of melodramas and light operatic farces that were to be the chief staples of the later eighteenth-century repertory.

Besides the comic opera, musical pieces of other types also reached the stage, but the new genre—along with the variations on it that soon came into being—was easily the most popular and influential. A comic opera by Bickerstaffe was usually in two or three acts, had a love plot similar to those employed in the sentimental comedies of Cumberland, Colman, and Kelly, and was well supplied with songs set to new airs especially composed for the piece. Although slighter than such works as *The Beggar's Opera* and *Comus,* the only musical pieces of an earlier day that still survived on the stage, the comic opera was more substantial as drama than was the operatic farce of about 1800, by which time music and spectacle had largely supplanted plot, dialogue, and character portrayal.

An examination of the audience that patronized such theatrical offerings shows that its members were present for several different reasons, not all of which do credit to contemporary taste. To illustrate, I have chosen as representative spectators three who attended the theater at ten-year intervals in the last two decades of the period, and who express three different— and representative—attitudes toward the musical entertainments of the time. In 1756 George Dempster, just arrived from Scotland, hurried to Drury Lane when he found that *Comus* was advertised for that evening. Here is the serious lover of music speaking: "Never was my soul so much enchanted as at seeing the representation of that Mask where poetry and music had lavished all their ornaments." [42] A letter Mrs. Montagu received from her sister in 1767 suggests that many attended musical performances because it was fashionable to do so: "I am just going to the Burletta; people are mad after them here. I believe the Duke and Duchess of Bedford came to enjoy them longer, for I can learn no other motive. . . . I own my raptures are many degrees below the fashion." [43] Finally, a letter from Samuel Johnson of Torrington to his sister in 1775 shows that some were impressed more by musical whimsicality and a kind of grotesque virtuosity than by either the music or the reigning fashion:

I have been at one play since I writ you my Journal, the Beggar's Opera with the Druids; my inducement for going was to hear Signor Rossignol's most amazing imitations of singing Birds, which He does to that perfection that it is impossible to distinguish them from the finest notes of the Nightingale, Canary Bird, Goldfinch, Linnet, etc., for all appearance of the human voice is entirely lost; the sound is produc'd with a very great effort and exertion of the lungs, and he is oblig'd to stop for breath and drink a glass of water in the middle of his performance.[44]

A genuine love for music, the desire to be fashionable, and the fascination of novelty—all three factors played their parts in determining the extent to which the theatrical repertory was given over to musical pieces. It would be impossible to determine their relative importance—and perhaps unprofitable as well—but it is clear that all three were continually operating in the audiences of the day.

Sheridan, whose tastes fortunately were refined, was benefiting those of the first group, the true lovers of music, when in 1777 he brought Tenducci, "the most delightful singer of Italy," to the London stage.[45] Although there were some who regretted that the "profuse Generosity of the present Age have [*sic*] lavished away on *French* Dancers and *Italian* Eunuchs" sums greater than Southampton's bounty to Shakespeare,[46] there were many genuine lovers of music who seized the opportunity to hear the great singers of the day. Colman, on the other hand, when he wrote *The Musical Lady,* was thinking of those who attended operatic performances only because it was fashionable to do so. This farce was produced just a month after Arne's *Artaxerxes* had made its appearance, and was intended to ridicule "the folly of pretending to a fine ear, without a true taste. . . ." [47] The whimsical Sterne was apparently thinking of the unmotivated oddities that marred too many of the musical pieces of the time while he was digressing into a facetious account of fictional and actual time lapses. The digression is occasioned by Obadiah's going for Dr. Slop, and concludes: "All which put together must have prepared the reader's imagination for the entrance of Dr. Slop upon the stage,—as much, at least (I hope), as a dance, a song, or a concerto between the acts." [48]

As long as Garrick was manager of Drury Lane, regular drama had at least one stout champion who refused to concede entirely to the rage for musicals. But when he retired in 1776, hardly a force remained that was strong enough to keep any considerable amount of serious drama on the stage. Colman, in his occasional prelude *New Brooms,* spoken at the opening of the 1776-1777 season at Drury Lane, refers to the change:

Crochet. . . . plays are worn out, Sir. Otway's a rag, Jonson obsolete, and Shakespeare worn threadbare. Plays!—plays might do well enough formerly indeed: but quite out of fashion now, Sir. Plays and little Roscius left the stage together, Sir!
Phelim. What will the stage do then?
Crochet. Do?—Musical pieces, to be sure—Operas, Sir—our only dependence now.—We have nothing for it now but wind, wire, rosin and catgut.[49]

But Garrick too had on occasion been forced by public opinion to resort to "mere opera," although at first he tried to resist. In 1763, for example, when Dr. Arne offered his promising pupil Miss Brent to the Drury Lane company, Garrick, who was said to lack musical taste, refused to employ her even against the advice of his friends. Beard then engaged her at Covent Garden, and she quickly became "his most powerful engine to demolish the success and humble the pride of Drury-lane." As Polly Peachum and later in *Artaxerxes,* she drew large audiences. Garrick's efforts to maintain the supremacy of

his theater were those which once had succeeded—but were now
to no avail:

In vain did Garrick oppose his prime characters in comedy and
tragedy, such as Ranger and Benedick, Hamlet and Lear, to Polly
Peachum. That bewitching Syren charmed all the world; and like
another Orpheus, drew crowds perpetually after her. . . . Shakespeare and Garrick were obliged to quit the field to Beard and
Brent.[50]

At least by 1770 Garrick had learned that to oppose the musical
fashion was to court failure; so in that year, recognizing that
"the rage for musical pieces was growing more and more into
fashion," when *A Word to the Wise* had been damned, he
brought out Dryden's *King Arthur,* reduced to two acts and
retitled *Arthur and Emmeline.* With the aid of Arne's music
and "splendid scenes and grand machinery," the piece succeeded.[51]

It has been previously noted that not only were musical
pieces, both new and old, becoming an ever larger part of the
repertory, but also that regular dramas were sometimes given
musical treatment to make them more palatable to the audience.
Nor were the plays of Shakespeare exempt from such "improvements." It is instructive to see how the taste for musical drama
affected many of Shakespeare's plays as they appeared on the
eighteenth-century stage, particularly when we remember that
it was this same public that in 1769 gathered by the thousands at
Stratford to pay tribute to Shakespeare's genius and for which
Rowe, Pope, Theobald, Tonson, and their successors were
making available the texts of the master whom they professed
to venerate. The operatizing of Shakespeare was of course not
new; many musical alterations date from the seventeenth century. But it is noteworthy that for the most part these pieces
showed great vitality in the eighteenth century; and even where
there was an attempt to restore the play in a form closer to the
original, the later alterer frequently retained many of the
operatic trimmings. Moreover, new alterations were being
produced that also had been given considerable musical decora-
tion. The musical treatment ranged in degree from the simple
interpolation of the song "When daisies pied" of *Love's Labour's
Lost* into *As You Like It,* to the wholesale operatizing of *The*

Taming of the Shrew, The Tempest, The Winter's Tale, A Midsummer Night's Dream, and *Macbeth.*

If music was often required to maintain the success of Shakespeare on the stage in the mid-century period, it is no wonder that new pieces, many of which were but slight in plot and often hackneyed and threadbare in dialogue and character, were sometimes completely dependent upon their musical content. The dramatist himself was often forced to admit that the musician rather than the poet was frequently the one who contributed most to the success of a piece. Thus, Colman, in the preface to the printed copy of *The Portrait: A Burletta* (1770), frankly stated that its success on the stage was owing to Dr. Arnold's music. Sir George Collier's *Selima and Azor* (1776), with music by Thomas Linley, Oulton says, "on account of the airs, was tolerated." [52] Dr. Arne's music for the songs added by John Dalton to *Comus,* a masque never long absent from the stage in the period, was regarded as contributing to make the piece "more fit for dramatic exhibition. . . ." [53] Such examples could readily be multiplied. It is apparent that Gentleman was not far wrong in his judgment that "three-fourths of every audience are more capable of enjoying sound and shew, than solid sense and poetical imagination."

But also the indications are that the audience's taste for music, even in the height of the fashion, was unpredictable—and not highly cultivated. Five acts of music, it was thought, would "tire the patience of a modern audience," [54] and consequently Dryden's masque, for example, was reduced to two acts. Cumberland, attempting to emulate Bickerstaffe's success with *Love in a Village* and *The Maid of the Mill,* produced his *The Summer's Tale* (1765), a musical comedy in three acts; its success was only slight, however, until he reduced it to two acts and produced it as *Amelia* the following year. [55] Such examples hint that the popular taste for musical pieces was based less upon a sincere love for music than upon the fashion of a novel and rather definite genre whose formal limits as well as content the leaders of the "ton" had dictated. Also, we may note a contemporary indication that such leaders might be followed blindly by the applauding public, with no really intelligent appreciation of what they heard. An anonymous critic remarks of Burgoyne's *The Maid of the Oaks* in the *Sentimental Magazine:* "If he has at all erred, he has erred in supposing that the plain dramatic palate of the multitude was calculated to relish a very refined dish, which is only just come into fashion with our nobility." [56] Yet this piece drew many large audiences at Drury Lane, at first as a five-act extension of Burgoyne's operetta and later with greater success as a musical comedy in the original two-act form, and caused Covent Garden to hurry onto the stage a masque called *The Druids,* which made use of the same theme. The public was ready to accept what it did not understand if only the connoisseurs gave it sanction.

In spite of the seriousness with which the eighteenth-century audience was generally inclined to regard its theater, it is apparent that often such superficial matters as the interest in the new and the desire for variety and change were the sole factors in determining the repertory. As long as the middle ranks of society felt their positions insecure or not completely validated, their theater inclined to be a laboratory wherein they could measure their own newly acquired powers and privileges. But once the middle class achieved a sense of equilibrium and came to trust itself, the theater as a communal forum tended to decline in importance, so that sheer amusement and escape supplanted social significance as desiderata. No theater, of course, can long remain vital if it fails to entertain and amuse; but during much of the eighteenth century there was a conscious attempt to make it do more—in the words of Aristotle, not only to delight but also to teach. But after about 1760 the stage gradually deserted its didactic function, and audiences became more and more content to follow the playwright into impossible realms where they were beguiled by pleasant melody and titillated by spectacular bustle.

CHAPTER THIRTEEN

Politics and Patriotism

The importance of the theater as a political institution had often been admitted before 1737, although it was not until the passing of the Licensing Act in that year that parliamentary cognizance was taken of its power. The stage thereafter could not be so outspoken, but it never completely ceased to reflect the audience's interests in national and patriotic matters. It is clear, moreover, that the theater was generally recognized as a political arena. The *Daily Gazetteer,* for example, which was controlled by Sir Robert Walpole's party, published in its columns a satire in which Lord Lyttelton, thinly disguised as Littledone, was attacked not only for undertaking the patronage of literature but especially for enlisting dramatists on the side of the Opposition.[1] Dean Swift, writing to Sanderson Miller from Dublin two years later, gives an insight into the methods by which audiences sometimes made their political views felt: "Ever since I came to Ireland I have been a daring Patriot for Liberty, and already by clapping and hissing properly I have got a small party in the Playhouse; and at this time I am soliciting subscribers for Gustavus Vasa. . . ."[2] *Gustavus Vasa,* it should be noted, was an antigovernment play. Even an innocent play like *The Rehearsal,* as I have shown, was used as a framework into which were thrown, for purposes of ridicule, references to "the public transactions—the flying follies of the day—the debates in parliament—the absurdities of playwriters, politicians, and players. . . ."[3] In Shakespeare's historical plays, most of which were acted many times in the period, were discerned

such general resemblances of character, in prince and subject, as must necessarily arise in a mixed government, like ours; where incroachments, on one side, must perpetually meet with resistance on

[1] For notes to chap. 13, see pp. 339-340.

the other, and will infallibly produce events not very unlike those which are described so affectingly by our inimitable poet.[4]

On one occasion the printer Haynes was prosecuted for publishing a letter in which he pointed out possible applications of passages in *Richard II* to Sir Robert Walpole and the ministry.[5]

Political interpretations were given not only to older plays but also to new pieces, even where they were not intended by the author. William Duncombe, the author of *Junius Brutus,* which was acted at Drury Lane in 1734, wrote to Mrs. Clayton, his patroness:

Mr. Fleetwood has told me, to my great surprise, that an invidious construction has been put on several passages . . . , as if intended to reflect on the Government, which was the furthest thing in the world from my thoughts, and gives him great uneasiness as well as me.[6]

The failure of this play resulted from the inadequate support given it by the actors, who, aware of popular sentiment, were chary about taking parts in a play that might make large numbers of political enemies for them. It is no wonder that Davies, speaking of the troublesome days of the mid-century when clamors for war were heard on every side, remarks that "the spectators were ready to apply all that was uttered in the theatre to the transactions of the day and to the ministry." [7]

The reception of single scenes from four of Shakespeare's plays furnishes a kind of standard of measurement as to the intensity of contemporary political interest in the drama. Such a scene is the one between Brutus and Cassius in *Julius Caesar* (IV, iii). Here the two Roman leaders almost come to blows before patching up their quarrel, but not before Cassius the pragmatist has shocked the idealistic Brutus by his willingness to exonerate Lucius Pella, even though the latter was guilty of accepting bribes. The possible application to Walpole is apparent; and it is notable that Davies remarks that the scene "has maintained its important character to this hour." [8] An account by the same contemporary leaves no doubt of the reception of a scene in *Richard II*. When Bridgewater, as the Earl of Northumberland, spoke the lines (II, i) "the king is not himself, but basely led/By flatterers," the noise from the clapping of hands and clattering of sticks was loud and boisterous. And when Ross said, "The earl of Wiltshire hath the state in farm," it was immediately applied to Walpole with the loudest shouts and huzzas I ever heard. Likewise the following observation of Northumberland, that the king's revenue was not diminished by war, was met, by the audience, with redoubled shouts —"War hath not wasted it; for warr'd he hath not./More hath he spent in peace than they [his ancestors] in war." [9]

In both examples the words of Shakespeare were made to serve the cause of the Opposition.

A more affirmative use in the cause of patriotism was made of *Timon of Athens*. Although this was not one of the popular Shakespearean plays in the eighteenth century, it was well received in Cumberland's alteration. How Cumberland had made the play carry a political burden is illustrated in an additional scene (II, iii), which contains the following notable lines:

> *Alcibiades.*   . . . ye are Lords:
> A lazy, proud, unprofitable crew:
> The vermin gender'd from the rank corruption
> Of a luxurious state—No soldiers, say you?
> And wherefore are ye none? Have ye not life,
> Friends, honour, freedom, country to defend?
> He, that hath these, by nature is a soldier,
> And when he wields his sword in their defense,
> Instinctively fulfils the end he lives for. . . .[10]

Finally, the restoration by Thomas Sheridan of IV, iv, to *Hamlet*, a scene long omitted in the representation,[11] is indicative of the patriotic feelings of the audience. Once more it could hear the soliloquy "How all occasions do inform against me," with its moralizing on man and his willingness to sacrifice even life itself for the national glory. It is perhaps also worthy of note that this scene contains the Norwegian captain's remark that his men are marching against Poland to contest for "a little patch of ground/That hath in it no profit but the name," a description reminiscent of a common remark of the day that Canada, for which so much blood was being shed, was "no more than a patch of snow."

The plays mentioned were, of course, innocent of deliberate reference to the political situation in the eighteenth century, since they were revived plays of an earlier time. But others in the repertory had a more explicit connection, frequently being written to support current patriotic interests or to attack political foes. A survey of England's history during the forty-year period in the light of theatrical and dramatic affairs reveals that there were at least five events that significantly affected the repertory or its reception by the audience: the Licensing Act of 1737, the Jacobite uprising, the mid-century war with France, the change of monarchs in 1760, and the sporadic outbursts of feeling against the Scots. Besides these, and closely related to them, was the continuing interest in the domestic policies of the government, which was often reflected in the theater.

Of these, only the effect of the Licensing Act of 1737 on the theater has received adequate treatment.[12] Such writers for the opposition as Dodsley, Fielding, Thomson, Mallet, and Brooke, who found their political center in the person of Frederick, Prince of Wales, turned naturally to the drama as a means of attacking Walpole, the ministry, corruption among officials close to the king, and the governmental policy of maintaining the long-continued but precarious peace in spite of the widespread demand for war. Before the passage of the act, such plays as Fielding's *Pasquin* and *The Historical Register for the Year 1736,* outspokenly antigovernment in tone, and Dodsley's *The King and the Miller of Mansfield,* with its jibes at courtiers, met with popular approval. But after the creation of a regular office of censorship under the authority of the lord chamberlain, only occasionally did a play containing outspoken attacks on the government manage to escape prohibition.

Two such plays that did escape were Thomson's *Agamemnon,* which has passages directed against the government's peace policy and the corruption of officials, and Mallet's *Mustapha,* an anti-Walpole tragedy in which the heir to the throne is made the hero.[13] *Alfred,* a play in which both these dramatists collaborated, and apparently written at the Prince of Wales' command,[14] was regarded at the time as containing "several party hints, and one invidious reflection," but it was also given performance. Of the plays that were less fortunate, the best-known are Brooke's *Gustavus Vasa,* which inspired Johnson's satirical pamphlet *A Complete Vindication of the Licensers of the Stage,* and Thomson's *Edward and Eleanora,* prohibited because of the resemblance of the play's hero to the Prince of Wales. Of the censorship of Brooke's play, one contemporary remarked, "I think the prohibition of it a more severe libel than any I have read." [15] The successful sales of the printed editions of the two plays are indicative of the temper of the public, which objected to such infringement of its cherished rights; these sales also suggest that the success on the stage of *Agamemnon, Mustapha, Alfred,* and their successors, however coldly conceived, was in part owing to the political opinions of the audience. For the same reason Hildebrand Jacob's *The Nest of Plays,* the "first fruits" of the Licensing Act, was irrevocably damned on its first appearance; for, as an abbé then visiting in England remarked, "The best play in the world would not have succeeded that night." [16]

Although the Licensing Act was nominally in force for more than a century, ways were soon found to circumvent many of its regulations. Giffard's successful seasons at Goodman's Fields and Foote's popular "Dish of Tea" are only the best known among the frequent violations of its provision restricting to two the number of theaters in London. As this provision became more honored in the breach than in the observance, there came about the recognized distinction between the "major" and "minor" theaters, and with it the rise of a new dramatic form— the burletta. Burlettas were originally shorter pieces containing a considerable number of songs, but the term was soon applied to any dramatic work acceptable for performance at a minor theater. Since the burletta, which was required to have the songs in order to escape censorship as "drama," stimulated the production of other types of musical pieces, the act is indirectly responsible for giving impetus to a movement that in the last quarter of the century determined a large part of the repertory—namely, the numerous operatic farces and melodramas. The regulation requiring that plays be submitted to the censor a fortnight before their stage representation also came to be disregarded, and, as already shown, the immediate purpose of the parliamentary measure—to prohibit attacks on the government from the stage—was only partly successful from the beginning. Thus the most famous attempt to regulate the stage in England's history, even though the law was not repealed for more than a century, was largely frustrated from the start—not only by the professionals whose livelihood and reputations were at stake, but by the spectators themselves, who would brook no interference where their favorite amusement was concerned.

Perhaps no single political event of the period was directly responsible for such an outburst of theatrical activity as was the Jacobite affair of 1744-1745. Interest in the attempt of Bonnie Prince Charlie to regain his grandfather's throne is reflected both in the revivals of older and almost forgotten plays and in new pieces apparently written purposely to exploit the popular excitement over the events in the north. Of the new plays, Charles Macklin's *King Henry VII, or the Popish Impostor,* and Cibber's *Papal Tyranny in the Reign of King John* (actually a free reworking of Shakespeare's historical play) are the most notable. As the titles suggest, the point of issue upon which the two dramatists seized was more sectarian than national. Cibber, apparently unaware that Shakespeare had rejected much of the anti-Roman spirit of his source, says in the prologue that he undertook the revision because Shakespeare had overlooked the opportunity to make the most of the rivalry between John and the pope. Although Cibber's play met with some success, its importance is chiefly owing to its influence in causing the original *King John* to be revived at Drury Lane to compete against the alteration then current at Covent Garden. Macklin's play was based on the story of Perkin Warbeck, which also furnished the plot for a play by Elderton, intended for the Covent Garden stage but finished too late in the season to be acted. In the meantime the rebellion was put down, and it was then "thought unreasonable to revive it on the stage." [17]

At this time almost every play that could be given an anti-Jacobite bias was revived, including Dennis' *Liberty Asserted* and *A Plot and No Plot,* Tomkis' *Albumazar,* Ford's *Perkin Warbeck,* Cibber's *The Nonjuror,* and Lee's *Massacre of Paris,* as well as Shakespeare's *King John.* Victor says that *The Nonjuror* was an "acknowledged Government Play";[18] of *Liberty Asserted* and *Plot and No Plot,* which were revived on the same night, Genest reports that they were staged respectively for "the invectives against the French" and "the cuts on the Jacobites." [19] *Albumazar's* brief stage history in the eighteenth century seems to have been owing partly to its reference to the Jesuits. It was brought to the stage again in 1773, with the reference strengthened, and made to allude to the order's suppression in that year.[20] Genest thought the prologue to *Massacre of Paris* "was as well suited to 1745 as if it had been written on purpose." [21]

Although the inclusion of such plays in the repertory was the most important effect of the Jacobite rebellion on the English stage, other events also show the influence on the theater of the intense popular feeling. When, in 1745, Mrs. Cibber offered to play the part of Polly in *The Beggar's Opera* three nights as a benefit performance, a writer in the *General Advertiser* who signed himself "Veteran Protestant" objected on the ground that she was a Catholic.[22] But her reply that she was a loyal subject of the king satisfied all but the most bigoted objectors. The actors were on the whole in sympathy with the government, as is suggested by an announcement in the *General Advertiser* that Lacy had asked leave to raise 200 men in defense of the country and that "the whole company of players are willing to engage." [23]

The intermittent wars with France that occupied much of the attention of the English in the mid-century are also reflected in the dramatic repertory. Two of Mallet's plays, *Britannia* and *Elvira,* were immediately inspired by contemporary events. *Britannia,* a masque with music by Arne, was written "to rouze the British spirit" [24] in the year that saw General Braddock defeated in America, and England on the verge of the Seven Years' War. *Elvira* contained an attack on Lord Bute at the time he had negotiated with France a peace treaty that the politicians considered disadvantageous.[25] A favorable reception was assured Glover's *Boadicia* in 1753, because the playwright, then famous as the author of the patriotic epic *Leonidas,* was highly regarded as "a patriot and a true lover of his country." [26] Dr. Brown's *Athelstan,* brought to the stage three years later, was described as "an excellent warning to every insurgent" who might be tempted to aid the French in an invasion of England.[27] This strongly nationalistic note was also struck frequently in the prologues and epilogues furnished the plays when they were performed. Typical of such pieces are the following passages from, respectively, the prologues to *Douglas* and to *Edward the Black Prince:*

> Oft has this audience soft compassion shown
> To woes of heroes, heroes not their own.

This night our scenes no common tear demand,
He comes, the hero of your native land!

Our bard tonight, no doubtful story brings,
Of native, genuine *English* feats he sings;
. . . sure that tale must have for *Britons* charms,
That shows you *France* subdu'd by *British* arms.

Similar sentiments are expressed in the prologue to *Britannia*, the epilogue to Brooke's *The Earl of Essex,* and a host of others, often so popular with the audience that the occasional piece outlived the play for which it was written. [28]

The theatrical fortunes of two early seventeenth-century plays were dependent upon the accession of George III. Shortly after the new king came to the throne, Garrick, in keeping with his practice of reviving older plays, put in rehearsal Beaumont and Fletcher's *King and No King.* While the parts were still being studied he turned against the projected revival, and the play was dropped. The inappropriateness of the title just at that time seems to have been one of the reasons for withdrawing the play.[29] Shakespeare's *Henry VIII* met with a different fate, however. Because this play gave the opportunity for spectacular processions and coronation scenes, it was performed frequently at this time, as it had been in 1727 when the new king's grandfather had ascended the throne. The differing tastes of the two Georges are also reflected in the repertory; but this manifestation, because it concerns morals rather than politics, is considered in the following chapter.

Enmity against the Scots—like that against the French—was often reflected in the theatrical history of the time. For example, when Home's *The Fatal Discovery* was brought to the stage (1769), the author, acting on Garrick's advice, concealed his name. The play was well received until Home revealed his authorship, after which the audiences immediately dwindled because of the intense feeling against the Scots.[30] Ten years earlier, Macklin's farce *Love à la Mode* had also been very favorably received. The two principal characters—a Scot and an Irishman—were played by the author and Moody, the latter a favorite in eccentric roles. The Scot was portrayed in such an odious light that Lord Bute tried to have the play prohibited. He failed in his attempt, but his intervention, says Walpole, "made the ridicule on the Scotch the more tasted." [31]

Internal affairs of government helped to determine the dramatic repertory during the later years of the mid-century also. Hugh Kelly's first play, *False Delicacy,* was given an "extraordinary reception," but at that time he had no political affiliations. Before his next play appeared, he had sided with the ministerial party in the Wilkes affair. As a result, when *A Word to the Wise* was brought out, a play that critics recognized as superior to his first attempt, a party was formed to damn it and riots ensued between Kelly's friends and the Wilkes faction. The antiministerial element in the audience succeeded, and thereafter Kelly's plays were produced without the author's name.[32] The plays of Brooke apparently succeeded because they kept alive the "spirit which [Bolingbroke] kindled during the administration of Walpole." [33] Frequent passages in new plays seem to allude to contemporary troubles in parliament and the ministry. For example, Southampton in Jones' *The Earl of Essex* probably reminded the audience of the current factionalism in the cabinet during the ministry of Pelham when he exclaimed:

> How ill had Providence
> Dispos'd the suffering world's opprest affairs,
> Had sacred right's eternal rule been left
> To crafty politicians' partial sway.[34]

The spirit that had made *Cato* a remarkable success when it first appeared was by no means extinct.

Correctly to assess the role of political and patriotic considerations in determining what plays were given performance and how they were received by the mid-eighteenth-century audience is to describe the British spirit in terms of one of its important manifestations. To recognize that Charles Bannister became especially popular because of "his truly English style of singing and acting . . . ";[35] to note that a new play—*The Spanish Lady*—could be quickly written and staged to take advantage of the news just received of an important victory in the West Indies;[36] to realize that even such an expensively mounted and spectacularly novel production as *The Chinese Festival* failed because the actors were believed to be French[37]—is to be aware that the audience's intense interest in both national issues and domestic policies had a far-reaching influence upon the actor, the playwright, and the manager in determining the theatrical repertory of the period. Naturally, the theater, as a medium of popular expression, had always reflected such interest although often faintly or indirectly; but never had it been so persistently affected for such a long period, nor—and here we seem to be dealing in paradox if we compare the period to that earlier time which culminated in the defeat of the Spanish Armada—was this propensity ever before detrimental to the quality of drama, as was true when the patriotic moralizer became a necessary and expected character in all new plays of a serious kind.

It will be noted that this stock character is here called a moralizer. In an age during which the British Empire was being forged, concurrently with the rise in importance of that class of society whose interests were most intimately connected with those of empire, references to national power and glory were an almost necessary and certainly a successful ingredient of drama. Moreover, if we consider that the philosopher-historians were industriously documenting popular interest by searching in the nation's and the world's past for universal principles that they could use as standards for the reconstruction of national society, it is no wonder that such references were frequently placed in the mouth of a "man in general," [38] the patriotic moralizer of the piece. How essential the playwrights felt it to be to satisfy the popular demand for moralizing in the patriotic vein is shown by the strenuous and well-intentioned, even if dramatically damaging, efforts to which they went, often providing such an opportunity only by unmotivated tragicomic denouements, by the use of the *deus ex machina,* or by distorting historical truth.

To what extent popular nationalism and anti-Rockinghamism might carry along the playwright is perhaps best illustrated by the apotheosis of England that ends Logan's *Runnamede,* a play written at the end of the period. The Archbishop, whom Logan has portrayed as the catalytic agent in making of the Normans and the Saxons a united nation ready to destroy any Continental foe (history is greatly telescoped in this play), after carrying out all his plans successfully, proclaims:

> The Queen of isles behold
> Sitting sublime upon her rocky throne,
> The region of the storms! She stretches forth
> In her right hand, the sceptre of the sea,
> And in her left the balance of the earth.
> The Guardian of the globe, she gives the law:

> She calls the winds, the winds obey her call,
> And bear the thunder of her power, to burst
> O'er the devoted lands, and carry fate
> To Kings, to nations, and the subject world.
> Above the Grecian or the Roman name,
> Unlike the great destroyers of the globe,
> She fights and conquers in fair Freedom's cause.
> Her song of victory the nations sing:
> Her triumphs are the triumphs of mankind.

There were no doubt many among the theatergoing populace who, with the laudable virtues of an eighteenth-century Brutus, must have agreed with the idealistic prelate of Logan's play.

England's manifest destiny was indeed the concern of moment during the later years of the century. And in 1800, when many writers felt it incumbent upon them to take stock of the passing era, there was much proclaiming that "the Close of this century, as the Close of the last, finds us again in the character of Saviours of Europe," and that "Religion, Virtue, Glory, shall adorn/Th'illustrious age of George. . . ." [39] But this recognition of England's cosmic role was not unmotivated; nor was it of sudden birth. Throughout the second half of the century there had been a growing preoccupation with the springs of national origin and with the process of historical development.[40] Complementing this was the heightened interest in foreign lands, especially those being incorporated gradually into the British Empire.

Both these interests—in distant lands and in distant ages—had a readily discernible effect upon the drama. The former influenced both the selection of subject matter for dramas written in the period and the popularity of older plays chosen for revival. Among the older plays, perhaps the most notable example is that of *Oroonoko,* which failed to reach the stage in only five seasons between 1737 and 1777. It was one of a relatively small number of serious dramas from the late seventeenth century considered worthy of revival, and it was therefore given the benefit of alteration that would make it congenial to the times. The alteration placed greater emphasis upon the humanitarian aspects of the play than was to be found in Southerne's original—a change in keeping with contemporary attitudes. The racial origin of Oroonoko and Imoinda was not only no obstacle for an age that could find in the "noble savage"

an image of its own humanitarian ideal, but also a manifestation of the universality of those human principles for which
the philosopher-historians were searching. Moreover, the setting in the West Indies, where many of England's mercantile
families had sent their sons and fathers, gave the play a sense
of immediacy that belied its considerable age.

It is, however, in the new drama that the popular interest
in America, Africa, and Asia, the three regions in which the
young British Empire was expanding, made itself felt most no-
ticeably. Early in the period a series of dramas had been based
on Eastern themes, such as Marsh's *Amasis* (1738), Mallet's
Mustapha (1739), Miller's *Mahomet* (1744), and Johnson's
Irene (1749). Some years later, Dow, while visiting the East
Indies, collected material for his *Zingis* (1768), a tragedy based
on a history of the Mogul Tartars written in Persian.[41] It is
worthy of note that about this same time Warren Hastings was
urging that the study of Persian be introduced into English
schools.[42] Africa furnished the setting for Mackenzie's *Prince
of Tunis* (1773) and Dow's *Sethona* (1774), and English imperial designs on that continent furnished the motive for Dr.
Bentley's *Philodamus* (published in 1767 although not acted
until 1782), a drama that "was meant to satirize our modern
Nabobs in Africa." [43] Of the plays based on American themes,
Cumberland's *The West Indian* (1771) was most favorably received; and although the West Indian planter was said not to
have been drawn with accuracy, the character was then new
to the stage and made the play a "favourite comedy at the
time." [44] Rogers' *Ponteach* (1766) was subtitled *Savages of
America* or, according to one contemporary play list, *An American Tragedy*. Murphy used a Peruvian setting for his *Alzuma*
(1773). The list of plays drawing upon foreign themes could
be readily expanded. It is apparent that drama was following
popular interest to distant lands in the choice of settings.

Dramatists apparently agreed with Dr. Johnson that anything
written of foreign lands and exploration would likely achieve
financial success.[45] Interest in the lands themselves, in their
peoples and manners, and in the activities there of English
merchants and government officers who were helping to extend
British prestige and dominion was widespread, as is illustrated
by the frequent references in contemporary documents. Walpole, for example, refers frequently in his letters to what he

calls "Nabob-land" even though he admits he understands Indian affairs no better than stocks.[46] A recent historian of the period concludes: "The fascination of the Orient in particular held the English mind under its spell, and played no small part in moulding the operation of English thought." [47] The increasingly large number of travel books that were published is another proof of the general interest in the remote.[48] Since it was from a populace thus interested in other lands that the theater drew its audiences, it is no wonder that dramatists tried to exploit that interest and that the theater managers gave such plays frequent performance.

England's own historical and legendary past also was widely used in various forms for the substance of drama during the mid-century. Nearly every period in British history was represented by one or more plays. Glover pictures the ancient Britons struggling against the Roman invaders in his *Boadicia* (1753). Mason's *Caractacus* (1764) is laid in the days of the Druids. Anglo-Saxon England furnished the subjects for Brown's *Athelstan* (1756), Mason's *Elfrida* (printed 1757, acted 1777), Home's *Alfred* (1778), and Mallet's play of the same title (1751). Historical events of the eleventh and twelfth centuries were used in Francklin's *Matilda* (1775), Mrs. More's *Percy* (1777), and Hull's *Henry the Second* (1773). The various Plantagenet reigns and the Hundred Years' War are represented by Hartson's *The Countess of Salisbury* (1765), Home's *Douglas* (1756), Shirley's *Edward the Black Prince* (1750), Thomson's *Edward and Eleanora* (1739), and Jackson's *The British Heroine* (1778). Both Francklin's *The Earl of Warwick* (1766) and Jerningham's *Margaret of Anjou* (1777) made use of the War of the Roses, and Macklin's *Henry VII* (1747) represents the early Tudor period. The reign of Elizabeth furnished the plots for Jones (1753) and Brooke (1750), both of whom wrote plays titled *The Earl of Essex*. The reign of James I was used for *Sir Thomas Overbury* (1777); the Civil Wars, for Harvard's *King Charles the First* (1737) and Greene's unacted *Oliver Cromwell* (1757); recent history, for Cockings' *The Conquest of Canada* (1766).

The popularity of older historical plays is a further indication of the audience's preoccupation with their nation's past. Three of John Banks' plays that were based upon English history in the late sixteenth century—*The Unhappy Favorite,*

Virtue Betray'd, and *The Island Queens*—were occasionally revived, and evidence shows that some of the interest in Rowe's popular pathetic tragedies *Jane Shore, Lady Jane Grey,* and *The Royal Convert* [49] may be ascribable to an interest in their historical settings. As already noted, most of Shakespeare's chronicle plays also were acted in the period, some with considerable frequency. The numerous performances of such a play as *Richard III* cannot be entirely explained on the basis of the audience's interest in its historical content;[50] the opportunity it afforded a powerful actor to portray the despotic king —particularly Garrick, who made his first London appearance in this play—is the more probable explanation for its success on the mid-century stage. The two parts of *Henry IV* were frequently acted because of the perennial popularity of Falstaff; but *Henry V,* which was performed even more often, succeeded without a Falstaff, and its success may be to a considerable extent owing to the nationalistic tone of the play. It is perhaps profitless to inquire how much of the popularity of others of the chronicle plays—for example, *King John, Henry VIII,* and *Richard II*—was owing to the contemporary interest in history, how much to the revived interest in earlier—especially Shakespearean—drama and how much to the strength of the principal roles. But it should be remembered, at least, that in a period when hardly a subject was more exploited by contemporary playwrights than was English history, these plays of Shakespeare, in spite of their violation of almost all the critical precepts of the day, were frequently brought to the stage and were outdistanced in popularity only by the tragedies from the hand of the same master.

The reason for this interest in historical drama is to be explained on several grounds. The British were becoming more intensely aware of their national integrity and of the increasingly important status of their nation as the center of a world empire. This awareness caused many to look to the past either for guidance or for explanation of origins and causes. Macpherson shows that he recognized the importance of history on both counts when he said, in the introduction to his *Secret History of Great Britain:* "The greatest part of mankind form their political opinions on the usages of past times." [51] The moral values of history to a doctrinaire age must also be assessed. "The Philosophers . . . tell us," says Becker, "that history, in connection with morality, is, of all subjects, one of the most important to be studied." [52] Finally, the antiquarian interest, the influence of which was becoming felt in all varieties of endeavor, naturally resulted in an increased interest in history as the antiquarians turned their attention to the customs, artifacts, and documents of past times. Thus political, moral, and cultural considerations were combining to influence the mid-century repertory in its historical content.

But the whole question of national morality must be examined more closely. That patriotism was rampant is frequently attested in the theater, sometimes to the point of petty chauvinism. No other explanation is possible for the alteration of *The Merchant of Venice,* for example, that omitted from the recital of Portia's unsuccessful suitors only the young English baron and the Scottish lord. And Garrick, even in a jesting epilogue (to *The Lying Valet*), shows that he believes the national character no jesting matter:

> *Sometimes you'll see a man* belye *his nation,*
> *Nor to his country shew the least relation.*
> *For instance now—*
> *A cleanly Dutchman, or a* Frenchman *grave,*
> *A sober* German, *or a Spaniard* brave,
> *An* Englishman *a coward or a slave.*

A complacent regard for the British character and reliance on the historical processes that were making England "the Guardian of the Globe" produced a feeling of national well-being that would have been impossible in the days of the "boy patriots" and the Jacobite troubles a half-century earlier. But there are signs that below the surface there were less admirable motives, that national eupepsia and patriotic ardor are not to be equated with sweetness and light. Burke, for example, felt it necessary to warn his countrymen that "mean thoughts and a great empire go ill together"; and later, when looking back over the course of English history during the century, he declared that the only war that originated in popular desire was that with Spain in 1739, one "which threatened little bloodshed, and which promised victories that were attended with something more solid than glory. A war with Spain was a war of plunder." [53] Indeed, British imperialism was resting also upon certain other qualities—to which the term "middle-class" is often affixed in a pejorative sense—qualities more earthly than spiritual, more prudential than idealistic.

CHAPTER FOURTEEN

Morals and Sentiment

The question of the extent to which the moral tone of the audience is reflected in the theatrical repertory of the period is a complex one. During the forty years there were many among the actors, critics, and playwrights, as well as among the people whose relation to the theater was amateur, who deplored the degraded state of public morality and insisted that the stage's moral laxity was not the cause but the result thereof. Thus, *Fog's Journal* proclaimed, "Nobody, of Morals, I may venture to say, but has long wish'd to see a Reformation of the Stage; but I fear, 'till we see a reformed Taste of the Town . . . the Theatres will continue as immoral as ever." [1] An anonymous writer in *The Craftsman* states the argument even more emphatically, using an excuse familiar since the days of Dryden: "The *Immorality of the People* is so far from being owing to the *Licentiousness of the Stage,* that the *Licentiousness of the Stage* is immediately owing to the *Immorality of the People,* which . . . obliges *necessitous Writers* to comply with the prevailing Humour of the Times." [2] He then defends the contemporary drama by pointing out that there are not "half so many Instances of Debauchery, Prophaneness and Blasphemy, in any of our *modern Plays,* as are to be found in those of *Dryden, Etherege, Wycherly, Congreve, Vanbrugh,* and others." Chesterfield, in his famous speech opposing passage of the Licensing Act of 1737, also blames the times rather than the theater: "When we complain of the Licentiousness of the Stage, I fear we have more Reason to complain of bad Measures in our Polity, and a general Decay of Virtue and good Morality among the People." [3]

Forty years later, times had apparently changed but little, for Cumberland, recalling the reception given his own *Fashionable Lover* in 1772, remarks that the play was "laudably directed against national prejudice, breach of trust, seduction, gaming,

[1] For notes to chap. 14, see pp. 341-344.

and the general dissipation of the time then present";[4] and one reviewer of *The School for Scandal* found that play not only an excellent but also a "seasonable" comedy because of the twofold "object of [its] satire . . . detraction and hypocrisy . . . the prevailing vices of the times. . . ." [5]

There is no gainsaying the fact that in many ways the times were corrupt. On the national level, the example set by Walpole, whose creed was that every man had his price, and the conduct and tastes of the king, who once dismissed his chaplain for preaching "A Persuasive to Chastity," [6] and found such morally lax plays as *The London Cuckolds* and *The Fair Quaker of Deal* most to his liking, naturally enough did not inspire moral behavior. Gaming, extravagance of various kinds, detraction, hypocrisy, and sexual immorality were prevalent. Yet there was a strong and largely beneficial leaven in that element of society which was beginning to make its power and influence felt—the middle class. Not only had this middle class inherited many of the puritan ideals of an earlier age, but, by the accumulation of wealth from growing industry and world trade, it was becoming more and more conscious of its obligations to society at large and to itself. Nor did the pursuit of bourgeois ideals leave either opportunity or inclination for the cultivation of time- and wealth-consuming follies and vices. Consequently, as the middle class grew stronger, moral ideals more frequently found expression, although it is apparent that their expression was often a result of the materialistic attitude that was developing—one more paradox of the eighteenth century.

Perhaps the external indications of an improved moral tone were sometimes blurred by a sanctimonious fastidiousness that demanded the expunging of the most innocuous oaths from Shakespeare's plays, and caused even the eminently sane Dr. Johnson to object to the words "O! by my soul" in Boswell's humorous verses "A Matrimonial Thought." [7] But there are also numerous indications that the sentiments that had found expression in Jeremy Collier and, a quarter-century later, in William Law had not been weakened. In spite of the apparent superficiality, the dominant attitude of the later eighteenth century, far from being merely negative, was becoming one of affirmation—one that drew upon prudential virtue for its ethic and upon the popular, however formal, emotionalism for its ontology. An institution as communal as the theater—especially when its audience came to include a large middle-class segment—may reasonably be expected to reflect this situation.

One of the most congenial methods of presenting moral substance in an age that preferred subtlety in its actors to subtlety in its playwrights was that of casting it in a moralizing vein and putting it in the mouth of a character whose chief function was often no more than to utter such remarks. Dubech notes the pervasiveness of this stock character:

Naturally enough, the prototype, in Cibber's *The Lady's Last Stake,* is called Sir Friendly Moral. Then this function is taken over by a father, as in *The West Indian,* and by a brother, as in *The Jealous Wife.* The roles are identical; they preach against dueling, gambling, jealousy, the fashionable vices.[8]

There were few new comedies and almost no new tragedies that did not have such a character.

But, not only was the moralizing strain used to attack current vices and follies; it also served to extol virtues highly regarded by the contemporary audiences. Of these, none seems to have been more frequently treated than domestic bliss. For example, when Garrick wished to "ensure success" of a benefit performance that he resolved to give for the indigent Cambridge scholar Christopher Smart, he completed the almost finished *The Guardian.*[9] This piece turns upon the happy union of Harriet and her guardian, and ends with a couplet promising that

> His friendly care shall change to grateful love,
> And the fond husband still the Guardian prove.

Not only was the piece considered by the spectators as truly edifying; the manager, the actors, and the beneficiary rightly anticipated its success for that very reason. Similarly, the revived *Rule a Wife and Have a Wife* owed much of its success to its "admirable lesson for proper conduct in the married state. . . ."[10]

Such a state of affairs is indeed a far remove from the *esprit gaulois* of Restoration comedy, but its *raison d'être* is not difficult to determine. Among the more restricted and more aristocratic audience of the later seventeenth century, cuckoldom was the privileged domain of comedy on the stage and of hardly more serious consideration in life. An idle and lax society, secure in its perquisites, risked neither material loss nor social ostracism through its debauchery. But later audiences, more heterogeneous and more representative of a wealth-minded middle class, recognized both the material consequences of such conduct and the stabilizing force of nuptial security. Davies inadvertently let the middle-class cat out of the bag: "I believe, since Collier's book was published, our magistrates of London have pretty much escaped the ridicule of theatrical horns." [11]

How universal was the opinion that moral teaching was a necessary ingredient of drama is typified by the stage history of two mid-century plays, one frequently revived and the other a near failure. The former, Miller's *Mahomet*, kept the stage, says a contemporary, because its subject was "of much importance to society, and, on account of its moral doctrine." [12] The latter, Whitehead's *Creusa*, although "ill adapted to the taste of a modern audience," owed what little success it had to its "excellent lessons of politicks and morals," and to Garrick's "skill in delivering didacticks." [13] That even a farce might be expected to have a didactic purpose is indicated by the anonymous "friend" who wrote the prologue to *Miss in Her Teens*.

Older plays were also given the moralizing treatment in alteration, from which several of Shakespeare's dramas did not escape. *Richard II* is so treated in Goodhall's version, which ends with the couplet:

> The Bad may please us in the guilty Part,
> But the Just only share the Monarch's Heart.

And Hazlitt later condemned the most popular of Shakespearean alterations in the eighteenth century, Cibber's *Richard III*, because of the "tedious whining morality of the uxorious king" that it contained.[14] Johnson's observations on two of Shakespeare's comedies illustrate more than just that critic's view of drama. Of *As You Like It*, he remarks: "By hastening to the end of his work, Shakespeare suppressed the dialogue between the usurper and the hermit, and lost an opportunity of exhibiting a moral lesson in which he might have found matter worthy of his highest powers," and of *Twelfth Night* he says that Shakespeare "fails to produce the proper instruction required in the drama. . . ." [15] Wilkinson gives an interesting account of the practice of introducing moral sentiments in the drama:

It must be admitted, that in modern comedies the players, as usual, are brought all together for the purpose of moralizing at the conclusion, but to very little purpose regarding the entertainment of the audience, except its being a kind of joy to the nodding auditory, and the hinting it is near bed time, and a good preparatory lull for their night's repose.[16]

We may accept Wilkinson's testimony as to the prevalence of the custom; but as to its reception by the audience—the fact that moralizing comedy continued to be written, even surviving the attacks of Goldsmith and Sheridan, and that it prepared the way for the fashionable melodrama of the later eighteenth century,[17] is sufficient proof of its welcome by the audience.

From what has been said, it is apparent that the audience regarded instruction as a proper end of drama—an end congenial with its own expanding horizons. Indeed, one recent student of the period concludes: "The overwhelming impression given by the century as a whole . . . is . . . that the *utile* took precedence over the *dulce*." [18] There are a few indications to the contrary. Cibber's *Love in a Riddle* (1729), even though, as the author proclaimed, it was an attempt to recommend virtue and innocence by means of a drama modeled upon the type popularized by *The Beggar's Opera*,[19] was damned by the audience after two nights, and a near riot ensued in spite of the Prince of Wales' presence. It is noteworthy that in 1729 the moral tone was not yet enough to counterbalance the audience's objections on other grounds. And an anonymous refutation of Caleb D'Anvers' statement in *The Craftsman* that the chief purpose of drama is to expose vice and folly in all ranks of people makes the claim that such a theory has long been exploded and has not been true since the days of Aristophanes.[20] But for the most part, authors and critics alike agreed that to the audiences moral doctrine was a not unpleasant ingredient in drama. Thus Aaron Hill, a dominant force among playwrights and playgoers until his death in 1750, had stated his views in his very first dramatic attempt:

> You know, who profit with your pleasure love,
> The stage shou'd both divert us and improve.[21]

At the close of the period a reviewer of *The School for Scandal* makes the same assumption: "Nothing is surely of more importance to the world than the proper regulation of the theatres, and the continually reminding them of the important duty they have undertaken, that of combating vice by every weapon which human ingenuity can invent, and supporting the cause of virtue." [22] Sheridan himself, whom this reviewer was attacking for his purported neglect of moral preachment, commented in his prologue to *A Trip to Scarborough*, which appeared in the same year (1777):

> Those writers well and wisely use their pens,
> Who turn our wantons into Magdalens.

Yet in spite of this academic view of drama, the moral tone of a considerable part of the repertory was of such a nature that we are led to suspect a divergence in the audience's mental processes between the social acceptance of a conventional ethical attitude and the practical enjoyment of the risqué and licentious situations which had amused earlier audiences. It was as if the populace reveled vicariously in sins that social code and materialistic necessity combined to make more hazardous in the personal commission than they had formerly been. Lyttelton's fictitious Persian, Selim, noted this strange circumstance:

As I now understand *English* pretty well, I went last night with some friends to see a play. The principal character was a young fellow, who in the space of three or four hours that the action lasted, cuckolds two or three husbands, and debauches as many virgins. I had heard that the English theatre was famous for killing people upon the stage: but this author was more for *propagating than destroying*. There were a great many ladies at the representation of this modest performance; and, though they sometimes hid their faces with their fans, (I suppose for fear of shewing that they did *not* blush) yet, in general, they seemed to be much delighted with the *fine gentleman's* heroical exploits.[23]

Selim was presumably observing London's customs about 1735; but there was no far-reaching change noticeable for another quarter of a century.

A moral stigma had long been attached to the stage and its

players, and statutes and proclamations had been necessary for their regulation as early as the reign of Henry VIII.[24] Indeed, for a brief period in the history of the English theater—the later seventeenth century—the audience, unwilling to give up its entertainment, demanded that its feminine members appear in masks. The fan of which Selim speaks was the successor to the mask of Restoration audiences; and, in spite of the prideful claims of contemporaries as to the reformation of the stage in the wake of Collier, Cibber, and Steele, fashionable accouterments that could represent ritualistic moral objection without hindering the enjoyment of the drama were still necessary. One critic found matters even worse than formerly: ". . . it is grown almost necessary for a Man's Reputation and Interest to appear in a *Mask.*" [25]

Walpole noted this curious discrepancy in mid-century audiences:

Our stage grew chaste; indecency dared not to show its face in a modern comedy, though it still remained in possession of the old ones; and what is remarkable, having been tolerated when women went to the theatre in masks, preserved its hold, now they went without them.[26]

Although Walpole locates the line of distinction between new and revived drama—a situation generally true—the matter is not quite so simple; for by 1758, the year of which he is speaking, many older plays had been expurgated before reaching the stage, and several of the new comedies had continued to slog through the moral swamps of the later seventeenth century. It seems more valid, therefore, to think of the temper of the contemporary audience as an imperfect fusion of its theoretical and practical moral views—a hypothesis that a consideration of certain indications of the audience's superficiality in matters of morality tends to reinforce; or, in Selim's terms, compared to the mask, the fan had the advantage in being able to disguise the blush (or its absence) without concealing its owner's identity.

The dichotomy just described can readily be seen in the inconsistency of attitude toward individual plays. On the side of improved moral tone may be mentioned the expunging of the most licentious passages from *The Provok'd Wife,* one of the most popular comedies of the eighteenth century, as early as 1725 when it was revived at Lincoln's Inn Fields.[27] Another change made in this play and kept in later performances was the substitution in the night scene of woman's disguise for Brute instead of that of an inebriated parson. Both changes reflect public recognition of the need for drama that was inoffensive to the moral sense. Three years later, Cibber, in continuing Vanbrugh's *The Journey to London* as *The Provok'd Husband,* although he largely followed the original, felt it necessary in the fifth act to recall "the lady's heart to a sense of her conjugal duties, as well as [to show] her the frivolities and miseries of her former conduct." [28] Here again an older play is made to conform outwardly to contemporary moral standards, although there may have been many who agreed with Edmund Burke that of Cibber's "morals or bawdry it is hard to judge which is most fulsome." [29]

On the other hand, *The Relapse* continued to be highly popular with eighteenth-century audiences, apparently without serious alteration in spite of its moral laxity; and it was not completely expurgated until 1776, when Lee thus advertised his alteration:

The Editor of these scenes thinks it proper to acquaint the public, that, if the play whence they are taken had been free from exception, in point of stile and moral, he should never have presumed to curtail it; but a long observation of the good taste of the town confirmed his opinion it was not so.[30]

Similarly, Wycherley's *The Country Wife* seems to have been acted in its original form until 1766, when it was altered by Garrick and brought to the stage as *The Country Girl;* the same author's *The Plain Dealer,* however, was denied performance until 1765, when Bickerstaffe's purified version was frequently acted. But perhaps the most notorious examples of the public's willingness to accept licentious drama undiluted from its original Restoration form are the plays of Mrs. Behn and Edward Ravenscroft, perhaps the most unrestrained manipulators of dramatic obscenity. *The Rover* and *London Cuckolds* were especially popular and frequently acted, although they seem to have disappeared from the stage about 1760.[31]

An examination of the repertory indicates, indeed, that the

year 1760 marks the approximate date of a considerable moral reformation of the theater. Although "Theatricus" complained as late as 1776 that *The Rehearsal* had not been pruned of all its "gross obscenity," [32] older drama that was still revived had for the most part been renovated and made to conform to the moral code.[33] This shift in attitude is also reflected in the reception of new plays. When Arthur's *The Lucky Discovery, or The Tanner of York* appeared in 1738, it was well received and had almost twenty performances in the next four seasons. The plot turns upon a bed-switch situation, which Shakespeare had twice used with grave moral significance, but which in Arthur's play becomes merely the exploitation of a risqué episode. Five years later, Fielding's *The Wedding Day* appeared and, though at first "refused by the Licenser, not as a reflecting one, but on account of its immorality," [34] somehow gained the stage. One member of its first audience called it "the most immoral and absurd performance he ever saw";[35] but it continued to be acted, and a month later Lord Beauchamp wrote to his mother: "I am very sorry Mr. Fielding's play has got admittance & hope it will not run, for I think we are corrupt enough already. . . ." [36] Twenty years later not only obscenity but vulgarity as well was found objectionable, and Mrs. Sheridan's new comedy *The Dupe* was damned after three performances because it "was so vulgar." [37]

We may therefore characterize the audiences between 1737 and 1777 in respect to their moral tone in two ways: first, that in spite of their numerous exclamations against the licentiousness of the drama, they often welcomed the very plays that when performed gave the theater of the period much of its immoral color; and second, that the later decades, judged by both new and revived drama, show a greater demand by the audiences for plays of unquestionable morality. It is apparent that in moral matters there had earlier been a period of indecision that was later supplanted by one of assurance and greater certainty. To consider this shift in attitude is to come face to face with the phenomenon of the increasing importance of the middle class to theatrical history.

On its most forthright level, the attitude of the audience may be described by quoting the youthful Burke, who wrote in 1748:

far from being disgusted at seeing any thing immoral represented we are seldom better pleased [than by] the luscious descriptions of which our Tragedies as well as Comedies are full, and the numberless indecent customs which are received not only with indifference, but approbation on the Stage.[38]

This attitude then was based upon the frank recognition of and pleasure in the immoral situations and dialogue of favorite plays. But there are always to be found in any audience those who wish to have their cake and eat it too. To resolve this paradox, arguments based on realistic, aesthetic, or historical considerations are usually called into play: drama blamable on moral grounds is acceptable, it may be argued, because it accurately reflects the society from which it sprung, because it has intrinsic and redeeming beauty, or because the admiration for the antique will find a sufficient apology for it. The first of these arguments, although frequently used in the later seventeenth century, was of little importance in the eighteenth. But of the second, more can be said, although curiously enough it operates inversely. One contemporary remarked, for example: "At present it is very genteel to think that the more immoral things are they have so much more beauty. . . . ";[39] and Mrs. Montagu was complaining of the same attitude just after the *Letters* of Chesterfield had been published: "As language grows delicate morals grow bad, for ugly things get pretty names." [40] The argument about respect for the ancients took form in drama chiefly in the attitude toward Shakespeare's plays, but it was not always powerful enough to prevent the "improvers" from tampering with them; even Garrick, instigator of the jubilee at Stratford as a tribute to Shakespeare's genius, was frequently moved to make alterations.

But none of these arguments, it is easily seen, is sufficient to explain the ready acceptance that the eighteenth-century audience accorded plays of immoral tendency. The explanation is rather to be found in a characteristic of the audience itself—one that at its harshest may be called hypocrisy or, less severely, superficiality. At its best, this quality applauded that virtue on the stage which the pit found conducive to its own material success. Domestic fidelity, as already shown, was such a virtue. It was no doubt Garrick's understanding of his audience that caused him to emphasize in his portrayal of Hamlet the element of filial piety—a virtue particularly important when sons were also apprentices and the future inheritors of merchant empires. Moore's *The Gamester* struck out at a vice that dissipated wealth, and it succeeded well enough to hold the stage for twelve performances. That it was then withdrawn is to be charged to the aristocracy, not to the middle class: "The polite inhabitants of the west end of the town, and the citizens addicted to play, did not like to see their ruling passion attacked by the moral doctrine of Mr. Moore." [41] It is noteworthy, however, that the play was revived in 1770 after an eighteen-year absence from the stage and was acted in the next seven seasons.

If we consider that one of the most influential and frequently performed comedies of the eighteenth century, *The Conscious Lovers,* defined merchants as "a species of gentry," [42] and that this note is struck in its numerous imitations as well as in plays as dissimilar as Garrick's *The Clandestine Marriage,* Cumberland's *The Fashionable Lover,* Whitehead's *The School for Lovers,* and Bickerstaffe's *Lionel and Clarissa,* the idea immediately suggests itself that contemporary drama was reflecting —perhaps even helping to originate—the ethical code for this new stratum of society.

At the same time, the respect shown by the middle classes for the aristocracy had not completely disappeared, and in numerous current comedies the plot turned on the wealthy merchant's efforts to bring a title into his family by marrying his daughter to a bankrupt lord. Not only was an ethical code necessary; the *nouveau riche* must also have social station. That the *mariage de convenance* was not limited to the world of the stage is aptly shown by a letter from Lord Lyttelton to Mrs. Montagu. He has just mentioned a young friend of Mrs. Montagu who would be a suitable bride for his son; "But," he adds, "she will probably be the prize of some needy Duke who will want her estate to repair the disasters of Newmarket and Arthur's." [43] This attitude toward the upper classes was based partly upon envy and partly upon the recognition of the worth of birth and breeding. For the latter quality, the middle class looked to the nobility as subjects of emulation and as arbiters in matters of taste. Thus, when Mrs. Clive, in *The Rehearsal: or, Bays in Petticoats,* made her heroine say, "The town never hiss anything that is introduced to them by a person of consequence and breeding, because they are sure they'll have nothing low," she was recording a fact whose truth her audience could appreciate. Another part of the regard for the aristocracy by the middle class was the result of envy—envy of its freedom from the restrictions that the acquisition and protection of material wealth had placed upon its owners. If this attitude were strong enough, the merchant might become such a person as the critic defined in *The Farmer's Return from London* as "a man that won't sin himself, and hates those that can." But this attitude also accounts for the numerous reformed rakes of title who appear in contemporary plays, for the most part likable and sympathetically treated, usually rewarded with the hand of the beautiful and virtuous daughter, but even when disappointed in love, like Lord Ogleby in *The Clandestine Marriage,* shown as generous and magnanimous to the last. Such a man had what the merchant needed to complete his happiness, recognition as a "connoisseur" and possession of the entree to society. But the middle classes were eventually to gain such recognition, and it is notable that thereafter fewer and fewer plays contained likable-though-dissipated noblemen. The shift in view is clearly reflected, for example, in the following disputation from *The Duenna* (1775):

Don Jer. Object to Antonio! I have said it. His poverty, can you acquit him of that?

Don Ferd. Sir, I own he is not over-rich; but he is of an ancient and honourable family as any in the kingdom.

Don Jer. Yes, I know the beggars are a very ancient family in most kingdoms; but never in great repute, boy.

Don Ferd. Antonio, sir, has many amiable qualities.

Don Jer. But he is poor; can you clear him of that, I say? Is he not a gay, dissipated rake, who has squandered his patrimony?

Don Ferd. Sir, he inherited but little; and that, his generosity, more than his profuseness, has stripped him of; but he has never sullied his honour, which, with his title, has outlived his means.

Don Jer. Psha! you talk like a blockhead! nobility without an estate, is as ridiculous as gold lace on a frieze coat.

Don Ferd. This language, sir, would better become a Dutch or English trader than a Spaniard.

Don Jer. Yes; and those Dutch and English traders, as you call them, are the wiser people. Why, booby, in England they were formerly as nice, as to birth and family, as we are: but they have long discovered what a wonderful purifier gold is; and now, no one there regards pedigree in anything but a horse. (II, iii)

At its worst, this quality, which I have variously called superficiality and hypocrisy, was a mere affectation of virtue, a perfunctory championing of the cause of morality. The fountainhead of this moral current was Colley Cibber, the actor-poet who had once remarked: " 'I am for the church, though I don't go to church,' . . . to illustrate his loving virtue in a play, &c. though he did not practice it." [44] It was this very quality that Sheridan, following in the footsteps of Fielding, castigated in *The School for Scandal*. And Sheridan's treatment, as might be expected, roused many of those who were sealed of the tribe of Colley. One commentator remarked, "However odious hypocrisy may be, it is for the interests of virtue that *some* attention should be paid to appearances," and continued, in defending the comedies of Cumberland against the ridicule of Sheridan, that although they "may tend to produce an affectation of sentiment . . . it is better to affect sentiment than vice." [45]

Here is to be found the reason for the change previously mentioned as having occurred by about 1760. Cumberland, Kelly, and their imitators in sentimental comedy were dealing in dramatic material already shaped to their hand. After a period of trial that followed the early experiments in this mode by Cibber and Steele, comedy had settled into a pattern with a superficial morality that was not disturbing to the audience, for it sketched in a background against which a nationalistic and materialistic populace could lead their accustomed lives. The period of uncertainty in drama, when the coarsest of Restoration plays were competing with the newer dramatized sermons, coincided with the period of uncertainty in the audience; the middle-class critics in the pit, finding themselves increasingly in a position of authority, little knew how best to exert their newly found powers, and were content for a time with merely flexing their muscles. But once a social code for the new "gentry" was established, apart from such occasional (and uniquely vital) exceptions as the plays of Goldsmith and Sheridan, the new drama was expected to reflect that code, and of course there was no longer a place for cuckoldry and erotic situation.

Regarded at this level, morality is virtually synonymous with sentimentality. Comedy, as shown, reflects this situation; but it is in tragedy, which felt the same influences, that the identification can most easily be seen. Long before, such playwrights as Otway, Southerne, and Rowe had popularized the type of tragedy in which the righteous are beaten down by evil fortune. And to it Addison had imparted his critical benediction:

the Instruction and Moral are much finer, where a Man who is virtuous in the main of his Character falls into Distress, and sinks under the Blows of Fortune at the end of a Tragedy, than when he is represented as Happy and Triumphant. Such an Example corrects the Insolence of Human Nature, softens the Mind of the Beholder with Sentiments of Pity and Compassion, comforts him under private Affliction, and teaches him not to judge of Men's Virtues by their Successes.[46]

Even where the identification was not complete, the interdependence of morality and sentiment remained striking. Thus, one contemporary observer, commenting on the character of Belvidera in *Venice Preserved*, remarks: "It is true, that, to complete the character of a heroine, she ought to have been perfectly virtuous. . . ." [47] Likewise, a letter from Birch to Lord Orrery concerning Moore's *The Foundling* emphasizes the juxtaposition that was regarded as necessary: "I was pleased to find the audience interest themselves so deeply in the virtuous distress which fills several most pathetic scenes." [48]

In short, sentimentality seems to have become confused with a feeling of moral approbation, which in time it largely supplanted. To be moved to tears by the distress of the persecuted heroine, the offended parent, or the dying hero was to give homage before the shrine of virtue. Those who witnessed the tragic ends of Lady Douglas and Norval in Home's famous play went home, therefore, according to the *London Chronicle,* "alive to the Loveliness of Virtue." [49] In comedy, much the same situation obtained, and to such an extent that to speak of "sentimental comedy" is to name a type that continued to bulk large in the repertory of the period. Chaste Thalia, so long nurtured by doting Morality, could not be expected easily to forget her decorous breeding. A return to something resembling Restoration comedy thus was manifestly impossible. So the comic operas, the melodramatic farces, even the laughing comedies of those scorners of sentimental comedy Goldsmith and Sheridan, all were largely moral, and the rakes had already reformed or were at least in the mood to do so with the opening curtain. In view of these circumstances it is necessary then to consider the matter of sentimentality and emotionalism as it finds expression in the theatrical repertory.

In contrast to the callousness of theater audiences in certain earlier periods, the sensibility rampant, not only in the boxes but in the pit and galleries during the mid-century, is especially striking. Its very pervasiveness therefore makes it necessary that this quality in its various degrees be considered for its effect upon the repertory of the time. It may be useful to premise that there is nothing pejorative in the term "sensibility"; it is merely a sensitiveness in emotion, more or less refined and often deliberately cultivated, with a particular responsiveness to the pathetic. Applied to the theater audience, it is therefore synonymous with "emotionalism," the tendency to respond to dramatic or histrionic stimuli with the feelings rather than with the reason or the aesthetic faculty. "Sentimentality" or "sentimentalism," on the other hand, suggests an overplus of sensibility, an immediate emotional response unrestrained by the judicial or other objective faculties, which is regarded as intensely pleasurable, is looked upon as a sufficient end in itself, and is exclusively egocentric. In contrast to sentimentalism, sensibility often expresses itself through benevolent and humanitarian outlets.

The mid-century period, during which manifestations of sentimentality in the drama were reaching their height, coincides with the period of the rediscovery of the feelings in literature generally. In the novel, sentimentality was given great impetus just three years after the passage of the Licensing Act by Richardson's *Pamela;* and in Mackenzie's *Man of Feeling,* written just five years before Garrick's retirement, it reached a point that could hardly be surpassed. In poetry, a decade before 1737 Thomson had begun his utilization of benevolence and the other social passions, drawing upon his observation of and trust in human sensibility. By 1780 this same sensibility brought Cowper to condemn the man who needlessly stepped on a worm.

In the drama itself, Nicoll notes that there was a "whole series of dramas almost purely of the sentimental pattern" written between 1732 and 1738; that in fact sentimentalism in comedy had gained "a new lease of life." [50] It is true that the same historian finds that far fewer purely sentimental comedies were written during the next decade,[51] a conclusion unquestionably just when only new plays are considered. But an examination of the entire theatrical repertory demonstrates that sentimental comedies continued to be frequently revived in the 'forties and in later decades as well, and that they successfully competed both with new plays and with other types of revived drama. *The Conscious Lovers,* for example, was performed more frequently in the 1742-1743, 1749-1750, and 1759-1760 seasons than it had been at any time except in its first run; and reached the stage every year between 1737 and 1777 except in the 1773-1774 season. Steele's, Cibber's, and Mrs. Centlivre's plays, as well as those of their successors later in the century, especially Kelly and Cumberland, were brought to the stage with considerable frequency; Hoadly's *The Suspicious Husband,* a comedy with strongly marked sentimental characteristics, was acted more often than *King Lear,* one of the most popular of Shakespeare's plays in the eighteenth century. In fact a statistical study of representative seasons at the patent theaters between 1737 and 1777 shows that there was actually an increase in the number of nights devoted to sentimental comedy, and that it was at the expense rather of the older comedies of manners and the comedies of humors than of the sentimental comedies that the newer realistic and farcical comedies and melodramas were making their inroads. Clearly, an age prone to moralize and proud of its improved moral tone would find sentimental comedy as congenial to its taste as it found such pathetic tragedies as *Jane Shore, The Orphan,* and *The Fair Penitent.*

The French theater of the time, according to one English contemporary, was a place where the spectators "sit in silence, and enjoy the beauty of sentiment, and energy of language; and are taught habitually to cry at scenes of distress." [52] But the distinguished French actress Mme Clairon, after seeing Garrick exhibit scenes from *Hamlet, Macbeth,* and *King Lear* while he was on the Continent, thought that "the English stage must be the spot where terror and pity were the great passions of the drama." [53] Similarly, Jean George Noverre, a famous French *maître de ballet* who had once been brought to England at great expense to stage *The Chinese Festival,* remarked of Garrick:

278

His pathos was touching; in tragedy he terrified with the successive movements with which he represented the most violent passions. And, if I may so express myself, he lacerated the spectator's feelings, tore his hair, pierced his soul, and made him shed tears of blood.[54]

It is not my purpose here to compare the two stages, nor to discover influences of one upon the other; but it is apparent that even the national theater where the *comédie larmoyante* was native could recognize in English drama the tear-provoking propensities of both playwrights and actors.

It is likewise instructive to note how two contemporary poets looked on the drama. Thomson speaks of both tragedy and comedy; and although he finds incentive to laughter in the comedy of manners, it is the comedy of sentiment that he finds sung in a higher strain:

> Dread o'er the Scene, the Ghost of Hamlet stalks;
> Othello rages; poor Monimia mourns;
> And Belvidera pours her Soul in Love.
> Deep-thrilling Terror shakes; the comely Tear
> Steals o'er the Cheek: or else the Comic Muse
> Holds to the World a Picture of itself,
> And raises sly the fair impartial Laugh.
> Sometimes she lifts her Strain, and paints the Scenes
> Of beauteous Life; whate'er can deck Mankind,
> Or charm the Heart, in generous Bevil shew'd.[55]

Thomas Warton, considering only tragedy, as befits the theme of his poem, finds numerous provocations to tears:

> Nor let me fail to cultivate my mind
> With the soft thrillings of the tragic Muse,
> Divine Melpomene, sweet Pity's nurse,
> Queen of the stately step, and flowing pall.
> Now let Monimia mourn with streaming eyes
> Her joys incestuous, and polluted love:
> Now let Juliet in the gaping tomb
> Print the last kiss on her true Romeo's lips,
> His lips yet reeking from the deadly draught:
> Or Jaffier kneel for one forgiving look.
> Nor seldom let the Moor on Desdemona
> Pour the misguided threats of jealous rage.
> By soft degrees the manly torrent steals

From my swoln eyes; and at a brother's woe
My big heart melts in sympathizing tears.[56]

The evidence is as overwhelming as it is varied in kind and
source that audiences of the mid-century responded to the
drama emotionally rather than intellectually, that their powers
of identification with the dramatis personae were cultivated to
a remarkable degree, and that the shock to one's sensibility—
whether it caused to be "melted into tenderness the heart of
every spectator," [57] or produced a feeling of terror[58]—was the
desideratum of drama. Almost as numerous are the indications
that the discriminatory powers of the audience were distinctly
biased by its sentimentality—that is, in every way but one (for
eighteenth-century audiences seem to have been remarkably
observant of the actors' methods of representation). Alterers
of older plays, actors, and playwrights alike were understand-
ably quick to exploit this predilection of audiences for the
sentimental.

The alterers of older drama found their great opportunity in
the plays of Shakespeare, although several works of Beaumont
and Fletcher, Jonson, and the Restoration dramatists were also
subjected to the kind of revision that the age felt made them
more suitable for the stage. As I have shown, alterations in
Restoration drama largely took the form of expurgation in the
interest of improved morality. Other alterations in both
Jacobean and Restoration plays attempted to bring order out of
what the eighteenth century regarded as dramatic chaos, to make
the dramas adhere more closely to the unities. But those who
would remake older plays by heightening their emotional appeal
went to Shakespeare's dramas, which were regarded as great
storehouses of raw materials. Cibber, for example, in altering
King John (1745), transferred most of Faulconbridge's lines to
Constance and, by intensifying the feminine element in the
play, provided the pathetic outlet for the audience's emotions.
The same author's version of *Richard III* attempted to strike
the same note of pathos by allowing Queen Margaret to see the
children in the Tower, a scene that Shakespeare had felt it
unnecessary to include. Although this alteration was made
early in the century, its popularity was never contested by the
original throughout the period under consideration. Garrick's
version of *King Lear* retained the Edgar-Cordelia love affair

popularized by Tate and, by bringing Cordelia on the stage in numerous scenes, gave added emphasis to the theme of virtue in distress. Perhaps the fate of *Timon of Athens* in the eighteenth century is most instructive of all. Shadwell earlier had provided the play with two new female characters: Evandra, an abandoned but still loyal mistress of Timon; and Melissa, whom Timon is about to marry but who leaves him in his adversity. When Love made further alterations in 1768, he retained Evandra but omitted Melissa—a significant change. The former fulfilled the century's demands of a tragic heroine: she is the virtuous and faithful female who meets a pathetic fate. But there was hardly a place for the Melissas in the tragedy of an age that could accept the virtuous, loyal Zenobias, Ormisindas, and Eleanoras who regularly pleaded, pined, and died to the satisfaction of the audience.

The actors were equally prone to exploit the emotionalism of their audiences. Garrick was the supreme master of this art, and his biographers make frequent mention of his effect on the spectators. Davies remarks of a performance of *King Lear:* "The audience, which had been sighing at the former part of the scene [IV, vii], could not sustain this affecting climax, but broke out into loud lamentations." [59] Mrs. Cibber, "the most pathetic of all actresses," [60] and Mrs. Pritchard had a similar power over the audience. Mrs. Yates "melted every audience that has seen her inimitable Medea [in Glover's tragedy of that name]," even though the subject was one "rather of admiration than pity." [61] On the other hand, Delane failed as Richard II because he could not "exhibit the tender feelings of the king's distressful situation";[62] and Miss Pritchard, though carefully trained by her mother, lacked the "sensibility" [63] to succeed on the stage. It is a commonplace that the age of Garrick was an age of great actors rather than great dramatists. It is not so well known, although it is equally true, that the reputation of an actor rested to a considerable extent upon his ability to exploit the sentimentality of his audience.

In the work of the playwright, however, the clearest examples of such exploitation can be found—that seem to have been as clearly recognized by contemporaries as they can be by the student of the drama today. Victor, for example, judges the relative merits of four separate plays based on the life of the Earl of Essex—by Banks, Ralph, Jones, and Brooke—on the numbers of tears shed by the audience.[64] James Hammond's prologue to Lillo's *Elmerio* condemns operas for not providing the opportunity to weep; and Lady Montagu, in "an Original Essay on Woman," praises Sheridan for providing that opportunity.[65] George Dempster was advised by his friends to "bring a white handkerchief" when he went to see *Douglas* acted, a play that was greeted "with much applause and many tears." [66] Lillo announced in his prologue to *The London Merchant* that he was about to tell a story that has filled "a thousand-thousand eyes with tears"; and Fielding's prologue to the same author's *Fatal Curiosity* promises scenes of tender passion and anguish. George Cumberland found More's *Percy* almost too "painful and distressing"; and of his brother's *Battle of Hastings,* then playing simultaneously at the other theater, he remarked: "I think [it] a pleasing tragedy—he has had a little more mercy on our feelings, which is objected to him as a fault. . . ." [67] The omission of a strong appeal to the emotions was indeed a fault; and Murphy goes so far as to say that Francis' *Eugenia* is not entitled even to be called a tragedy, because it is "without any incident to raise tears and pity, and without a circumstance of distress in the catastrophe. . . ." [68]

Such a conception of tragedy was indeed far removed from that held in the days of Shakespeare. The interplay of emotions had given way almost entirely to whatever would provoke a feeling of pity in the audience; instead of the varied passions of Elizabethan heroes and heroines, contemporary tragic characters were activated solely by love—the human being in distress had taken the place of the whole man of the Renaissance. Tragedy was thus circumscribed to a narrow compass in the eighteenth century, whether it was expressed in the romanticism of *Douglas, Percy,* and the other successors of the tragedies of Otway and Southerne or in the cold and classical cadences of those inspired by an admiration for Addison's *Cato.* Shakespeare's tragedies were, of course, frequently acted, sometimes even without "improvement"; but mid-eighteenth-century audiences found their chief pleasure in scenes that most readily provoked tears—Juliet's dying kisses, the distress of the mad Ophelia, the pitiable reunion of Lear and Cordelia—that is, in scenes most closely resembling the situations in contemporary tragedy. This propensity for sentimentalism had two notable results on the theatrical repertory of the time: the older tragedies chosen for revival were those most congenial to this spirit, and the new tragedies were likely to be written in the strain of the "she-tragedy" of Rowe or of the domestic tragedy of Otway and Lillo.

Except for four of Shakespeare's plays, no tragedies were revived more frequently than *Jane Shore, The Orphan, Venice Preserved, The Fair Penitent,* and *The Mourning Bride.* What these plays have in common is immediately apparent. And it was because of this pathetic quality, contemporary comments show, that they enjoyed such popularity. Johnson, for example, remarks of *The Orphan:* "This is one of the few plays that keep possession of the stage, and has pleased for almost a century, through all the vicissitudes of dramatic fashion. . . . Its whole power is upon the affections." [69] Contemporaries frequently commented in a similar vein on the popular plays of Rowe. Likewise, *The Mourning Bride* pleased because of its pathetic possibilities; and that Venice was preserved "by the resistless charms and pressing remonstrances of a virtuous woman" [70] was satisfying both to the audience's sensibility and to its moral sense.

Two of Southerne's tragedies—*The Fatal Marriage* and *Oroonoko*—both of which belong to this genre, were only slightly less popular. An examination of their mid-century alterations is instructive. *The Fatal Marriage* originally had two unconnected plots, one tragic and one comic, a practice Southerne justified by saying he was following "the present humour of the town." As it was altered by Garrick, the comic plot is entirely excised and the pathos of Isabella's situation, when she discovers on the day following her marriage to Willeroy that her beloved first husband is still alive, is exploited to the full. [71] The final scene, when Isabella and the fatally wounded Biron are reunited and she stabs herself after he dies at her feet, was obviously calculated to give Garrick and Mrs. Cibber, the two most effective tear inciters of the day, the opportunity to melt the hardest heart in the audience. Hawkesworth's treatment of *Oroonoko* is similar. By removing the low-comedy characters, he concentrated the entire attention upon the hero and Imoinda. The result is that those elements most dependent for their full appreciation upon a highly sensible audience—the pathetic separation and joyful reunion of the African lovers, and the humanitarian concern for slavery and its evils—are unrelieved by scenes of lighter or less distressing import.

Among the new tragedies the most frequently acted and revived were: *Barbarossa* (1754), *Cleone* (1758), *Cyrus* (1768), *Douglas* (1756), Jones' *The Earl of Essex* (1753), *The Earl of Warwick* (1766), *The Gamester* (1753), *The Grecian Daughter* (1772), *The London Merchant* (1731), *Mahomet* (1744), *Merope* (1749), *The Orphan of China* (1759), *The Roman Father* (1750), *Tancred and Sigismunda* (1745), *Zara* (1736), and *Zenobia* (1768). Although these may be classified into various categories,[72] most of them share one element in common: the heightened emphasis upon the pathetic, usually centering this quality in the person of a distressed female—mother, daughter, wife, or mistress. The "she-tragedy," as Rowe had developed the species, was not of course entirely an invention of the eighteenth century,[73] but never before had there been the persistent preoccupation with the tragic heroine.

Contemporaries, remarking on the reception given these tragedies, almost invariably speak chiefly of the audience's emotional response. *Barbarossa* succeeded because of its pathos;[74] Mrs. Pritchard and Garrick as mother and son in *Merope* "made the spectators pant with terror and pity, and at last drew tears of joy from every eye";[75] *Cleone* struck "to the heart." [76] The reason for one of the most famous fiascos of the mid-century—that of Johnson's *Irene*—arises from the same quarter. Boswell thought the play "deficient in pathos, in that delicate power of touching the human feelings, which is the principal end of the drama";[77] and Murphy, agreeing as to the reason for its failure, comments: "The business proceeds without an incident to alarm the passions . . . it has no emotion to agitate the heart." [78] The lone tragedy by Dr. Johnson's friend Richard Savage fared hardly better, but its later history indicates that pathos was still regarded as necessary in 1777. His tragedy *Sir Thomas Overbury* was originally performed in 1724 at Drury Lane. In 1738 the author revised his play, but it was apparently not acted at that time. It was then lost until 1777, when it was revived with further alterations by William Woodfall.[79] Of this revival, the critic in the *London Chronicle* noted that the additions—of pathos and "trying incidents" and (premonitions of the increasingly important melodrama) the heightened contrast between virtuous and vicious characters—had made the tragedy more suitable for the stage.[80] Pathos was still, at the very end of the period, regarded as an essential ingredient of drama. We may safely conclude that whether the tragedy announced for the evening at Covent Garden or Drury Lane playhouses was new or old, domestic or kingly, historical or fictional, had less to do with its reception than did its ability to arouse pity and tears in the audience.

Tragedy, however, was not the only dramatic form that evoked tears from the audience; comedy, or such plays as were currently called by that name, also produced its share. The plight of comedy is well characterized in the prologue to Jephson's *Braganza*:

> While in these days of sentiment and grace,
> Poor comedy in tears resigns her place,
> And smit with novels, full of fancies crude,
> She, that was frolick once, now turns a prude . . .
>   The comic sister, in hysteric fit,
> You'd swear, has lost all memory of wit:
> Folly, for her may now exult on high;
> Feather'd by ridicule no arrows fly,
> But, if you are distress'd, she's sure to cry.
> She that could jig, and nick-name all heaven's creatures,
> With sorrows not her own deforms her features;
> With stale reflections keeps a constant pother;
> Greece gave her one face, and she makes another,
> So very pious, and so full of woe,
> You may well bid her, "To a Nun'ry go."

The great precursor of this type of comedy, to which both audiences and critics looked back as a kind of model, was *The Conscious Lovers*, a play whose continued popularity has already been noted. The scene in Steele's comedy that so particularly affected audiences and seems always to have called forth tears was that in which Indiana is acknowledged by her father.[81] Here was the opportunity for a highly sensible audience to give release to its feelings previously dammed up by the uncertainty of the outcome; at the same time it could, by so doing, show its approval of both the virtuous conduct of the heroine and the plot manipulation of the dramatist who had thereby reached a denouement in which the predilection of the audience for poetic justice was satisfied. But we need not limit our consideration to those plays written specifically in this genre. *As You Like It* is a far remove from *The Conscious Lovers;* yet Berry, as Adam, regularly brought his audience to tears, and apparently they wept for the same reasons.[82] How deeply entrenched was this attitude toward comedy is demonstrated by the remark a friend made to Goldsmith just after he had finished writing *She Stoops to Conquer.* Goldsmith described the action of the plot to his friend, whose critical opinions he valued, and then asked for his judgment. The friend "shook his head, observing at the same time, that he was afraid the audience, under their then *sentimental impressions,* would think it too broad and farcical for comedy." [83] The friend's judgment was obviously sound, for the play made almost no headway against the popular genre in spite of its superior merit.

Indeed, the audience seems generally to have had its way where sensibility was concerned. The critics, even before the days of Goldsmith and Sheridan, were making a stand against sentimental comedy, but without much success. Murphy implies as much when he speaks of Kelly's *False Delicacy.* The prologue had announced: " 'Tis quite a sermon,—only preach'd in acts"; and Murphy comments, "The critics considered it in the same light, but the general voice was in favour of the play, during a run of near twenty nights." [84] Spectators continued to find it satisfying to pay homage to virtue while weeping at the misfortunes of the distressed heroine.

By the mid-century, to arouse pity and tears was hardly a difficult undertaking, for the sensibilities of audiences were then developed to a high degree. A certain Dr. Barrowby was once called to attend upon a young apprentice, whom he found "extremely indisposed and low-spirited." After being questioned by the doctor for some time, the apprentice finally admitted that "his distemper was owing to his having lately seen the tragedy of George Barnwell." [85] James Grainger confessed that, although he had not yet seen *Cleone* on the stage, the mere reading of the play had made him weep.[86] We need not even limit our view to the theater to find these traits. Charles James Fox is said to have resorted secretly to his handkerchief after listening to the tale of woes that had befallen Lady Lindsay, a total stranger[87]—a kind of behavior that is hardly expected of a secretary of war and admiralty lord (as Fox then was) in any age.

The altruistic counterpart of such sensibility is of course humanitarianism. I have already mentioned the humanitarian interests of Thomson and Cowper. Furthermore, two of the century's greatest achievements are monuments to the humanitarian concern of the time—in poetry, *An Elegy Written in a Country Churchyard,* in which Gray celebrated "the short and simple annals of the poor"; and in practical affairs, the Foundling Home, established in 1740.

The same "social passion" that resulted in the founding of this institution also had its effect upon the theater. It is noteworthy, for example, that the same decade also saw the production of Moore's tragedy *The Foundling* and, incidentally, the publication of *Tom Jones,* the history of a foundling. But the greatest influence was probably exerted through benefit performances, for crowds could be regularly expected when it was announced that the benefit was for a charitable cause. Garrick's benefits for aged and retired actors were heavily patronized, as were those for the families of deceased playwrights, for the various hospitals, and for philanthropic societies. How willing audiences sometimes were to subordinate aesthetic and personal considerations to their feelings is revealed by the history of *The Rout's* single performance. This farce was written by Aaron Hill, then at odds with Garrick, and anonymously offered to the latter as by a "person of quality," with the request that it be performed for the benefit of the Marine Society. Later, when the author's identity was revealed, a paper war ensued; but on the night of its performance, and in spite of its utter lack of merit, "being for a charity, [it] was endured with a remarkable degree of patience." [88] Humanitarian concern for those in need was in fact sometimes a sufficient incentive to draw crowded houses regardless of the night's stage offering, and allowance for this motive must be taken into account in considering the factors that influenced the theatrical repertory. The audience was essentially benevolent, in spite of its willingness to riot when it felt its liberty had been infringed; easily moved to tears, whether by the misfortunes of acquaintances or of imaginary persons in stage drama; and yet often prone to indulge in and to be satisfied by the mere sentimental thrill of vicarious experience.

Vicarious experience of this kind also helps to account for the simultaneous popularity of the novel. The novel apparently owed much to the older genre, especially in the work of a man like Fielding, for example, who turned from one to the other. But some influence was exerted in the other direction also— particularly by the vogue of the Richardsonian kind of fiction. To what extent the audience's preference for sentimental comedy is owing to the popularity of the sentimental novel would be difficult to determine with any precision, but it is evident that the new literary form was making itself felt in the theater. Colman's first piece, a farce called *Polly Honeycombe,* ridiculed "the follies of a young girl, whose imagination was bewildered by romances and novels from circulating libraries," [89] and Sheridan's Lydia Languish in *The Rivals* is well known. Foote wrote *Piety in Pattens* expressly to ridicule the sentimental taste.[90] The prologue to *Braganza* previously quoted regards "Poor comedy in tears" as "smit with novels."

The novel had a variety of effects upon the theater. It furnished situations and sometimes entire plots for stage pieces. It offered a character type for purposes of ridicule. According to Foote's biographer, it increased the number of spectators at a play they could attend with the smugly satisfying assurance of being competent critics, gained from reading the popular novels of the day.[91] But if novel reading became a more and more prevalent practice, it must not be forgotten that the reading of printed plays also became popular; and there were apparently those who were more familiar with drama in print than on the stage. It must also be remembered, however, that the full enjoyment of a stage play did not depend upon the ability to read, and thus for a considerable part of the populace the novel could not replace the stage as a means of entertainment. But it is clear that the novel, particularly the sentimental novel, had an effect upon drama and the repertory.

The popularity of the sentimental novel, the increasingly humanitarian interests of the time, the nebulous identification of pathos and virtue, qualities traditionally subsumed under the term "Romanticism"—all these were at work in shaping the history of the mid-century theater. But no matter how various and indefinable the causes, the results are easily assessed: that what the audience regarded as excellence in acting was often the skill with which the actor could draw tears from the spectators; that those writers who altered older plays for stage presentation in the mid-eighteenth century were attempting to increase their emotional power over the audience; that most of the new tragedies and a large number of the new comedies deliberately exploited the sensibilities of the spectators; that indeed the theatrical repertory of the period as a whole seems to be provided for audiences whose sentimental propensities were developed to a marked degree.

CHAPTER FIFTEEN

The Spectator as Critic

The theatrical repertory between 1737 and 1777 was thus subjected to a variety of influences because of certain predilections of the audiences of the time. Current fads and fashions also made themselves felt in the theater, although sometimes only briefly and without far-reaching consequences. The typical mid-century audience was miscellaneous in its composition, although the composition itself remained quite constant. It remains to be seen how well the spectators who made up such an audience were qualified to sit as judges of drama and of dramatic performance.

Contemporary opinion was divided. There were many who thought that at least certain parts of the audience were not possessed of critical judgment. Authors particularly were inclined not to credit the fashionable part of the audience with much critical power. The epilogue to *Virginia* contains a typical comment of this kind:

> May I approach unto the boxes pray,
> And there search out a judgment on the play?
> In vain alas! I should attempt to find it!
> Fine ladies see a play, but never mind it:
> 'Tis vulgar to be mov'd by acted passion,
> Or form opinions till they're fixed by Fashion.

The people of fashion in the boxes seem to have held a similarly unfavorable view of those in the pit. Miss Crotchet (in the epilogue to *The Clandestine Marriage*) had "made a party" to damn a new comedy at Drury Lane, but she did not succeed because the "crowds of City-folks" were determined to let the play run its course. Thereupon Lord Minim consoles her by saying that, except for the "Folks of Fashion" in the audience, "The rest have no more judgment than my horse."

It was apparently not difficult to set oneself up as a critic.

What seems to have been the common practice is described in *Town and Country Magazine:*

Dick is always the first night at a new play in the pit; and though he never read Aristotle, or understands a syllable of Horace, he is one of the greatest critics of the age. He has learnt a few set-phrases at the Bedford: these he utters promiscuously upon all such occasions, and he blends them in so curious a manner that they will do for any performance of every degree of merit. He, nevertheless, has frequently a crowd about him at the coffee-house; and his decisions, indecisive as they be, are considered as the opinion of the town.[1]

Similar is Dr. Johnson's earlier account of the brewer's apprentice (also named Dick) who becomes a critic with a large following and heads a party in the pit.[2] We must of course allow for the dramatic and satirical motives of the authors just cited. Nevertheless, doubt is cast on the audience's discriminatory powers when we learn that the town was about equally divided in its judgment of Glover's epic poem, *Leonidas.* Although one group relegated it to the lowest rank, the other preferred it to Milton's greatest works.[3] On the other hand, one contemporary called the mid-century audience "the most critical, as well as the most candid, audience in Europe." [4] In the face of such conflicting testimony, a reasonable conclusion as to the audience's critical ability can be reached only by examining its reception of theatrical offerings in typical instances.

The evidence falls naturally into two classes: that which shows the audience primarily concerned with the actors, and that which illustrates its views of the drama itself. This distinction can often be rather sharply drawn, with the result that in considering the spectator as a critic (as differentiated from the professional critic who ordinarily published his views in essays and periodicals) it is helpful to distinguish between what may be called histrionic and dramatic criticism. Of the first kind, an incident that complimented the audience's judicial powers occurred at a performance of *Macbeth,* in which Macklin played the leading role. His conception of the character was not "calculated to impress the idea of a dignified warrior," and did not make a favorable impression on the audience. In addition, Macklin had many enemies who were eager, for personal reasons, to prolong the hissing to which he had been subjected during

[1] For notes to chap. 15, see pp. 344-345.

the evening. Yet, when he spoke the lines to the messenger who had just informed Macbeth that Birnam Wood was seen to move, the audience recognized the actor's skill in registering the transition of emotion from a threatening attitude to one of despondency and applauded loudly.[5] The value of this evidence is clear because it shows the audience forced into approbation where its natural propensity would have been to deny it.

Contemporary audiences seem also to have been able to discriminate in the matter of the appropriateness of roles for the various actors, even where to do so meant to deny themselves a performance by a favorite player. The parts of Lord Townly, Sir Harry Wildair, Othello, Lord Foppington, and Pierre were popularly considered as unsuitable for Garrick; the West Indian, for Mossop; Varanes, for Ryan; Lady Townly and Lady Brute, for Mrs. Cibber; Richard, for Barry; Zara, for Mrs. Clive; and Chamont and Young Bevil, for Quin. Yet all these actors were popular and had strong followings among the audiences of the day. That the actors often did appear in some of these roles is apparently to be charged to the actors' rather than the audience's lack of judgment.[6]

Audiences were inclined to receive a new actor with sympathy, and reserved their show of disapproval until the novice had had the chance to adjust himself to his new situation. Both Mrs. Cibber and Wilkinson, for example, frequently refer to "the candour of the public, which they ever grant to a new performer and novice on the stage." [7] Mrs. Clive's advice to Miss Pope just before her second performance illustrates how the audience felt toward new actors:

The violent thunder of applause last Saturday on your first appearance was not all deserved, it was only benevolently bestowed to give you the pleasing information that they were well delighted, and had their warmest wishes that you would hereafter merit the kindness they bestowed on you.[8]

But, except in such instances, eighteenth-century audiences made great demands upon the actors.

Indeed, the audience regarded the theater as so much its own province that innovation in acting, particularly in well-known and popular roles, was dangerous, and more often than not met with discouragement and failure. Mrs. Abington's original difficulty in the role of Beatrice was owing to the "remembrance of Mrs. Pritchard's excellence in that favourite part [which] had stamped a decisive mark on the mode of representing it. . . ." [9] Woodward's complete failure as Polonius resulted from his departure from the traditional representation of the character as a low-comedy type.[10] There were, however, several notable exceptions. Sheridan's Hamlet became popular although it was not in the Betterton-Garrick tradition, and Garrick's Macbeth was immediately preferred to previous representations. There were also those in the audience who objected to one actor's imitation of another in the same role. Lord Bath, for example, condemned Love's Falstaff because the actor was "too servile an imitator of Quin." [11] But on the whole the tendency of audiences was to resent innovation by the actors. The tendency might on occasion be so strong as to have ludicrous results. Thus, when Cibber played Cardinal Pandolph in his own alteration of *King John*, a part he had frequently acted in the original, the audience was prepared to applaud his performance even though "his Auditors could only be entertained with his Attitudes and Conduct . . ." because he had recently lost all his teeth and was consequently inaudible.[12] Here, the respect for the actor and for the traditional portrayal apparently blinded the audience to the inadequacy of the performance. The same situation prevailed when Foote acted Ben in *Love for Love*, which was, except for Othello, his worst role.[13]

From the testimony of the numerous contemporaries who mention the theater in their letters and memoirs, we must inevitably conclude that, in spite of the peculiar prejudices in which it sometimes indulged, the mid-century audience was made up of connoisseurs of acting. The representative spectator was one who knew the theater well and had seen a surprising number of stock pieces quite a number of times; who had a fixed idea about the manner in which the characters should be performed; who was outspoken and certain in his criticism of the actor; and who, because of the frequency with which he attended the theater, had developed a certain facility in discriminating between superior and inferior techniques of acting.[14] Such an audience would find pleasure in discussing the relative merits of the portrayals of Romeo or Othello by rival actors; and, by the very fact that it did so, the theater came to play an even greater part in the daily life of the time. At the same time, we must quite as inevitably conclude that contemporary audiences were bound by custom—that only supremely good innovations in acting had the power to alter tastes that had long been formed and were jealously guarded.

We cannot, however, allow the audience equal discriminatory power as judges of dramatic quality. As already shown, plays were often applauded or condemned quite apart from their intrinsic merit. Current fashions, the popular sensibility, national pride, topical allusions, and similar matters too frequently furnished the sole basis upon which the survival of a new piece or the run of a revived play depended. Yet numerous indications show that the audience sometimes attempted to judge a play apart from such extraneous considerations. The evidence of this kind is, however, disparate, often contradictory, and not equally reliable. Victor, for example, in remarking that eighteenth-century audiences were inclined to laugh at the "bombastical strokes" in *King Arthur* which Restoration audiences received with "great Gravity," felt that the theater had reached an "improved, enlightened Age." Murphy, on the other hand, noting the relative failure of *The Foundling,* charged it to the bad judgment of the audience,[15] and says of Home's *The Fatal Discovery* and Dow's *Zingis,* "That both were endured nine nights is a disgrace to the audience of that day." [16]

Yet there can be discerned in the maze of conflicting testimony a small number of qualities that at least the more discriminating members of the audience demanded of drama. One of these is probability. *Timanthes* failed because it was thought "too remote from common life to interest one." [17] The outcry against *The Faithful Shepherdess* was raised because "the spectators have no resemblances in their minds" to the dramatis personae.[18] *Philoclea's* ridiculous number of decapitations, after which the victims returned to the stage with their heads on, caused the audience to laugh but resulted in the play's condemnation.[19]

Besides the result to the stage careers of individual plays, the insistence on probability had a larger effect on the repertory in making certain types of plays popular. Of these, the two most notable are the tragedy based upon English history and the domestic drama. Not only were Shakespeare's chronicle plays frequently acted, but also scores of tragedies that drew upon the nation's past for plot and characters were produced by contemporary playwrights, often in imitation of Shakespeare. The frequent success of these plays is to be attributed partly of course to their appeal to the patriotic sentiments of the audience. Yet, it should be added, that in place of the verisimilitude that Shakespeare achieved quite apart from the historical context, the eighteenth-century playwright depended almost exclusively for his sense of reality upon the knowledge that the audience would accept as probable situations and characters that were known to have had actual existence.

The success of domestic drama was also considerable during the period. Besides such perennial favorites as *The Orphan* and *Jane Shore,* newer plays that made use of domestic themes were consistently popular. Lillo's *The London Merchant* was acted in almost every season between 1737 and 1777 at Drury Lane and frequently at Covent Garden; Moore's *The Gamester,* after being banished for almost twenty years, was revived in 1770 and thereafter was often performed. *Cleone,* Dodsley's tragedy once rejected by Garrick, enjoyed a long run in its first season and was revived in the following five seasons at Covent Garden. Of this tragedy Mrs. Bellamy remarked: "The subject being a family distress, that pre-determined the public in its favor." [20] Grainger seems to be expressing the attitude of the audiences that found domestic tragedy congenial: "What the deuce have we to do with kings and emperors? What's Hecuba to me, or I to Hecuba? Let me have a lively representation of life." [21] The appeal of such tragedies was perhaps owing primarily to their heavy reliance upon pathetic situation. Yet it must be added that the time-spirit was right for the revival of dramatic activity along the lines laid out by Lillo and Moore; and if playwrights had been willing and able to follow their example, they would have found audiences capable of appreciating the new drama.

As a kind of counterbalancing effect on the repertory, plays felt to be particularly remote from actuality—dramas based upon Greek and Roman myth—were less frequently performed than formerly, and relatively few new plays on such themes were written. Of older plays, only Philips' *The Distrest Mother,* which retold the story of Phaedra and Hyppolitus, was performed with any frequency. Dr. Johnson, while discussing Smith's play based on the same myth, declared such plays unacceptable: "The fable is mythological, a story which we are accustomed to reject as false; and the manners are so distant from our own, that we know them not from sympathy, but by study; the ignorant do not understand the action; the learned reject it as a schoolboy's tale; *incredulus odi.*" [22] New drama on mythological themes met with no greater success, apparently for the same reason. Murphy says that Mallet's revived *Eurydice* (1759), an alteration of his 1731 drama, "met with as cold a reception in it's [*sic*] altered state, as it did on its first appearance . . . loitered on the stage nine nights, and sunk into oblivion"; [23] whereas John Delap, according to Victor, was "only unhappy in the Choice of his Subject" in *Hecuba* (1761). [24]

Besides the insistence on probability, contemporary audiences seem to have been agreed that certain themes were too horrible or too unnatural to serve as dramatic situations. *Titus Andronicus* was one of the few Shakespearean dramas denied revival in the period. Incest, a vice frequently treated in Restoration drama, was nearly unknown in the acted drama of the mid-century except in Otway's *The Orphan,* where it is given dignified and profound treatment; and such plays as Ford's *'Tis Pity she's a Whore* and Dryden's *Oedipus* had either completely disappeared from the repertory or met with failure if revived, [25] whereas new plays using the same theme, such as Walpole's *Mysterious Mother,* were deemed unsuitable for the stage. Patricide was also thought unsuitable for dramatic presentation. Hill's *Roman Revenge,* based upon the story Shakespeare had used in *Julius Caesar,* was unacceptable, not only because it departed from the outlines of the story as they were known from Shakespeare's play, but also because the audience would not "have borne with a patriot who could lift the murdering sword against his own father." [26] But it must not be concluded that the audience objected to death and blood in drama. The frequent revivals of *Hamlet, Macbeth,* and *Richard III,* to name but three popular tragedies, are strong evidence to the contrary. In fact, Count Kilmansegg, an envoy from Hanover at the coronation of George III, after witnessing a performance of *Richard III,* remarked that it was "quite in the English taste—very bloody." It was only when the deeds of horror were also unnatural that they conflicted with the prevailing sensibilities and moral sense of mid-century audiences. [27]

Other requirements demanded by the audience are harder

to determine. Contemporaries sometimes suggest that the audience preferred plays that maintained the unities. Garrick was supposed to have reduced *The Winter's Tale* to the three-act *Florizel and Perdita* because he saw that the public "would be little obliged to him for a revival of the entire play, and therefore, with great judgement, extracted from the chaos before him a clear and regular fable." [28] Many new plays, however, as well as successfully revived older dramas, violated the unities and nevertheless held the stage. It is apparent that the critic rather than the audience at large made such demands. Similarly, there were some who demanded that drama be typologically "pure," but these were apparently in the minority. When Garrick published his alteration of *The Fatal Marriage,* which had been produced at Drury Lane as *Isabella,* he accompanied it with the comment, "though the mixed drama of the last age, called Tragi-Comedy, has been generally condemned by the critics, and not without reason; yet it has been found to succeed on the stage; both the comic and the tragic scenes have been applauded by the audience without any particular exceptions." [29] A sufficient amount and variety of incident and stage business was also demanded. Thus Hill's *Alzira* (1736), based upon a play by Voltaire that was then succeeding on the French stage, failed because it had "too little of incident, and too much of declamation, to suit the taste of an English audience." [30] But this requirement is not peculiar to the period.

It seems clear that no formal and extensive critical code can be reconstructed that would satisfactorily represent the audience's requirements of the drama. The mid-eighteenth-century audience may perhaps be best characterized by saying that it was theater- rather than drama-minded, and also that it was composed of spectators, a large number of whom attended the theater with such frequency that they were thoroughly acquainted with actors and acting traditions. In such matters they were capable critics, but at the same time they were less qualified to penetrate into the deeper significance of the playwright's language and characters. They could follow and appreciate an actor's interpretation, but they were not equally capable of striking out independently in their critical evaluation of the drama. The former ability was owing to a certain facility that comes from frequent playgoing, and depended upon an intermediary—that is, the actor. That such a situation could exist points to a lack of original genius in mid-century audiences, to a propensity to accept what is time-honored, to an unwilling-ness to depart from the customary, and to a need for guidance.

CHAPTER SIXTEEN

Conclusion

The theater of the eighteenth century—with its repertory, its professionals, and its audience—marks an important chapter in literary history in spite of the generally moribund state of the drama; but more important perhaps is its use as a means of understanding the *Zeitgeist,* as a useful measuring stick for determining the direction and the extent of interests larger and more humanely significant than those of the theater itself. Certain elements can be called the constants in the equation—the repertory, the actors, the managers, and the playwrights. After these have been established, it becomes more nearly possible to assess with some precision the variable factor, the audience—which represents fairly, with only minor omissions, the general public of the years 1737 to 1777.

The interrelations of audience and theater company are numerous and not easily disassociated. It is frequently impossible to distinguish clearly between the relative importance of popular taste and that of managerial dictates or potentialities of actors. And often the greatest influence of the various factors upon the repertory must have been exerted when in combination one with another. The prevailing taste of the audience, for example, necessarily made itself felt in the theater, particularly in a way that immediately came under the notice of the manager; for frequent thin houses would cause him at once to consider the advisability of making the changes necessary in the repertory or the company to recapture the audience. Consequently, the requirements laid on the theater by the audience might take effect through the medium of the manager. On the other hand, the manager himself was sometimes the principal determining force. If he introduced or revived plays in such a way as to strike the fancy of the audience, or supported them on the stage with the "strength of the house," he was setting rather than following fashions in drama. And in rejecting plays, because he needed to consult only his own preferences, he alone often determined the repertory—although, to be sure, the shrewd manager usually took into account popular taste before doing so.

Similarly there are close connections between the actors and the audience. It was the audience that expressed its desire to see a particular actor in a favorite role—"by particular desire" the playbills called it—and, by doing so, prolonged the life of a play that might otherwise reach the stage infrequently or even not at all. Conversely, an actor's failure to portray certain roles or types of roles to the satisfaction of the audience often resulted in the removal of plays from the prompter's list—even of plays that were superior to those which were then enjoying success on the stage. But the actor might also directly influence the repertory. When a principal—and occasionally a minor—actor refused a part, was taken ill, or left the company, his importance in determining what the audience could see became apparent immediately. And of course certain plays were impossible of successful performance except when special talents were available in the personnel of the acting company, even though the audience might have been ready to greet such plays with immediate approbation.

The playwrights also are involved in this complex interrelationship. Occasionally they influenced the repertory directly, but for the most part their influence was exerted through the manager, the actors, or the audience. Naturally, the writers who depended upon the performance of their plays for their livelihood catered to popular taste insofar as they were able; but on occasion they also wrote to the manager's order or were attempting to provide an appropriate vehicle for an actor friend. But— except for the almost uniformly mediocre level of their output —they had little direct influence upon theatrical history. Goldsmith, who tried to retrieve comedy from its sentimental dumps, had little effect in restoring to drama the *vis comica,* and Moore's and Lillo's attempts at tragedy that interpreted contemporary life were isolated phenomena. But they are the exceptions. Also, quite a number of writers, exploiting a then current interest, opened a vein that might have been eminently rewarding both to the contemporary stage and to dramatic history. By delving into English history, they were able to fit out their plays with characters and events in which the eighteenth-century audience was becoming increasingly interested; but the resulting dramas were too often so frigid or so diffuse that they failed to survive—sometimes even for the customary run accorded a new tragedy.

A host of playwrights wrote for the stage. Many of them consciously attempted to imitate Shakespeare; others imitated his imitators. A few succeeded in writing plays that were retained for a time in the repertory, but most had little more than their labor as their reward. Many tried comedy; still more wrote tragedy. Fewer wrote farces and musical pieces, but those who did were likely to see their pieces survive when the more ambitious dramas had been forgotten. Many confined their efforts to the reworking of older plays, but for the most part the alterations, unless leaning so heavily upon their source as to be no more than shortened acting versions, were soon supplanted by the originals. In short, original legitimate drama was moribund, and the only vitality remaining was to be found in the afterpiece.

The reasons for this decay are rather obvious. The playwrights' blind veneration of Shakespeare—blind because those who sought to imitate him too often did not understand the source of his greatness and were looking for mannerisms rather than for his great spirit—and often their too ready acquiescence to the demands of the professional critics combined to produce drama that fell far short of their ambitions. Finding the accidents instead of the substance in Shakespeare and being compelled by the critics to accept a formalism based upon a priori rule, at the same time lacking the genius or simply the ingenuity to strike out independently, the playwright failed to contribute to the theater a drama that was intensely meaningful and significant for his audience. The result was a series of plays that were reminiscent of older drama—characters, situations, and plots drawn from Shakespeare, Fletcher, Dryden, Otway, Rowe, and Steele—but with nothing to contribute to the present or the future.

The time was ripe for the production of drama dealing with the problems of a changing society—a society that offered varied and appropriate matter for comedy and tragedy, one that was curious about itself, its milieu, and its origins. Such a society was in the mood to welcome drama that was contemporary, vital, and organic. But no dramatist came along who found the means to translate the melancholy Dane or the fat knight of Boar's-Head Tavern into the universal man who might walk the streets of Georgian London.

Since the dramatist failed, the destiny of the theater depended largely upon the actor and the stock piece. In both respects the age was fortunate. Some of the greatest actors and actresses in England's theatrical history graced the boards during the mid-century. They gave to the stock play renewed life, and to the new play whatever vitality it had. In pathetic scenes they moved the spectators to tears; they regaled them with caricature and farcical situation; they could even stir them with "didacticks." But, except for the few who also wrote farces and entertainments or revised older plays, they could not contribute to the development of drama. They did, however, contribute in numerous and important ways to theatrical history. Their special abilities, their rivalries, their possession of parts—all aided in determining what plays could be performed. Moreover, the longevity or the sudden demise of a drama, whether new or revived, was sometimes the direct result of their efforts. The repertory, consequently, often reflected the propensities of the players, and trivial and unrecorded motives must often have determined whether *King Lear* or *The Rover* would be "given out" for the following night. But the theater and its company could not thrive on thin houses. No matter how much power the actors exerted, that power was ultimately circumscribed by the audience.

As for stock pieces, not only was the seasonal repertory planned to make the greatest possible use of them, but it was heavily dependent upon them in the absence of viable new plays. The persistence of the pathetic and sentimental dramas of Otway, Rowe, Cibber, and Steele is noteworthy evidence. At the same time, fifteen plays by Shakespeare, on the average, were revived each year, and many were also continually present on the acting list. The recurring alternation of plays of these two groups must have struck the frequent theatergoer by their very contrast. Yet they have one element in common. No one will question the "literary" quality of Shakespeare's plays. Otway and Rowe too regarded themselves as followers of the great Elizabethan, and their plays demonstrate that they strove, however feebly at times, to emulate him. Cibber and Steele, exploiting the vein of sentimental comedy, were followers at a much greater distance; but their work also is substantial. The age had, then, a large body of older drama that it regarded as not alien to its own temperament and that at the same time had both respectable fullness and dramatic worth. Until quite late in the eighteenth century the theater as an institution was concerned principally with mounting such plays, whether stock pieces or new plays, thought substantial enough to compete for a place in the repertory. But conditions were soon to change; in fact the changes had already begun to take place. Extensive alteration and rebuilding of the older theaters brought into being larger and larger structures where regular drama might sometimes be performed—a kind of nominal justification of their status as "playhouses"—but which, because of their size and their more elaborate stage equipment, were more suitable for various kinds of spectacular performance that had little in common with the drama of an earlier day. Eventually the large theaters began to decline. But meanwhile stock drama was largely to be found in the newer, smaller theaters that came into being in considerable numbers, especially in the early nineteenth century. There the audiences were of a different social order from the one that had come to dominate at Drury Lane and Covent Garden. Ultimately stock drama moved again, this time to the more congenial "little" theater with its "intimate" audience. Those developments served to remove from the center of the theatrical world the stock plays and the literary drama, which were then largely supplanted by short-lived melodramas and spectacular extravagancies that found no need for poetry or dramatic substance.

Such changes could not come about *in vacuo*. In an institution as close to everyday life as is the theater, there could be changes only as the audience approved. And audiences too were changing. In 1737, spectators as well as critics believed that the purpose of the drama was as much to teach virtue as to give pleasure. But by 1777, although the critic might still cry out against new plays that had little didactic content, audiences were content to seek in the theater enjoyment and escape from growing materialistic burdens. Hence the playwrights, recognizing the necessity of taking their cues from the audience rather than from the critic, provided a fare of operatic farce and melodrama. Horace wrote that the aim of poets is *"aut prodesse aut delectare,"* a dictum that the earlier eighteenth century had often interpreted as *"cum delectare tum prodesse"*; but audiences were willing enough later to make no such double requirement of those who wrote for their stage. If they delighted, that was sufficient.

It is this great variable in our equation, interrelated though it is with the other factors that contributed to theatrical history, that must ultimately be our chief concern. For the audience then as now exerted the final control, even in an age that is known chiefly today for the excellence and versatility of its acting companies and for the sufficiency and striking individualism of its managers. Fortunately for us, there was sufficient uniformity in the professional theater of the mid-eighteenth century to enable us to see with some clarity the changes that were taking place in the audience itself and in the age it represents. The typical mid-century audience, although not yet completely democratic, was greatly different from the smaller, more homogeneous audience of the Restoration theater. The aristocracy was still an important element, and its approval was still sought; but the merchants and clerks—and their wives and children— were making their presence felt, and "Mr. Town" or the "voice of the pit" could damn a play just as surely as, perhaps even more effectively than, "Milord" in the stage box. The galleries also, where sat those of lesser station in life, were ready to direct at the stage either loud cries of approval or the showers of dried peas that made walking about on the stage a precarious business. And, to insure his success, many an actor felt it necessary to play to the galleries or to commend those "hearts of oak" who sat there. But in this very heterogeneity there was a surprising degree of uniformity, a situation that can be explained only when it is realized that the typical audience contained a large number of those, whether in box, pit, or gallery, who were constant theatergoers. Fortunate also is it for our purpose that there was such a large proportion of habitués. Box and pit might disagree, as they frequently did, in their dramatic tastes or in their preferences in actors; but still it was possible to "form a party" either to support or damn a play, and once the leaders gave the cue the rest of the audience could usually be counted on to fall in line. Feeling sometimes ran so high that the ladies were escorted out of the theater, and the men "went to work on the house." Or in a less belligerent mood, they were satisfied if an offending actor knelt on the stage and begged their pardon.

Conclusion

But the noteworthy fact is that the mid-century audience had a sense of its own continuity in the theater—a situation that is possible only when a considerable segment of the public attends the theater with great frequency—and as a result that audience felt to a remarkable degree that the theater was its own—its forum and its arena.

Given such an audience, it should be expected that the repertory would reflect closely the contemporary interests and fashions. As long as spectators enjoyed weeping, therefore, the plight of Jane Shore and the touching reunion of Indiana and her father were the proper subjects for histrionic representation. And spectators still liked to weep when Sheridan wrote *The School for Scandal*. To assume, then, that it was the audience and not Sheridan who was the rebel is to miss the significance of the part that the theater was playing in the development toward the romanticism of the following generation. For drama, just as surely as poetry and fiction, was preparing the way for the later Scotts, Wordsworths, and Shelleys; and the playwrights and managers who catered to the sensibilities of their audience must be given a place beside Richardson, Sterne, Walpole, Thomson, Collins, and Cowper, who in various ways were helping to usher in the romantic movement of the next century.

Similarly, as long as England's development was in the direction of empire the repertory reflected the interests of the "new gentry" of Sealand and Sterling, upon whose backs the burden of empire largely rested. And empire was still England's destiny in 1777. Consequently, throughout the mid-century the repertory continued to demonstrate the patriotism and the nationally oriented interests of the time, and the middle classes were gaining their dominant position not only in the audience but even in the drama itself. Concurrent with this development, and to a considerable extent as a consequence of it, was an intensified interest in remote parts—the lands of the nabobs and the West Indians—and a serious-minded curiosity about national origins and the days of the Athelstans and the Burghleys. This interest in the distant and the remote is also a manifestation of the romantic temperament. We may conclude that the history of the theater during the mid-century goes far to substantiate the findings of such students of the time as Carl Becker and F. J. Fisher, who, by examining the intellectual and economic backgrounds, have come to regard the period as marking an important seminal stage in the development of British national and imperial greatness. But we may also conclude that the history of the theater helps to define the means, both materialistic and spiritual, that brought about the important changes that were taking place in the later eighteenth century both in the social structure of Britain and in the minds of Britons.

The theater reflects also the great moral revolution that was concomitant with the rise of the middle class. This movement was to bring about such sweeping changes by the nineteenth century that the Elizabethan and Restoration periods seemed then to the man on the street to have receded into antiquity, for they had become separated by the chasm of the eighteenth century from his own day and its conception of the "modern" man. Several times in this book the date 1760 has been mentioned. It was approximately then that the stock plays inherited from earlier times were being purified of their obscenity and vulgarity in keeping with the demands of a somewhat sterner moral code. It was approximately then also that music and spectacle began to usurp the place of legitimate drama. A third development is noticeable in literary works outside of drama that were being written at the time. The Briton was taking stock of himself: of his language (Johnson's *Dictionary*, 1755); of his culture (Goldsmith's *An Enquiry into the Present State of Polite Learning*, 1759); of his aesthetics (Burke's *Origin of Our Ideas of the Sublime and Beautiful*, 1756); of his ethics and religion (Hume's *Four Dissertations*, 1757, and Hutcheson's *System of Moral Philosophy*, 1755); of his political history (Smollett's *Complete History of England*, 1757, and Robertson's *History of Scotland*, 1759); even of his hagiography (Butler's *Lives of the Saints*, 1756) and his theatrical history ' (Wilkes' *General View of the Stage*, 1759). Moreover, Adam Smith was furnishing a reasoned apologia for the prevailing sensibility (*Theory of Moral Sentiments*, 1759). In spite of some provincial cross currents (for example, Walpole's *Catalogue of the Royal and Noble Authors*, 1758, and Akenside's "Ode to the Country Gentlemen of England," 1758), the Briton was ready to emerge as *A Citizen of the World* (1760), at, it will be noted, the precise mid-point between those two events of far-reaching importance—the Revolution of 1688 and the Reform Bill of 1832.

What was the result of these developments for the theater?

Conclusion

No sooner had the eighteenth century, as represented by its theater audience, found itself in the drama—that is, had replaced the earlier uncertainty with certainty about its nature, its morality, and its destiny—than it began to desert drama altogether, so that in less than two decades a literary form that had prevailed for two centuries was virtually defunct. It is not, therefore, accidental that the expurgation of older plays and the increased importance of music and spectacle are simultaneous phenomena. A public that took itself seriously—that was inclined to reflect gravely upon its mores and its feelings, upon its rights and its manifest destiny, that in short was made up of a gradually emancipated middle class—had found in highly moral sentimental comedy and pathetic tragedy congenial theatrical fare, only to renounce that fare for mere sound and show at, significantly, the very time that it was changing in its own sphere of activity from the self-conscious newcomer to the established leader. Drama, hence, changed also—from ethics and emotions to distraction and escape. It is worthy of note that this cycle was completed in the following century. Just as the drama was substantial and socially significant while the middle classes were establishing themselves in the early and middle eighteenth century, so in the later nineteenth century, when the lower classes were benefiting from such developments as the passing of the Third Reform Bill, the founding of the Labour party, and the rise of unions, the drama ceased to be merely entertaining and escapist and once again became respectably belletristic and socially important. The conclusion is obvious. Only so long as an important segment of society is struggling to find its place in the sun can that society engender significant drama. Once it is established, its drama tends toward decadence.

But the point need not be labored here. It is clear that the history of the theater as one of man's cherished institutions reflects in its own peculiar ways the changes that were going on in the nation that gave that theater existence. But it was an existence that became precarious for the drama that had long been its staple. The mid-eighteenth-century period began under favorable conditions. There were considerable dramatic activity, abundant critical counsel, and histrionic excellence. But the theater, ever in pursuit of novel attractions to hold increasingly sophisticated audiences, virtually sold out to spec-

307

tacle and music, so that it eventually abandoned literary drama and poetic illusion for acting scenario and scenic display. A literary form highly respected and widely practiced for more than two centuries—one that, while maintaining its dominant position, had accurately reflected the community of interest, had indeed been a major expression of the peculiarly English genius—was now exhausted. Thereafter, literary masters found their media in other forms or, if they occasionally cast their sentiments in the dramatic mold, they regarded the final product as fit rather for the closet than the stage.

Notes

NOTES TO CHAPTER ONE

[1] Cf. Herbert Spencer Robinson, "English Shakespearian Criticism in the Eighteenth Century," *Abstracts of Dissertations Approved for the Ph.D., M.Sc. and M.Litt. Degrees in the University of Cambridge for the Academical Year 1929-30* (Cambridge, 1931): "the interest . . . in Shakespeare's *characters* [is] a feature which distinguishes the later criticism of the century from the earlier."

[2] Thomas Davies, *Memoirs of the Life of David Garrick, Esq.* (Boston, 1818, 2 vols.), I, 46.

[3] *Memoirs* (London, 1807, 2 vols.), I, 81.

NOTES TO CHAPTER TWO

[1] That this was the general practice is indicated by the records of performances in John Genest, *Some Account of the English Stage, from the Restoration in 1660 to 1830* (Bath, 1832, 10 vols.); but note also the remark in the diary of Hopkins, prompter at Drury Lane: "This evening [September 15, 1767] Covent Garden played against us unexpected, on which Account both Houses performed every Night" (see Dougald MacMillan, *Drury Lane Calendar, 1747-1776*, Oxford, 1938, p. 126).

[2] Such circumstances were of quite frequent occurrence. For example, both theaters were closed for a time in 1757 because of the death of Princess Caroline; in the 1767-1768 season there were no performances from September 28 through October 5, and on the first three days of November because of the death of the Duke of York, and from May 13 through May 22 because of the death of the king's sister.

[3] Genest, *op. cit.*, IV, 249.

[4] Two projects have been undertaken, however, that may make a larger part of the total record more readily available: the revision of Genest's work being prepared by W. B. Van Lennep and G. W. Stone, Jr., and a calendar of theatrical performances in London from 1700 to 1800 by Arthur H. Scouten and E. L. Avery.

[5] The statistics upon which the conclusions are based and some of which appear throughout the text have been compiled by checking in a large number of works of various kinds; the following may be regarded as representative: periodicals, such as the *London Chronicle*, the *London Magazine*, and *Gentleman's Magazine;* theater annals, such as those of Genest, Benjamin Victor, and Walley C. Oulton; memoirs, such as those of Tate Wilkinson, Richard Cumberland, and William Cooke; diaries, such as those of George Bubb Dodington, Isaac Reed, and William Hickey; the letters of such contemporaries as Horace Walpole, the Bluestocking ladies, the Duke of Bedford, and the Rev. Battista Angeloni; and early biographies, such as Boswell's of Johnson and Arthur Murphy's and Thomas Davies' of Garrick. There is no complete set of playbills extant for the entire period and for both theaters; however, MacMillan (*op. cit.*) gives a full account for the years from 1747 to 1776 at Drury Lane, which is based upon the playbills in Huntington Library. From these and similar sources, I have been able to compile a list of 10,824 performances of full-length plays.

[6] See *Gentleman's Magazine*, XX (1750), 439, and XXII (1752), 535.

[7] Tate Wilkinson, *Memoirs of His Own Life* (York, 1790, 4 vols.), quoted in Genest, *op. cit.*, IV, 341.

Notes

NOTES TO CHAPTER THREE

[1] *Correspondence Between Frances, Countess of Hartford, and Henrietta Louisa, Countess of Pomfret, Between the Years 1738 and 1741* (Second ed., London, 1806, 3 vols.), I, 88; cf. the letter from Sir John Guise, Bart., to Mrs. Clayton, later Viscountess Sundon, with which he enclosed a copy of his new tragedy *Palmyra*, in *Memoirs of Viscountess Sundon, Mistress of the Robes to Queen Caroline* (Katherine Thomson, ed., London, 1847, 2 vols.), I, 397.

[2] Letter to the Rev. Thomas Percy, Oct. 22, 1756, in John Nichols, *Illustrations of the Literary History of the Eighteenth Century* (London, 1817-1858, 8 vols.), VII, 241.

[3] Letter to George Montagu, Oct. 16, 1769, in *The Letters of Horace Walpole* (Peter Cunningham, ed., Edinburgh, 1906, 9 vols.), V, 197.

[4] Letter to his sister, Feb. 6, 1775, in *Sir Joshua's Nephew, Being Letters Written, 1760-1778, by a Young Man to his Sisters* (Susan M. Radcliffe, ed., London, 1930), p. 38.

[5] The careful preparation and the general air of expectancy attending the performance of a new tragedy, which contemporaries customarily record, suggest that no other event in the course of an ordinary season was of such consequence.

[6] See Ashley Thorndike, *English Comedy* (New York, 1929), p. 388.

[7] *Adventurer* for Nov. 14, 1752.

[8] *Ibid.*, for Jan. 9, 1753; cf. Arthur Murphy, *The Life of David Garrick, esq.* (London, 1801, 2 vols.), I, 360.

[9] Isaac Bickerstaffe's *The Padlock*, a comic opera, is called a farce in Hopkins' Diary (see MacMillan, *Drury Lane Calendar, 1747-1776*, p. 134).

[10] Eighteenth-century masques, however, in comparison with those of Jonson, Chapman, Beaumont, and Campion, are so in name only; rather, they are pastoral dramas, with elements taken over from and first popularized by the masques of pre-Civil War England. Even *Comus*, either as written by Milton or as altered by Dalton and Colman, does not completely conform to the traditional masque form. See Herbert Arthur Evans, *English Masques* (London, 1897), p. xxxiii, n. 2, and pp. liv-lviii.

[11] This reaction is sometimes overdrawn; for an adequately restrained treatment see Thorndike, *op. cit.*, chaps. XVII-XVIII, and Ernest Bernbaum, *The Drama of Sensibility* (Boston, 1915), chaps. XI-XIII.

[12] James Boswell, *Life of Johnson* (Hill-Powell, ed., Oxford, 1934, 6 vols.), I, 198.

[13] See, for example, David E. Baker, *Biographia Dramatica* (London, 1812, 3 vols.), I:1, 136; and Murphy, *op. cit.*, I, 118-127.

NOTES TO CHAPTER FOUR

[1] Thorndike, *English Comedy*, p. 372.

[2] See Baker, *Biographia Dramatica*, II, 384, 387, 391; the second of these operas, written by Cibber, was according to Baker (I:1, 130-131), strongly hissed because of its author's unpopularity at the time.

[3] See, for example, Wilkinson, *Memoirs of His Own Life*, II, 219.

[4] For example, Dr. Johnson; see Boswell, *Life of Johnson*, II, 367.

[5] Samuel Johnson, *Works* (Oxford, 1825, 9 vols.), V, 404.

[6] Arthur Murphy, *The Life of David Garrick, esq.*, I, 148.

[7] *Ibid.*, I, 243.

[8] This unsatisfactory term, as used here, includes all the drama written between

Notes

1660 and 1700 and all the comedies of Vanbrugh and Farquhar, even though some of them were written after 1700. It seems better to regard these two writers with the earlier dramatists, with whom they are more congenial, than to establish an arbitrary date that would exclude their later work.

[9] David E. Baker, *The Companion to the Playhouse* (London, 1764, 2 vols.), Vol. I, under "Rival Queens" and "Theodosius." Because this work has no pagination but has subject entries listed alphabetically, reference here and in later notes is made by volume and subject heading; G. P. Baker, *Some Unpublished Correspondence of David Garrick* (Boston, 1907), p. 35.

[10] A definitive book on this subject, Emmet L. Avery's *Congreve's Plays on the Eighteenth-Century Stage* (Modern Language Association, 1951), appeared too recently for me to make much use of the author's exhaustive data. His conclusions and mine, however, do not differ significantly.

[11] Thomas Davies, *Dramatic Miscellanies* (London, 1783-1784, 3 vols.), III, 232.

[12] Cf. Joseph W. Krutch, *Comedy and Conscience after the Restoration* (New York, 1924), pp. 24ff.

[13] Davies, *op. cit.*, II, 385.

[14] See *ibid.*, II, 401; cf. Fletcher's note "To The Reader," prefixed to the play.

[15] See Thorndike, *op. cit.*, p. 353.

[16] Murphy, *op. cit.*, I, 294.

[17] *Ibid.*, I, 262-263.

[18] See Lord Bath's letter to Mrs. Montagu in 1764, in *Mrs. Montagu, "Queen of the Blues,"* (Reginald Blunt, ed., London, 1923, 2 vols.), I, 99-100; that Garrick held a similar opinion of this play is indicated by a letter written to John Hoadley eighteen years earlier: "I have been looking into Philaster or Love lies a Bleeding; there is good stuff; but ye Intrigue between Megra & Pharamond, upon wch ye Whole turns, is very indecent & requires great alterations," G. P. Baker, *Some Unpublished Correspondence of David Garrick,* p. 35.

[19] William Cooke, *Memoirs of Samuel Foote* (London, 1805, 3 vols.), III, 95-96.

[20] Genest, *Some Account of the English Stage,* V, 188.

[21] See the table of performances of Jonson's plays in Robert Gale Noyes, *Ben Jonson on the English Stage, 1660-1776* (Cambridge, Mass., 1935), pp. 319-333.

[22] See *ibid.*, p. 80.

[23] Davies, *op. cit.*, II, 100-101.

[24] *Ibid.*, II, 102.

[25] *Ibid.*, II, 103.

[26] *Ibid.*, II, 107.

[27] See Allardyce Nicoll, *A History of Late Eighteenth Century Drama* (Cambridge, 1927), p. 266.

[28] Noyes, *op. cit.*, p. 145.

[29] Murphy, *op. cit.*, I, 205-209.

[30] Davies, *op. cit.*, II, 64.

[31] Murphy, *op. cit.*, I, 205-209.

[32] See the hand list in Nichol, *op. cit.*, p. 325; Noyes seems to have overlooked these two pieces.

[33] See p. 29 n. 10 above.

[34] Francis Gentleman, *Sejanus, As it was intended for the Stage, With a Preface, wherein the Manager's Reasons for refusing it are set forth* (London, 1752); the preface to this work is particularly valuable because seldom were disgruntled playwrights so frank; most such accounts come either from the managers and their friends, and so give the other side of the picture, or from disappointed authors who could find only acrimony to print in their prefaces.

[35] Davies, *op. cit.*, II, 385-386.

[36] Murphy, *op. cit.*, I, 307.

[37] Davies, *op. cit.*, II, 64, 95, 103.

[38] See Earl Reeves Wasserman, "The Scholarly Origin of the Elizabethan Revival," *ELH*, IV (1937), 213-243.

[39] See Robert D. Williams, "Antiquarian Interest in Elizabethan Drama Before Lamb," *PMLA*, LIII (1938), 434-444.

[40] John Genest, *op. cit.*, IV, 530-531.

[41] Baker, *The Companion to the Playhouse*, I, "The City Madam."

[42] See Hugh G. Dick, *Albumazar: A Comedy* (Berkeley and Los Angeles, Univ. Calif. Publ. English, Vol. 13, 1944), pp. 56-61.

[43] Baker, *Biographia Dramatica*, III, 243.

[44] Baker, *The Companion to the Playhouse*, I, "The Jovial Crew"; this play is not listed in Dougald MacMillan, *Drury Lane Calendar, 1747-1776.*

[45] See Genest, *op. cit.*, IV, 179.

[46] Baker, *The Companion to the Playhouse*, I, " 'Tis Pity she's a Whore."

[47] See George Otto Trevelyan, *The Early History of Charles James Fox* (London, 1884), pp. 85-86.

[48] See Genest, *op. cit.*, III, 533-534, and Baker, *The Companion to the Playhouse*, I, "Comus." See also Alwin Thaler, "Milton in the Theatre," *SP*, XVII (1920), 289-308.

[49] The song is included in a letter written by the Countess of Hartford; see *Correspondence Between Frances, Countess of Hartford, and Henrietta Louisa, Countess of Pomfret, Between the Years 1738 and 1741*, II, 86-88.

[50] Boswell, *Life of Johnson*, I, 227-228; see also Johnson's postscript to his "Preface to an Essay on Milton's Use and Imitations of the Moderns in His Paradise Lost," in *Works*, IV, 271-272.

[51] Cited in Genest, *op. cit.*, V, 186.

[52] It should be noted, however, that both Day (c. 1600) and Dodsley (1739) wrote pieces titled *The Blind Beggar of Bethnal Green*, which make use of the same theme. Dodsley's play was acted at Drury Lane but met with little success.

[53] This play was actually altered by Benjamin Victor as *The Fatal Error*, which was published in 1776 but was not acted.

[54] Davies, *op. cit.*, I, 61.

[55] *London Chronicle*, I (1757), 238-239.

NOTES TO CHAPTER FIVE

[1] This number takes into account *The Fairies* (Garrick's alteration of *A Midsummer Night's Dream*), which was performed as a first piece, but not the various reworkings of Shakespearean plays that served only as afterpieces, such as *Katharine and Petruchio* and Colman's abridgement of Garrick's alteration of *A Midsummer Night's Dream*, or such anomalous plays as Lillo's *Marina*, a three-act adaptation of *Pericles*. A more nearly complete statistical record will be available when the second part of Charles B. Hogan's *Shakespeare in the Theatre, 1701-1800* is published. The first part (Oxford, 1952), which covers the period 1701-1750, lists 1,054 performances of Shakespearean plays as first pieces for 1737-1750. If we assume that the rate of performance remained about constant for the period 1750-1777, we get, as a projection of Hogan's statistics for 1737-1777, performances numbering 3,123; in other words, my figure of 2,472 represents about 80 per cent of the conjectured total number, a ratio somewhat more favorable than the 75 per cent of possible performances

of plays of all kinds, on the basis of which all conclusions in this book have been correspondingly qualified.

[2] Sometimes announced as a tragedy, following the first folio, but more usually regarded as a comedy.

[3] Advertised in the playbill as "Not acted these hundred years" (Genest, *Some Account of the English Stage*, IV, 167), but actually it was eighty-two years.

[4] Quoted in Thomas Davies, *Memoirs of the Life of David Garrick, Esq.* (Boston, 1818, 2 vols.), I, 91.

[5] Gisbert Freiherrn Vincke, "Bearbeitungen and Aufführungen Shakespeare'scher Stücke vom Tode des Dichters bis zum Tode Garrick's" *Shakespeare Jahrbuch*, IX (1874), 54.

[6] Davies, *Dramatic Miscellanies*, III, 4-5.

[7] Quoted in *ibid.*, III, 30.

[8] *Ibid.*, III, 126.

[9] *Ibid.*, III, 68-69.

[10] *Ibid.*, III, 126-127.

[11] *Ibid.*

[12] *Ibid.*, III, 41-42.

[13] The business of the waistcoats is mentioned in Brander Matthews, "Shaksperian Stage Traditions," *Shakespearian Studies* (New York, 1916), pp. 12-13; but cf. George W. Stone, Jr., "Garrick's Long Lost Alteration of *Hamlet*," *PMLA*, XLIX (1934), 901. There are numerous contemporary indications that the public, unlike the critics, did not object to an infusion of comedy, even of a low kind, into tragedy.

[14] Davies, *Dram. Misc.*, III, 32-33.

[15] Quoted in George C. D. Odell, *Shakespeare from Betterton to Irving* (New York, 1920, 2 vols.), I, 334-335.

[16] According to Odell (*op. cit.*, I, 225), it had been restored by Wilks as early as 1718; Davies (*Dram. Misc.*, III, 80) and Vincke (*op. cit.*, p. 54) say that it was first restored by Garrick. The pamphlet from which Odell quotes seems to settle the matter in favor of Wilks.

[17] Davies, *Dram. Misc.*, III, 85.

[18] *Ibid.*, I, 129.

[19] Stone, *op. cit.*, pp. 898ff.; the description of this play which follows is partly drawn from Stone's account.

[20] Davies, *Dram. Misc.*, III, 142.

[21] *Ibid.*, III, 146-147.

[22] See Frederick W. Kilbourne, *Alterations and Adaptations of Shakespeare* (Boston, 1910), pp. 153-157; the alteration appears in *The Wandering Patentee*, I, 167-173.

[23] Stone, *op. cit.*, pp. 893-894.

[24] Davies, *Dram. Misc.*, III, 145-147.

[25] Vincke (*op. cit.*, p. 54) lists *The Three Conjurers: A Political Interlude Stolen from Shakespeare* (1763) as if it were indebted to *Hamlet;* but he adds that this satire, directed against Lord Bute, may not be based on Shakespeare in spite of its subtitle, and that "vielleicht war das *'stolen from Shakespeare'* bloss ein scherzhafter Zusatz."

[26] According to the anonymous *Literary and Graphical Illustration of Shakespeare and the British Drama* (London, 1831), p. 48, it was acted seventy-two times "about 1747." It is doubtful, however, that the entire play was performed that many times; it is more likely that only the coronation procession was given seventy-two nights and that the anonymous author misunderstood his source.

[27] Quoted in Genest, *op. cit.*, III, 578.

Notes

[28] Davies, *Dram. Misc.*, I, 353-56; cf. Vincke, *op. cit.*, p. 48.

[29] Davies, *Dram. Misc.*, I, 386.

[30] Davies, *Memoirs*, I, 35.

[31] Davies, *Dram. Misc.*, I, 427-428.

[32] *Ibid.*, I, 391.

[33] *Ibid.*, I, 382-383.

[34] Davies, *Memoirs*, II, 82.

[35] Vincke, *op. cit.*, p. 47.

[36] Davies, *Dram. Misc.*, I, 243ff.

[37] Davies, *Memoirs*, II, 90-91.

[38] Davies, *Dram. Misc.*, I, 227.

[39] *Ibid.*, I, 273-275.

[40] *Ibid.*, I, 239.

[41] *Ibid.*

[42] *Ibid.*, I, 255.

[43] *Ibid.*, I, 229.

[44] See William Jaggard, *Shakespeare Bibliography* (Stratford, 1911).

[45] *Literary and Graphical Illustration*, p. 68.

[46] Baker, *The Companion to the Playhouse*, I, "The Revenge."

[47] See Henry B. Wheatley, "Post-Restoration Quartos of Shakespeare's Plays," *Library*, 3rd series, IV (July, 1913), pp. 252-253.

[48] Davies, *Dram. Misc.*, II, 212; Vincke, *op. cit.*, pp. 49-50.

[49] Davies, *Dram. Misc.*, II, 255.

[50] Davies, *Memoirs*, I, 81.

[51] For the same reason he refused the part of Caesar in Aaron Hill's *Roman Revenge*; cf. Davies, *Memoirs*, I, 118. Note also the indication that *Julius Caesar* was staged in Roman costume.

[52] Davies, *Dram. Misc.*, II, 213.

[53] *Literary and Graphical Illustration*, p. 60; Genest says the play is "wrongly" attributed to Dryden and Davenant, but cf. Vincke, *op. cit.*, p. 49.

[54] Baker, *The Companion to the Playhouse*, I, "The Death of Marcus Brutus."

[55] Genest, *op. cit.*, III, 94-97.

[56] Davies, *Dram. Misc.*, II, 261.

[57] Wheatley, *op. cit.*, p. 236.

[58] Cf. Vincke, *op. cit.*, p. 51. Parts of the following account of the alterations are drawn from D. Nichol Smith, *Shakespeare in the Eighteenth Century* (Oxford, 1928), pp. 20-24; Kilbourne, *op. cit.*, pp. 157-172; *Literary and Graphical Illustration*, p. 66. For the text of Tate's alteration, see Montague Summers, *Shakespeare Adaptations* (Boston, 1922).

[59] *Works*, I, 263.

[60] Victor, *The History of the Theatres of London and Dublin, from the Year 1730 to the present time* (London, 1761-1771, 3 vols.), III, 119-120.

[61] George Colman, Sr., *Dramatick Works* (London, 1777, 4 vols.), III, 103.

[62] Davies, *Dram. Misc.*, II, 263.

[63] *Ibid.*, II, 266-267.

[64] Colman, *op. cit.*, III, 105; Smith, *op. cit.*, p. 23, n. 1.

[65] Davies, *Dram. Misc.*, II, 304.

[66] *Ibid.*, II, 322-325.

[67] *London Chronicle* for May 21-23, 1776.

[68] Quot. in Vincke, *op. cit.*, p. 50.

[69] Davies' observation (*Memoirs*, II, 197-198); Genest (*op. cit.*, IV, 317-319) gives an account of this play.

[70] Davies, *Memoirs*, II, 197-198.

[71] Walley Chamberlain Oulton, *The History of the Theatres of London* (London, 1796, 2 vols.), I, 3.

[72] Wheatley (*op. cit.,* pp. 267-268) speaks of a version by Love printed in 1771 and one by Dance printed in 1768 as if they were different alterations; he was apparently unaware that the actor-author was known by both names.

[73] Genest, *op. cit.,* III, 609.

[74] Odell, *op. cit.,* I, 224-235.

[75] It is likely that it was performed earlier, perhaps in 1703, for it was announced in 1720 as not having been acted for seventeen years; since this play is the work of Betterton, it seems highly probable that he would have brought it to the stage.

[76] See Genest for an account of this alteration (*op. cit.,* III, 46-48).

[77] *Ibid.,* III, 554-555; this revival was inspired by the "Shakespeare Club."

[78] See Jaggard, *op. cit.*

[79] Davies, *Dram. Misc.,* I, 294; Genest, *op. cit.,* III, 425.

[80] Vincke, *op. cit.,* p. 47.

[81] Davies, *Dram. Misc.,* I, 307-308.

[82] *Ibid.,* I, 309.

[83] Davies, *Memoirs,* I, 125.

[84] Vincke, *op. cit.,* p. 43.

[85] See Baker, *The Companion to the Playhouse,* I, "The Universal Passion."

[86] Genest (*op. cit.,* III, 482) believed that this was the original.

[87] See Kilbourne, *op. cit.,* pp. 101-103; Vincke, *op. cit.,* p. 47.

[88] Genest, *op. cit.,* III, 38.

[89] *Ibid.,* III, 555; see n. 86, above. Victor (*op. cit.,* II, 121) says it was revived under Lacy and Garrick, which would place it after 1746; but Victor apparently was referring to the short-lived revival at Drury Lane only (ten performances between 1746 and 1749). The evidence seems to warrant regarding the 1735 revival as that of the original, and I have consequently discussed the play here rather than in the next chapter. The performance at Covent Garden in 1738 is sometimes regarded as the first revival of the original.

[90] Baker, *The Companion to the Playhouse,* I, "The Life of Henry V."

[91] Genest, *op. cit.,* IV, 648, 654-658.

[92] *Literary and Graphical Illustration,* p. 46.

[93] Edmond Malone, "An Historical Account of the Rise and Progress of the English Stage," *The Plays and Poems of William Shakespeare* (London, 1790), I:2, 280-281.

[94] Cf. Thomas R. Lounsbury, *Shakespeare as a Dramatic Artist* (London, 1901), p. 309; note that this was the basic formula for almost all new tragedies.

[95] William Hazlitt, *Characters of Shakespeare's Plays* (London, 1934), p. 188.

[96] See *Literary and Graphical Illustration.*

[97] Genest, *op. cit.,* V, 497-498.

[98] See Alice I. P. Wood, *The Stage History of Shakespeare's King Richard the Third* (New York, 1909), p. 107, n. 13.

[99] Davies, *Memoirs,* I, 41-42.

[100] Hazlitt, *op. cit.,* pp. 191-192.

[101] Hazelton Spencer, *The Art and Life of William Shakespeare* (New York, 1940), p. 163.

[102] Genest, *op. cit.,* III, 567.

NOTES TO CHAPTER SIX

[1] Davies, *Dram. Misc.,* I, 15; Vincke, "Bearbeitungen und Aufführungen Shakespeare'scher Stücke vom Tode des Dichters bis zum Tode Garricks," *Shakespeare Jahrbuch,* IX (1874), 46.

[2] Davies, *Dram. Misc.,* I, 55-56.

[3] *Literary and Graphical Illustration,* p. 30 (the italics are mine).

[4] Davies, *Dram. Misc.,* I, 102.

[5] *Ibid.,* I, 51-52.

[6] See W. Allwardt, *Die englischen Bühnenbearbeitungen von Shakespeares "King Richard the Second"* (Doberan, 1909), pp. 64-93.

[7] Baker, *The Companion to the Playhouse,* I, "Richard II."

[8] "Advertisement" to Wroughton's edition (London, 1815) quoted in Allwardt, *op. cit.,* p. 94.

[9] Quoted in Genest, *Some Account of the English Stage,* III, 554.

[10] Note, for example, that the abdication scene was not printed until the fourth quarto (1608), before which time it had been excised by the censor; that it was the play used at the famous Globe performance in 1601 on the eve of the Essex rebellion; and, as noted above, that the Stuart king suppressed the play, after only two nights, when Tate's alteration was staged in 1680. The Theobald version (1719) went unsuppressed, however, and had a moderate success for a couple of seasons.

[11] See George W. Stone, Jr., "Garrick's Presentation of *Antony and Cleopatra,*" *RES,* XIII (1937), 36, for the full account and the text of the letters, one of which was previously unpublished; Genest (*op. cit.,* III, 554) also notes that Garrick had contemplated reviving the play.

[12] Davies, *Dram. Misc.,* I, 179.

[13] *Ibid.,* I, 180.

[14] See *ibid.,* I, 142-143, and Genest, *op. cit.,* III, 553.

[15] Vincke (*op. cit.,* p. 48), for example, makes this mistake.

[16] See Jaggard, *Shakespeare Bibliography,* and Wheatley, "Post-Restoration Quartos of Shakespeare's Plays," p. 254.

[17] Conjectured to be J. Carrington by Odell (*Shakespeare from Betterton to Irving,* I, 247); Wheatley (*op. cit.,* p. 249) assumes that it is.

[18] Reprinted in Odell, *op. cit.,* I, facing p. 262.

[19] *Grove's Dictionary of Music and Musicians,* I, 114.

[20] See Genest, *op. cit.,* III, 638.

[21] For an account of the various versions, see Kilbourne, *Alterations and Adaptations of Shakespeare,* pp. 84-90; Vincke, *op. cit.,* pp. 45-46; Davies, *Memoirs,* I, 199-201; and Walter Schneider, *Über das Verhältnis von David Garricks "Florizel and Perdita" zu Shakespeares "The Winters Tale,"* passim.

[22] Wilkinson, *Memoirs of His Own Life,* II, 55.

[23] Quoted in Genest, *op. cit.,* III, 629.

[24] See *ibid.* for the whole account.

[25] See Otto Burmeister, *Nachdichtungen und Bühneneinrichtungen von Shakespeares Merchant of Venice* (Rostock, 1902), pp. 52-55.

[26] Genest, *op. cit.,* III, 641, and Edmond Malone, "An Historical Account of the Rise and Progress of the English Stage," I:2, 283. Malone adds that the revival at Drury Lane was made "to make a stand against Macklin." Since Macklin was apparently then at Drury Lane, Malone's statement is, however, difficult to understand.

[27] Davies, *Dram. Misc.,* II, 10; Genest, *op. cit.,* III, 645-646; but cf. Hogan, p. 88.

[28] Davies, *Dram. Misc.,* II, 11.

[29] Wheatley, *op. cit.,* p. 248.

[30] *Literary and Graphical Illustration,* p. 10; cf. Wheatley, *op. cit.,* p. 249, and Kilbourne, *op. cit.,* p. 56.

[31] Davies (*Memoirs,* I, 93-94), followed by Vincke (*op. cit.,* p. 53), credits Garrick with this restoration.

[32] Garrick's purpose in removing the rhyme was "to clear the original as much as possible from the jingle and quibble which were always the objection to the

reviving it." Rosaline was omitted to remove a "blemish" in Romeo's character, for according to popular opinion the rapid change of affection from Rosaline to Juliet was a sign of fickleness; and Garrick remarked that this change in the play was "made more in complaisance to that opinion, than from a conviction that Shakespear, the best judge of human nature, was faulty" ("Advertisement" to *Romeo and Juliet* in Garrick's *Dramatic Works*, I, 207).

[33] Why the Friar's speech is necessary to Shakespeare's conception of the tragedy is for the first time adequately explained by Bertrand Evans, in "The Brevity of Friar Laurence," *PMLA*, LXV (1950), 841-865.

[34] Samuel Johnson, "General Observations on Shakespeare's Plays," in *Works*, I, 264.

[35] Davies, *Dram. Misc.*, II, 166-167.

[36] *Ibid.*, II, 149; Davies, *Memoirs*, I, 93.

[37] Davies, *Dram. Misc.*, II, 23, 118-120.

[38] Garrick, who was perhaps the best judge in this matter, remarked in the "Advertisement" to *Isabella* (*Works*, II, 219): "Though the mixed drama of the last age, called Tragi-Comedy, has been generally condemned by the critics, and not without reason; yet it has been found to succeed on the stage; both the comic and the tragic scenes have been applauded by the audience without any particular exceptions."

[39] Davies (*Memoirs*, II, 135-136) describes her manner of acting in this scene.

[40] See below, "The Spectator as Critic," pp. 290ff.

[41] George W. Stone, Jr., "Garrick's Handling of *Macbeth*," *SP*, XXXVIII (1941), 622.

[42] Davies, *Dram. Misc.*, II, 117.

[43] See Stone, "Macbeth," pp. 609-628, for an account of this play.

[44] *Literary and Graphical Illustration*, p. 22; Genest, *op. cit.*, IV, 450.

[45] *Literary and Graphical Illustration*, p. 22.

[46] Davies, *Memoirs*, I, 199.

[47] See Genest (*op. cit.*, IV, 450-451), who cites the testimony of Murphy, Wilkinson, and Davies.

[48] See Vincke, *op. cit.*, p. 49; that the original was revived, at least by 1761, is indicated by Victor (*The History of the Theatres of London and Dublin*, II, 166-167), who wonders why Thomson should have altered *Coriolanus* when he had the unsuccessful examples of Dennis' *Coriolanus*, Hill's *Henry V*, and Cibber's *King John* before him, and then adds: "but the immortal Shakespear's three Plays on those Subjects, written above one hundred and sixty years ago, are, at this day, the Stock Plays in our Theatres, and apparently superior in merit."

[49] Quoted in Genest, *op. cit.*, IV, 405.

[50] Reprinted in W. Winter, *Shakespeare on the Stage* (New York, 1911-1916, 3 series), III, facing p. 198.

[51] From Cross' Diary, quoted in George W. Stone, Jr., "*A Midsummer Night's Dream* in the Hands of Garrick and Colman," *PMLA*, LIV (1939), 469.

[52] The solution of this puzzling problem was worked out by Stone, who discovered the Tonson edition in the Folger Library.

[53] See the entry in Hopkins' Diary, quoted in MacMillan, *Drury Lane Calendar*, p. 100.

[54] *Literary and Graphical Illustration*, p. 16.

[55] Kilbourne, *op. cit.*, pp. 65-68; Vincke (*op. cit.*, p. 44) gives additional details.

[56] Stone, "*Antony and Cleopatra*," p. 25.

[57] Davies, *Dram. Misc.*, II, 368-369. The occasional references to stage per-

formance found in contemporary documents probably allude to *All for Love;* for example, Mrs. Slipslop is described as casting on Fanny a look "not unlike that which Cleopatra gives Octavia in the play" (Fielding, *Joseph Andrews,* II, xiii).

[58] Based upon the Furness *Variorum* edition. Note that Stone says the play is shorter than the original by 657 lines.

[59] For example, III, vi, 1-2; see Furness' note, p. 197. This kind of emendation indicates that the actor as well as the editor took an active part in preparing the stage version.

[60] See Spencer, *The Art and Life of William Shakespeare,* p. 342.

[61] Victor, *op. cit.,* III, 18.

[62] Genest, *op. cit.,* V, 205-211.

[63] G. P. Baker, *Some Unpublished Correspondence of David Garrick,* p. 36.

[64] Genest, *op. cit.,* IV, 564.

[65] Baker, *The Companion to the Playhouse,* I, "Cymbeline."

[66] Quoted in Odell, *op. cit.,* I, 372-373.

[67] Seven, according to Genest, but he apparently counted all the nights for which the play was *announced;* the author of *Literary and Graphical Illustrations* says, (p. 4), there were only five performances; Murphy (*Life of Garrick,* I, 371) says it was acted nine nights, and that it was on the tenth night that Fitzpatrick and his "malevoli" threatened to start a riot.

[68] Kilbourne, *op. cit.,* pp. 37-38.

[69] Davies, *Memoirs,* II, 13-15; see also MacMillan, *op. cit.,* p. xiv.

[70] This statement is based on the assumption that the 1777 revival at Drury Lane by Sheridan was not an operatic version. Genest (*op. cit.,* V, 551) lists it as "Tempest revived." Note, however, that Hogan (p. 434) lists six performances at Drury Lane in 1746 as of the original.

[71] Quoted in Wheatley, *op. cit.,* p. 265.

[72] Quoted in Kilbourne, *op. cit.,* p. 36.

[73] *Literary and Graphical Illustration,* p. 74.

[74] Steevens' letter is quoted by Stone; see n. 11, above.

[75] By George W. Stone, Jr.; see his article, "Garrick, and an Unknown Operatic Version of *Love's Labour's Lost,*" *RES,* XV (1939), 323-328, from which the following account is drawn.

[76] *Ibid.,* p. 326.

[77] *Ibid.,* p. 328.

[78] For example, Cibber's *Richard III,* already mentioned, and Ambrose Philips' *Humphrey, Duke of Gloster,* which used about thirty lines.

[79] Genest, *op. cit.,* III, 611.

[80] The pamphlet that contains this contemporary comment is quoted in J. R. Sutherland, "Shakespeare's Imitators in the Eighteenth Century," *MLR,* XXVIII (1933), 31.

[81] Pointed out by Odell, *op. cit.,* I, 233; see also Sutherland, *op. cit.,* 25-28.

[82] See Dougald MacMillan, *Catalogue of the Larpent Plays in the Huntington Library* (San Marino, Calif., 1939).

[83] Emmet L. Avery and A. H. Scouten, "A Tentative Calendar of Daily Theatrical Performances in London, 1700-1701 to 1704-1705," *PMLA,* LXIII (1948), 114-180.

NOTES TO CHAPTER SEVEN

[1] This brief summary of theatrical affairs is drawn from accounts contained in the works of Victor, Oulton, Genest, Wyndham, Maude, Stirling, Nicoll, and Nicholson.

Notes

[2] Wilkinson, *Memoirs of His Own Life*, II, 138-139.

[3] Victor, *The History of the Theatres of London and Dublin*, I, 194.

[4] Thomas Wilkes, *A General View of the Stage* (London, 1759), p. 334; Oulton (*A History of the Theatres of London*, II, 162) says that the position was "attended with infinite trouble" and "subject to the little paragraph invectives of every disappointed would-be writer."

[5] See the letter written by Thomas King, September 30, 1778, after he had retired as acting manager of Drury Lane, which lists his duties and rights as acting manager (Oulton, *op. cit.*, II, 20-30).

[6] Arthur Murphy, *The Life of David Garrick, esq.*, II, 156-157.

[7] Wilkes, *op. cit.*, pp. 334-335.

[8] Quoted in *The Life of Mrs. Abington* (London, 1888), pp. 76-77.

[9] Murphy, *op. cit.*, II, 158-159; Murphy says that "not one good play was produced at Covent-Garden, from the days of Booth, Wilkes [sic] and Cibber," obviously an overstatement, but indicative of Rich's detrimental influence nevertheless.

[10] Davies, *Dram. Misc.*, I, 165.

[11] Wilkinson, *op. cit.*, I, 33.

[12] John Genest, *Some Account of the English Stage*, IV, 654.

[13] Wilkinson, *op. cit.*, II, 135; Rich had also of course his loyal supporters, notably Quin and Mrs. Bellamy.

[14] Besides the inference that can be drawn in support of this statement by examining the seasonal repertory, a letter from Garrick to Sir Joshua Reynolds gives direct evidence. Reynolds had sent Palmer's *Zaphira* to Garrick to read. Garrick replied that even if he found it acceptable he would not be able to use it for two years. Reynolds was offended, thinking Garrick's reply an unfriendly refusal, and said so in a letter to the manager. To this Garrick replied: "What I wrote to Sir Joshua was, upon my honour, the real situation of my affairs at present. I have no less than seven plays, each of five acts, and two smaller pieces for presentation. These, with our revived plays will be as much as any manager can thrust with all his might into two seasons" (Susan M. Radcliffe, ed., *Sir Joshua's Nephew, Being Letters Written 1670-1778, by a Young Man to His Sisters*, pp. 47-49).

[15] The generally accepted view is that Garrick refused them because they did not provide him with adequate roles; but see n. 43, below.

[16] Cf. Allardyce Nicoll, *An Introduction to Dramatic Theory* (London, 1923), *passim*.

[17] See chaps. LXII-LXIII; the notes to the Shakespeare Head edition (Oxford, 1926), II, 332, give the following identifications: Mr. Melopoyn—Smollett; Brayer—Lacy; Marmozet—Garrick; Sheerwit—Lord Lyttelton.

[18] For example, Murphy (*op. cit.*, II, 104-105) mentions Dow's *Sethona* as an instance. Davies, Wilkinson, and several anonymous writers make similar comments.

[19] As an example of the latter kind of patronage, we may note a passage in a letter from Samuel Johnson of Torrington to his sister in 1775; Samuel's uncle, Sir Joshua Reynolds, had just seen *Braganza* and had sat with Garrick in the orchestra. Johnson remarked, "I suppos'd Garrick appear'd to support the great enconium [sic] which He had bestow'd on the Play. . . ." (Radcliffe, *op. cit.*, 62-63).

[20] Boswell, *Life of Johnson*, II, 438-439.

[21] Besides his excellence as Harlequin and his love of cats, Rich is famous for his conviction that he was a master in the art of training actors. Whenever a young actor agreed to submit to his direction, he was likely to be given

his own choice of roles (so subject to flattery was Rich), often with unfortunate results (see Davies, *Dram. Misc.*, I, 166).

[22] Murphy, *op. cit.*, I, 205.

[23] See chap. six, above.

[24] For another poetic effusion, we may note Hannah More's *Ode to Dragon:*

> For he shall shine while Taste survives,
> And he shall shine while Genius lives,
> A never-setting sun.

(This is the original ending, which was altered as included in her *Collected Works;* see Mary Alden Hopkins, *Hannah More and Her Circle* [New York, 1947], p. 75.)

Wilkinson prosaically agrees: "Garrick had a wonderful power of that kind over his hearers, as they mostly held him invaluable, and put great faith in what he recommended to their sanction and good opinion" (*op. cit.*, II, 160). Testimony of another kind is seen in Murphy's remark about Garrick's alteration of *The Country Wife:* "The manager had it in his power to repeat it as often as he pleased, and his own patronage was sufficient to keep the piece alive for some time" (*Life of Garrick*, II, 38).

Finally, we may note, as an example of the extreme view that some modern scholars have taken, based apparently upon similar evidence but with some misstatement of the case, and in itself a kind of evidence, Walter Schneider's conclusion: Garrick "gab [dem Publikum] einen anderen Geschmack, zog es durch sein geniales Spiel von den Harlekinaden und franzödien ab und gewöhnte es allmählich an festere, kräftigere Kost" (*Uber das Verhältnis von David Garricks "Florizel and Perdita" zu Shakespeares "The Winters Tale"* [Halle, 1902], p. 7).

[25] Theophilus Cibber, *Two Dissertations on the Theatres* (1756), quoted in Odell, *Shakespeare from Betterton to Irving*, I, 365.

[26] P. 5.

[27] *Theatrical Biography: or, Memoirs of the Principal Performers of the Three Theatres Royal* (London, 1772, 2 vols.), I, 84.

[28] Esther K. Sheldon, "Walker's Influence on the Pronunciation of English," *PMLA*, LXII (1947), 142; Miss Sheldon mentions, for example, Walker's attempt to establish the pronunciation of *transition*. Walker stated: "When I asked Mr. Garrick to pronounce this word, he, without premeditation, gave it in the first manner [trans-sizhun]; but when I desired him to repeat the pronunciation, he gave it in the second [tran-sishun]." Both pronunciations, in that order, were entered in the dictionary.

[29] Davies, *Dram. Misc.*, II, 157.

[30] The following verse appeared in *Gentleman's Magazine*, XX (1750), 471:

On the Run of Romeo and Juliet

> Well—what to night? says angry Ned,
> As up from bed he rouses:
> *Romeo* again!—and shakes his head,
> Ah! pox on both your houses.

Murphy's version of this verse (*op. cit.*, I, 194), which he says appeared in the newspapers, is substantially the same.

[31] Murphy, *op. cit.*, I, 195.

[32] *Ibid.*, I, 203-204.

[33] *Ibid.*, II, 10.

[34] Victor, *op. cit.*, III, 113.

[35] See *ibid.*, 113-115, and Oulton, *op. cit.*, II, 84-91.

[36] H. Barton Baker (*The London Stage: Its History and Traditions from 1576*

Notes

to 1888 [London, 1889, 2 vols.], I, 89) says that Covent Garden was especially popular for its musical entertainments in 1763 and that about that time Drury Lane fell off in popularity.

[37] Oulton (*op. cit.*, II, 160-166) remarks that Colman "was not a *Colley Cibber* that delighted in crushing *Singing birds*. . . ."

[38] Davies, *Memoirs*, I, 126 n.; Davies also points out in this connection, however, that Garrick, who had brought out in the 1753-1754 season four new tragedies (*The Gamester, The Brothers, Creusa,* and *Boadicea*) and two revived pieces (*Don Sebastian* and *Coriolanus*), was hardly outdone by Harris or Sheridan in bringing novelty to the stage.

[39] Thomas Whincop (*Scanderbeg* [London, 1747], p. 183) uses this phrase, which he says was the common term; the practice is noted by all contemporary theatrical historians.

[40] Davies, *Memoirs*, I, 68-69.

[41] Murphy, *op. cit.*, I, 330-341.

[42] See William Cooke, *Memoirs of Samuel Foote*, II, 192-193.

[43] The letter, written to Percy, April 4, 1758, is contained in John Nichols, *Illustrations of Literature*, VII, 251; this seems to be a more valid explanation than the one usually given—that the play did not provide an adequate role for Garrick (cf. n. 15, above) or that Garrick accepted the play he had previously rejected because he had become friends with Home. The latter view is set forth in Henry G. Graham, *Scottish Men of Letters in the Eighteenth Century* (London, 1901), p. 68.

[44] Horace Bleackley, *The Beautiful Duchess* (London, 1927), p. 66, and cf. Margaret Barton, *David Garrick* (London, 1948), p. 135; although Bleackley gives the author's first name as Samuel and does not name the play, the reference may be to Henry Crisp's tragedy, *Virginia*, which was acted at Drury Lane in the year mentioned (1754); see also Murphy, *op. cit.*, I, 244-249.

[45] Reginald Blunt, *Mrs. Montagu, "Queen of the Blues,"* I, 353.

[46] See Rose Mary Davis, *The Good Lord Lyttelton* (New York, 1939), p. 303; Boswell was among those who helped to obtain subscriptions.

[47] G. P. Baker, *Some Unpublished Correspondence of David Garrick* (Boston, 1907), p. 37.

[48] See Murphy, *op. cit.*, II, 85-86; Mme Celisia was the daughter of Mallet, who was also befriended by Garrick. Friendship for the author is also given by Graham (*op. cit.*, pp. 69-74) as the reason for Garrick's acceptance of Home's *The Siege of Aquileia* and *The Fatal Discovery;* but see n. 43, above.

[49] Murphy, *op. cit.*, I, 387; Garrick himself acted the part of Sir Anthony Branville, said to be the last role he undertook in a new play.

[50] *Ibid.*, I, 381-384; Murphy says that Garrick and Mrs. Cibber, who played the principal characters, gave *Elvira* their best efforts.

[51] Johnson gives the same reason for the acceptance of *Alfred* in his life of Mallet (*Works,* VI, 242-243), and is quoted with approval by George W. Cooke in his *Memoirs of Lord Bolingbroke* (London, 1835, 2 vols.), II, 249 n. It seems improbable that Mallet could succeed in hoodwinking Garrick twice with the same trick; and if a choice must be made between the evidence of Murphy and that of Johnson, the former's more circumstantial account must be given credence.

[52] George Anne Bellamy, *Apology* (London, 1785, 6 vols. in 3), II, 205.

[53] Bellamy, *op. cit.*, II, 194-195.

[54] David E. Baker, *Biographia Dramatica*, I:1, 279.

[55] *Ibid.*, p. 316.

[56] See the "Preface" to Francis Gentleman's *Sejanus* (London, 1752).

[57] See *A History of Early Nineteenth Century Drama.*

[58] Garrick was apparently considering a revival of *Richard II*, as is indicated by his correspondence with Steevens. The revived play was probably to be an alteration made by the manager. For the text of the letters, see George W. Stone, Jr., "Garrick's Presentation of *Antony and Cleopatra*," *RES*, XIII (1937), 36; see also Genest, *op. cit.*, III, 554. Although Goodhall's alteration was published in 1772, a year before the date of Garrick's letter, the manager, who was persistently concerned with reviving older plays, particularly those of Shakespeare, may well have had in mind the possibility of reviving *Richard II* even long before 1772.

[59] Gordon Goodwin, "Mark Anthony Meilan," *DNB*, XXXVII, 215.

[60] Such, for example, as the rejection of three plays by Mrs. Hoper, which were later acted at Goodman's Fields and the Haymarket. Of their performance at the minors, Baker remarks (*Biographia Dramatica*, I:1, 365): "Their small success vindicated the judgment of the managers who had refused them"; but the reason for their refusal remains unstated. Similarly, Mrs. Frances Brooke had several plays and an opera rejected by Garrick, for which she later took revenge by caricaturing Garrick in her novel, *The Excursion;* Dr. Johnson suggested that she might put one of the plays, *The Siege of Sinope,* in the fire (see Hopkins, *op. cit.*, pp. 73-74).

[61] Baker, *Biographia Dramatica*, III, 338-339.

[62] Davies, *Memoirs*, I, 90.

[63] Murphy, *op. cit.*, I, 324-325.

[64] Bellamy, *op. cit.*, II, 137-138; it was acted the next evening, but only because "Mr. Town *begged* a third night for the author."

[65] See Oulton, *op. cit.*, I, 13.

[66] Davies, *Dram. Misc.*, II, 238.

[67] *Ibid.*, p. 370.

[68] Cf. H. B. Baker, *The London Stage*, I, 218.

[69] Davies, *Dram. Misc.*, II, 106.

[70] Bellamy, *op. cit.*, II, 113-114; Garrick, who was on the stage during the scene, was much disgusted.

[71] Boswell, *Life of Johnson*, II, 348-349.

[72] Davies, *Dram. Misc.*, II, 106.

NOTES TO CHAPTER EIGHT

[1] Davies, *Dram. Misc.*, I, 180.

[2] For example, Casca, who in the original does not appear after Act III, was given the lines of Titinius. It is noteworthy that in Queen Anne's time this play was acted when the "united strength" of the two companies was available (see *ibid.*, II, 212-213).

[3] Hopkins' diary, quoted in Dougald MacMillan, *Drury Lane Calendar, 1747-1776*, p. 104.

[4] Arthur Murphy, *The Life of David Garrick, esq.*, I, 298.

[5] John Galt, *Lives of the Players* (London, 1803, 2 vols. in one), I, 185.

[6] *Theatrical Biography*, I, 19-22.

[7] For example, in Davies, *Memoirs,* chaps. III and IV.

[8] *Theatrical Biography*, I, 85.

[9] Davies, *Dram. Misc.*, II, 408.

[10] Wilkinson remarks (*Memoirs of His Own Life*, II, 126): "Young actors think of nothing but tragedy . . ."; he then notes how the actor King failed in tragedy because "Mrs. Chance decided otherwise." Oulton (*The History of the Theatres of London*, II, 59-60) mentions several comedians who tried tragedy.

[11] Davies, *Memoirs*, II, 132-133.

[12] Wilkinson, *op. cit.*, II, 55.

[18] Davies, *Memoirs*, I, 122; cf. *London Chronicle*, I (1757), 335: "the most gentlemanlike actor on the stage." From many possibilities, we may note the description of Winstone (Davies, *Dram. Misc.*, I, 38-39) as "an actor of singular skill in two or three parts," apparently those which represented the country booby.

[14] *Theatrical Biography*, I, 10; Romeo was another such role.

[15] *Ibid.*, I, 114; among those who excelled in particular kinds of tragic roles was Thomas Hull, who was highly regarded as a "heavy father" (see Joseph Knight, "Thomas Hull," *DNB*, XXVIII, 195-196).

[16] See her *Apology*, I, 56.

[17] Mrs. Pritchard was long a favorite Beatrice, but when she "resigned it in favour of her daughter, . . . the play lost half its value" (Murphy, *Life of Garrick*, I, 156); Davies (*Memoirs*, II, 127) mentions the difficulties and prejudices that Mrs. Abington encountered because of the remembrance of Mrs. Pritchard in the part.

[18] Davies, *Memoirs*, II, 140; see also Victor, *op. cit.*, III, 145. Of Macklin's Shylock, Reynolds remarked: "I can venture boldly to assert that, for *identity* of character from the first scene to the last, probably as a performance it was never surpassed" (quoted in Percy Fitzgerald, *A New History of the English Stage*, II, 111).

[19] XL (1776), 63.

[20] Before the days of Garrick it was commonly believed that the character of Macbeth could not hold audiences after the first two acts, that by then "all the pith of it was exhausted"; but Garrick made it one of his most effective roles (Davies, *Dram. Misc.*, II, 149ff.).

[21] The *London Chronicle* (I, 231) remarks that this play "owes its present Reception on the Stage, to the inimitable Performance of Mr. Garrick."

[22] Ranger was one of Garrick's favorite and most popular roles; when he decided that Richard was too taxing for his last performances, he took his farewell in the part of Ranger, a role with which he had long been identified by the public.

[23] Murphy (*op. cit.*, I, 261) states: "Whenever Garrick appeared in any of his capital parts, either in tragedy or comedy, he was sure of attracting crowded audiences"; the truth of this statement is borne out by the record of receipts at Drury Lane. An illuminating comment is supplied by the anonymous pamphleteer who brought out *D--ry-L-ne P--yh--se Broke Open, in a Letter to Mr. G------* (p. 17); he criticizes the revival of *Albumazar*, not because of the play, but because Garrick had not acted in it: ". . . if you think a Score of Rhimes, repeated by way of Prologue, will satisfy your Guests, you are mistaken."

[24] The *London Chronicle* (I, 231) calls Othello Barry's "first and greatest part."

[25] Davies, *Memoirs*, I, 36.

[26] *The Thespian Dictionary*, "Woffington" (this work has no pagination).

[27] Genest, *op. cit.*, III, 633.

[28] I, 310-311; see also Victor, *op. cit.*, III, 1-8.

[29] In a letter to Mrs. Abington dated Nov. 11, 1785, quoted in *The Life of Mrs. Abington*, pp. 39-40.

[30] *Theatrical Biography*, I, 131.

[31] *The Life of Mr. James Quin*, p. 41; almost the identical words appear, without ascription, in *Biographia Dramatica* (I:1, 131). To what extent this play's success depended upon the actress is suggested in a letter from Lady Hertford to her son, written in 1744: "I went to the play (as I told you I intended) on Monday night. Mr. Garrick I own answered my expectation and acted so well that I am almost tempted to see him once in tragedy. Mrs. Clive

either was really suddenly taken ill or was not in the humor to act Nell, so that the part was done by a frightful Mrs. Philips, who could neither sing, laugh, or do any one thing that was fit for a cobbler's wife; in short she spoiled the whole thing" (Helen Sard Hughes, *The Gentle Hertford, Her Life and Letters*, p. 233). The play was later given renewed life when Miss Pope, the protégée of Mrs. Clive, undertook the part of Nell, in which she also won great success (*Theatrical Biography*, I, 50-51).

[32] Victor, *op. cit.*, III, 138.

[33] *Ibid.*, III, 146.

[34] Oulton, *op. cit.*, II, 204-209.

[35] Thomas Francklin, *Matilda* (London, 1775).

[36] Murphy, *op. cit.*, I, 263-269.

[37] *Ibid.*, I, 102.

[38] Victor, *op. cit.*, II, 163.

[39] Genest, *op. cit.*, V, 297-298.

[40] *Ibid.*, IV, 491.

[41] *Ibid.*, V, 517; in this instance, the audience's pleasure in seeing a new actor, as well as his success as Norval, must have contributed in prolonging the run of the play.

[42] *Theatrical Biography*, II, 52-53; later, the continued success of the play seems to have depended largely upon Garrick, and on one occasion Garrick's sudden illness caused *The West Indian* to be substituted for *Every Man in His Humour*.

[43] Victor, *op. cit.*, III, 53-54.

[44] Murphy, *op. cit.*, II, 6-7; this practice is one of the results of the possession of parts.

[45] Wilkinson, *op. cit.*, II, 39; it is noteworthy, as evidence of the close knowledge by the audience of theatrical affairs, that in the very next year Wilkinson's imitation of Garrick as Biron in this play was immediately recognized, although he spoke only "a few words."

[46] Oulton, *op. cit.*, I, 45.

[47] Bellamy, *op. cit.*, III, 17-18; Miss Nossiter was a protégée of Barry, who "was obliged to adopt such a measure, the possession of characters being . . . esteemed at this time the property of the performer. And it was an invariable rule at the theatre, not to make the smallest encroachment on a custom so long established."

[48] Genest, *op. cit.*, IV, 198.

[49] *Biographia Dramatica*, I:1, 286-287.

[50] Murphy, *op. cit.*, II, 20-21.

[51] Quoted in MacMillan, *op. cit.*, p. 190. Similarly, the title role in Garrick's *The Male-Coquette* was expressly written for Woodward (see the "Advertisement" to the play printed in Garrick's *Works*, I, 44).

[52] Wilkinson, *op. cit.*, II, 60.

[53] Oulton, *op. cit.*, I, 32.

[54] This substitution, here regarded as representative, actually took place; see Genest, *op. cit.*, IV, 333-334; one tragedy was sometimes substituted for another also if it furnished a different type of role; for example, *All for Love* instead of *King John* at Covent Garden, February 26, 1751.

[55] Davies, *Dram. Misc.*, II, 10.

[56] Bellamy, *op. cit.*, III, 112.

[57] Genest, *op. cit.*, V, 323.

[58] Oulton, *op. cit.*, I, 6.

[59] The author of *D--ry-L-ne P--yh--se Broke Open* (p. 6) charged that Gar-

Notes

rick, by pretending illness, could put "a Stop to a Play, by which *R—h* would have been so considerable a Gainer."

⁶⁰ Cooke, *Memoirs of Samuel Foote,* II, 190.

⁶¹ Genest, *op. cit.,* IV, 413.

⁶² Henry Saxe Wyndham, *The Annals of Covent Garden Theatre from 1732 to 1897,* I, 114.

⁶³ Genest, *op. cit.,* IV, 349; similarly, many tragedies depended upon Mrs. Cibber, the coincidence of her presence in the company and *King John* in the repertory being particularly notable (see Davies, *Memoirs,* I, 213).

⁶⁴ Murphy, *op. cit.,* I, 325-327; but cf. Wilkinson (see note 65).

⁶⁵ Wilkinson, *op. cit.,* II, 5; led by Woodward, quite a number of actors deserted from Drury Lane at this time.

⁶⁶ *The Thespian Dictionary,* "Susanna Maria Cibber."

⁶⁷ Richard Cumberland, *Memoirs,* I, 380-381.

⁶⁸ Victor, *op. cit.,* III, 121; this actor, who married Miss Pritchard, is not to be confused with the more famous John Palmer, who died in 1798.

⁶⁹ Oulton, *op. cit.,* I, 4.

⁷⁰ Davies, *Memoirs,* I, 81; Davies referred to *Julius Caesar* in 1784 as *"now laid aside and almost forgotten" (Dram. Misc.,* II, 255).

⁷¹ See Genest, *op. cit.,* IV, 490-491.

⁷² Whincop, *Scanderbeg,* pp. 182-183.

⁷³ *The Playhouse Pocket-Companion,* p. 53.

⁷⁴ Genest, *op. cit.,* III, 601-603; Genest, presumably drawing upon the playbill, dates the performance of this play November 12, 1739, the date I have accepted even though Victor, Whincop, and *The Playhouse Pocket-Companion* give 1741. Quin had originally agreed to play Ceron in this tragedy, but he gave it up; and his action caused the others to neglect the study of their parts, so that on the night of the performance it was poorly received. Quin was hissed for several nights afterward for his part in bringing about the play's condemnation, until he finally came forward and told the audience that he had read the play and found it the worst he had ever seen. The audience was apparently satisfied with his explanation.

⁷⁵ Cooke, *op. cit.,* II, 23-24.

⁷⁶ The dispute between the two actresses was continued in their correspondence, quoted in Oulton, *op. cit.,* II, 204-209.

⁷⁷ Davies, *Dram. Misc.,* II, 368-369; Garrick's person was not "sufficiently important and commanding," Mrs. Yates was then a young actress lacking the experience required for the difficult role of Cleopatra, and Mossop "wanted the essential part of Enobarbus, humour"; see *Literary and Graphical Illustration,* p. 70.

⁷⁸ Davies, *Dram. Misc.,* I, 159.

⁷⁹ Murphy, *op. cit.,* I, 106; Contemporaries thought that Garrick's relative failure as Othello was due, not only to his slight stature, but to the blackening that "disguised his features, and the expression of the mind was wholly lost." Garrick depended heavily upon the remarkable mobility of his features, which would of course be less effective in black face.

⁸⁰ Murphy, *op. cit.,* I, 364; Murphy said that the three principal actors acted their parts "to perfection."

⁸¹ Davies, *Dram. Misc.,* II, 238; Garrick was not the only one displeased, for the king, who had commanded one of the six performances, expressed "some displeasure at Garrick's portrayal of the Bastard," and Garrick thereupon stopped the play although the boxes had been taken for several nights (Davies, *Memoirs,* I, 212-216); see also Genest, *op. cit.,* IV, 605-606.

[82] Whincop, *op. cit.*, p. 183; there were, of course, many possible causes for the damning of a new play—popular dislike of the author or of an actor, disapproval of a play because it was licensed, the unpopularity of a change in the manager's policies—which are discussed elsewhere in this study, as well as causes too trivial or various to be recorded by contemporaries; to represent those failures resulting from an unfortunate relationship between actor and audience, we may mention Mrs. Griffith's *A Wife in the Right* (1772). This comedy was damned at its only performance, because Shuter, whose carelessness had once caused the comedy to be postponed, was hissed from the stage by an audience that resented being trifled with (Genest, *op. cit.*, V, 333-334).

[83] Thomas Moore, *Memoirs of the Life of the Right Honourable Richard Brinsley Sheridan,* quoted in Genest, *op. cit.,* V, 459; the play's ultimate success was due in part to the revisions made by the author, but contemporaries almost invariably mention the substitution of actors as an important factor; it should be noted also that out of gratitude to Clinch, Sheridan gave him the new farce, *St. Patrick's Day,* for his benefit.

[84] Davies, *Memoirs,* I, 30.

[85] Murphy (*op. cit.,* I, 116) says that it "was regarded as their strong play and was used on Saturday nights to compete with the opera."

[86] *Ibid.,* I, 222-223; two years earlier, before Barry left for Covent Garden, that actor had made possible the revival of similar plays.

[87] *Ibid.,* I, 224-225; Victor (*op. cit.,* II, 129) notes that *The Brothers* was once in rehearsal at Drury Lane in 1726.

[88] Genest, *op. cit.,* V, 205-211; the dispute between the actresses was further aggravated by the notorious lack of harmony that existed among the four patentees, who seem to have played favorites among the members of the company.

[89] The matter of salary was occasionally of direct importance in influencing the repertory, as in the case of Woodward mentioned above (p. 152), and of Macklin during the management of Fleetwood; but since such instances are relatively rare, I have not thought it necessary to deal specifically with actors' salaries.

[90] Murphy, *op. cit.,* II, 32.

[91] *Ibid.,* I, 36.

[92] Bellamy, *op. cit.,* II, 136.

[93] *Ibid.,* I, 100; cf. Percy Fitzgerald, *Life of Mrs. Catherine Clive,* pp. 41-42: "The 'stock' pieces brought forward at regular intervals belong to fixed 'castes,' and each character belongs to one regular performer. His or her special gifts become associated in the mind of the public with the particular part,—the appearance, the tones, and manner, are curiously associated with it,—while a new performer appears strange and unfamiliar."

[94] Bellamy, *op. cit.,* III, 11.

[95] *Ibid.,* I, 100.

[96] *Ibid.,* III, 17-18.

[97] Quoted in The Earl of Ilchester and Mrs. Langford Brooke, *The Life of Sir Charles Hanbury-Williams, Poet, Wit and Diplomatist,* p. 84; note also Mrs. Montagu's letter to her husband (November, 1762): "I do not expect to see Falstaffe [*sic*] acted in the same perfection I have seen it by Quin," and she continues by pointing out how little different Quin was from Falstaff (Reginald Blunt, *Mrs. Montagu, "Queen of the Blues,"* II, 39); and Garrick's tribute in his prologue to *Florizel and Perdita:*
But should you call for *Falstaff,* where to find him?
He's gone,—nor left one cup of sack behind him (Murphy, *op. cit.,* II, 297).

[98] "Benedict war eine Lieblingsrolle Garrick's" (Gisbert Freiherrn Vincke, "Bearbeitungen und Aufführungen Shakespeare'scher Stücke vom Tode des

Notes

Dichters bis zum Tode Garricks," *Shakespeare Jahrbuch*, IV, 43); see also Davies, *Memoirs*, I, 125, and *Literary and Graphical Illustration*, p. 12.

[99] George C. D. Odell, *Shakespeare from Betterton to Irving*, I, 338; note that, a page earlier, Odell remarked that the revivals of Shakespeare's comedies were "somewhat inexplicable," an inconsistency suggesting that his later statement was inadequately considered.

[100] Note that Edmond Malone ("An Historical Account of the Rise and Progress of the English Stage, and of the Economy and Usages of Ancient Theatres," *The Plays and Poems of William Shakespeare*, I:2, 283-284), although giving the greatest share of credit to that tribe of which he himself was a member, yet was willing to pay tribute to Garrick: "Since [1741], in consequence of Mr. Garrick's admirable performance of many of his [that is, Shakespeare's] principal characters, the frequent representation of his plays in nearly their original state, and above all, the various researches which have been made for the purpose of explaining and illustrating his works, our poet's reputation has been yearly increasing, and is now fixed upon a basis, which neither the lapse of time nor the fluctuation of opinion will ever be able to shake."

[101] *An Essay on the Writings and Genius of Shakespeare* (London, 1769), pp. 15-16.

[102] Oulton, *op. cit.*, I, 150.

[103] Wilkinson, *op. cit.*, I, 111.

[104] Davies, *Dram. Misc.*, III, 85-88.

[105] *Ibid.*, I, 102.

[106] *Ibid.*, III, 101.

[107] Cf. Vincke, *op. cit.*, p. 51.

[108] Bellamy, *op. cit.*, II, 138; the author, of course, had his own interests in mind when he made the alteration, for a strong role for Garrick was a certain recipe for success.

[109] Genest, *op. cit.*, IV, 178.

[110] Cumberland, *Memoirs*, I, 293.

[111] Boswell, *Life of Johnson*, II, 219.

[112] See above, pp. 53-54. Note also that one reason for the omission of Rosaline from *Romeo and Juliet* was to avoid the appearance of fickleness in the hero.

[113] Bellamy, *op. cit.*, II, 134-136.

[114] *Lives of the Poets*, in *Works*, V, 404.

[115] *Reformer* for February 11, 1747/48.

NOTES TO CHAPTER NINE

[1] *Tristram Shandy*, Bk. IV, Chap. 7.

[2] *Correspondence Between Frances, Countess of Hartford, and Henrietta Louisa, Countess of Pomfret*, I, 86.

[3] Blunt, *Mrs. Montagu, "Queen of the Blues,"* I, 354; see also the correspondence between Garrick and Reynolds referred to in chap. seven, n. 14, above.

[4] The count mentioned here includes the 323 first pieces, as well as the afterpieces, for which the records are less complete.

[5] I have thought it best not to distinguish between new plays and new alterations at this point. Since both are largely the work of the same playwrights, to separate them here would be profitless.

[6] Victor, *The History of the Theatres of London and Dublin*, III, 174.

[7] Murphy, *The Life of David Garrick*, II, 11.

[8] *The Thespian Dictionary*, "Arne."

[9] *Ibid.*, "Forrest"; the author's name is here given as Theophilus Forrest, but he is the same as the Theodosius Forrest listed by Nicoll, *A History of Late Eighteenth Century Drama*, p. 261.

[10] *The Thespian Dictionary*, "Hitchcock."

[11] *Ibid.*, "Massink"; Nicoll (*A History of Late Eighteenth Century Drama*, p. 28) gives his name as Messink and does not mention his attachment to the Drury Lane theater under Garrick.

[12] See Oulton, *The History of the Theatres of London*, II, 191-192.

[13] Murphy, *op. cit.*, II, 91-92; he finally, however, gave the role to Barry.

[14] Galt, *Lives of the Players*, II, 125.

[15] David E. Baker, *The Companion to the Playhouse*; see also *The Dramatic Works of David Garrick, Esq.* (London, 1774, 2 vols.), I, 51, n., where this passage appears verbatim.

[16] Boswell, *Life of Johnson*, II, 95, n. 2.

[17] Letter written to the Countess of **** at Rome, in [John Shebbeare, tr.], *Letters on the English Nation by Battista Angeloni, A Jesuit, Who resided many years in London* (London, 1775, 2 vols.), II, 247.

[18] Boswell, *op. cit.*, II, 127.

[19] Oulton, *op. cit.*, I, 36.

[20] To list merely the titles of such pieces would require several pages; but it may be noted that authors usually acknowledged their indebtedness, realizing that to do so often enhanced the value of the piece in the public eye.

[21] This is one of the many alterations of relatively recent plays (Murphy [*op. cit.*, II, 82] called the practice of altering plays a "rage," which he felt was "the very error of the times"). Savage had left his play in pawn with the jailor at Bristol, with whom it remained when the author died in 1743. It was then sold for seven guineas (*The Thespian Dictionary*, "Woodfall"), but whether Woodfall was the purchaser is unrecorded. Perhaps the actor, seeing an opportunity to gain fame easily as a playwright, determined to acquire the tragedy and bring it to the stage.

[22] George W. Stone, Jr., "Garrick's Handling of *Macbeth*," SP, XXXVIII (1941), 622.

[23] Gisbert Freiherrn Vincke, "Shakespeare und Garrick," *Shakespeare Jahrbuch*, IX (1874), 21. It may be helpful to quote here Murphy's statement of Garrick's definitions of tragedy and comedy (*op. cit.*, I, 136). He regarded comedy, Murphy says, "as the mirror of life, in which may be seen the follies, humours, and foibles, of the mind, exposed to ridicule; at once to delight and to reform the manners of the age"; and tragedy "as the school of virtue, representing the actions, passions, and sufferings, of human nature, for the instruction of mankind." It will be noted that these are not greatly different from the views held by such classicists and scholars as Mason and Cumberland; and in this connection it is instructive to recall another statement by Murphy (I, 263) —that Garrick "had kindled a spirit of emulation in the minds of classic scholars, who now employed their leisure hours in writing for the stage."

[24] Murphy, *op. cit.*, I, 295-296.

[25] *Literary and Graphical Illustration*, p. 22.

[26] Cf. Victor, *op. cit.*, II, 138.

[27] *Florizel and Perdita*, Garrick's alteration, is printed in his *Dramatic Works*, II, 37ff., and in the Furness *Variorum* ed. of *The Winter's Tale*, pp. 399ff.; see also Walter Schneider, *Uber das Verhältnis von David Garricks "Florizel and Perdita" zu Shakespeares "The Winters Tale."*

[28] *Morning Post* for Jan. 20, 1775, quoted in George Henry Nettleton, *English Drama of the Restoration and Eighteenth Century*, 1642-1780 (New York, 1923), p. 296.

Notes

[29] Bernbaum remarks (*The Drama of Sensibility*, p. 253): "It was rather the extraordinary brilliance of the comic portions of *The Rivals* than the conventional sentimentalism of its sub-plot that commanded admiration"; but comments in contemporary periodicals suggest that such a statement is not wholly accurate. It is significant that Sheridan shows in *The Rivals* his indebtedness to two men thoroughly familiar with the requirements of the stage, Garrick and Colman (see Miriam Gabriel and Paul Mueschke, "Two Contemporary Sources of Sheridan's *The Rivals*," *PMLA*, XLIII, 249-50).

[30] For example, the May-December marriage as a plot situation in English literature is at least as old as Chaucer; and the similarity of the Surface brothers to the two youths in *Tom Jones* was at once recognized by the audience (*London Chronicle*, LXI, 444).

[31] Thomas Moore, *Memoirs of the Life of the Right Honourable Richard Brinsley Sheridan*, I, 210: "his original intention was too satirise some of the gossips at Bath"; see also R. Crompton Rhodes, ed., *The Plays and Poems of Richard Brinsley Sheridan*, II, 13ff.

[32] For the account of its composition, see Moore, *op. cit.*, I, 208-262.

[33] *Ibid.*, I, 210; note that the original title was "The Slanderers—A Pump-Room Scene."

[34] When he came to join what were originally independent sketches, it is significant that he named the play after the Scandalous Club, and that, although he suppressed elements in the Surface-Teazle plot, he kept Lady Sneerwell and her colleagues, even though they do not advance the action. Moore (I, 252) said that those whom he attacked "richly deserve such ridicule." The *London Chronicle* critic agreed, for he called the play a "seasonable" comedy because of its satire of "detraction and hypocrisy . . . the prevailing vices of the time." Critics who disagreed with this view of the times, for example the author of "Animadversions on the School for Scandal" (*Gentleman's Magazine*, XLVIII [1778], 57-59), give similar testimony even while they are disagreeing.

[35] *An Apology for the Life of George Anne Bellamy*, II, 137.

[36] *Ibid.*, II, 197; Garrick kept it on the stage for nine nights as a "compliment to the translator of Horace" (Murphy, *op. cit.*, I, 216-218), but he foresaw its failure and had ready a revival of *Love's Last Shift* in order to win back the audience. The same author's *Eugenia* met with a similar fate in spite of the author's reputation and Garrick's best efforts (Bellamy, *op. cit.*, II, 138).

[37] Oulton, *op. cit.*, I, 51.

[38] Such seems to be the implication, for example, of Birch's letter to Lord Orrery, written Sept. 30, 1748 (*The Orrery Papers* [London, 1903, 2 vols.], II, 43); and cf. Davies, *Memoirs of the Life of David Garrick, Esq.*, I, 96: "no play, I will venture to assert, would draw together a larger audience than this tragedy, not only for its intrinsick merit, but also the great love and veneration which the publick bear to the author. . . ."

[39] In a letter to the Rev. Mr. Colson, March 2, 1737, quot. in Davies, *Memoirs*, I, 19-20; Boswell also mentions the incident.

[40] Leslie Stephen, "William Mason," *DNB*, XXXVI, 440.

[41] Davies, *Memoirs*, I, 104.

[42] Boswell, *op. cit.*, II, 335.

[43] *Ibid.*; Johnson's remark is explicit testimony for those who hold that the history of blank verse in the eighteenth century is the history of the attempt to assimilate the blank verse of Milton.

[44] John W. Draper, *William Mason: A Study of Eighteenth Century Culture* (New York, 1924), p. 202.

[45] *DNB*.

[46] Mary Alden Hopkins, *Hannah More and Her Circle*, p. 213.

47 Cf. Bernard H. Stern, *The Rise of Romantic Hellenism in English Literature, 1732-1786* (New York, 1940), *passim.*

48 Cumberland, *Memoirs,* I, 116-117.

49 *Ibid.,* I, 272.

50 *Ibid.,* I, 274.

51 Davies, *Memoirs,* II, 197-198.

52 This attitude was pervasive, being expressed, for example, by men as dissimilar as Aaron Hill, William Mason, and General Burgoyne.

53 W. P. Courtney, "Thomas Francklin," *DNB,* XX, 183.

54 *Letters . . . by Battista Angeloni,* II, 247.

55 Cf. Stern, *op. cit.,* pp. 162-164.

56 Murphy, *op. cit.,* I, 182-187.

57 *Ibid.,* I, 236-241; see also *Memoirs by a Celebrated Literary and Political Character* (London, 1814), p. ix, and Stern, *op. cit.,* p. 124.

58 According to MacMillan (*Drury Lane Calendar,* p. 213); Murphy (*op. cit.,* I, 241) says that it ran twelve nights.

59 For example, he read it to Doddington; see Henry P. Wyndham, ed.,. *The Diary of the Late George Bubb Doddington* (4th ed., London, 1809), p. 192.

60 See Baker, *Biographia Dramatica,* I:1, 34, and Lloyd Sanders, *Patron and Place-Hunter, a Study of George Bubb Doddington Lord Melcombe* (London, 1919), pp. 257-258.

61 Murphy, *op. cit.,* I, 315-318.

62 Graham, *Scottish Men of Letters in the Eighteenth Century,* p. 61; his heroic escapades included an escape from Doune Castle by making a rope of the bed clothes.

63 He was, of course, influenced also by Shakespeare, whom he deliberately attempted to imitate. This does not seem to be the place for a discussion of Shakespeare's influence upon the eighteenth-century dramatists, which would be more appropriately dealt with in a study of critical theory; it may be noted, however, in connection with Home's work that the public was divided in its opinion, Hume, for example, thinking that he had "corrupted his taste by imitation of Shakespeare," whereas the Duke of Argyle, Lyttelton, and Pitt gave their approval (Rose Mary Davis, *The Good Lord Lyttelton* [New York, 1939], p. 231).

64 "Preface."

65 See, for example, the account of Cooke, *Memoirs of Samuel Foote,* III, 77-78.

66 II, i.

67 V, iii.

68 Johnson said he knew "of no comedy for many years that has so much exhilarated an audience" (Boswell, *op. cit.,* II, 233); it was revived in every season throughout the remainder of the period.

69 See Bernbaum, *The Drama of Sensibility,* pp. 247-251.

70 Similarly, Hugh Kelly, though he recognized the absurdities of sentimental drama, and satirized it in the epilogue of *A Word to the Wise,* could not change his style of writing, for the "pathetic was his forte . . ." (*London Chronicle,* LXI, 313).

71 V, ii.

72 *The Thespian Dictionary,* "Bickerstaffe."

73 "Advertisement" to *Lionel and Clarissa* (London, 1770).

74 II, xiii.

75 Horace Bleackley, *The Beautiful Duchess,* pp. 182-183.

76 See H. M. Stephens, "John Burgoyne," *DNB,* VII, 340-342.

77 *The Thespian Dictionary,* "Hawkesworth."

[78] The two oratorios, according to *The Thespian Dictionary,* were produced at Covent Garden and Drury Lane respectively; they are not listed by Nicoll in his hand lists.

[79] Murphy, *op. cit.,* II, 43.

[80] See Bernbaum, *op. cit.,* p. 230.

[81] *The Thespian Dictionary,* "Jones."

[82] *The Dramatic Mirror,* I, 398-399.

[83] Baker, *The Companion to the Playhouse,* I, "Cleone."

[84] See the account of its rehearsal and first run in Bellamy, *op. cit.,* III, 105-112; she remarks: "And the subject of it being a family distress, that predetermined the public in its favour."

[85] Carl L. Becker, *The Heavenly City of the Eighteenth-Century Philosophers* (New Haven, 1932), p. 99.

NOTES TO CHAPTER TEN

[1] Boswell, *Life of Johnson,* I, 461.

[2] Murphy, *The Life of David Garrick, esq.,* II, 201.

[3] *Ibid.,* II, 173.

[4] "Introduction," (I, ii).

[5] Murphy, *op. cit.,* I, 41.

[6] See, for example, Helen Sard Hughes, *The Gentle Hertford, Her Life and Letters* (New York, 1940), p. 220; John Beresford, ed., *The Diary of a Country Parson: The Reverend James Woodforde* (London, 1924-1931, 5 vols.), I, 17-18; the *Adventurer* for Jan. 27, 1753 (I, 203-214).

[7] Cecil Aspinall-Oglander, *Admiral's Wife* (London, 1940), pp. 128-129.

[8] James Fergusson, ed., *Letters of George Dempster to Sir Adam Fergusson, 1756-1813* (London, 1934), p. 11.

[9] Philip C. Yorke, ed., *The Diary of John Baker* (London, 1931), p. 107.

[10] Peter Cunningham, ed., *The Letters of Horace Walpole* (Edinburgh, 1906, 9 vols.), IV, 118-119.

[11] Reginald Blunt, ed., Mrs. Montagu, *"Queen of the Blues,"* I, 99-100.

[12] C. E. Vulliamy, *Aspasia, the Life and Letters of Mary Granville, Mrs. Delany* (London, 1935), p. 180.

[13] Yorke, *op. cit.,* p. 230.

[14] Susan M. Radcliffe, ed., *Sir Joshua's Nephew, Being Letters Written, 1769-1778, by a Young Man to His Sisters,* p. 39.

[15] Clementina Black, ed., *The Cumberland Letters* (London, 1912), p. 98.

[16] Thomas Whincop, *Scanderbeg* (London, 1747), p. 237.

[17] See Henry Saxe Wyndham, *The Annals of Covent Garden Theatre from 1732 to 1897* (London, 1906, 2 vols.), I, 32-33.

[18] William Cooke, *Memoirs of Samuel Foote,* II, 22.

[19] R. Brimley Johnson, ed., *Bluestocking Letters* (New York, 1826), pp. 150-151 (italics mine). No student of theatrical history has looked into the attendance of children at the theaters, a point that may be of some importance to the question of morality in the drama. That children did attend plays when adequately chaperoned is seen from Mrs. Boscawen's letter quoted above. In another letter this same lady also notes that she took her daughters, the oldest then about ten, to Drury Lane in April, 1755, to see *Richard III* and *"Tommy Thumb"* (Aspinall-Oglander, *op. cit.,* pp. 174-175). Another, and somewhat different, view may be gained from the *Memoirs of William Hickey* (2nd ed., London, 1914, 4 vols.): In 1765, Hickey, then sixteen years old, and two recent acquaintances who were spending a short vacation with him at

Notes

Streatham, slipped off to London, where Hickey introduced them to "two females," who suggested that they go to Covent Garden, where a new play was being performed. Hickey records in his journal, "Though at all times prone to mischief, the boldness of such a proposal nevertheless staggered me . . ." (I, 49-50).

[20] Lewis Melville, *Lady Suffolk and Her Circle* (London, 1924), pp. 277-278.

[21] Francis Coventry, *Pompey the Little,* quoted in Susan Hale, *Men and Manners of the Eighteenth Century* (Philadelphia, 1897), p. 285.

[22] William Hay, "Epigram I," Book I, in *The Works* (London, 1794), p. 227.

[23] Hughes, *op. cit.,* p. 220.

[24] *D--ry-L-ne P--yh--se Broke Open, in a Letter to Mr. G------* (London, 1748), p. 18.

[25] *London Magazine,* VI (1737), 107, 163 (italics mine). Horace Walpole specifically called it the "Footman's Gallery" in his *Memoirs of the Reign of King George the Second* (2nd ed., London, 1846, 3 vols.), I, 61.

[26] Radcliffe, *op. cit.,* p. 39.

[27] *The Dramatick Works* (London, 1777, 4 vols.), IV, 325.

[28] See, for example, *Theatrical Biography,* I, 118; John Nichols, *Illustrations of the Literary History of the Eighteenth Century* (London, 1817-1858, 8 vols.), I, 140; Baker, *Biog. Dram.,* II, 206-207, 287; Davies, *Dram. Misc.,* I, 427-428; Fielding, *Joseph Andrews,* III, x; Davies, *Memoirs,* II, 133.

[29] Note that Fielding speaks of the "critics in embroidery transplanted from the boxes to the pit, whose ancient inhabitants were exalted to the galleries, where they played on catcalls" (*Joseph Andrews,* III, vi).

[30] Edward Abbott Parry, *Charles Macklin* (London, 1891), p. 58.

[31] *Craftsman* for May 28, 1737.

[32] Quoted in Percy Fitzgerald, *The Life of Mrs. Catherine Clive* (London, (1888), p. 13.

[33] Quoted in Parry, *op. cit.,* p. 162.

[34] Richard Cumberland, *Memoirs,* (London, 1807, 2 vols.), I, 364-365.

[35] Quoted in Radcliffe, *op. cit.,* p. 84.

[36] *D--ry-L-ne P--yh--se Broke Open,* p. 8.

NOTES TO CHAPTER ELEVEN

[1] *The Connoisseur* (1755), quoted in Elizabeth Wheeler Manwaring, *Italian Landscape in Eighteenth Century England* (London, 1925), p. 28.

[2] Garrick's *A Peep Behind the Curtain* gives a revealing picture of the contemporary theater, where "ridiculous pretenders to virtu and taste" attend the rehearsal of an opera; see also Murphy, *Life of Garrick,* II, 51.

[3] *London Chronicle,* I, 558.

[4] Wilkinson, *Memoirs of His Own Life,* I, 182.

[5] *Ibid.,* I, 101.

[6] *Ibid.,* I, 183.

[7] *Ibid.,* II, 240.

[8] Davies, *Memoirs of the Life of David Garrick, Esq.,* I, 45.

[9] Cunningham, *The Letters of Horace Walpole,* I, 168.

[10] Genest, *Some Account of the English Stage,* IV, 331.

[11] Wilkinson, *op. cit.,* II, 20.

[12] See Odell, *Shakespeare from Betterton to Irving,* I, 334.

[13] Wilkinson, *op. cit.,* I, 113.

[14] See *ibid.,* II, 183.

[15] Boswell, *Life of Johnson,* II, 330.

[16] Davies, *Memoirs*, I, 219.

[17] Genest, *op. cit.*, IV, 618.

[18] Cumberland, *Memoirs*, I, 294-295.

[19] Wilkinson, *op. cit.*, I, 146.

[20] *Ibid.*, II, 230.

[21] Hughes, *The Gentle Hertford*, p. 412.

[22] *Correspondence Between Frances, Countess of Hartford, and Henrietta Louisa, Countess of Pomfret, Between the Years 1738 and 1741*, I, 95.

[23] *Ibid.*, I, 126.

[24] Countess of Cork and Orrery, ed., *The Orrery Papers* (London, 1903, 2 vols.), II, 64.

[25] Bellamy, *Apology*, I, 53.

[26] *Ibid.*, II, 209. Such interest in stage queens was of course not new. About 1706, Wilks and Mrs. Rogers acted Jaffier and Belvidera in a revival of *Venice Preserved*. They had previously been lover and mistress in real life also; but as Wilks had been unfaithful, the conjugal embraces on the stage were regarded as a "perversion of courtship [and] brought crowds of curious spectators. . . . from their close embrace she left visible and bloody marks of her jealous resentment" (Davies, *Dramatic Miscellanies*, III, 238-239).

[27] Murphy, *op. cit.*, I, 171-175.

[28] Davies, *Dram. Misc.*, I, 192-193.

[29] Violet Biddulph, *Kitty, Duchess of Queensberry* (London, 1935), pp. 172-175.

[30] Wilkinson, *op. cit.*, I, 142-143.

[31] *The Thespian Dictionary*, "Clinch," "Sheridan." See also Thomas Moore, *Memoirs of the Life of the Right Honourable Richard Brimsley Sheridan*, I, 148; and cf. Jeremy Bagster-Collins, *George Colman the Younger, 1762-1836* (New York, 1946), p. 19, and Murphy, *op. cit.*, II, 94-95.

[32] Whincop, *Scanderbeg*, pp. 146-147.

[33] Davies, *Memoirs*, I, 25.

[34] Davies, *Dram. Misc.*, II, 299-300.

[35] Audiences were so well acquainted with the manner in which various roles were played by the different actors that talented mimics like Foote and Wilkinson were enthusiastically received in their "imitations." Wilkinson relates how his imitations of Luke Sparks as Capulet, Mrs. Woffington as Lady Macbeth, and Barry as Macbeth were immediately recognized even by Dublin audiences. See Percy Fitzgerald, *A New History of the English Stage* (London, 1882, 2 vols.), II, 204-213.

[36] *London Chronicle*, LXI, 444; cf. Rhodes, *The Plays and Poems of Richard Brinsley Sheridan*, II, 12-13; see Ralph L. Collins, "Moore's *The Foundling*—An Intermediary," *PQ*, XVII (1938), 139-143.

[37] Cooke, *Memoirs of Samuel Foote*, I, 183-184.

[38] Murphy, *op. cit.*, I, 200-203.

[39] See Bertrand Evans, *Gothic Drama from Walpole to Shelley* (Univ. Calif. Publ. English, Vol. XVIII [Berkeley and Los Angeles, 1947]), chaps. I and II.

[40] I. Giberne Sieveking, *The Memoir of Sir Horace Mann* (London, 1912), pp. 150-151.

[41] It has been stated at various times that the effect of the Gothic revival upon literature was the result of a cyclic trend in historical progression—that just as the Augustan age of literature emulated Greece and Rome and scorned the Middle Ages, the later period in its antirationalistic pursuits turned away from the classical and toward the medieval. It is necessary, however, also to recall the pervasive influence of sentimentalism upon literature even early in the century. The argument advanced here, which so far as I

know has never previously been stated, although admittedly materialistic, seems more in accord with the evidence provided by the literary works themselves and by the contemporary literary scene in general. Moreover, such an explanation seems to be supported by the fact that Gothicism received its initial impetus, not as a cultural movement, but as a fashionable interest in tangible objects—the architectural remains of the Middle Ages.

[42] Quoted in Allardyce Nicoll, *A History of Late Eighteenth Century Drama* (Cambridge, 1927), p. 59.

[43] Davies, *Dram. Misc.*, I, 134.

[44] Genest, *op. cit.*, IV, 639; see also Victor, *The History of the Theatres of London and Dublin*, III, 22-24. Boswell (I, 406-407) includes the account of Johnson's part in "exorcising" this famous ghost.

[45] Hugh Dick, *Albumazar: A Comedy* (Univ. of Calif. Publ. English, Vol. XIII [Berkeley and Los Angeles, 1944]), p. 61.

[46] See above, p. 52.

[47] Cooke, *op. cit.*, II, 28-29.

[48] Davies, *Dram. Misc.*, II, 361.

[49] Bleackley, *The Beautiful Duchess*, p. 182; a detailed account of this affair is given in *ibid.*, pp. 172-183; besides this play at Drury Lane and a similar piece quickly mounted at the rival theater, the fashionable fete inspired numerous private imitations, including one given by the Garricks at their Hampton home.

[50] Interest in contemporary events could of course have the opposite effect upon the repertory. For example, it happened that the public was engrossed in the "Douglas Cause" at the time when Home's *The Fatal Discovery* reached the stage, and the playwright attributed the failure of his play to the general preoccupation with the details of that affair (see Bleackley, *op. cit.*, p. 135). The play was acted eleven nights, however—a good run for the time. It may well have been that political considerations, particularly the hatred of the Scots, were the real reason for the play's withdrawal; but Home's attribution of failure to the Douglas affair suggests at least how the energies of the theater-going public might on occasion be diverted into other channels to the detriment of the manager, the actors, and the playwright.

[51] See Cooke, *op. cit.*, I, 77-82; Wilkinson, *op. cit.*, II, 52-53; Davies, *Memoirs*, I, 145-147.

[52] Cooke, *op. cit.*, I, 198ff.

[53] Baker, *The Companion to the Playhouse*, I, "Miss Lucy in Town."

[54] Cooke, *op. cit.*, II, 33.

[55] Actually, as Cooke remarks, their complacency biased their judgment so that they could hardly have been discriminating critics.

[56] *London Chronicle*, LXI, 468.

[57] Murphy, *op. cit.*, I, 117-118.

[58] *Ibid.*, I, 308-309.

[59] "Advertisement" to *The Male-Coquette* in Garrick's *Works* (London, 1774, 2 vols.), I, 144.

[60] Murphy, *op. cit.*, I, 345.

[61] See Victor, *op. cit.*, III, 16-17.

[62] See, for example, the illustrations in T. Wright, *Caricature History of the Georges* (London, 1876).

[63] Murphy, *op. cit.*, I, 296-298.

[64] *London Chronicle*, LXI, 468.

[65] Erroll Sherson, *The Lively Lady Townshend and Her Friends* (London, 1926), p. 243.

Notes

[66] For a list of the pamphlets, see Nicoll, *A History of Late Eighteenth Century Drama*, p. 172, n. 4.

[67] Cooke, *op. cit.*, I, 96-97, 104-105.

[68] Dr. Johnson thought the portrait better suited to the Non-jurors than the Methodists (Boswell, *op. cit.*, II, 321); Cooke (*op. cit.*, I, 105), who was much less likely than Johnson to look for redeeming qualities in those with whom he disagreed, thought that Foote had captured "the enthusiastic manner of Whitfield."

[69] Lloyd Sanders, *Patron and Place-Hunter, a Study of George Bubb Doddington Lord Melcombe* (London, 1919), p. 259.

[70] Murphy, *op. cit.*, I, 212-213.

[71] *London Chronicle*, LXI, 336.

[72] For example, Garrick wrote to the Duke of Bedford (Sept. 11, 1744): "I had obeyed your Grace's commands sooner in sending the account of the scenes and other things, but the person whom I employed to make the fasces, asps, and garlands for the play of 'All for Love' was out of town. . . ." With the letter he sent a statement of the expenses, which amounted to forty-eight pounds. See Lord John Russell, ed., *Correspondence of John, Fourth Duke of Bedford* (London, 1842, 3 vols.), I, 21.

NOTES TO CHAPTER TWELVE

[1] Murphy, *The Life of David Garrick, esq.*, I, 297.

[2] *Adventurer* for Nov. 14, 1752.

[3] Wilkinson, *Memoirs of His Own Life*, II, 261.

[4] Murphy, *op. cit.*, I, 346-347.

[5] Boswell, *Life of Johnson*, I, 197, and see Burney's note in *ibid.*, pp. 197-198, n. 5.

[6] Edmond Malone's note to Boswell's *Life of Johnson*, quoted by Augustine Birrell in his edition (London, 1912), I, 156.

[7] Bellamy, *Apology*, III, 105-110.

[8] Murphy, *op. cit.*, I, 339; this account, given by the author of the play in question, differs from that given by Cooke (*Memoirs of Samuel Foote*, II, 190), who suggests that Mrs. Cibber's illness was feigned and that Murphy, anticipating such a move by the actress, had requested Mrs. Yates to study the part so that Garrick would have no excuse to put the play over until the following season.

[9] See above, 290-298.

[10] Cf. Murphy, *op. cit.*, I, 262: "the public derived a two-fold pleasure [from Garrick's revival of old plays]; their love of novelty was gratified, and they saw with pride the literary merit of ancient times."

[11] *Poetics* (tr. S. H. Butcher), VI, 19.

[12] H. Barton Baker, *The London Stage* (London, 1889, 2 vols.), I, 122.

[13] *Craftsman* for Aug. 13, 1737.

[14] *Adventurer* for Feb. 3, 1753.

[15] Murphy, *op. cit.*, I, 374.

[16] Quoted in Odell, *Shakespeare from Betterton to Irving*, I, 419.

[17] *London Magazine*, VI, 433; pantomime had been attacked quite early, for example, by Fielding's *Pasquin* (see Charles W. Nichols, "Fielding's Satire on Pantomime," *PMLA*, XLVI, 1107-1112).

[18] Murphy, *op. cit.*, II, 164.

[19] Wilkinson, *op. cit.*, II, 158.

[20] Davies, *Memoirs of the Life of David Garrick, Esq.*, I, 101.

[21] See Genest, *Some Account of the English Stage*, IV, 320.

[22] Davies, *Memoirs*, I, 101.

[23] Murphy, *op. cit.*, I, 276-282.

[24] Blunt, *Mrs. Montagu, "Queen of the Blues,"* I, 280-281.

[25] *London Chronicle*, LXI, 468.

[26] *General Advertiser* for Nov. 20, 1744, quoted in Genest, *op. cit.*, IV, 138-139.

[27] Bellamy, *op. cit.*, III, 45.

[28] *Ibid.*, II, 210-211.

[29] This situation, rather unique among Shakespeare's plays, is perhaps due to the partial authorship of Fletcher, who, according to Marjorie H. Nicolson ("The Authorship of Henry the Eighth," *PMLA*, XXXVII, 485-502), completed *Henry VIII* in the new style of "oratory, and spectacles, and sentiment, and tears."

[30] George W. Stone, Jr., "Garrick's Presentation of *Antony and Cleopatra*," *RES*, XIII, 20-38.

[31] *A Letter to the Hon. Author of the New Farce call'd the Rout*, quoted in Stone, *op. cit.*, p. 35; note the indication here of the widening divergence between poetry and the theater.

[32] George Steevens, quoted in Genest, *op. cit.*, III, 554.

[33] Wilkinson, *op. cit.*, II, 182.

[34] Davies, *Memoirs*, I, 84.

[35] Davies, *Dramatic Miscellanies*, II, 11.

[36] See Alice I. P. Wood, *The Stage History of Shakespeare's King Richard the Third*, p. 107, n. 13.

[37] Murphy, *op. cit.*, II, 45; cf. *Dram. Misc.*, III, 250.

[38] *London Chronicle*, LXI, 144.

[39] Rae Blanchard, "The Songs in Steele's Plays," *Pope and His Contemporaries: Essays presented to George Sherburn* (Oxford, 1949), p. 185.

[40] Quoted in Genest, *op. cit.*, V, 128.

[41] Victor, *The History of the Theatres of London and Dublin*, III, 113-115; see also Oulton, *The History of the Theatres of London*, II, 84-91.

[42] Fergusson, *Letters of George Dempster to Sir Adam Fergusson, 1756-1813*, p. 11.

[43] Blunt, *op. cit.*, I, 153-154.

[44] Radcliffe, *Sir Joshua's Nephew*, p. 83.

[45] *London Chronicle*, LXI, 144.

[46] See Whincop, *Scanderbeg*, p. 140.

[47] Murphy, *op. cit.*, I, 368-369; Genest remarked: "the rage for Music is well ridiculed" (*op. cit.*, IV, 641).

[48] Laurence Sterne, *Tristram Shandy*, II, viii.

[49] *Works*, IV, 334.

[50] Davies, *Memoirs*, II, 55-56; Baker, *Biographia Dramatica* (I:1, 11), gives further details.

[51] Murphy, *op. cit.*, II, 76-79.

[52] Oulton, *op. cit.*, I, 50.

[53] Baker, *Biog. Dram.*, I:1, 166.

[54] Murphy, *op. cit.*, II, 79; cf. the passage from Mrs. Montagu's letter quoted above, p. 235.

[55] Cumberland, *Memoirs*, I, 248-256.

[56] *Sentimental Magazine* for Nov., 1774, quot. in *The Life of Mrs. Abington* (London, 1888), p. 60. As was noted above, interest in contemporary affairs was also operative in maintaining the popularity of this piece.

Notes

NOTES TO CHAPTER THIRTEEN

[1] See Rose Mary Davis, *The Good Lord Lyttelton*, pp. 53-55.

[2] Lillian Dickens and Mary Stanton, eds., *An Eighteenth Century Correspondence* (London, 1910), p. 26.

[3] Cooke, *Memoirs of Samuel Foote*, II, 28-29.

[4] Davies, *Dramatic Miscellanies*, I, 359.

[5] *Ibid.*, I, 117.

[6] Katherine Thomson, ed., *Memoirs of Viscountess Sundon*, I, 393-396. Note also that Kelly's *A Word to the Wise* was damned for political reasons at its first appearance; but when it was revived later for the benefit of the author's widow, Dr. Johnson in the prologue written for that occasion remarked that it was "unconscious of offence" (Murphy, *The Life of David Garrick, esq.*, II, 74-75).

[7] Davies, *Dram. Misc.*, I, 152-153.

[8] *Ibid.*, II, 250; Professor B. H. Bronson informs me that this scene was parodied (and similarly understood) in *The Beggar's Opera*.

[9] *Ibid.*, I, 153-154.

[10] See Cumberland, *Memoirs*, I, 387-388.

[11] Davies, *Dram. Misc.*, III, 120-121.

[12] See especially Watson Nicholson, *The Struggle for a Free Stage in London*, chaps. III and IV. An account sympathetic to the act is contained in Walpole's *Memoirs of George II* (I, 13). The most virulent attack I have found is one in *London Magazine* (VI, 261-262), signed "Pasquin" (Fielding?). He is defending the play of the same name against a recent attack on it in the *Gazetteer*, which had charged that the comedy represented all government as farce: "Ridicule, like *Ward's* Pill, passes innocently thro' a sound Constitution; but when it meets with a Complication of foul Distempers in a gross corrupt Carcase, it is apt to give a terrible Shock, to work the poor Patient most immoderately; in the Course of which Working, it is ten to one but he bes--ts his Breeches."

[13] See Davis, *op. cit.*, 59-60.

[14] Hartford-Pomfret *Correspondence*, II, 61-62.

[15] *Ibid.*, I, 210.

[16] G. M. G., *The Stage Censor*, p. 90; see also Genest, *Some Account of the English Stage*, III, 551.

[17] Genest, *op. cit.*, IV, 179.

[18] Benjamin Victor, *The History of the Theatres of London and Dublin*, III, 131-133.

[19] Genest, *op. cit.*, IV, 194.

[20] *The Life of Mrs. Abington*, p. 54; but see Dick, *Albumazar: A Comedy*, pp. 59-60.

[21] Genest, *op. cit.*, IV, 188.

[22] *Ibid.*, IV, 190.

[23] Quot. in *ibid.*, IV, 172-173.

[24] Murphy, *op. cit.*, I, 269.

[25] *Ibid.*, I, 386.

[26] *Memoirs by a Celebrated Literary and Political Character*, p. ix.

[27] Murphy, *op. cit.*, I, 291.

[28] For example, the prologue to *Britannia*, written and spoken by Garrick, "was called for when Britannia was laid aside" (Murphy, *op. cit.*, I, 270).

[29] Davies, *Dram. Misc.*, II, 41-49.

Notes

[30] Henry G. Graham, *Scottish Men of Letters in the Eighteenth Century,* p. 74.

[31] Walpole, *Memoirs of George II,* III, 250-251.

[32] *London Chronicle,* LXI, 313-314; Kelly had become a ministerial hack writer and had been granted a pension through the efforts of Lord North.

[33] John C. Collins, *Bolingbroke, A Historical Study,* p. 15.

[34] I, i.

[35] John Adolphus, *Memoirs of John Bannister, Comedian,* I, 7.

[36] The "Advertisement" of the play written by its author, Thomas Hull, quoted in Genest, *op. cit.,* V, 76.

[37] There are numerous contemporary accounts of this infamous affair; for example, the works of Cooke, Murphy, Davies, Victor, and Genest. That there was on occasion a soberer element in the audience who were less chauvinistic than bent on being entertained is indicated by an account of a riot at the Haymarket Theatre in 1748, contained in *The Life of Mr. James Quin, Comedian* (p. 43).

[38] Carl F. Becker, *The Heavenly City of the Eighteenth-Century Philosophers,* p. 99; Becker regards (p. 83) Hume's turning from philosophic speculation to the study of history and economics "symptomatic of a certain change in the climate of opinion—of an increasing interest in the concrete political and social activities of men, and of the disposition to approach such matters in a more earnest temper, a mood more highly charged with emotion."

[39] Joseph Moser, "The Close of the Century," *Scots Magazine,* LXII (1800), 153-159; Henry James Pye, *Carmen Seculare for the Year 1800;* see also *Gentlemen's Magazine,* LXX, 4-7, and *Universal Magazine,* CVI, 30-32.

[40] Cf. James M. Osborn, "The First History of English Poetry," in *Pope and His Contemporaries: Essays presented to George Sherburn* (Oxford, 1949), p. 233: "England in the eighteenth century was a nation that derived an almost narcissistic pleasure from contemplating its political and economic growth."

[41] Victor, *op. cit.,* III, 135-136.

[42] Boswell, *Life of Johnson,* IV, 68.

[43] Oulton, *The History of the Theatres of London,* I, 120.

[44] Murphy, *op. cit.,* II, 88.

[45] Boswell, *op. cit.,* II, 247-248, cited in Jay Barrett Botsford, *English Society in the Eighteenth Century* (New York, 1924), p. 22.

[46] Cunningham, *The Letters of Horace Walpole,* IV, 180.

[47] Botsford, *op. cit.,* p. 16.

[48] *The Annual Register for 1773* states: "Books of travel are read with as much relish as ever, though the number of publications of that sort might well be supposed to have long since satiated the public curiosity" (cited in Botsford, *op. cit.,* pp. 22-23).

[49] Cf. Ashley H. Thorndike, *Tragedy,* p. 283: "*The Royal Convert* turns to early English history, a field which literary patriotism was appropriating for tragedy."

[50] But cf. Davies, *Memoirs of the Life of David Garrick, Esq.,* I, 41-42: "The play *Richard III* has always been popular on account of its comprehending such variety of *historical* and domestick facts. . . ." (The italics are mine.)

[51] James Macpherson, *Original Papers Containing the Secret History of Great Britain from the Restoration to the Accession of the House of Hannover* (London, 1776, 2 vols.), I, 3.

[52] Carl L. Becker, *The Heavenly City of the Eighteenth-Century Philosophers,* p. 93.

[53] Edmund Burke, "Letters on a Regicide Peace," in *Works,* V, 288.

Notes

[1] For June 18, 1737.

[2] For June 4, 1737.

[3] See *London Magazine*, VI, 403.

[4] *Memoirs*, I, 347.

[5] *London Chronicle*, LXI, 444.

[6] Albert Hartshorne, ed., *Memoirs of a Royal Chaplain, 1729-1763* (London, 1905), p. 363.

[7] Boswell, *Life of Johnson*, II, 111; similarly, the word "God" was removed from most of the older dramas that were revived during the century.

[8] Lucien Dubech, *et al.*, *Histoire Générale Illustrée du Théâtre* (Paris, 1933, 5 vols.), IV, 291.

[9] Murphy, *The Life of David Garrick, esq.*, I, 346-347.

[10] *Ibid.*, I, 293-294.

[11] *Dramatic Miscellanies*, III, 172.

[12] Murphy, *op. cit.*, I, 97-98.

[13] Davies, *Memoirs of the Life of David Garrick, Esq.*, I, 133.

[14] *Characters of Shakespeare's Plays* (London, 1934), p. 191.

[15] *General Observations on Shakespeare's Plays*, in *Works*, I, 251-252.

[16] Wilkinson, *Memoirs of His own Life*, II, 136.

[17] Cf. Alan Reynolds Thompson, *The Anatomy of Drama* (2nd ed., Berkeley, 1946), pp. 230-231.

[18] Clarence C. Green, *The Neo-Classic Theory of Tragedy in England During the Eighteenth Century* (Cambridge, Mass., 1934), p. 136.

[19] See Percy Fitzgerald, *The Life of Mrs. Catherine Clive* (London, 1888), p. 13.

[20] See *London Magazine*, VI, 309.

[21] Prologue to *Elfrid*.

[22] "Animadversions on the School for Scandal," *Gentleman's Magazine*, XLVIII, 57.

[23] George Edward Ayscough, ed., *The Works of George Lord Lyttelton* (London, 1774), p. 119; the passage quoted is from *Letters from a Persian* (1735).

[24] The statute of 1543 is quoted in J. P. Collier, *The History of English Dramatic Poetry* (London, 1879, 2 vols.), I, 127-128. It is perhaps unnecessary here to distinguish between the objections to drama for its immortality and those to the theater as the milieu of a licentious segment of society. Mrs. Delany had the latter in mind when she wrote to Mrs. Port in 1772: "My friend *Mason* is much chagrined at his daughter Elfrida's having eloped without his consent. I knew, when I heard it was brought to the stage, that he was not consulted, and they say it is sadly performed. It vexes one to think that a poem of such delicacy and dignity should be prostituted, and the charms of *virgins* represented by the abandoned nymphs of Drury Lane . . ." (C. E. Vulliamy, *Aspasia, the Life and Letters of Mary Granville, Mrs. Delany* [London, 1935], p. 204).

[25] *London Magazine*, VI, 433.

[26] *Memoirs of the Reign of King George the Second* (2nd ed., London, 1846, 3 vols.), III, 99.

[27] *The Life of Mr. James Quin, Comedian*, pp. 27-28.

[28] Cooke, *Memoirs of Samuel Foote*, III, 10.

[29] *Reformer* for Feb. 4, 1747/48.

[30] A. E. H. Swaen, ed., *The Best Plays of the Old Dramatists: Sir John Vanbrugh* (London, 1896), p. 55, n. 2.

Notes

[31] I have found no records for a performance of *The Rover* after the 1759-1760 season, or for *London Cuckolds* after 1758-1759. Garrick is credited with abolishing the latter play, which had apparently been annually staged on Lord Mayor's Day; the Covent Garden manager then followed his example, recognizing "the propriety of the measure" (*The Life of Mr. James Quin, Comedian*, p. 14).

[32] *London Chronicle*, XL, 63.

[33] Cf. Baker, *Biographia Dramatica* (I:1, 266): Although public taste had made some beginning toward purification of the stage, it was to a great extent the influence of Garrick that banished from the stage "all those plays which carry with them an immoral tendency; and to prune from those which do not absolutely on the whole promote the interests of vice . . . scenes of licentiousness and libertinism."

[34] Helen Sard Hughes, *The Gentle Hertford, Her Life and Letters* (New York, 1940), p. 238.

[35] *Ibid.*, p. 244.

[36] *Ibid.*, p. 451.

[37] Cunningham, *The Letters of Horace Walpole*, IV, 151.

[38] *Reformer* for Feb. 11, 1747/48.

[39] Hughes, *op. cit.*, p. 451.

[40] Reginald Blunt, *Mrs. Montagu, "Queen of the Blues"* (London, 1923, 2 vols.), I, 284.

[41] Murphy, *op. cit.*, I, 234.

[42] IV, ii.

[43] Blunt, *op. cit.*, I, 64.

[44] Joseph Spence, *Anecdotes, Observations, and Characters, of Books and Men* (2nd ed., London, 1858), pp. 264-265; the passage quoted is from "Supplemental Anecdotes."

[45] *Gentleman's Magazine*, XLVIII, 57-59.

[46] *Spectator*, No. 548 (Nov. 28, 1712).

[47] *Correspondence Between Frances, Countess of Hartford, and Henrietta Louisa, Countess of Pomfret, Between the Years 1738 and 1741* (2nd ed., London, 1806, 3 vols.), II, 66.

[48] *The Orrery Papers*, II, 20.

[49] *London Chronicle*, I, 256.

[50] Allardyce Nicoll, *A History of Early Eighteenth Century Drama, 1700-1750*, pp. 199-200.

[51] *Ibid.*, p. 216.

[52] Davies, *Memoirs*, I, 110.

[53] Murphy, *op. cit.*, II, 17.

[54] *Letters on Dancing and Ballets*, trans. Cyril W. Beaumont (London, 1930), p. 82.

[55] *Winter*, lines 649-658.

[56] *The Pleasures of Melancholy*, lines 211-225.

[57] Davies, *Dram. Misc.*, III, 184; this is a typical contemporary comment.

[58] Although Mrs. Delany recognized this power in *Richard III*, she resolved not to "go to any more such deep tragedies, they shock the mind too much" (Vulliamy, *op. cit.*, p. 102); it is clear, however, that the majority of playgoers enjoyed that play's intensity, for only *Hamlet* among tragedies outranked it in popularity.

[59] *Dram. Misc.*, II, 318.

[60] *Ibid.*, II, 320.

[61] Davies, *Memoirs*, I, 132.

[62] Davies, *Dram. Misc.*, I, 159.

Notes

[63] See the letter from Dr. Grainger to the Rev. Thomas Percy, in Nichols, *Illustrations of Literature*, VII, 241.

[64] *The History of the Theatres of London and Dublin*, II, 167-168.

[65] See Johannes Hendrik Harder, *Observations on Some Tendencies of Sentiment and Ethics Chiefly in Minor Poetry and Essay in the Eighteenth Century* (Amsterdam, 1933), pp. 74-76.

[66] James Fergusson, *Letters of George Dempster to Sir Adam Fergusson, 1756-1813* (London, 1934), pp. 25-29.

[67] Clementina Black, *The Cumberland Letters* (London, 1912), pp. 175-176.

[68] *Op. cit.*, I, 217.

[69] *Lives of the Poets*, in *Works*, V, 151.

[70] Davies, *Dram. Misc.*, III, 213.

[71] See Murphy, *op. cit.*, I, 318-323; Garrick himself said that he altered the play, not because it was a "mixed drama," but because some of the scenes were "exceptionable in themselves, not only as indelicate, but as immoral" ("Advertisement" to *Isabella* in *Works*, II, 219).

[72] See, for example, the classifications of Allardyce Nicoll and George H. Nettleton; it quickly becomes obvious that no system is adequate, many of the plays being in-between types.

[73] In nondramatic tragedy it was already 150 years old: "The discovery which Churchyard made [in the 1563 extension of *Mirror for Magistrates* (the complaint of Jane Shore)] was that the prince's mistress could be as moving a subject for tragedy as the prince, and could have a special appeal in her femininity. . . . hitherto the authors of the Mirror had been severely content to recognize only men" (Willard E. Farnham, *The Medieval Heritage of Elizabethan Tragedy*, Berkeley, 1936, p. 293). That there were no female actors before the closing of the theaters must of course be taken into account; and when they were introduced in the later seventeenth century, feminine roles in revived plays were often expanded and in new plays were made more important; cf. D. Nicol Smith, *Shakespeare in the Eighteenth Century* (Oxford, 1928), p. 23. Frederick W. Kilbourne (*Alterations and Adaptations of Shakespeare*, Boston, 1910, p. 93) remarks of the year 1745: "That the woman element must be made an important one was . . . an article of the dramatic faith of the time."

[74] Murphy, *op. cit.*, I, 263-269.

[75] *Ibid.*, I, 170.

[76] Bellamy, *An Apology for the Life of George Anne Bellamy*, III, 105.

[77] Boswell, *Life of Johnson*, I, 198.

[78] Murphy, *op. cit.*, I, 159.

[79] The history of this play as given here seems the most likely conjecture. Nicoll, *A History of Late Eighteenth Century Drama, 1750-1800* (p. 317), on the basis of the Larpent MS, calls the 1777 play Woodfall's revision of Savage's tragedy. The *London Chronicle* for Feb. 1-4, 1777 (the play was acted on Feb. 1) does not name Woodfall, and apparently regards the revived play as Savage's 1738 revision, which it does mention. If the latter is the true account, then of course the alterations reflect not the later but the earlier part of the period.

[80] *London Chronicle*, LXI, 117.

[81] See Murphy, *op. cit.*, II, 54-55.

[82] See Bellamy, *op. cit.*, IV, 56.

[83] Cooke, *op. cit.*, III, 77-78.

[84] *Op. cit.*, II, 52.

[85] Davies, *Dram. Misc.*, III, 62.

[86] Letter to Percy, in Nichols, *op. cit.*, VII, 269.

[87] Bellamy, *op. cit.*, III, 37-38.

[88] Murphy, *op. cit.*, I, 327-328.

[89] *Ibid.*, I, 354-355. That eighteenth-century maidens of real life as well as those of literature took their reading seriously is aptly illustrated by this notice, headed simply "Missing," in the *London Chronicle* of 1757 (I, 587): "Supposed to be stolen from a Boarding School near ———, a beautiful young Lady, aged Seventeen, Daughter of the late Earl of ———, and Heiress to Thirty Thousand Pounds, independent of her Mother. She was observed to walk in the Back Garden after Dinner with Mr. Macmulla the Dancing Master, and is supposed to have made her Escape with him through the Yew Hedge. She took Nothing with her but a Bottle of Aqua Vitae from her Governess' China Closet, the Second Volume of Pamela, and the Marriage-Service torn out of her Common-Prayer Book. If offered to be married to Mr. Macmulla, pray stop her." Indeed a deliberate and calculating young miss!

[90] Cooke, *op. cit.*, I, 182

[91] *Ibid.*, I, 183-184.

NOTES TO CHAPTER FIFTEEN

[1] II (1770), 94-95; from "A Hunter of Oddities," conjectured to be by Thomas Chatterton (see Donald S. Taylor, "A Critical Edition of the Journalistic Prose and the Letters of Thomas Chatterton," unpubl. Ph.D. diss., Univ. of California, Berkeley, 1950, p. 190).

[2] *The Idler*, nos. 60-61.

[3] Helen Sard Hughes, *The Gentle Hertford, Her Life and Letters*, p. 362.

[4] Thomas Davies, *Memoirs of the Life of David Garrick, Esq.*, I, 51.

[5] John Genest, *Some Account of the English Stage*, V, 426-428.

[6] See Tate Wilkinson, *Memoirs of His Own Life*, I, 112.

[7] *Ibid.*, II, 11; see also his account of Mrs. Wier's reception (II, 223), and Mrs. Bellamy's remarks on the subject (*An Apology for the Life of George Anne Bellamy*, I, 53-54, 60).

[8] See Wilkinson, *op. cit.*, II, 128.

[9] Davies, *Memoirs*, II, 127.

[10] Davies, *Dramatic Miscellanies*, III, 41-42.

[11] Reginald Blunt, *Mrs. Montagu, "Queen of the Blues,"* I, 35.

[12] Benjamin Victor, *The History of the Theatres of London and Dublin*, II, 163.

[13] William Cooke, *Memoirs of Samuel Foote*, II, 22.

[14] How detailed the connoisseur's criticism of an actor might be is suggested by a letter from Hartson to Garrick, Jan. 22, 1762, quoted in Stone, "Garrick's Handling of *Macbeth*," SP, XXXVIII, 622-623. The burlesque that such self-appointed critics would inevitably provoke is given its supreme expression by Sterne: "And how did Garrick speak the soliloquy last night?—Oh, against all rule, my Lord,—most ungrammatically! betwixt the substantive and the adjective, which should agree together in number, case, and gender, he made a breach thus,—stopping, as if the point wanted settling;—and betwixt the nominative case, which your lordship knows should govern the verb, he sus-pended his voice in the epilogue a dozen times three seconds and three fifths by a stop-watch, my Lord, each time.—Admirable grammarian!—but in sus-pending his voice—was the sense suspended likewise? Did no expression of attitude or countenance fill up the chasm?—Was the eye silent? Did you narrowly look?—I looked only at the stop-watch, my Lord.—Excellent ob-server! (*Tristram Shandy*, III, xii).

[15] Victor, *op. cit.*, III, 172-173; Murphy, *Life of David Garrick, esq.*, I, 145-148. The two widely differing attitudes expressed by these two men, both of whom were closely connected with the theater, illustrate on a small scale how critical judgments must be carefully assessed before an adequate conclusion about contemporary dramatic theory can be reached.

[16] Murphy, *op. cit.*, II, 66.

[17] Genest, *op. cit.*, V, 284-285.

[18] Davies, *Dram. Misc.*, II, 401.

[19] Bellamy, *op. cit.*, III, 17-18.

[20] *Ibid.*, III, 105; this type of comment is frequent: Davies says of *The Orphan*, "The characters, by being brought nearer to the condition of the audience, more deeply interest their passions than the fate and fortune of persons who are eminently placed above them" (*Dram. Misc.*, III, 183); Johnson remarks of *Timon of Athens:* "The play . . . is a domestic tragedy, and therefore strongly fastens on the attention of the reader" (*General Observations on Shakespeare's Plays*); of *The Fair Penitent:* "The story is domestic, and therefore easily received by the imagination and assimilated to common life"; and of *Jane Shore:* "This play, consisting chiefly of domestic scenes and private distress, lays hold upon the heart. . . . This, therefore, is one of those pieces which we still welcome on the stage" (*Lives of the Poets*).

[21] Letter to Percy, in Nichols, *Illustrations of Literature*, VII, 241.

[22] *Lives of the Poets*, in *Works*, V, 322.

[23] Murphy, *op. cit.*, I, 329-330; but cf. Whincop (*Scanderbeg*, p. 259), who says that the original play was successful.

[24] Victor, *op. cit.*, III, 18; Johnson makes a similar remark of Rowe's *Ulysses:* "with the common fate of mythological stories, [it] is now generally neglected" (*Lives of the Poets*).

[25] It should be noted that Garrick finally decided against reviving *King and No King* partly because of its incest theme (Davies, *Dram. Misc.*, II, 41-49).

[26] Davies, *Dram. Misc.*, II, 207.

[27] Cf. Leo Kirschbaum, "Shakespeare's Stage Blood and Its Critical Significance," *PMLA*, LXIV (1949), 517-529.

[28] Murphy, *op. cit.*, I, 284-286.

[29] *Works*, II, 219.

[30] Bellamy, *op. cit.*, III, 51-52.

Indexes

349

355

INDEX OF PLAYS

357

Index of Plays